THIRD EDITION

Java™ & XML

Brett D. McLaughlin and Justin Edelson

Beijing · Cambridge · Farnham · Köln · Paris · Sebastopol · Taipei · Tokyo

Java™ & XML

by Brett D. McLaughlin and Justin Edelson

Copyright © 2007, 2001, 2000 O'Reilly Media, Inc. All rights reserved.
Printed in the United States of America.

Published by O'Reilly Media, Inc., 1005 Gravenstein Highway North, Sebastopol, CA 95472.

O'Reilly books may be purchased for educational, business, or sales promotional use. Online editions are also available for most titles (*safari.oreilly.com*). For more information, contact our corporate/institutional sales department: (800) 998-9938 or *corporate@oreilly.com*.

Editor: Mike Loukides	**Indexer:** Ellen Troutman Zaig
Production Editor: Laurel R.T. Ruma	**Cover Designers:** Ellie Volckhausen and Karen Montgomery
Copyeditor: Linley Dolby	**Interior Designer:** David Futato
Proofreader: Laurel R.T. Ruma	**Illustrators:** Robert Romano and Jessamyn Read

Printing History:

June 2000:	First Edition.
August 2001:	Second Edition.
December 2006:	Third Edition.

Nutshell Handbook, the Nutshell Handbook logo, and the O'Reilly logo are registered trademarks of O'Reilly Media, Inc. *Java & XML*, the image of lions, and related trade dress are trademarks of O'Reilly Media, Inc.

Java™ and all Java-based trademarks and logos are trademarks or registered trademarks of Sun Microsystems, Inc., in the United States and other countries.

Many of the designations used by manufacturers and sellers to distinguish their products are claimed as trademarks. Where those designations appear in this book, and O'Reilly Media, Inc. was aware of a trademark claim, the designations have been printed in caps or initial caps.

While every precaution has been taken in the preparation of this book, the publisher and authors assume no responsibility for errors or omissions, or for damages resulting from the use of the information contained herein.

 This book uses RepKover™, a durable and flexible lay-flat binding.

ISBN-10: 0-596-10149-X
ISBN-13: 978-0-596-10149-7
[M]

Table of Contents

Preface

Welcome to the third edition of *Java & XML*. Whether you've read either of the prior editions, both, or neither, I think you'll find something interesting in the chapters that follow. Quite a bit has changed since the second edition appeared. Specifications that were drafts have been finalized, new APIs have been introduced, and new uses for XML have emerged. Perhaps most significantly, two APIs discussed in the second edition—JDOM and JAXB—saw important changes between the prerelease versions available at the time of writing and their eventual final releases. Although I hope that the text of this edition never becomes out of date, the rate of change in the Java and XML universe makes this unlikely. Nevertheless, I'm confident the bulk of what's ahead will be useful for years to come, even if some of the details change.

Organization

This book is organized into three sections. The first section, composed of Chapters 1 and 2, provides a basic introduction to XML and related standards. The second— Chapters 3 through 11—explains a wide variety of APIs for creating, manipulating, outputting, and pretty much doing anything else to XML documents. The last section—Chapters 12 and 13—describes two important applications for XML. There's also a final chapter and an appendix.

Chapter 1, *Introduction*
> We'll begin with the basics of XML. If you've never used XML before, this chapter will give you all the information you need to proceed with the remainder of the chapters. We briefly touch on the changes between XML 1.0 and 1.1 before introducing XSLT and XPath.

Chapter 2, *Constraints*
> This chapter covers three ways of defining the structure of XML documents: DTDs, W3C XML Schemas, and RELAX NG schemas. It covers how to use these standards to define a structure and how to ensure that a document

matches that definition (in other words, to validate a document). You'll also learn how to convert between the various constraint document types.

Chapter 3, *SAX*

The Simple API for XML (SAX), our first Java API for handling XML, is introduced in this chapter. The parsing lifecycle is detailed, and the events that can be caught by SAX and used by developers are demonstrated.

Chapter 4, *Advanced SAX*

We'll push further with SAX in this chapter, covering less-used but still powerful items in the API. You'll learn how to use SAX features and properties to alter the behavior of the SAX parser, use XML filters to chain callback behavior, use XML writers to output XML with SAX, and look at some of the less commonly used SAX handlers like LexicalHandler and DeclHandler.

Chapter 5, *DOM*

This chapter moves forward through the XML landscape to the next Java and XML API, the Document Object Model (DOM). You'll learn DOM basics, find out what is in the current specification (DOM Level 3), and how to read and write DOM trees.

Chapter 6, *DOM Modules*

Moving on through DOM, you'll learn about the various Level 2 and Level 3 DOM modules like Traversal, Range, Events, Style, HTML, Load and Save, and Validation.

Chapter 7, *JAXP*

This chapter examines the Java API for XML Processing (JAXP), including the XPath and Validation APIs introduced with JAXP 1.3.

Chapter 8, *Pull Parsing With StAX*

The Streaming API for XML (StAX) is the newest standard Java XML API. You'll learn how to use StAX and how it compares to both SAX and DOM. We also briefly look at a precursor to StAX named XMLPull, which is still in use.

Chapter 9, *JDOM*

This chapter examines JDOM, a Java-specific object model API. It contains complete coverage of the JDOM 1.0 release.

Chapter 10, *dom4j*

This chapter examines another Java-specific object model API, dom4j. You'll see how it compares to both JDOM and DOM including the features unique to dom4j like its object-orientated transformation API.

Chapter 11, *Data Binding with JAXB*

With data binding, your application code does not concern itself with the details of XML documents, only a Java object model. Sun has developed a standard for XML data binding: the Java Architecture for XML Binding (JAXB). In this chapter, you'll learn about JAXB 1.0 and 2.0, as well as the general basics of data binding. We also discuss when it is (and is not) appropriate to use data binding.

Chapter 12, *Content Syndication with RSS*

This chapter covers using XML documents to syndicate content. Specifically, the RSS standards are examined along with a brief discussion of Atom. You'll see how to create and read RSS feeds using APIs discussed in the earlier chapters as well as an RSS-specific API named ROME. You'll even see how to create your own podcast feed for submission to Apple's iTunes Podcast directory.

Chapter 13, *XML As Presentation*

In this chapter, we'll look at a variety of techniques for using XML in the presentation, or visual, portion of web applications. You'll see how XML is a key component of the dynamic web application techniques quickly moving from the bleeding edge to the mainstream.

Chapter 14, *Looking Forward*

This final chapter provides some brief overviews of technologies not covered in depth in this book. Readers hungry for more may want to pursue these topics further.

Appendix, *SAX Features and Properties*

This appendix details the features and properties available to SAX 2.0 parser implementations.

Conventions Used in This Book

The following typographical conventions are used in this book:

Constant width

Indicates command-line elements, computer output, and code examples.

Constant width italic

Indicates placeholders (for which you substitute an actual name) in examples and in registry keys.

Constant width bold

Indicates user input and is used to highlight key portions of code.

Italic

Introduces new terms and example URLs, commands, file extensions, filenames, and directory or folder names

 Indicates a tip, suggestion, or general note.

 Indicates a warning or caution.

Using Code Examples

This book is here to help you get your job done. In general, you may use the code in this book in your programs and documentation. You do not need to contact us for permission unless you're reproducing a significant portion of the code. For example, writing a program that uses several chunks of code from this book does not require permission. Selling or distributing a CD-ROM of examples from O'Reilly books *does* require permission. Answering a question by citing this book and quoting example code does not require permission. Incorporating a significant amount of example code from this book into your product's documentation *does* require permission.

We appreciate, but do not require, attribution. An attribution usually includes the title, author, publisher, and ISBN. For example: "*Java & XML*, Third Edition, by Brett McLaughlin and Justin Edelson. Copyright 2007 O'Reilly Media, Inc., 978-0-596-10149-7."

If you feel your use of code examples falls outside fair use or the permission given above, feel free to contact us at *permissions@oreilly.com*.

We'd Like Your Feedback!

We at O'Reilly have tested and verified the information in this book to the best of our ability, but mistakes and oversights do occur. Please let us know about errors you may find, as well as your suggestions for future editions, by writing to:

O'Reilly Media, Inc.
1005 Gravenstein Highway North
Sebastopol, CA 95472
800-998-9938 (in the U.S. or Canada)
707-829-0515 (international or local)
707-829-0104 (fax)

There is a web page for the book where we list errata, examples, or any additional information. You can access this page at:

http://www.oreilly.com/catalog/9780596101497

To comment or ask technical questions about this book, send email to:

bookquestions@oreilly.com

For more information about our books, conferences, software, Resource Centers, and the O'Reilly Network, see our web site at:

http://www.oreilly.com

Safari® Enabled

 When you see a Safari® Enabled icon on the cover of your favorite technology book, that means the book is available online through the O'Reilly Network Safari Bookshelf.

Safari offers a solution that's better than e-books. It's a virtual library that lets you easily search thousands of top tech books, cut and paste code samples, download chapters, and find quick answers when you need the most accurate, current information. Try it for free at *http://safari.oreilly.com*.

Acknowledgments

This book would not be possible without the efforts of the O'Reilly staff, especially our editor, Mike Loukides; his associate, Caitrin McCullough; and the production talents of Marlowe Shaeffer and Linley Dolby. Additional thanks goes out to everyone who reviewed this book, in whole or part; valuable input from Colin Chow, Greg Graf, Noah Jones, Michael Rosencrantz, Victor Toni, and Deepak Vohra improved the book you're reading now.

Everyone stands on the shoulders of giants, but this is especially true for writers of a book such as this. For obvious reasons, without the efforts and contributions of developers around the world, the technologies discussed in this book wouldn't exist. There are far too many of you to thank, but you know who you are.

Brett D. McLaughlin

Seeing this book as it prepares to publish as a third edition is one of the coolest events of my year, mostly because it's become such a team effort. As I've been pulled into the "dark side" of technical books—the world of Head First—I began to wonder if there ever would *be* a third edition of *Java & XML*. Thanks to the wonderful talents of Justin Edelson, though, you've got an even better book than the first and second editions. Justin came onto this project, added polish and technical detail to the work I'd already done, and cranked out an amazing amount of spectacular material in just a few short months. Justin, I'm proud to have my name next to yours on the cover; you've really added such tremendous value to the book.

I always want to thank the O'Reilly team, and in particular Mike Loukides, for driving this book to completion. This was the book that got me started at O'Reilly, and it's really gratifying to see so many people pitch in and get this third edition out. Thanks, everyone, it's always a joy writing an O'Reilly book.

Justin Edelson

First and foremost, thanks to Brett and Mike. You took a chance on me, and I can't express how grateful I am. To my wife, Elizabeth, there's no way I could have done this without your help and support. To Owen, it'll be a few years before you read this, but know that you are already an inspiration to me every day. To both my and Beth's parents as well as my sisters and brothers, thanks for everything. To our dogs, Burt and Lola, thanks for occasionally making room on the couch.

Thanks to everyone at MTV—especially Lily Chang, Dmitry Grinberg, Steven Hsu, Glenn Goldstein, Greg Clayman, and Nick Rockwell—for all of your support. Thanks to Dan Brustein for being such a great officemate. To the pod, thanks for the last decade; it wouldn't have been the same without you. To Michael Joyce, thanks for the words of wisdom.

Finally, I'd like to dedicate this work to my grandfather, Max Edelson, without whom most of the good things in my life (including co-authoring this book) never would have happened.

## CHAPTER 1

Introduction

In the next two chapters, I'm going to give you a crash course in XML and constraints. Since there is so much material available on XML and related specifications, I'd rather cruise through this material quickly and get on to Java. For those of you who are completely new to XML, you might want to have a few of the following books around as reference:

- *XML in a Nutshell*, by Elliotte Rusty Harold and W. Scott Means
- *Learning XML*, by Erik Ray
- *Learning XSLT*, by Michael Fitzgerald
- *XSLT*, by Doug Tidwell

These are all O'Reilly books, and I have them scattered about my own workspace. With that said, let's dive in.

XML 1.0

It all begins with the XML 1.0 Recommendation, which you can read in its entirety at *http://www.w3.org/TR/REC-xml*. Example 1-1 shows an XML document that conforms to this specification. I'll use it to illustrate several important concepts.

Example 1-1. A typical XML document is long and verbose

```
<?xml version="1.0" encoding="UTF-8"?>
<rdf:RDF xmlns:rdf="http://www.w3.org/1999/02/22-rdf-syntax-ns#"
         xmlns:dc="http://purl.org/dc/elements/1.1/"
         xmlns="http://purl.org/rss/1.0/" xmlns:admin="http://webns.net/mvcb/"
         xmlns:l="http://purl.org/rss/1.0/modules/link/"
         xmlns:content="http://purl.org/rss/1.0/modules/content/">
  <!--Generated by Blogger v5.0-->
  <channel rdf:about="http://www.neilgaiman.com/journal/journal.asp">
    <title>Neil Gaiman's Journal</title>
    <link>http://www.neilgaiman.com/journal/journal.asp</link>
    <description>Neil Gaiman's Journal</description>
```

Example 1-1. A typical XML document is long and verbose (continued)

```
    <dc:date>2005-04-30T01:57:38Z</dc:date>
    <dc:language>en-US</dc:language>
    <admin:generatorAgent rdf:resource="http://www.blogger.com/" />
    <admin:errorReportsTo rdf:resource="mailto:rss-errors@blogger.com" />
    <items>
      <rdf:Seq>
        <rdf:li
  rdf:resource="http://www.neilgaiman.com/journal/2005/04/three-photographs.asp" />
        <rdf:li
  rdf:resource="http://www.neilgaiman.com/journal/2005/04/jetlag-morning.asp" />
        <rdf:li
  rdf:resource="http://www.neilgaiman.com/journal/2005/04/demon-days.asp" />
        <rdf:li
  rdf:resource="http://www.neilgaiman.com/journal/2005/04/more-from-mailbag.asp" />
        <rdf:li
  rdf:resource="http://www.neilgaiman.com/journal/2005/04/two-days.asp" />
        <rdf:li
  rdf:resource="http://www.neilgaiman.com/journal/2005/04/finishing-things.asp" />
      </rdf:Seq>
    </items>
  </channel>

  <!-- and so on... -->
</rdf:RDF>
```

 For those of you who are curious, this is the RSS feed for Neil Gaiman's blog (*http://www.neilgaiman.com*). It uses a lot of RSS syntax, which I'll cover in Chapter 12 in detail.

A lot of this specification describes what is mostly intuitive. If you've done any HTML authoring, or SGML, you're already familiar with the concept of elements (such as items and channel in Example 1-1) and attributes (such as resource and content). XML defines how to use these items and how a document must be structured. XML spends more time defining tricky issues like whitespace than introducing any concepts that you're not at least somewhat familiar with. One exception may be that some of the elements in Example 1-1 are in the form:

```
[prefix]:[element name]
```

Such as rdf:li. These are elements in an *XML namespace*, something I'll explain in detail shortly.

An XML document can be broken into two basic pieces: the *header*, which gives an XML parser and XML applications information about how to handle the document, and the *content*, which is the XML data itself. Although this is a fairly loose division, it helps us differentiate the instructions to applications within an XML document from the XML content itself, and is an important distinction to understand. The header is simply the XML declaration, in this format:

```
<?xml version="1.0" encoding="UTF-8"?>
```

This header includes an encoding, and can also indicate whether the document is a standalone document or requires other documents to be referenced for a complete understanding of its meaning:

```
<?xml version="1.0" encoding="UTF-8" standalone="no"?>
```

The rest of the header is made up of items like the DOCTYPE declaration (not included in the example):

```
<!DOCTYPE RDF SYSTEM "DTDs/RDF-gaiman.dtd">
```

In this case, the declaration refers to a file on the local system, in the directory *DTDs/* called *RDF-gaiman.dtd*. Any time you use a relative or absolute file path or a URL, you want to use the SYSTEM keyword. The other option is using the PUBLIC keyword, and following it with a public identifier. This means that the W3C or another consortium has defined a standard DTD that is associated with that public identifier. As an example, take the DTD statement for XHTML 1.0:

```
<!DOCTYPE html PUBLIC "-//W3C//DTD XHTML 1.0 Transitional//EN"
  "http://www.w3.org/TR/xhtml1/DTD/xhtml1-transitional.dtd">
```

Here, a public identifier is supplied (the funny little string starting with -//), followed by a system identifier (the URL). If the public identifier cannot be resolved, the system identifier is used instead.

You may also see processing instructions at the top of a file, and they are generally considered part of a document's header, rather than its content. They look like this:

```
<?xml-stylesheet href="XSL/JavaXML.html.xsl" type="text/xsl"?>
<?xml-stylesheet href="XSL/JavaXML.wml.xsl" type="text/xsl"
                 media="wap"?>
<?cocoon-process type="xslt"?>
```

Each is considered to have a *target* (the first word, like xml-stylesheet or cocoon-process) and *data* (the rest). Often, the data is in the form of name-value pairs, which can really help readability. This is only a good practice, though, and not required, so don't depend on it.

Other than that, the bulk of your XML document should be content; in other words, elements, attributes, and data that you have put into it.

The Root Element

The root element is the highest-level element in the XML document, and must be the first opening tag and the last closing tag within the document. It provides a reference point that enables an XML parser or XML-aware application to recognize a beginning and end to an XML document. In Example 1-1, the root element is RDF:

```
<rdf:RDF xmlns:rdf="http://www.w3.org/1999/02/22-rdf-syntax-ns#"
         xmlns:dc="http://purl.org/dc/elements/1.1/"
         xmlns="http://purl.org/rss/1.0/" xmlns:admin="http://webns.net/mvcb/"
         xmlns:l="http://purl.org/rss/1.0/modules/link/"
```

```
                xmlns:content="http://purl.org/rss/1.0/modules/content/">

        <!-- Document content -->
    </rdf:RDF>
```

This tag and its matching closing tag surround all other data content within the XML document. XML specifies that there may be only one root element in a document. In other words, the root element must enclose all other elements within the document. Aside from this requirement, a root element does not differ from any other XML element. It's important to understand this, because XML documents can reference and include other XML documents. In these cases, the root element of the referenced document becomes an enclosed element in the referring document and must be handled normally by an XML parser. Defining root elements as standard XML elements without special properties or behavior allows document inclusion to work seamlessly.

Elements

So far, I have glossed over defining an actual element. Let's take an in-depth look at elements, which are represented by arbitrary names and must be enclosed in angle brackets. There are several different variations of elements in the sample document, as shown here:

```
    <!-- Standard element opening tag -->
    <items>

    <!-- Standard element with attribute -->
    <rdf:li
        rdf:resource="http://www.neilgaiman.com/journal/2005/04/three-photographs.asp">

    <!-- Element with textual data -->
    <dc:creator>Neil Gaiman</dc:creator>

    <!-- Empty element -->
    <l:permalink l:type="text/html"
         rdf:resource="http://www.neilgaiman.com/journal/2005/04/finishing-things.asp"
    />

    <!-- Standard element closing tag -->
    </items>
```

 This isn't actual XML; it's just a collection of examples. Trying to parse something like this would fail, as there are opening tags without corresponding closing tags.

The first rule in creating elements is that their names must start with a letter or underscore, and then may contain any amount of letters, numbers, underscores, hyphens, or periods. They may not contain embedded spaces:

```
    <!-- Embedded spaces are not allowed -->
    <my element name>
```

XML element names are also case-sensitive. Generally, using the same rules that govern Java variable naming will result in sound XML element naming. Using an element named tcbo to represent *Telecommunications Business Object* is not a good idea because it is cryptic, while an overly verbose tag name like beginningOfNewChapter just clutters up a document. Keep in mind that your XML documents will probably be seen by other developers and content authors, so clear documentation through good naming is essential.

Every opened element must in turn be closed. There are no exceptions to this rule as there are in many other markup languages, like HTML. An ending element tag consists of the forward slash and then the element name: </items>. Between an opening and closing tag, there can be any number of additional elements or textual data. However, you cannot mix the order of nested tags; the first opened element must always be the last closed element. If any of the rules for XML syntax are not followed in an XML document, the document is not *well-formed*. A well-formed document is one in which all XML syntax rules are followed, and all elements and attributes are correctly positioned. However, a well-formed document is not necessarily *valid*, which means that it follows the constraints set upon a document by its DTD or schema. There is a significant difference between a well-formed document and a valid one; the rules I discuss in this section ensure that your document is well-formed, while the rules discussed in Chapter 2 ensure that your document is valid.

As an example of a document that is not well-formed, consider this XML fragment:

```
<tag1>
 <tag2>
</tag1>
 </tag2>
```

The order of nesting of tags is incorrect, as the opened <tag2> is not followed by a closing </tag2> within the surrounding tag1 element. However, even if these syntax errors are corrected, there is still no guarantee that the document will be valid.

While this example of a document that is not well-formed may seem trivial, remember that this would be acceptable HTML, and commonly occurs in large tables within an HTML document. In other words, HTML and many other markup languages do not require well-formed XML documents. XML's strict adherence to ordering and nesting rules allows data to be parsed and handled much more quickly than when using markup languages without these constraints.

The last rule I'll look at is the case of empty elements. I already said that XML tags must always be paired; an opening tag and a closing tag constitute a complete XML element. There are cases where an element is used purely by itself, like a flag stating a chapter is incomplete, or where an element has attributes but no textual data, like an image declaration in HTML. These would have to be represented as:

```
<admin:generatorAgent rdf:resource="http://www.blogger.com/">
</admin:generatorAgent>

<img src="/images/xml.gif"></img>
```

This is obviously a bit silly, and adds clutter to what can often be very large XML documents. The XML specification provides a means to signify both an opening and closing element tag within one element:

```
<admin:generatorAgent rdf:resource="http://www.blogger.com/" />
<img src="/images/xml.gif" />
```

What's with the Space Before the End Slash?

Well, let me tell you. I've had the unfortunate pleasure of working with Java and XML since late 1998, when things were rough at best. And some web browsers at that time (and some today, to be honest) would only accept XHTML (HTML that is well-formed) in very specific formats. Most notably, tags like <br> that are never closed in HTML must be closed in XHTML, resulting in <br/>. Some of these browsers would completely ignore a tag like this; however, oddly enough, they would happily process
 (note the space before the end slash). I got used to making my XML not only well-formed, but consumable by these browsers. I've never had a good reason to change these habits, so you get to see them in action here.

This nicely solves the problem of unnecessary clutter, and still follows the rule that every XML element must have a matching end tag; it simply consolidates both start and end tag into a single tag.

Attributes

In addition to text contained within an element's tags, an element can also have attributes. Attributes are included with their respective values within the element's opening declaration (which can also be its closing declaration!). For example, in the channel element, a URL for information about the channel is noted in an attribute:

```
<channel rdf:about="http://www.neilgaiman.com/journal/journal.asp">
```

In this example, rdf:about is the attribute name; the value is the URL, "http://www.neilgaiman.com/journal/journal.asp". Attribute names must follow the same rules as XML element names, and attribute values must be within quotation marks. Although both single and double quotes are allowed, double quotes are a widely used standard and result in XML documents that model Java programming practices.

In addition to learning how to use attributes, there is an issue of *when* to use attributes. Because XML allows such a variety of data formatting, it is rare that an attribute cannot be represented by an element, or that an element could not easily be converted to an attribute. Although there's no specification or widely accepted standard for determining when to use an attribute and when to use an element, there is a good rule of thumb: use elements for multiple-valued data and attributes for single-valued data. If data can have multiple values, or is very lengthy, the data most likely belongs in an element. It can then be treated primarily as textual data, and is easily searchable and usable. Examples are the description of a book's chapters, or URLs detailing related links from a site. However, if the data is primarily represented as a single value, it is best represented by an attribute. A good candidate for an attribute is the section of a chapter; while the section item itself might be an element and have its own title, the grouping of chapters within a section could be easily represented by a `section` attribute within the `chapter` element. This attribute would allow easy grouping and indexing of chapters, but would never be directly displayed to the user. Another good example of a piece of data that could be represented in XML as an attribute is if a particular table or chair is on layaway. This instruction could let an XML application used to generate a brochure or flyer know to not include items on layaway in current stock; obviously this is a true or false value, and has only a singular value at any time. Again, the application client would never directly see this information, but the data would be used in processing and handling the XML document. If after all of this analysis you are still unsure, you can always play it safe and use an element.

Namespaces

Note the use of namespaces in the root element of Example 1-1:

```
<rdf:RDF xmlns:rdf="http://www.w3.org/1999/02/22-rdf-syntax-ns#"
         xmlns:dc="http://purl.org/dc/elements/1.1/"
         xmlns="http://purl.org/rss/1.0/" xmlns:admin="http://webns.net/mvcb/"
         xmlns:l="http://purl.org/rss/1.0/modules/link/"
         xmlns:content="http://purl.org/rss/1.0/modules/content/">
```

An *XML namespace* is a means of associating one or more elements in an XML document with a particular URI. This means that the element is identified by both its name *and* its namespace URI. In many complex XML documents, the same XML name (for example, author) may need to be used in different ways. For instance, in the example, there is an author for the RSS feed, as well as an author for each journal entry. While both of these pieces of data fit nicely into an element named author, they should not be taken as the same *type* of data.

The XML namespaces specification nicely solves this problem. The namespace specification requires that a unique URI be associated with a prefix to distinguish the elements in one namespace from elements in other namespaces. So you could assign a URI of *http://www.neilgaiman.com/entries*, and associate it with the prefix journal, for use by journal-specific elements. You could then assign another URI, like *http://www.w3.org/1999/02/22-rdf-syntax-ns,* and a prefix of rss, for RSS-specific elements:

```
<rdf:RDF xmlns:rss="http://www.w3.org/1999/02/22-rdf-syntax-ns#"
         xmlns:journal="http://www.neilgaiman.com/entries">
```

Now you can use those prefixes in your XML:

```
<rss:author>Doug Hally</rss:author>
<journal:author>Neil Gaiman</journal:author>
```

You can actually use a namespace prefix on the same element where that namespace is declared. For example, this is perfectly legal XML:

```
<rss:author xmlns:rss="http://www.w3.org/1999/02/22-rdf-
syntax-ns#">Doug Hally</rss:author>
```

An XML parser can now easily distinguish these two different types of author; as an added benefit, the XML is a lot more human-readable now.

Entity References

One item I have not discussed is escaping characters, or referring to other constant type data values. For example, a common way to represent a path to an installation directory in online documentation is <path-to-Ant> or <TOMCAT_HOME>. Here, the user would replace the text with the appropriate choice of installation directory. In the following journal entry, there are several HTML tags within the entry itself:

```
When the shoot was done, my daughter Holly, who had been doing her
homework in the room next door, and occasionally coming out to laugh
at me, helped use up the last few pictures on the roll. She looks like
she's having fun. I think I look a little dazed.<br /><br />
<img src="http://www.neilgaiman.com/journal/Neil_8313036.jpg" ><br />
<br />This is the one we're going to be using on the book jacket of
ANANSI BOYS.
```

The problem is that XML parsers attempt to handle these bits of data (
 and <img>) as XML tags. This is a common problem, as any use of angle brackets results in this behavior. *Entity references* provide a way to overcome this problem. An entity reference is a special data type in XML used to refer to another piece of data. The entity reference consists of a unique name, preceded by an ampersand and followed by a semicolon: &*[entity name]*;. When an XML parser sees an entity reference, the specified substitution value is inserted, and no processing of that value occurs. XML defines five entities to address the problem discussed in the example: < for the less-than bracket, > for the greater-than bracket, & for the ampersand sign itself, " for a double quotation mark, and ' for a single quotation mark or apostrophe. Using these special references, the entry can contain the HTML tags without having them interpreted as XML tags by the XML parser:

```
When the shoot was done, my daughter Holly, who had been doing her
homework in the room next door, and occasionally coming out to laugh
at me, helped use up the last few pictures on the roll. She looks like
she's having fun. I think I look a little dazed.&lt;br /&gt;
&lt;br /&gt;&lt;img src="http://www.neilgaiman.com/journal/Neil_8313036.jpg"
/&gt;&lt;br /&gt;&lt;br /&gt;This is the one we're going to be using
on the book jacket of ANANSI BOYS.
```

Once this document is parsed, the data is interpreted as normal HTML br and img tags, and the document is still considered well-formed.

Also be aware that entity references are user-definable. This allows a sort of shortcut markup; for example, you might want to reference a copyright notice online somewhere. Because the copyright is used for multiple books and articles, it doesn't make sense to include the actual text within hundreds of different XML documents; however, if the copyright is changed, all referring XML documents should reflect the changes:

```
<ora:copyright>&OReillyCopyright;</ora:copyright>
```

Although you won't see how the XML parser is told what to reference when it sees &OReillyCopyright; until the next chapter, you need to realize that there are more uses for entity references than just representing difficult or unusual characters within data.

Unparsed Data

The last XML construct to look at is the CDATA section marker. A CDATA section is used when a significant amount of data should be passed on to the calling application without any XML parsing. It is used when an unusually large number of characters would have to be escaped using entity references, or when spacing must be preserved. In an XML document, a CDATA section looks like this:

```
<content:encoded><![CDATA[Lot of flying yesterday and now I'm home again.
For a day. Last night's useful post was written, but was eaten by weasels.
Next week is the last week of <em>Beowulf-</em>with-Avary-and-Zemeckis work
for a long while, and then I get to be home for about a month, if you
don't count the trip to New York for Book Expo, and right now I just
like the idea of sleeping in my own bed for a couple of nights running.
<br /><br /> </p>]]></content:encoded>
```

In this example, the information within the CDATA section does not have to use entity references or other mechanisms to alert the parser that reserved characters are being used; instead, the XML parser passes them unchanged to the wrapping program or application.

At this point, you have seen the major components of XML documents. Although each has only been briefly described, this should give you enough information to recognize the parts of an XML document when you see them and know their general purpose.

XML 1.1

In February of 2004, the XML 1.1 specification was released by the World Wide Web Consortium (W3C; *http://www.w3.org*). If you don't recall hearing much about XML 1.1, it's no surprise; XML 1.1 was largely about Unicode conformance, and really didn't affect XML as a whole that much, particularly for document authors and programmers not working with unusual character sets.

While XML was undergoing fairly minor maintenance updates, Unicode moved from Version 2.0 to 4.0. Since XML relies on Unicode for the characters allowed in XML element and attribute names, this had a ripple effect on document authors who wanted to use the new Unicode 4.0 characters in their documents. In XML 1.0, the specification had to explicitly permit characters to be in element and attribute names; as a result, new characters in later versions of Unicode were excluded for name usage by parsers. In XML 1.1—in an effort to avoid similar problems in the future—characters not explicitly forbidden are permitted. This means that if new characters are added in future Unicode versions, they can immediately be used in XML 1.1 documents.

If all of this doesn't mean anything to you, then you probably don't need to be too concerned about XML 1.1. Personally, I still type in version="1.0" and haven't needed to change that yet. If you want to understand more about the intricacies of Unicode and XML 1.1, check out the complete specification at *http://www.w3.org/TR/xml11*.

 All the tools and parsers used throughout this book will work with XML 1.0 and 1.1 documents.

XML Transformations

One of the cooler things about XML is the ability to transform it into something else. With the wealth of web-capable devices these days (computers, personal organizers, phones, DVRs, etc.), you never know what flavor of markup you need to deliver. Sometimes HTML works, sometimes XHTML (the XML flavor of HTML) is required, sometimes the Wireless Markup Language (WML) is supported; and sometimes you need something else entirely. In all of these cases, though, the basic data being displayed is the same; it's just the formatting and presentation that changes. A great technique is to store the data in an XML document, and then transform that XML into various formats for display.

As useful as XML transformations can be, though, they are not simple to implement. In fact, rather than trying to specify the transformation of XML in the original XML 1.0 specification, the W3C has put out three separate recommendations to define how XML transformations work.

Because these three specifications are tied together tightly and are almost always used in concert, there is rarely a clear distinction between them. This can often make for a discussion that is easy to understand, but not necessarily technically correct. In other words, the term XSLT, which refers specifically to extensible stylesheet transformations, is often applied to both XSL and XPath. In the same fashion, XSL is often used as a grouping term for all three technologies. In this section, I distinguish among the three recommendations, and remain true to the letter of the specifications outlining these technologies. However, in the interest of clarity, I use XSL and

XSLT interchangeably to refer to the complete transformation process throughout the rest of the book. Although this may not follow the letter of these specifications, it certainly follows their spirit, as well as avoiding lengthy definitions of simple concepts when you already understand what I mean.

XSL

XSL is the Extensible Stylesheet Language. It is defined as a language for expressing stylesheets. This broad definition is broken down into two parts:

- XSL is a language for transforming XML documents.
- XSL is an XML vocabulary for specifying the formatting of XML documents.

The definitions are similar, but one deals with moving from one XML document form to another, while the other focuses on the actual presentation of content within each document. Perhaps a clearer definition would be to say that XSL handles the specification of how to transform a document from format A to format B. The components of the language handle the processing and identification of the constructs used to do this.

XSL and trees

The most important concept to understand in XSL is that all data within XSL processing stages is in tree structures (see Figure 1-1). In fact, the rules you define using XSL are themselves held in a tree structure. This allows simple processing of the hierarchical structure of XML documents. Templates are used to match the root element of the XML document being processed. Then "leaf" rules are applied to "leaf" elements, filtering down to the most nested elements. At any point in this progression, elements can be processed, styled, ignored, copied, or have a variety of other things done to them.

A nice advantage of this tree structure is that it allows the grouping of XML documents to be maintained. If element A contains elements B and C, and element A is moved or copied, the elements contained within it receive the same treatment.

This makes the handling of large data sections that need to receive the same treatment fast and easy to notate concisely in the XSL stylesheet. You will see more about how this tree is constructed when I talk specifically about XSLT in the next section.

Formatting objects

The XSL specification is almost entirely concerned with defining *formatting objects*. A formatting object is based on a large model, not surprisingly called the formatting model. This model is all about a set of objects that are fed as input into a formatter. The formatter applies the objects to the document, and what results is a new document that consists of all or part of the data from the original XML document in a format specific to the objects the formatter used. Because this is such a vague, shadowy

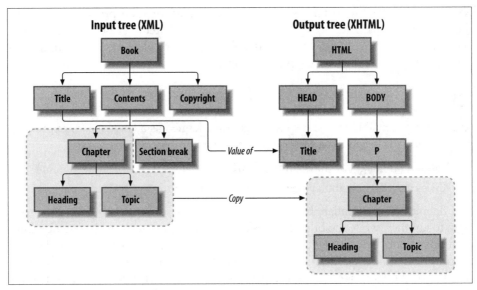

Figure 1-1. Tree operations within XSL

concept, the XSL specification attempts to define a concrete model to which these objects should conform. In other words, a large set of properties and vocabulary make up the set of features that formatting objects can use. These include the types of areas that may be visualized by the objects; the properties of lines, fonts, graphics, and other visual objects; inline and block formatting objects; and a wealth of other syntactical constructs.

Formatting objects are used heavily when converting textual XML data into binary formats such as PDF files, images, or document formats such as Microsoft Word. For transforming XML data to another textual format, these objects are seldom used explicitly. Although an underlying part of the stylesheet logic, formatting objects are rarely invoked directly, since the resulting textual data often conforms to another predefined markup language such as HTML. Because most enterprise applications today are based at least in part on web architecture and use a browser as a client, I spend the most time looking at transformations to HTML and XHTML. While formatting objects are covered only lightly, the topic is broad enough to merit its own coverage in a separate book. For further information, consult the XSL specification at *http://www.w3.org/TR/xsl*.

XSLT

The second component of XML transformations is XSL Transformations. XSLT is the language that *specifies* the conversion of a document from one format to another (where XSL defined the means of that specification). The syntax used within XSLT is generally concerned with textual transformations that do not result in binary data output. For example, XSLT is instrumental is generating HTML or WML from an

XML document. In fact, the XSLT specification outlines the syntax of an XSL stylesheet more explicitly than the XSL specification itself!

Just as in the case of XSL, an XSLT stylesheet is always well-formed, valid XML. A DTD is defined for XSL and XSLT that delineates the allowed constructs. For this reason, you should only have to learn new syntax to use XSLT, and not new structural rules (if you know how XML is structured, you know how XSLT is structured). Just as in XSL, XSLT is based on a hierarchical tree structure of data, where nested elements are leaves, or children, of their parents. XSLT provides a mechanism for matching patterns within the original XML document, and applying formatting to that data. This results in anything from outputting XML data without the unwanted element names to inserting the data into a complex HTML table and displaying it to the user with highlighting and coloring. XSLT also provides syntax for many common operators, such as conditionals, copying of document tree fragments, advanced pattern matching, and the ability to access elements within the input XML data in an absolute and relative path structure. All these constructs are designed to ease the process of transforming an XML document into a new format.

XPath

As the final piece of the XML transformations puzzle, XPath provides a mechanism for referring to the wide variety of element and attribute names and values in an XML document. As I mentioned earlier, many XML specifications are now using XPath, but this discussion is concerned primarily with its use in XSLT. With the complex structure that an XML document can have, locating one specific element or set of elements can be difficult. It is made more difficult because access to a set of constraints that outlines the document's structure cannot be assumed; documents that are not validated must be able to be transformed just as valid documents can. To accomplish this addressing of elements, XPath defines syntax in line with the tree structure of XML, and the XSLT processes and constructs that use it.

Referencing any element or attribute within an XML document is most easily accomplished by specifying the path to the element relative to the current element being processed. In other words, if element B is the current element and element C and element D are nested within it, a relative path most easily locates them. This is similar to the relative paths used in operating system directory structures. At the same time, XPath also defines addressing for elements relative to the root of a document. This covers the common case of needing to reference an element not within the current element's scope; in other words, an element that is not nested within the element being processed. Finally, XPath defines syntax for actual pattern matching: find an element whose parent is element E and that has a sibling element F. This fills in the gaps left between the absolute and relative paths. In all these expressions, attributes can be used as well, with similar matching abilities:

```
<!-- Match the element named link underneath the current element -->
<xsl:value-of select="link" />
```

```
<!-- Match the element named title nested within the channel element -->
<xsl:value-of select="channel/title" />

<!-- Match the description element using an absolute path -->
<xsl:value-of select="/rdf:RDF/description" />

<!-- Match the resource attribute of the current element -->
<xsl:value-of select="@rdf:resource" />

<!-- Match the resource attribute of the errorReportsTo element -->
<xsl:value-of select="/rdf:RDF/channel/admin:errorReportsTo/@rdf:resource" />
```

Because the input document is often not fixed, an XPath expression can result in the evaluation of no input data, one input element or attribute, or multiple input elements and attributes. This ability makes XPath very useful and handy; it also causes the introduction of some additional terms. The result of evaluating an XPath expression can be a *node set*. This name is in line with the idea of a hierarchical structure, which is dealt with in terms of *leaves* and *nodes*. The resultant node set can be empty, have a single member, or have 5 or 10 members. It can be transformed, copied, ignored, or have any other legal operation performed on it. Instead of a node set, evaluating an XPath expression could result in a Boolean value, a numerical value, or a string value.

In addition to expressions that select node sets, XPath defines several functions that operate on node sets, like not( ) and count( ). These functions take in a node set as input and operate upon that node set. All of these expressions and functions are part of the XPath specification and XPath implementations; however, XPath is also often used to signify any expression that conforms to the specification itself. As with XSL and XSLT, this makes it easier to talk about XSL and XPath, though it is not always technically correct.

With all that in mind, you're at least somewhat prepared to take a look at a simple XSL stylesheet, shown in Example 1-2.

Example 1-2. XSL stylesheet for Example 1-1

```
<?xml version="1.0" ?>
<xsl:stylesheet xmlns:xsl="http://www.w3.org/1999/XSL/Transform" version="1.0"
                xmlns:rss="http://purl.org/rss/1.0/"
                xmlns:dc="http://purl.org/dc/elements/1.1/"
                xmlns:rdf="http://www.w3.org/1999/02/22-rdf-syntax-ns#">
<xsl:output method="xml" omit-xml-declaration="yes" indent="yes"/>

<xsl:template match="/rdf:RDF">
<p>
 <a><xsl:attribute name="href">
    <xsl:value-of select="rss:channel/rss:link"/>
    </xsl:attribute>
```

Example 1-2. XSL stylesheet for Example 1-1 (continued)

```
    <xsl:value-of select="rss:channel/rss:title"/></a>
</p>
<p>

<!-- Make the date presentable -->
 <xsl:variable name="datetime" select="rss:channel/dc:date"/>
 <xsl:variable name="day" select="substring($datetime, 9, 2)"/>
 <xsl:variable name="month" select="substring($datetime, 6, 2)"/>
 <xsl:variable name="year" select="substring($datetime, 0, 5)"/>
 <xsl:value-of select="concat($day, '/', $month, '/', $year)"/> -
 <xsl:value-of select="substring($datetime, 12, 5)"/>
</p>

<dl>
<xsl:for-each select="rss:item">
    <dt>
        <a><xsl:attribute name="href">
            <xsl:value-of select="rss:link"/>
          </xsl:attribute>
        <xsl:value-of select="rss:title"/></a>
    </dt>
    <dd>
        <xsl:value-of select="rss:description"
            disable-output-escaping="yes" />
        <!-- Format the publish date -->
        (<xsl:variable name="pubdate" select="dc:date"/>
        <xsl:variable name="pubday" select="substring($pubdate, 9, 2)"/>
        <xsl:variable name="pubmonth" select="substring($pubdate, 6, 2)"/>
        <xsl:variable name="pubyear" select="substring($pubdate, 0, 5)"/>
        <xsl:value-of select="concat($pubday, '/', $pubmonth, '/', $pubyear)"/> -
        <xsl:value-of select="substring($pubdate, 12, 5)"/>)
    </dd>
</xsl:for-each>
</dl>

<p>
 <xsl:value-of select="rss:channel/dc:rights"/>
</p>
</xsl:template>

</xsl:stylesheet>
```

Template matching

The basis of all XSL work is template matching. For any element on which you want
some sort of output to occur, you generally provide a template that matches the element. You signify a template with the template keyword, and provide the name of
the element to match in its match attribute:

```
    <xsl:template match="/rdf:RDF">
    <p>
     <a><xsl:attribute name="href">
        <xsl:value-of select="rss:channel/rss:link"/>
```

```
    </xsl:attribute>
    <xsl:value-of select="rss:channel/rss:title"/></a>
</p>

    <!-- etc... -->
</xsl:template>
```

Here, the RDF element (in the rdf-associated namespace) is being matched (the / is an XPath construct). When an XSL processor encounters the RDF element, the instructions within this template are carried out. In the example, several HTML formatting tags are output (the p and a tags). Be sure to distinguish your XSL elements from other elements (such as HTML elements) with proper use of namespaces.

You can use the value-of construct to obtain the value of an element, and provide the element name to match through the select attribute. In the example, the character data within the title element is extracted and used as the title of the page, and a link is constructed using the link element as the target.

On the other hand, when you want to cause the templates associated with an element's children to be applied, use apply-templates. Be sure to do this, or nested elements can be ignored! You can specify the elements to apply templates to using the select attribute; by specifying a value of * to that attribute, all templates left will be applied to all nested elements.

Looping

You'll also often find a need for looping in XSL:

```
<xsl:for-each select="rss:item">
    <dt>
        <a><xsl:attribute name="href">
            <xsl:value-of select="rss:link"/></xsl:attribute>
            <xsl:value-of select="rss:title"/></a>
    </dt>
    <dd>
        <xsl:value-of select="rss:description"
            disable-output-escaping="yes" />
        <!-- Format the publish date -->
        (<xsl:variable name="pubdate" select="dc:date"/>
        <xsl:variable name="pubday" select="substring($pubdate, 9, 2)"/>
        <xsl:variable name="pubmonth" select="substring($pubdate, 6, 2)"/>
        <xsl:variable name="pubyear" select="substring($pubdate, 0, 5)"/>
        <xsl:value-of select="concat($pubday, '/', $pubmonth, '/', $pubyear)"/> -
        <xsl:value-of select="substring($pubdate, 12, 5)"/>)
    </dd>
</xsl:for-each>
```

Here, I'm looping through each element named item using the for-each construct. In Java, this would be:

```
for (Iterator i = item.iterator( ); i.hasNext( ); ) {
    // take action on each item
}
```

Within the loop, the "current" element becomes the next item element encountered. For each item, I output the description (the entry text) using the value-ofconstruct. Take particular note of the disable-output-escaping attribute. In the XML, the description element has HTML content, which makes liberal use of entity references:

```
When the shoot was done, my daughter Holly, who had been doing her
homework in the room next door, and occasionally coming out to laugh
at me, helped use up the last few pictures on the roll. She looks like
she's having fun. I think I look a little dazed.&lt;br /&gt;
&lt;br /&gt;&lt;img src="http://www.neilgaiman.com/journal/Neil_8313036.jpg"
/&gt;&lt;br /&gt;&lt;br /&gt;This is the one we're going to be using
on the book jacket of ANANSI BOYS.
```

Normally, value-of outputs text just as it is in the XML document being processed. The result would be that this escaped HTML would stay escaped. The output document would end up looking like Figure 1-2.

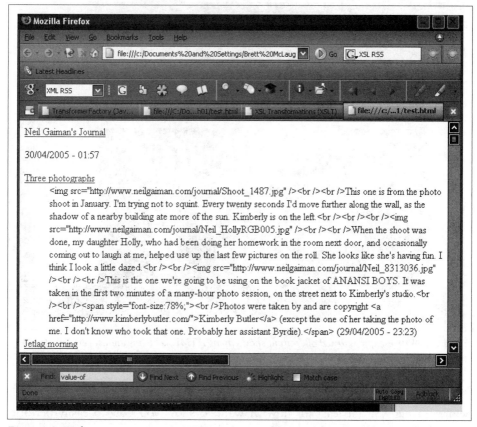

Figure 1-2. With output escaping on, HTML content within XML elements often won't look correct

To ensure that your output is not escaped, set `disable-output-escaping` to yes.

 Be sure you think this through. I used to get confused, thinking that I wanted to set this attribute to no so that escaping would *not* happen. However, a value of no results in escaping being enabled (not being disabled). Make sure you get this straight, or you'll have some odd results.

Setting this attribute to yes and rerunning the transform results in the output shown in Figure 1-3.

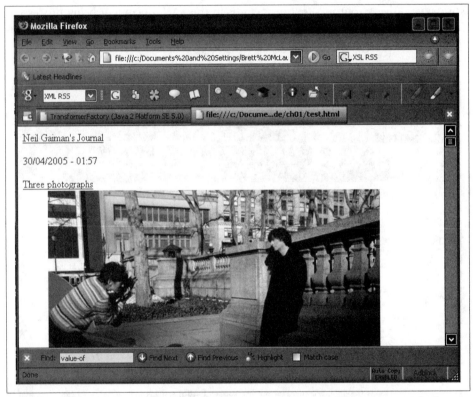

Figure 1-3. With escaping turned off, output shows up as HTML, which is almost certainly the desired result

Performing a transform

Before leaving XSL (at least for now), I want to show you how to easily perform transformations from the command line. This is a useful tool for quick-and-dirty tests; in fact, it's how I generated the screenshots used in this chapter.

Download Xalan-J from the Xalan web site, *http://xml.apache.org/xalan-j*. Expand the archive (on my Windows laptop, I use *c:/java/xalan-j_2_6_0*).

Then add *xalan.jar*, *xercesImpl.jar*, and *xml-apis.jar* to your classpath. Finally, run the following command:

```
java org.apache.xalan.xslt.Process -IN [XML filename]
                                   -XSL [XSL stylesheet]
                                   -OUT [output filename]
```

For example, to generate the HTML output for Neil Gaiman's feed, I used the tool like this:

```
> java org.apache.xalan.xslt.Process -IN gaiman-blogger_rss.xml
                                     -XSL rdf.xsl -OUT test.html
```

You'll get a file (*test.html* in this case) in the directory in which you run the command. Use this tool often; it will really help you figure out how XSL works, and what effect small changes have on output.

And More...

Lest I mislead you into thinking that's all that there is to XML, I want to make sure that you realize there are a multitude of other XML-related technologies. I can't possibly get into them all in this chapter, or even in this book. You should take a quick glance at things like Cascading Style Sheets (CSS) and XHTML if you are working on web design. Document authors will want to find out more about XLink and XPointer. XQuery will be of interest to database programmers. In other words, there's something XML for pretty much every technology space right now. Take a look at the W3C XML activity page at *http://www.w3.org/XML* and see what looks interesting.

CHAPTER 2

Constraints

It's rare that you'll be able to author XML without worrying about anyone else modifying your document, or anyone having to interpret the meaning of the document. The majority of the time, someone (or something) will have to figure out what your tags mean, what data is allowed within those tags, and how your document is structured. This is where constraint models come into play in the XML world. A *constraint model* defines the structure of your document and, to some degree, the data allowed within that structure.

In fact, if you take XML as being a data representation, you really can't divorce a document (often called an *instance*) from its constraints (the *schema*). The instance document contains the data, and the schema gives form to that data. You can't have one without the other; at least, not without introducing tremendous room for error. An instance document without a schema must be interpreted by the recipient; and do you really want him deciding what your elements and attributes meant?

 There's an argument that essentially goes like this: "Good XML should be structured so that it's self-documenting." That's a good goal, but practically impossible. As a programmer, I often think my code is well documented and easily understood; but I'm assuming a certain level of expertise, and a certain approach to coding. Change just a few bits here and there, and someone else might reasonably interpret my "well-documented" code (or XML) completely differently than I might. Taking the time to write a schema solves this problem much more definitively.

There are three basic models for constraints in use today:

DTDs
> Introduced as part of the XML 1.0 specification, DTDs are the oldest constraint model around in the XML world. They're simply to use, but this simplicity comes at a price: DTDs are inflexible, and offer you little for data type validation as well.

XML Schema (XSD)

XML Schema is the W3C's anointed successor to DTDs. XML Schemas are literally orders of magnitude more flexible than DTDs, and offer an almost dizzying array of support for various data types. However, just as DTDs were simple and limited, XML Schemas are flexible, complex, and (some would argue) bloated. It takes a lot of work to write a good schema, even for 50- or 100-line XML documents. For this reason, there's been a lot of dissatisfaction with XML Schema, even though they are widely being used.

RELAX NG

RELAX NG is largely a result of the backlash against the complexity of XML Schema. An alternate schema language, RELAX NG attempts to merge the flexibility of XML Schema with the simplicity of DTDs. While it's not as fully featured as XML Schema, it serves most of the common use cases, making it a great tool for the "everyday" XML developer.

There's some confusion around terminology in constraint models. To clarify, the term *schema* is used in this chapter to refer to any constraint model, whether it be a DTD, XML Schema, or Relax NG schema. In cases where the XSD specification is specifically referenced, "schema" will be capitalized, and preceded by "XML," as in XML Schema.

DTDs

A DTD defines how data is formatted. It must define each allowed element in an XML document, the allowed attributes, and—when appropriate—the acceptable attribute values for each element; it also indicates the nesting and occurrences of each element, and any external entities. DTDs can specify many other things about an XML document, but these basics are what I'll focus on here.

This chapter is by no means an extensive treatment of DTDs, XML Schema, or RELAX NG. For more detail on all of these schema types, check out *XML in a Nutshell* by Elliotte Rusty Harold and W. Scott Means (O'Reilly), and *RELAX NG* by Eric van der Vlist (O'Reilly), both exhaustive works on XML and RELAX NG.

DTD Semantics

There's remarkably little to a DTD's semantics, although you will have to use a totally different syntax for notation than you do in XML (an annoyance corrected in both XML Schema and RELAX NG).

Elements

The bulk of the DTD is composed of ELEMENT definitions (covered in this section) and ATTRIBUTE definitions (covered in the next section). An element definition begins with the ELEMENT keyword, following the standard <! opening of a DTD tag, and then the name of the element. Following that name is the *content model* of the element. The content model is generally within parentheses and specifies what content can be included within the element. Take the item element, from the RSS 0.91 DTD (*http://my.netscape.com/publish/formats/rss-0.91.dtd*) as an example:

```
<!ELEMENT item (title | link | description)*>
```

This says that for any item element, there may be a title element, a link element, or a description element nested within that item. The "or" relationship is indicated by the pipe (|) symbol; the OR applies to all elements within a group, indicated by the parentheses. In other words, for the grouping (title | link | description), one and only one of title, link, or description may appear. The asterisk after the grouping indicates a recurrence. Table 2-1 lists the complete set of DTD recurrence modifiers.

Table 2-1. When an element needs to appear multiple times, recurrence operators must be used

Operator	Description
[Default]	Must appear once and only once (1)
?	May appear once or not at all (0..1)
+	Must appear at least once, up to an infinite number of times (1..N)
*	May appear any number of times, including not at all (0..N)

So, revisiting the item definition, for an item, a title, link, or description may appear; but then the group can appear multiple times, meaning that you can have any number of title, link, and/or description elements within an item, and the XML would still be valid.

> This can get tricky pretty quickly if you're not used to working with these operators. All the item definition really does is say that it can have any number of title, link, and description elements, in any order. Since there is no modifier that tells DTDs that order doesn't matter, this basically becomes a hack to get around that limitation.

As an example of recurrence applying to just one element, take a look at the skipHours element definition:

```
<!ELEMENT skipHours (hour+)>
```

Here, the skipHours element must have at least one hour element within it, but has no maximum number of occurrences.

You can specify ordering using the comma (,) operator:

```
<!ELEMENT subscribers (url, email, comment*)>
```

In the subscribers element, there must be one (and only one) url element, followed by a single email element, followed by zero or more comment elements.

If an element has character data within it, the #PCDATA keyword is used as its content model:

```
<!ELEMENT title (#PCDATA)>
```

If an element should always be an empty element, the EMPTY keyword is used:

```
<!ELEMENT topic EMPTY>
```

 You won't find the topic or subscribers elements in the RSS 0.91 DTD. There are no elements with ordered content in that DTD, nor are there empty elements, so I made these elements up.

Attributes

Once you've handled the element definition, you'll want to define attributes. These are defined through the ATTLIST keyword. The first value is the name of the element, and then you have various attributes defined. Those definitions involve giving the name of the attribute, the type of attribute, and then whether the attribute is required or implied (which means it is not required, essentially). Most attributes with textual values will simply be of the type CDATA, as shown here:

```
<!ATTLIST rss
          version      CDATA #REQUIRED> <!-- must be "0.91"> -->
```

You can also specify a set of values that an attribute must take on for the document to be considered valid (this sample is from a hypothetical DTD describing a technical book):

```
<!ATTLIST title
          series   (C | Java | Linux | Oracle | Perl | Web | Windows)
                   #REQUIRED
>
```

Entities

You can specify entity reference resolution in a DTD using the ENTITY keyword. This works a lot like the DOCTYPE reference detailed in Chapter 1, where a public ID and/or system ID may be specified:

```
<!ENTITY OReillyCopyright SYSTEM
    "http://www.oreilly.com/copyright.xml"
>
```

This results in the *copyright.xml* file at the specified URL being loaded as the value of the O'Reilly copyright entity reference in a sample document that uses this reference:

```
<legal>
 <legal-notice>&OReillyCopyright;</legal-notice>
</legal>
```

Example 2-1 shows the complete RSS 0.91 DTD, so you can see several of these constructs in action.

Example 2-1. The RSS 0.91 DTD is a pretty simple example of a DTD; but then, DTDs are best for simple applications

```
<!--
Rich Site Summary (RSS) 0.91 official DTD, proposed.
RSS is an XML vocabulary for describing
metadata about websites, and enabling the display of
"channels" on the "My Netscape" website.
RSS Info can be found at http://my.netscape.com/publish/
XML Info can be found at http://www.w3.org/XML/
copyright Netscape Communications, 1999
Dan Libby - danda@netscape.com
Based on RSS DTD originally created by
Lars Marius Garshol - larsga@ifi.uio.no.
$Id$
-->
<!ELEMENT rss (channel)>
<!ATTLIST rss
version    CDATA #REQUIRED> <!-- must be "0.91"> -->
<!ELEMENT channel (title | description | link | language | item+ | rating? | image? |
textinput? | copyright? | pubDate? | lastBuildDate? | docs? | managingEditor? | webMaster?
| skipHours? | skipDays?)*>
<!ELEMENT title (#PCDATA)>
<!ELEMENT description (#PCDATA)>
<!ELEMENT link (#PCDATA)>
<!ELEMENT image (title | url | link | width? | height? | description?)*>
<!ELEMENT url (#PCDATA)>
<!ELEMENT item (title | link | description)*>
<!ELEMENT textinput (title | description | name | link)*>
<!ELEMENT name (#PCDATA)>
<!ELEMENT rating (#PCDATA)>
<!ELEMENT language (#PCDATA)>
<!ELEMENT width (#PCDATA)>
<!ELEMENT height (#PCDATA)>
<!ELEMENT copyright (#PCDATA)>
<!ELEMENT pubDate (#PCDATA)>
<!ELEMENT lastBuildDate (#PCDATA)>
<!ELEMENT docs (#PCDATA)>
<!ELEMENT managingEditor (#PCDATA)>
<!ELEMENT webMaster (#PCDATA)>
<!ELEMENT hour (#PCDATA)>
<!ELEMENT day (#PCDATA)>
<!ELEMENT skipHours (hour+)>
<!ELEMENT skipDays (day+)>
```

 I've omitted the ISO Latin-1 character entities for clarity.

Generating DTDs from XML Instance Documents

If you need to quickly get a DTD up and running, and already have XML on hand, you may just want to autogenerate a DTD from an XML document. Relaxer is a cool tool for doing just this (as well as generating XML Schemas and RELAX NG schemas). Download Relaxer from *http://www.relaxer.org/download/index.html*, and drop the archived folder somewhere accessible. Install it like this:

```
[bmclaugh:/usr/local/java/relaxer-1.0] sudo java -cp . setup

We trust you have received the usual lecture from the local System
Administrator. It usually boils down to these three things:

    #1) Respect the privacy of others.
    #2) Think before you type.
    #3) With great power comes great responsibility.

Password:
Install directory [default: /usr/local/lib/relaxer]:
Command directory [default: /usr/local/bin]:

[Configuration]
Install directory = /usr/local/lib/relaxer
Command directory = /usr/local/bin

Type "yes" to install, "no" to re-enter, "exit" to exit
> yes
Extract archives...
Generate script...
   script = /usr/local/bin/relaxer
Done.
[bmclaugh:/usr/local/java/relaxer-1.0]
```

 On Unix or Mac OS X, you'll probably need to use *sudo* to install Relaxer; */usr/local/lib* (if it even exists on your system) is probably only root-writable. You may also need to make the resulting installed files accessible by non-root users:

```
sudo chmod -R 755 /usr/local/bin
```

Now you can run Relaxer:

```
[bmclaugh:/usr/local/java/relaxer-1.0] relaxer
Copyright(c) 2000-2003 ASAMI,Tomoharu. All rights reserved.
Relaxer Version 1.0 (20031224) by asami@relaxer.org

Usage: relaxer [-options] [args...]
   for more information, use -help option
```

To generate a DTD, just give it the name of your XML file, and specify the *-dtd* option:

```
relaxer -dtd toc.xml
```

You can specify an alternate output directory using the *-dir:[output dir]* option. You should also ensure that the input XML has no DOCTYPE reference referring to an existing DTD, as that generally causes Relaxer to error out. Just comment out the reference if you have one already.

By default, Relaxer uses the name of your input XML as the name of the DTD, and replaces the XML extension with *.dtd*. Example 2-2 is the output from this command, using the table of contents from Eclipse's documentation set as input (*toc.xml* is available from the online examples).

Example 2-2. The DTD generated here by Relaxer is simple; Relaxer works best with simple XML, and gets progressively worse at generation as your XML gets more complicated

```
<!-- Generated by Relaxer 1.0 -->
<!-- Wed Jul 06 13:39:26 CDT 2005 -->

<!ELEMENT topic (link)>
<!ATTLIST topic href CDATA #IMPLIED>
<!ATTLIST topic label CDATA #REQUIRED>

<!ELEMENT toc (topic+)>
<!ATTLIST toc label CDATA #REQUIRED>

<!ELEMENT link EMPTY>
<!ATTLIST link toc CDATA #REQUIRED>
```

While you'll often need to tweak the generated DTD to match your needs, it's a great start, and can save a lot of tedious DTD authoring. If you do get errors, they'll most likely crop up in recurrence operators. To try and avoid these sorts of errors, you can supply multiple instance documents in an effort to get an even better first cut:

```
relaxer -dtd toc.xml toc_gr.xml toc_jp.xml
```

A lot of times a few extra files will really help nail any optional elements, as well as refine the recurrence operators that Relaxer uses. In the case of Example 2-2, this line is incorrect:

```
<!ELEMENT topic (link)>
```

You need to add an optional modifier, as link is not always required to be present in topic elements:

```
<!ELEMENT topic (link)?>
```

Aside from these glitches, I still use Relaxer on a regular basis.

Validating XML Against a DTD

If you just can't wait until I talk about SAX, DOM, and JAXP for validation, it's simple to use a few nifty tools for validating your XML documents against a DTD. I like

---

using *xmllint*, an application that comes with Red Hat, but can be downloaded for a variety of platforms at *http://www.xmlsoft.org/downloads.html*. Installation varies by platform, but you'll find the program simple and well-documented; just make sure you have the *xmllint* binary somewhere on your path. To validate against a DTD, first make sure your XML has a DOCTYPE declaration in it:

```
<?xml version="1.0" encoding="UTF-8"?>
<!DOCTYPE toc SYSTEM "toc.dtd">
```

Then, execute *xmllint* with the *--valid* option:

```
xmllint --valid toc.xml --noout
```

 xmllint will actually echo the XML you supply it, unless you supply the *--noout* option. With this option on, you'll only receive errors from validation. Further, in some cases, *xmllint* errors out when *--noout* is anywhere other than at the end of the command; always place it last to avoid these problems.

xmllint is a great tool for validating documents against generated DTDs; you'll often uncover errors, and be able to quickly correct them.

XML Schema

XML Schema seeks to improve upon DTDs by adding more typing and quite a few more constructs than DTDs, as well as using XML as the constraint representation format. I'm going to spend relatively little time here talking about schemas, because they are a behind the scenes detail for Java and XML. In the chapters where you'll be working with schemas, I'll address any specific points you need to be aware of. However, the specification for XML Schema is so enormous that it would take up an entire book of explanation on its own. As a matter of fact, *XML Schema* by Eric van der Vlist (O'Reilly) is just that: an entire book on XML Schema.

XML Schema Definitions

Before getting into the actual schema constructs, take a look at a typical XML Schema root element:

```
<xsd:schema xmlns:xsd="http://www.w3.org/2001/XMLSchema"
    xmlns:dw="http://www.ibm.com/developerWorks/"
    elementFormDefault="unqualified"
    attributeFormDefault="unqualified" version="4.0">
```

There's quite a bit going on here, including two different namespace declarations. First, the XML Schema namespace itself is attached to the xsd prefix, allowing separation of XML Schema constructs from the elements and attributes being constrained. Next, the dw namespace is defined; this particular example is from the IBM Developer-Works XML article template, and dw is used for DeveloperWorks-specific constructs.

Then, the values of `attributeFormDefault` and `elementFormDefault` are set to "unqualified". This allows XML instance documents to omit namespace declarations on elements and attributes. Qualifications are a fairly tricky idea, largely because attributes in XML do not fall into the default namespace; they must explicitly be assigned to a namespace. For a lot more on qualification, check out the relevant portion of the XML Schema specification at *http://www.w3.org/TR/2004/REC-xmlschema-1-20041028/structures.html#element-schema*.

Finally, the `version` attribute is given a value of "4.0". This is used to indicate the version of this particular schema, not of the XML Schema specification being used. The namespace assigned to the xsd prefix, *http://www.w3.org/2001/XMLSchema*, is actually the indicator as to which schema spec is being used, rather than an explicit version attribute.

Elements and attributes

Elements are defined with the element construct. You'll generally need to define your own data types by nesting a `complexType` tag within the `element` element, which defines the name of the element (through the `name` attribute). For example, here's an element definition from IBM's schema; this particular fragment constraints the code element:

```
<xsd:element name="code">
    <xsd:annotation>
      <xsd:documentation xml:lang="en">
        <title>Define a code listing</title>
        <desc>The stylesheet allows code to be inline or section.  The contents of
this element are displayed in a monospaced font, with all whitespace preserved from
the original XML source.</desc>
      </xsd:documentation>
    </xsd:annotation>
    <xsd:complexType mixed="true">
      <xsd:choice minOccurs="0" maxOccurs="unbounded">
        <xsd:element ref="a"/>
        <xsd:element ref="b"/>
        <xsd:element ref="br"/>
        <xsd:element ref="font"/>
        <xsd:element ref="heading"/>
        <xsd:element ref="i"/>
        <xsd:element ref="sub"/>
        <xsd:element ref="sup"/>
        <xsd:group ref="specialCharacters"/>
      </xsd:choice>
      <xsd:attribute name="type" type="inline" use="required">
        <xsd:annotation>
          <xsd:documentation xml:lang="en">
            <desc>The type of code listing.</desc>
          </xsd:documentation>
        </xsd:annotation>
      </xsd:attribute>
```

```
    <xsd:attribute name="width">
      <xsd:annotation>
        <xsd:documentation xml:lang="en">
          <desc>The width in characters of this code listing.</desc>
        </xsd:documentation>
      </xsd:annotation>
    </xsd:attribute>
  </xsd:complexType>
</xsd:element>
```

In this case, the element's name (code) is supplied, and then annotation is used to provide some basic commenting and documentation.

 annotation is notoriously underused. Consider yourself lucky when you get an XML Schema as well documented as this example is. I've removed annotations from the remaining examples, just to save space and add some clarity (albeit while losing documentation).

complexType simply informs the schema parser that the element is not a predefined schema type, like string or integer. Setting the mixed attribute to true lets the schema parser know that the code element can have textual content, as well as nested elements. The default value for mixed is false; you have to explicitly specify when an element has both text and subelements.

Next, choice is used to supply a selection of subelements. If you omit choice and just list the elements, the order matters (elements must appear in the order that they are declared in the schema). But, by using choice, order becomes unimportant. Further, the minimum and maximum number of each element is unbounded (minOccurs="unbounded" and maxOccurs="unbounded" takes care of this). This effectively allows any number of any of these elements to appear, in any order. For each of these elements referenced (using ref), there must be a definition somewhere else in the schema (and may have its own complexType, referencing other elements).

Finally, the type and width attributes are defined and annotated, using the attribute keyword. So, there should be two things to take away from this definition:

- Once you get the basic constructs in your head, it's fairly easy to read an XML Schema.
- Even the definition of very simple elements is verbose; you'll rarely see an XML Schema that's fewer than several hundred lines.

Simple types

If you did have a so-called "simple type," you can avoid the complexType construct altogether:

```
<xsd:element name="text-data" type="xsd:string" />
```

Extending base types

You'll often want the simplicity of a simple type but the flexibility of XML Schema's more advanced constraints. For example, if you were defining a `colorname` element, you would probably want it as a simple string:

```
<xsd:element name="colorname" type="xsd:string" />
```

But, you can use XML Schema's enumeration feature to ensure only certain colors are allowed. In these cases, you have to use extension; but, since you're actually restricting the base type of string, rather than expanding on it, you'd use the `restriction` keyword:

```
<xsd:simpleType name="colorname">
  <xsd:restriction base="xsd:string">
    <xsd:enumeration value="blue" />
    <xsd:enumeration value="green" />
    <xsd:enumeration value="red" />
  </xsd:restriction>
</xsd:simpleType>
```

On the other hand, extension is used when you're taking a base type and adding to it:

```
<xsd:element name="title">
  <xsd:complexType>
    <xsd:simpleContent>
      <xsd:extension base=" xsd:string">
        <xsd:attribute name="isbn" type="xsd:string"/>
      </xsd:extension>
    </xsd:simpleContent>
  </xsd:complexType>
</xsd:element>
```

Here, the `title` element is based on a simple string, but adds an additional attribute (isbn, also a string).

> For Java programmers, the distinction between extension and restriction is not as obvious; we're used to extending (even if the subclass ends up adding restrictions to types it might accept). In XML Schema, you use restriction to further constrain a type, and you use extension to broaden a type.

Although I've barely scratched the surface of XML Schema, this should at least give you a rough idea of the major constructs; it's certainly enough to get you through this book without too much trouble.

Generating XML Schemas from Instance Documents

You already know about Relaxer from the previous section "Generating DTDs from XML Instance Documents." The same tool works with XML Schemas, using the *-xsd* option:

```
relaxer -xsd toc.xml
```

You'll get an XSD file (in this case, *toc.xsd*). For the Eclipse table of contents, the resulting schema is shown in Example 2-3.

Example 2-3. The XML Schema generated by Relaxer automatically assigns a no-URL namespace as the default, if none is specified in the instance document

```
<?xml version="1.0" encoding="UTF-8" ?>
<xsd:schema xmlns=""
            xmlns:xsd="http://www.w3.org/2001/XMLSchema"
            targetNamespace="">
  <xsd:element name="toc" type="toc"/>
  <xsd:complexType name="toc">
    <xsd:sequence>
      <xsd:element maxOccurs="unbounded" minOccurs="1"
                   name="topic" type="topic"/>
    </xsd:sequence>
    <xsd:attribute name="label" type="xsd:token"/>
  </xsd:complexType>
  <xsd:complexType name="topic">
    <xsd:sequence>
      <xsd:element name="link" type="link"/>
    </xsd:sequence>
    <xsd:attribute name="href" type="xsd:token"/>
    <xsd:attribute name="label" type="xsd:token"/>
  </xsd:complexType>
  <xsd:complexType name="link">
    <xsd:sequence/>
    <xsd:attribute name="toc" type="xsd:token"/>
  </xsd:complexType>
</xsd:schema>
```

Compare this to Example 2-2, and you begin to see how verbose XML Schema really is! As in the case of autogeneration of DTDs, the more instance documents you can supply to Relaxer, the more accurate the resulting XML Schema.

Generating XML Schemas from a DTD

As the XML community moves away from DTDs to either XML Schema or RELAX NG, you'll need to convert many of your DTDs to a new constraint model. The DTD2XS tool at *http://www.lumrix.net/xmlfreeware.php* is perfect for just this use-case. Download the tool, and expand it to somewhere easily added to your classpath (like */usr/local/java/dtdxs*). On Unix/Linux/Mac OS X:

```
export CLASSPATH=$CLASSPATH:/usr/local/java/dtd2xs
```

and on Windows:

```
set CLASSPATH=%CLASSPATH%;c:\java\dtd2xs
```

Unfortunately, you have to copy the *complextype.xsl* file, from the DTD2XS distribution, into the directory you're working from (or always convert from the *dtdxs* directory, which is equally inconvenient).

Now just give the tool a DTD to convert:

```
[bmclaugh] java dtd2xsd toc.dtd > toc-schema.xsd

dtd2xs: dtdURI file:////Users/bmclaugh/Documents/O'Reilly/Writing/Java and XML 3rd/
subs/code/ch02/toc.dtd
dtd2xs: resolveEntities true
dtd2xs: ignoreComments true
dtd2xs: commentLength 100
dtd2xs: commentLanguage null
dtd2xs: conceptHighlight 2
dtd2xs: conceptOccurrence 1
dtd2xs: conceptRelation element attribute
dtd2xs: load DTD ... done
dtd2xs: remove comments from DTD ... done
dtd2xs: DOM translation ...
... done
dtd2xs: complextype.xsl ... done
dtd2xs: add namespace ... done
```

The name of the tool is DTD2XS, but the Java class to execute is dtd2xsd. Another slightly confusing aspect of the tool; but, it's workable, and that's what's important.

The resulting XML Schema is shown in Example 2-4.

Example 2-4. The output from DTD2XS isn't the prettiest you'll ever see, but it usually gets the job done just fine

```
<?xml version="1.0" encoding="UTF-8"?>
<xs:schema xmlns:xs="http://www.w3.org/2001/XMLSchema">
<xs:element name="topic">
<xs:complexType>
<xs:sequence minOccurs="0">
<xs:element ref="link"/>
</xs:sequence>
<xs:attribute name="href" type="xs:string"/>
<xs:attribute name="label" type="xs:string" use="required"/>
</xs:complexType>
</xs:element>
<xs:element name="toc">
<xs:complexType>
<xs:sequence>
<xs:element maxOccurs="unbounded" ref="topic"/>
</xs:sequence>
<xs:attribute name="label" type="xs:string" use="required"/>
</xs:complexType>
</xs:element>
<xs:element name="link">
<xs:complexType>
<xs:attribute name="toc" type="xs:string" use="required"/>
</xs:complexType>
</xs:element>
</xs:schema>
```

Validating XML Against an XML Schema

Finally, you should be able to validate your documents against an XML Schema (without resorting to programming, which is detailed in later chapters). As in "Validating XML Against a DTD," *xmllint* does the trick. First, though, you need to reference your schema in your instance document; this is quite a bit different from using a DOCTYPE definition, though.

Referencing a schema for nonnamespaced documents

If you're not using namespaces in the instance document, here's what you'd use:

```
<dw-document xsi:noNamespaceSchemaLocation="dw-document-4.0.xsd"
             xmlns:xsi="http://www.w3.org/2001/XMLSchema-instance">
```

> You can use URLs, like *http://www.ibm.com/xsd/dw-document-4.0.xsd*, as well as local references, when pointing to an XML Schema.

dw-document is the root element here, and it defines the xsi namespace. You should always use the same URI for this declaration (*http://www.w3.org/2001/XMLSchema-instance*), as that's what schema-aware parsers are expecting.

> Some parsers ignore the URI, while others check against it. In either case, it's better to just use the same (correct) URI in every document, and not worry about it.

Since there is no namespace being constrained, use the noNamespaceSchemaLocation attribute to indicate where to find the XML Schema (again, used to constrain all portions of the document not in a namespace).

Referencing a schema for namespaced documents

If you are using namespaces, you'll need to pair each namespace with a schema to validate against:

```
<dw-document xmlns="http://www.ibm.com/developerWorks"
   xmlns:xsi="http://www.w3.org/2001/XMLSchema-instance"
   xsi:schemaLocation="http://www.ibm.com/developerWorks
                       dw-document-4.0.xsd">
```

schemaLocation is used, instead of noNamespaceSchemaLocation, and it takes two arguments (separated by a space; that space appears as a line break in the printed book). The first value is the namespace to constrain, and the second is the schema location.

> The XML Schema specification allows for multiple pairs of namespace URI/schema URI combinations, although that becomes difficult to accurately represent in a fixed-margin book.

Validating against a schema

Now invoke *xmllint* with the *--schema* option:

```
[bmclaugh] xmllint --schema dw-document-4.0.xsd index.xml --noout
index.xml validates
```

Errors are reported, and you can easily fix them.

RELAX NG

RELAX NG is, in many senses, the rebel child in the constraint family. While DTDs and XML Schema are both W3C specifications (or at least part of a specification, in the case of DTDs), RELAX NG is not endorsed or "blessed" by the W3C. And, even though it has been developed underneath the OASIS umbrella (*http://www.oasis-open.org/home/index.php*), RELAX NG is still seen as almost a grassroots effort to compete with—or at least provide an alternative to—XML Schema. Whatever you think about the political standing of RELAX NG, though, any good XML programmer should have RELAX NG in her constraint toolkit.

Constraining XML with RELAX NG

RELAX NG, like XML Schema, is pure XML. You start out by nesting everything within a grammar element:

```
<grammar xmlns="http://relaxng.org/ns/structure/1.0"
         datatypeLibrary="http://www.w3.org/2001/XMLSchema-datatypes">
  <!-- Content model for XML -->
</grammar>
```

This sets up the namespace for all the elements you used, which are of course all part of the RELAX NG syntax. datatypeLibrary lets the schema know where to pull data types (covered in the "Data types" section later) from, when you type elements and attributes. You don't have to put this on your root element, but you'll find that's the best place to locate the reference; otherwise, you end up burying it somewhere in the middle of your schema, and that's a maintenance pain.

 Like the XML Schema specification, you should always use the same URI for the namespace here (*http://relaxng.org/ns/structure/1.0*).

You'll find that most of the RELAX NG constructs are pretty intuitive; I'll run through the highlights.

Elements

You define elements using the element keyword, and nestings within an XML document are represented by nestings with the RELAX NG schema:

```
<element name="phonebook">
  <element name="entry">
    <element name="firstName">
      <text/>
    </element>
    <element name="firstName">
      <text/>
    </element>
    <!-- etc... -->
  </element>
</element>
```

In fact, you should already be seeing one of the cooler features of RELAX NG: its structure closely mirrors the structure of the document it's constraining.

Cardinality and recurrence

In DTDs, you used *, +, and ? to indicate how many times an element can occur; XML Schema uses minOccurs and maxOccurs. In RELAX NG, you use elements, like zeroOrMore, oneOrMore, or optional:

```
<zeroOrMore>
  <element name="phonebook">
    <oneOrMore>
      <element name="entry">
        <element name="firstName">
          <text/>
        </element>
        <optional>
          <element name="middleName>
        </optional>
        <element name="firstName">
          <text/>
        </element>
        <!-- etc... -->
      </element>
    </oneOrMore>
  </element>
</zeroOrMore>
```

This is a little different from anything you've seen so far, but turns out to be pretty simple to remember. Any element (or attribute) without a cardinality modifier like this is assumed to appear once and only once (just like in XML Schema).

Attributes

Attributes are equally easy to specify:

```
<zeroOrMore>
  <element name="phonebook">
    <oneOrMore>
      <element name="entry">
        <element name="firstName">
```

```
          <text/>
        </element>
        <optional>
          <element name="middleName">
        </optional>
        <element name="firstName">
          <text/>
        </element>
        <zeroOrMore>
          <element name="address">
            <attribute name="type">
              <choice>
                <value>home</value>
                <value>work</value>
                <!-- and so on -->
              </choice>
            </attribute>
          </element>
        </zeroOrMore>

        <!-- etc... -->
      </element>
    </oneOrMore>
  </element>
</zeroOrMore>
```

I also tossed in the choice operator, which allows you to indicate specific values that
are allowed for the attribute.

Data types

Last but not least (in this RELAX NG crash course, at least), you can type your data
in RELAX NG, using the data element. Here's the definition of a point type, from the
RELAX NG tutorial, for example:

```
<element name="point" datatypeLibrary="http://www.w3.org/2001/XMLSchema-datatypes">
  <element name="x">
    <data type="double"/>
  </element>
  <element name="y">
    <data type="double"/>
  </element>
</element>
```

If you placed the datatypeLibrary attribute on your root element, then
you don't need to repeat that declaration here.

When you use the string data type (instead of the <text/> tag) for an element, you
have to specify the length allowed as well; for this reason, only use the string data
type when you have a maximum length in mind:

```
<element name="email">
  <data type="string">
    <param name="maxLength">127</param>
  </data>
</element>
```

That's not much on RELAX NG, but it's plenty to help you get started. As mentioned earlier, *RELAX NG* by Eric van der Vlist (O'Reilly) is available for a more in-depth look at the schema language.

Generating RELAX NG from an XML Instance

Relaxer (used previously in the "Generating DTDs from XML Instance Documents" and "Generating XML Schemas from Instance Documents" sections) handles RELAX NG schema generation easily enough, using the *-rng* option:

```
relaxer -rng toc.xml
```

The resultant RELAX NG schema, *toc.rng*, is shown in Example 2-5.

Example 2-5. Relaxer generates RELAX NG schemas, in XML format, of course

```
<?xml version="1.0" encoding="UTF-8" ?>
<grammar xmlns="http://relaxng.org/ns/structure/1.0"
        xmlns:a="http://relaxng.org/ns/compatibility/annotations/1.0"
        xmlns:java="http://www.relaxer.org/xmlns/relaxer/java"
        xmlns:relaxer="http://www.relaxer.org/xmlns/relaxer"
        xmlns:sql="http://www.relaxer.org/xmlns/relaxer/sql"
        datatypeLibrary="http://www.w3.org/2001/XMLSchema-datatypes"
        ns="">
  <start>
    <ref name="toc"/>
  </start>
  <define name="toc">
    <element name="toc">
      <attribute name="label">
        <data type="token"/>
      </attribute>
      <oneOrMore>
        <ref name="topic"/>
      </oneOrMore>
    </element>
  </define>
  <define name="topic">
    <element name="topic">
      <optional>
        <attribute name="href">
          <data type="token"/>
        </attribute>
      </optional>
      <attribute name="label">
        <data type="token"/>
      </attribute>
```

```
        <ref name="link"/>
      </element>
    </define>
    <define name="link">
      <element name="link">
        <attribute name="toc">
          <data type="token"/>
        </attribute>
      </element>
    </define>
</grammar>
```

Converting DTDs to RELAX NG Schemas

To convert DTDs to RELAX NG, use Sun's RELAX NG Converter, which you download from *https://msv.dev.java.net*. The RELAX NG Converter began as its own project, but is now part of Sun's Multi-Schema XML Validator project

Move the downloaded and extracted folder into somewhere useful; I moved mine into */usr/local/java*, and then renamed the folder (*rngconv-20030225*) to a more manageable name (*rngconv*). Then just run *java* and supply the converter JAR file as the module to run:

```
java -jar /usr/local/java/rngconv/rngconv.jar toc.dtd > toc-dtd.rng
```

Every bit of documentation I found insisted you supply RELAX NG Converter the *-dtd* flag for converting DTDs, but I couldn't get the tool to work with that flag. It's only when I removed the flag that I had successful results.

The result—piped into the *toc-dtd.rng* file—is shown in Example 2-6.

Example 2-6. I'm not a fan of all the whitespace that RELAX NG Converter introduces, but other than that, it does a great job

```
<?xml version="1.0"?>
<grammar ns="" xmlns="http://relaxng.org/ns/structure/1.0"
         datatypeLibrary="http://www.w3.org/2001/XMLSchema-datatypes">
    <start>
        <choice>
            <ref name="topic"/>
            <element name="toc">
                <attribute name="label">
                    <data type="normalizedString"/>
                </attribute>
                <oneOrMore>
                    <ref name="topic"/>
                </oneOrMore>
            </element>
```

Example 2-6. I'm not a fan of all the whitespace that RELAX NG Converter introduces, but other than that, it does a great job (continued)

```
                <ref name="link"/>
            </choice>
        </start>
        <define name="link">
            <element name="link">
                <attribute name="toc">
                    <data type="normalizedString"/>
                </attribute>
            </element>
        </define>
        <define name="topic">
            <element name="topic">
                <optional>
                    <attribute name="href">
                        <data type="normalizedString"/>
                    </attribute>
                </optional>
                <attribute name="label">
                    <data type="normalizedString"/>
                </attribute>
                <optional>
                    <ref name="link"/>
                </optional>
            </element>
        </define>
</grammar>
```

Converting XML Schemas to RELAX NG Schemas

You can use the Sun RELAX NG Converter (see the previous section "Converting DTDs to RELAX NG Schemas" for installation instructions) for converting XML Schema to RELAX NG:

```
java -jar /usr/local/java/rngconv/rngconv.jar toc.xsd > toc.rng
```

Example 2-7 shows what the tool did with my XSD file as input.

Example 2-7. Although the semantics are slightly different in a DTD schema, versus this one from an XML Schema, the constraints are remarkably similar

```
<?xml version="1.0"?>
<grammar ns="" xmlns="http://relaxng.org/ns/structure/1.0"
        datatypeLibrary="http://www.w3.org/2001/XMLSchema-datatypes">
    <start>
        <choice>
            <notAllowed/>
            <element name="toc">
                <optional>
                    <attribute name="label">
                        <data type="token"/>
                    </attribute>
```

Example 2-7. Although the semantics are slightly different in a DTD schema, versus this one from an XML Schema, the constraints are remarkably similar (continued)

```
            </optional>
            <oneOrMore>
                <element name="topic">
                    <optional>
                        <attribute name="label">
                            <data type="token"/>
                        </attribute>
                    </optional>
                    <optional>
                        <attribute name="href">
                            <data type="token"/>
                        </attribute>
                    </optional>
                    <element name="link">
                        <optional>
                            <attribute name="toc">
                                <data type="token"/>
                            </attribute>
                        </optional>
                    </element>
                </element>
            </oneOrMore>
        </element>
    </choice>
  </start>
</grammar>
```

Validating XML Against a RELAX NG Schema

No surprise here; *xmllint* does the job once again (*xmllint* was introduced in "Validating XML Against a DTD" and used again in "Validating XML Against an XML Schema"). You just need to use the *--relaxng* option, and you're off to the races:

```
xmllint --relaxng toc-dtd.rng toc.xml --noout
```

> You may have noticed that I supplied no instructions for referencing a RELAX NG schema in your XML document. That's because there's no need to; the schema to use is controlled by the tool validating, rather than the input document.

I realize that I've assaulted you with tools in this chapter, but you just can't have enough conversion utilities in your back pocket. You never know when it will be easier to quickly convert a DTD to a RELAX NG schema, and work with that, rather than trying to reengineer a DTD; the same is true for validation, and working with XML Schema. And, this will all be even more useful as we begin to explore introducing Java into the XML equation.

## CHAPTER 3

SAX

XML is fundamentally about data; programming with XML, then, has to be fundamentally about getting at that data. That process, called *parsing*, is the basic task of the APIs I'll cover in the next several chapters. This chapter describes how an XML document is parsed, focusing on the events that occur within this process. These events are important, as they are all points where application-specific code can be inserted and data manipulation can occur.

I'm also going to introduce you to one of the two core XML APIs in Java: SAX, the Simple API for XML (*http://www.saxproject.org*). SAX is what makes insertion of this application-specific code into events possible. The interfaces provided in the SAX package are an important part of any programmer's toolkit for handling XML. Even though the SAX classes are small and few in number, they provide a critical framework for Java and XML to operate within. Solid understanding of how they help in accessing XML data is critical to effectively leveraging XML in your Java programs.

For the impatient, the other of those two core APIs is DOM. Coverage of DOM begins in Chapter 5.

Setting Up SAX

I'm increasingly of the "learning is best done by doing" philosophy, so I'm not going to hit you with a bunch of concept and theory before getting to code. SAX is a simple API, so you only need to understand its basic model, and how to get the API on your machine; beyond that, code will be your best teacher.

Callbacks and Event-Based Programming

SAX uses a *callback model* for interacting with your code; you may also have heard this model called *event-based programming*. Whatever you call it, it's a bit of a departure for object-oriented developers, so give it some time if you're new to this type of programming.

In short, the parsing process is going to hum along, tearing through an XML document. Every time it encounters a tag, or comment, or text, or any other piece of XML, it *calls back* into your code, signaling that an event has occurred. Your code then has an opportunity to act, based on the details of that event.

For example, if SAX encounters the opening tag of an element, it fires off a startElement event. It provides information about that event, such as the name of the element, its attributes, and so on, and then your code gets to respond. You, as a programmer, have to write code for each event that is important to you—from the start of a document to a comment to the end of an element. This process is summed up in Figure 3-1.

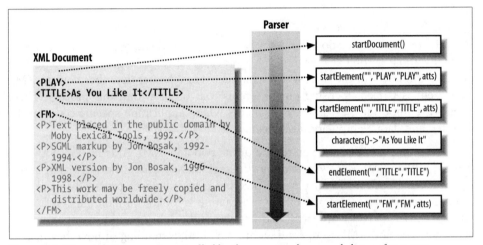

Figure 3-1. The parsing process is controlled by the parser and your code listens for events, responding as they occur

What's different about this model is that your code is not active, in the sense that it doesn't ever instruct the parser, "Hey, go and parse the next element." It's passive, in that it waits to be called, and *then* leaps into action. This takes a little getting used to, but you'll be an old hand by the end of the chapter.

 Swing and AWT programmers, as well as EJB experts, are familiar with this approach to programming.

The SAX API

Unsurprisingly, the SAX API is made up largely of interfaces that define these various callback methods. You would implement the ContentHandler interface, and provide an implementation for the characters() method (for example) to handle events triggered by character processing. Figure 3-2 provides a visual overview of the API; you'll see that it's remarkably simple.

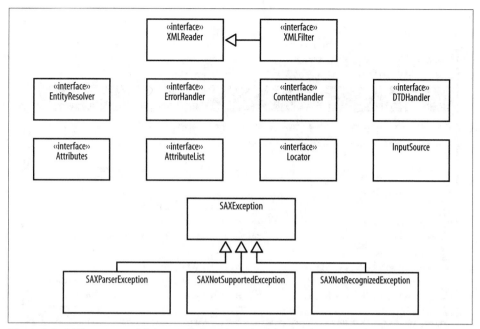

Figure 3-2. SAX is a powerful API, even though it's largely interfaces and a few helper classes

Keep in mind that a SAX-compliant parser will *not* implement many of these interfaces (EntityResolver, ContentHandler, ErrorHandler, etc.); that's the job of you, the programmer. The parser from your vendor will implement the XMLReader interface—and a few helper interfaces like Attributes—and provide parsing behavior; everything else is left up to you.

SAX Parsing Setup

Like most APIs, getting setup to work with SAX just involves a download or two. You'll need the SAX classes and interfaces, obviously, as well as a concrete implementation of those interfaces. This is all usually bundled into one download; for example, the Apache Xerces project allows you to download one large file that contains several JAR files, containing everything from the SAX API to several parser implementations to examples and help files.

Choose the parser you want to use (or, if you're at a big company, ask your boss or co-workers what parser they're using), and download that parser's implementation. For Xerces, visit *http://xml.apache.org/xerces2-j*, and click the Download link on the left. Navigate to the correct download (the binary release is what most users want), and grab the file from Apache's server, or a mirror (see Figure 3-3).

You'll need to consult your parser documentation as to what your classpath should look like. For Xerces, you'll want to include the *xml-apis.jar* and *xercesImpl.jar* files

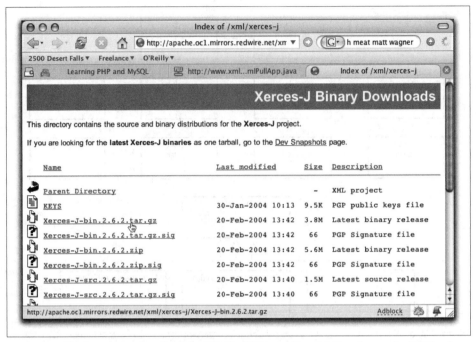

Figure 3-3. *Windows users, download the ZIP file; Unix and Mac OS X geeks, try the GZIPped TAR file*

on your classpath; both are in the Xerces distribution's *bin/* directory. For example, here's a fragment of my *.profile* on Mac OS X:

```
export JAVA_BASE=/usr/local/java
export XERCES_HOME=$jAVA_BASE/xerces-2_6_2
export XALAN_HOME=$JAVA_BASE/xalan-j_2_6_0

export CVS_RSH=ssh
export PS1="[`whoami`:\w] "

export CLASSPATH=$XERCES_HOME/xml-apis.jar:$XERCES_HOME/xercesImpl.jar
```

 If you're unclear on how to set your classpath, ask a friend or co-worker; that's what they're there for.

In the Xerces case, *xml-apis.jar* contains XML standard APIs like SAX and DOM, and (you never would have guessed this) *xercesImpl.jar* is the Xerces implementation of these APIs.

Parsing with SAX

Without spending any further time on the preliminaries, it's time to code. As a sample to familiarize you with SAX, this chapter details the SAXTreeViewer class. This utility uses SAX to parse an XML document, and displays the document visually as a Swing JTree.

> If you don't know anything about Swing, don't worry; I don't focus on that, but just use it for visual purposes. The focus will remain on SAX, and how events within parsing can be used to perform customized action.

The first thing you need to do in any SAX-based application is get an instance of a class that implements the SAX org.xml.sax.XMLReader interface; remember, this is why you downloaded a SAX-compliant parser in the first place.

Instantiating a Reader

SAX provides the org.xml.sax.XMLReader interface for all SAX-compliant XML parsers to implement. For example, the Xerces SAX parser implementation, org.apache.xerces.parsers.SAXParser, implements the XMLReader interface. If you have access to the source of your parser, you should see the same interface implemented in your parser's main SAX parser class. Each XML parser must have one class (and sometimes has more than one) that implements this interface, and that is the class you need to instantiate to allow for parsing XML:

```
// Instantiate a Reader
XMLReader reader =
  new org.apache.xerces.parsers.SAXParser( );

// Do something with the parser
reader.parse(uri);
```

> For newcomers to SAX, you may be wondering why XMLReader isn't called Parser. In fact, it was in SAX 1.0, and then so many changes were introduced that the class had to be deprecated and renamed. As a result, you'll call the parse( ) method on the XMLReader class.

This approach ties you tightly to your parser vendor, though; you can use SAX's org.xml.sax.helpers.XMLReaderFactory to get away from this:

```
XMLReader reader = XMLReaderFactory.createXMLReader( );
```

Just set the org.xml.sax.driver system property, and you can get your vendor's XMLReader implementation, without importing your vendor's classes:

```
java -Dorg.xml.sax.driver=org.apache.xerces.parsers.SAXParser
  [MyClassName]
```

Even better, most vendor's will set this property internally, meaning you don't have to worry about this system property at all; just call createXMLReader( ), and go.

 As you might expect, Apache Xerces is one of these vendors.

With that in mind, it's worth looking at a more realistic application. Example 3-1 is the skeleton for the SAXTreeViewer class, which allows viewing of an XML document as a graphical tree.

Example 3-1. This class sets up an XMLReader and then lists the basic parsing steps

```
public class SAXTreeViewer extends JFrame {

  // Swing-related variables and methods, including
  //    setting up a JTree and basic content pane

  public void buildTree(DefaultTreeModel treeModel,
                        DefaultMutableTreeNode base, String xmlURI)
    throws IOException, SAXException {

    // Create instances needed for parsing
    XMLReader reader =
      XMLReaderFactory.createXMLReader( );

    // Register content handler

    // Register error handler

    // Parse
  }

  public static void main(String[] args) {
    try {
      if (args.length != 1) {
        System.out.println(
          "Usage: java javaxml3.SAXTreeViewer " +
          "[XML Document]");
        return;
      }
      SAXTreeViewer viewer = new SAXTreeViewer( );
      viewer.init(args[0]);
      viewer.setVisible(true);
    } catch (Exception e) {
      e.printStackTrace( );
    }
  }
}
```

In this and the rest of this book's examples, I've tried to cut down all but the crucial portions of code. Import statements and code that isn't related to the concepts at hand (in this case, Swing details) have been excised, and relegated to the online examples.

The buildTree( ) method is where we'll be spending our time in this chapter; you can already see I've placed a few comments to outline the basic steps involved in parsing with SAX.

Parsing the Document

Once a reader is loaded and ready for use, use the parse( ) method to parse XML; this method accepts either an org.xml.sax.InputSource or a simple string. It's a much better idea to use the SAX InputSource class, because it can be constructed with an I/O InputStream, Reader, or a string URI.

U-R-What?

A URI is a *uniform resource identifier*. As the name suggests, it provides a standard means of identifying (and thereby locating, in most cases) a specific resource; this resource is almost always some sort of XML document, for the purposes of this book. URIs are also related to URLs, *uniform resource locators*. In fact, a URL is always a URI (although the reverse is not true). So in the examples in this and other chapters, you could specify a filename or a URL, like *http://www.ibiblio.org/xml/examples/shakespeare/othello.xml*, and either would be accepted.

Because the code loads an XML document, either locally or remotely, a java.io. IOException may result, and must be caught. In addition, the org.xml.sax. SAXException will be thrown if problems occur while parsing the document. Notice that the buildTree method can throw both of these exceptions:

```
public void buildTree(DefaultTreeModel treeModel,
                      DefaultMutableTreeNode base, String xmlURI)
    throws IOException, SAXException {

    // Create instances needed for parsing
    XMLReader reader =
      XMLReaderFactory.createXMLReader();

    // Register content handler

    // Register error handler
```

```
    // Parse
    InputSource inputSource = new InputSource(xmlURI);
    reader.parse(inputSource);
}
```

Using InputSource for input

The advantage to using an InputSource instead of directly supplying a URI is simple:
InputSource can provide more information to the parser. An InputSource encapsulates information about a single object, the document to parse. In situations where a
system identifier, public identifier, or stream may all be tied to one URI, using an
InputSource for encapsulation can become very handy. The class has accessor and
mutator methods for its system ID and public ID, a character encoding, a byte
stream (java.io.InputStream), and a character stream (java.io.Reader). When
passed as an argument to the parse( ) method, SAX also guarantees that the parser
will never modify the InputSource. The original input to a parser is still available
unchanged after its use by a parser or XML-aware application.

To put this in perspective, consider parsing a document with a simple DTD reference:

```
<!DOCTYPE PLAY SYSTEM "play.dtd">
```

By using an InputSource and wrapping the supplied XML URI, you have set implicitly the system ID of the document. This effectively sets up the path to the document
for the parser and allows it to resolve all relative paths within that document, like the
play.dtd file. If instead of setting this ID, you parsed an I/O stream, the DTD
wouldn't be able to be located (as it has no frame of reference); you could simulate
this by changing the code in the buildTree( ) method to what is shown here:

```
    // Parse
    InputSource inputSource =
      new InputSource(new java.io.FileInputStream(
                      new java.io.File(xmlURI)));
    reader.parse(inputSource);
```

You'll now get the following exception when running the viewer:

```
/usr/local/writing/javaxml3>java javaxml3.SAXTreeViewer /usr/local/contents.xml
org.xml.sax.SAXParseException: File
    "file:///usr/local/writing/javaxml3/play.dtd" not found.
```

While this seems a little silly (wrapping a URI in a file and I/O stream), it's actually
quite common to see people using I/O streams as input to parsers. You just need to set
a system ID for the XML stream (using the setSystemID( ) method on InputSource). So
the above code sample could be "fixed" by changing it to the following:

```
    // Parse
    InputSource inputSource =
      new InputSource(new java.io.FileInputStream(
                      new java.io.File(xmlURI)));
    inputSource.setSystemID(xmlURI);
    reader.parse(inputSource);
```

Not much going on...

If you compile and run the program now, nothing of any real interest seems to happen. Despite appearance, though, the XML document is parsed.

 By default, Xerces looks for any DTD referred to in a DOCTYPE listing. This means that you'll need to be able to access the DTD referred to in any XML document you parse, either locally or via the network. Otherwise, you'll get an error indicating the DTD isn't available. Xerces won't actually validate XML by default, but does require the DTD referenced be accessible.

However, you've provided no callbacks to take action during the parsing; without these callbacks, a document is simply parsed quietly. Parser callbacks let you insert action into the program flow, and turn the rather boring, quiet parsing of an XML document into an application that can react to the data, elements, attributes, and structure of the document being parsed, as well as interact with other programs and clients along the way.

Content Handlers

To let an application do something useful with XML data, you must register *handlers* with the SAX parser. A handler is nothing more than a set of callbacks that SAX defines; a group, if you will, of related events to which you might want to attach code.

There are four core handler interfaces defined by SAX 2.0: org.xml.sax. ContentHandler, org.xml.sax.ErrorHandler, org.xml.sax.DTDHandler, and org.xml. sax.EntityResolver.

 In this chapter, I will discuss ContentHandler and ErrorHandler. I'll leave discussion of DTDHandler and EntityResolver for the next chapter; it is enough for now to understand that EntityResolver and DTDHandler work just like the other handlers, but just group different behaviors.

Your classes implement one or more of these handlers and fill in the callback methods with working code (or, if you desire, no code at all; this effectively ignores a certain type of event). You then register your handler implementations using setContentHandler( ), setErrorHandler( ), setDTDHandler( ), and setEntityResolver( ), all on the XMLReader class (see Figure 3-4). Then the reader invokes the callback methods on the appropriate handlers during parsing.

For the SAXTreeViewer example, start by implementing the ContentHandler interface. ContentHandler, as the name implies, details events related to the content of an XML

```
                    «interface»
                    XMLReader

    +getFeature(name:String):boolean
    +setFeature(name:String,value:boolean):void
    +getProperty(name:String):Object
    +setProperty(name:String,value:Object):void
    +setEntityResolver(resolver:EntityResolver):void
    +getEntityResolver():EntityResolver
    +setDTDHandler(handler:DTDHandler):void
    +getDTDHandler():DTDHandler
    +setContentHandler(handler:ContentHandler):void
    +getContentHandler():ContentHandler
    +setErrorHandler(handler:ErrorHandler):void
    +getErrorHandler():ErrorHandler
    +parse(input:InputSource):void
    +parse(systemId:String):void
```

Figure 3-4. The handler classes are all passed into the XMLReader interface, and then used during parsing to trigger programmer-defined behaviors

document: elements, attributes, character data, etc. Add the following class to the end of your *SAXTreeViewer.java* source listing:

```
class JTreeHandler implements ContentHandler {

    /** Tree Model to add nodes to */
    private DefaultTreeModel treeModel;

    /** Current node to add sub-nodes to */
    private DefaultMutableTreeNode current;

    public JTreeHandler(DefaultTreeModel treeModel,
                        DefaultMutableTreeNode base) {
      this.treeModel = treeModel;
      this.current = base;
    }

    // ContentHandler callback implementations
}
```

> Most of this early version is Swing-related. The handler will respond to each SAX event by adding a node to the Swing tree, building up a visual representation of the XML document.

Don't bother trying to compile the source file at this point; you'll get a ton of errors about methods defined in ContentHandler not being implemented. The rest of this section walks through each of these methods. Now you're ready to look at the various ContentHandler callbacks and implement each. They're all listed for you in Figure 3-5.

```
                        «interface»
                      ContentHandler
+setDocumentLocator(locator:Locator):void
+startDocument():void
+endDocument():void
+startPrefixMapping(prefix:String,uri:String):void
+endPrefixMapping(prefix:String):void
+startElement(uri:String,localName:String,qName:String,atts:Attributes):void
+endElement(uri:String,localName:String,qName:String):void
+characters(ch:char[],start:int,length:int):void
+ignorableWhitespace(ch:char[],start:int,length:int):void
+processingInstruction(target:String,data:String):void
+skippedEntity(name:String):void
```

Figure 3-5. Each of these callbacks returns void; it's not OO programming, but it gets the job done

The Document Locator

The first callback you need to implement is setDocumentLocator( ); this allows you to save a reference to an org.xml.sax.Locator for use within your other SAX events. When a callback event occurs, the class implementing a handler often needs access to the location of the SAX parser within an XML file. The Locator class has several useful methods—such as getLineNumber( ) and getColumnNumber( )—that return the current location of the parsing process within an XML file when invoked.

Since this might be handy to use later, the code shown here saves the provided Locator instance to a member variable:

```
class JTreeHandler implements ContentHandler {

    /** Hold onto the locator for location information */
    private Locator locator;

    // Constructor

    public void setDocumentLocator(Locator locator) {
        // Save this for later use
        this.locator = locator;
    }
}
```

 The Locator should be used only within the scope of the ContentHandler implementation; data it reports outside of the parsing process is unpredictable (and useless, anyway).

The Beginning and the End of a Document

In any lifecycle process, there must always be a beginning and an end. These important events should each occur once: the former before all other parsing events and the latter after all other events. This rather obvious fact is critical to your applications, as it allows you to know exactly when parsing begins and ends. SAX provides callback methods for each of these events, aptly named startDocument( ) and endDocument( ).

startDocument( ) is called before any other parsing callbacks, including the callback methods within other SAX handlers, such as DTDHandler. In other words, startDocument( ) is not only the first method called within ContentHandler, but also within the entire parsing process, aside from setDocumentLocator( ). This ensures a finite beginning to parsing, and lets the application perform any tasks it needs to before parsing takes place.

endDocument( ), is always the last method called, again across all handlers. This includes situations in which errors occur that cause parsing to halt.

> Even if an unrecoverable error occurs, the ErrorHandler's callback method is invoked, and then a final call to endDocument( ) completes the attempted parsing.

In the example code, no visual event should occur with these methods; however, as with implementing any interface, the methods must still be present:

```
public void startDocument( ) throws SAXException {
  // No visual events occur here
}

public void endDocument( ) throws SAXException {
  // No visual events occur here
}
```

Both of these callback methods can throw SAXExceptions. The only types of exceptions that SAX events ever throw, SAXException provides another standard interface to the parsing behavior. However, these exceptions often wrap other exceptions that indicate what problems have occurred. For example, if an XML file is parsed over the network via a URL, and the connection becomes invalid, a java.net.SocketException can occur. Within the SAX reader, the original exception is caught and rethrown as a SAXException, with the originating exception stuffed inside the new one. This allows your applications to trap for one standard exception, while allowing specific details of what errors occurred within the parsing process to be wrapped and made available to the calling program through this standard exception. The SAXException class provides a method called getException( ) that returns the underlying Exception (if one exists).

Processing Instructions

Chapter 1 mentioned processing instructions (PIs) within XML as a bit of a special case. They were not considered XML elements, and were handled differently by being made available to the calling application. Because of these special characteristics, SAX defines a specific callback for handling processing instructions. This method, processingInstruction( ), receives the target of the processing instruction and any data sent to the PI. For this chapter's example, the PI can be converted to a new node and displayed in the tree viewer:

```
public void processingInstruction(String target, String data)
  throws SAXException {

  DefaultMutableTreeNode pi =
    new DefaultMutableTreeNode("PI (target = '" + target +
                               "', data = '" + data + "')");
  current.add(pi);
}
```

This method allows an application to receive instructions and set variable values, or even execute additional code to perform application-specific processing. For example, the Apache Cocoon publishing framework might set flags to perform transformations on the data once it is parsed, or to display the XML as a specific content type. This method, like the other SAX callbacks, throws a SAXException when errors occur.

 This method will not receive notification of the XML declaration:

> `<?xml version="1.0" standalone="yes"?>`

In fact, SAX provides no means of getting at this information (and you'll find out that it's not currently part of DOM Level 2, either!). The general underlying principle is that this information is for the XML parser or reader, not the consumer of the document's data. For that reason, it's not exposed to the developer.

Namespace Callbacks

From the discussion of namespaces in Chapters 1 and 2, you should be starting to realize their importance and impact on parsing and handling XML. Alongside XML Schema, XML Namespaces is one of the more significant concepts added to XML since the original XML 1.0 Recommendation. With SAX 2, support for namespaces was introduced at the element level. This allows a distinction to be made between the namespace of an element, associated with an element prefix and URI, and the local name of an element. *Local name* refers to the unprefixed name of an element. For example, the local name of the rdf:li element is simply li. The namespace prefix is rdf, and the namespace URI might be declared as http://www.w3.org/1999/02/22-rdf-syntax-ns#. You'll also see the term *Q name* (sometimes written *QName*), which refers to the prefixed name of the element; so li is the local name in this case, and rdf:li is the Q name.

There are two SAX callbacks specifically dealing with namespaces. These callbacks are invoked when the parser reaches the beginning and end of a *prefix mapping*. Although this is a new term, it is not a new concept; a prefix mapping is simply an element that uses the xmlns attribute to declare a namespace. This is often the root element (which may have multiple mappings) but can be any element within an XML document that declares an explicit namespace. For example:

```
<catalog>
  <books>
    <book title="XML in a Nutshell"
          xmlns:xlink="http://www.w3.org/1999/xlink">
      <cover xlink:type="simple" xlink:show="onLoad"
             xlink:href="xmlnutCover.jpg" ALT="XML in a Nutshell"
             width="125" height="350" />
    </book>
  </books>
</catalog>
```

In this case, an explicit namespace is declared several element nestings deep within the document. That prefix and URI mapping (in this case, xlink and http://www.w3. org/1999/xlink, respectively) are then available to elements and attributes within the declaring element.

The startPrefixMapping( ) callback is passed the namespace prefix, as well as the URI associated with that prefix. The mapping is considered "closed" or "ended" when the element that declared the mapping is closed, which triggers the endPrefixMapping( ) callback. The only twist to these callbacks is that they don't quite behave in the sequential manner in which SAX is usually structured; the prefix mapping callback occurs directly *before* the callback for the element that declares the namespace, and the ending of the mapping results in an event just *after* the close of the declaring element. However, it actually makes a lot of sense: for the declaring element to be able to use the declared namespace mapping, the mapping must be available before the element's callback. It works in just the opposite way for ending a mapping: the element must close (as it may use the namespace), and then the namespace mapping can be removed from the list of available mappings.

In the JTreeHandler, there aren't any visual events that should occur within these two callbacks. However, a common practice is to store the prefix and URI mappings in a data structure. You will see in a moment that the element callbacks report the namespace URI, but not the namespace prefix. If you don't store these prefixes yourself (reported through startPrefixMapping( )), they won't be available in your element callback code. The easiest way to do this is to use a Map, add the reported prefix and URI to this Map in startPrefixMapping( ), and then remove them in endPrefixMapping( ). This can be accomplished with the following code additions:

```
/** Store URI to prefix mappings */
private Map namespaceMappings;

public JTreeHandler(DefaultTreeModel treeModel,
                    DefaultMutableTreeNode base) {
  this.treeModel = treeModel;
  this.current = base;
  this.namespaceMappings = new HashMap( );
}
```

```
public void startPrefixMapping(String prefix, String uri) {
  // No visual events occur here.
  namespaceMappings.put(uri, prefix);
}

public void endPrefixMapping(String prefix) {
  // No visual events occur here.
  for (Iterator i = namespaceMappings.keySet().iterator();
              i.hasNext(); ) {
    String uri = (String)i.next( );
    String thisPrefix = (String)namespaceMappings.get(uri);
    if (prefix.equals(thisPrefix)) {
      namespaceMappings.remove(uri);
      break;
    }
  }
}
```

Notice that I used the URI as a key to the mappings, rather than the prefix. The startElement( ) callback reports the namespace URI for the element, not the prefix. So keying on URIs makes those lookups faster. However, as you see in endPrefixMapping( ), it does add a little bit of work to removing the mapping when it is no longer available.

 The solution shown here is far from a complete one in terms of dealing with more complex namespace issues. It's perfectly legal to reassign prefixes to new URIs for an element's scope, or to assign multiple prefixes to the same URI. In the example, this would result in widely scoped namespace mappings being overwritten by narrowly scoped ones (in the case where identical URIs were mapped to different prefixes). In a more robust application, you would want to store prefixes and URIs separately, and have a method of relating the two without causing overwriting. However, you get the idea in the example of how to handle namespaces in the general sense.

Element Callbacks

More than half of SAX callbacks have nothing to do with XML elements, attributes, and data. Remember, the process of parsing XML is intended to do more than simply provide your application with the XML data; it should give the application instructions from XML PIs so your application knows what actions to take, let the application know when parsing begins and when it ends, and even tell it when there is whitespace that can be ignored!

Of course, there certainly are SAX callbacks intended to give you access to the XML data within your documents. The three primary callbacks involved in accessing that data are the start and end of elements and the characters( ) callback. These tell you that the start tag for an element has been parsed, the data found within that element, and when the closing tag for that element is reached.

The first of these, startElement( ), gives an application information about an XML element and any attributes it may have. The parameters to this callback are the name of the element (in various forms) and an org.xml.sax.Attributes instance (see Figure 3-6). The Attributes interface (or, rather, your parser's implementation of the interface) holds references to all of the attributes within an element. It allows easy iteration through the element's attributes in a form similar to a Vector. In addition to being able to reference an attribute by its index (used when iterating through all attributes), it is possible to reference an attribute by its name. Of course, by now you should be a bit cautious when you see the word "name" referring to an XML element or attribute, as it can mean various things. In this case, either the attribute's Q name can be used, or the combination of its local name and namespace URI if a namespace is used. There are also helper methods such as getURI(int index) and getLocalName(int index) that help give additional namespace information about an attribute. Used as a whole, the Attributes interface provides a comprehensive set of information about an element's attributes.

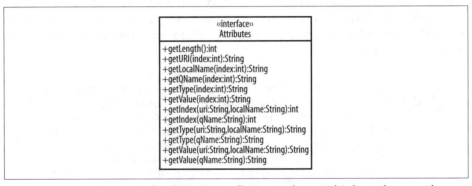

Figure 3-6. The Attributes interface isn't a Java collection (unfortunately), but it does provide collection-like behavior

In addition to its attributes, you get several forms of the element's name. This again is in deference to XML namespaces. The namespace URI of the element is supplied first. This places the element in its correct context across the document's complete set of namespaces. Then the local name of the element is supplied, which is the unprefixed element name. In addition (and for backward compatibility), the Q name of the element is supplied.

Now, back to the actual implementation of startElement( ). First, a new node is created and added to the tree with the local name of the element. Then, that node is set as the current node, so all nested elements and attributes are added as leaves.

 Technically, an attribute is not nested within an element. Attributes are usually said to be on the element, and usually describe the element. That's a bit tricky to display though, so I've opted for simply nesting them; you're a smart reader and will know what I mean, though, won't you?

Next, the namespace is determined, using the supplied namespace URI and the namespaceMappings object (to get the prefix) that you just added to the code from the "Namespace Callbacks" section. This is added as a node, as well. Finally, the code iterates through the Attributes interface, adding each (with local name and namespace information) as a child node. The code to accomplish all this is shown here:

```java
public void startElement(String namespaceURI, String localName,
                         String qName, Attributes atts)
  throws SAXException {

  DefaultMutableTreeNode element =
    new DefaultMutableTreeNode("Element: " + localName);
  current.add(element);
  current = element;

  // Determine namespace
  if (namespaceURI.length( ) > 0) {
    String prefix =
      (String)namespaceMappings.get(namespaceURI);
    if (prefix.equals("")) {
      prefix = "[None]";
    }
    DefaultMutableTreeNode namespace =
      new DefaultMutableTreeNode("Namespace: prefix = '" +
        prefix + "', URI = '" + namespaceURI + "'");
    current.add(namespace);
  }

  // Process attributes
  for (int i=0; i<atts.getLength( ); i++) {
    DefaultMutableTreeNode attribute =
      new DefaultMutableTreeNode("Attribute (name = '" +
                                 atts.getLocalName(i) +
                                 "', value = '" +
                                 atts.getValue(i) + "')");
    String attURI = atts.getURI(i);
    if (attURI.length( ) > 0) {
      String attPrefix = (String)namespaceMappings.get(attURI);
      if (attPrefix.equals("")) {
        attPrefix = "[None]";
      }
      DefaultMutableTreeNode attNamespace =
        new DefaultMutableTreeNode("Namespace: prefix = '" +
                  attPrefix + "', URI = '" + attURI + "'");
      attribute.add(attNamespace);
    }
    current.add(attribute);
  }
}
```

The end of an element is much easier to code. Since there is no need to give any visual information, all that must be done is to walk back up the tree one node, leaving the element's parent as the new current node:

```
public void endElement(String namespaceURI, String localName,
                       String qName)
  throws SAXException {

  // Walk back up the tree
  current = (DefaultMutableTreeNode)current.getParent( );
}
```

Element Data

Once the beginning and end of an element block are identified and the element's attributes are enumerated, the next piece of important information is the actual data contained within the element itself. This generally consists of additional elements, textual data, or a combination of the two. When other elements appear, the callbacks for those elements are initiated, and a type of pseudorecursion happens: elements nested within elements result in callbacks "nested" within callbacks. At some point, though, textual data will be encountered. Typically the most important information to an XML client, this data is usually either what you show to the client or what you process to generate a client response.

In SAX, textual data within elements is sent to your application via the characters( ) callback. This method provides your application with an array of characters as well as a starting index and the length of the characters to read. Generating a String from this array and applying the data is a piece of cake:

```
public void characters(char[] ch, int start, int length)
  throws SAXException {

  String s = new String(ch, start, length);
  DefaultMutableTreeNode data =
    new DefaultMutableTreeNode("Character Data: '" + s + "'");
  current.add(data);
}
```

Seemingly a simple callback, this method often results in a significant amount of confusion. A SAX parser may choose to return all contiguous character data in one invocation, or split this data up into multiple method invocations. For any given element, this method will be called not at all (if no character data is present within the element) or one or more times. Parsers implement this behavior differently, often using algorithms designed to increase parsing speed. Never count on having all the textual data for an element within one callback method; conversely, never assume that multiple callbacks would result from one element's contiguous character data.

Getting Ahead of the Data

The characters() callback method accepts a character array, as well as start and length parameters, to signify which index to start at and how far to read into the array. This can cause some confusion; a common mistake is to include code like this to read from the character array:

```java
public void characters(char[] ch, int start, int length)
  throws SAXException {

  for (int i=0; i<ch.length; i++)
    System.out.println(ch[i]);
}
```

The mistake here is in reading from the beginning to the end of the character array, instead of from start to start+length. This common mistake results from years of iterating through arrays, either in Java, C, or another language. However, in the case of a SAX event, this can cause quite a problem. SAX parsers are required to pass starting and length values on the character array that any loop constructs should use to read from the array. This allows lower-level manipulation of textual data to occur in order to optimize parser performance, such as reading data ahead of the current location as well as array reuse. This is all legal behavior within SAX, as the expectation is that a wrapping application will not try to "read past" the length parameter sent to the callback.

Mistakes as in the example shown can result in gibberish data being output to the screen or used within your application, and is almost always problematic. The loop construct looks very normal and compiles without a hitch, so this can be a very tricky problem to track down. Remember to always simply convert this data to a String and use it directly:

```java
String data = new String(ch, start, length);
```

Sequencing mixups

As you write SAX event handlers, be sure to keep your mind in a hierarchical mode. In other words, you should not get in the habit of thinking that an element *owns* its data and child elements, but only that it serves as a parent. Also keep in mind that the parser is moving along, handling elements, attributes, and data as it comes across them. This can make for some surprising results. Consider the following XML document fragment:

```xml
<parent>This element has <child>embedded text</child> within it.</parent>
```

Forgetting that SAX parses sequentially, making callbacks as it sees elements and data, and forgetting that the XML is viewed as hierarchical, you might make the assumption that the output here would be something like Figure 3-7.

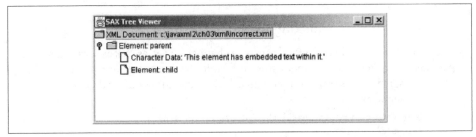

Figure 3-7. If you're not careful, your assumptions about XML will result in a mismatch between what you see and what you get

This seems logical, as the parent element completely "owns" the child element. But what actually occurs is that a callback is made at each SAX event point, resulting in the tree shown in Figure 3-8.

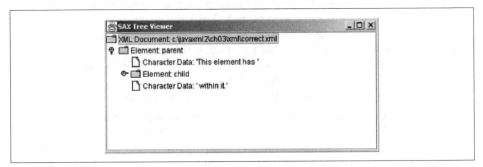

Figure 3-8. If you keep the parsing cycle in mind, you'll keep element data with its correct element, rather than a parent element further up the hierarchy

Whitespace

Whitespace is also often reported by the characters( ) method. This introduces additional confusion, as another SAX callback, ignorableWhitespace( ), also reports whitespace. You can avoid this confusion by remembering this simple rule: if no schema is referenced, ignorableWhitespace( ) will never be invoked.

 As explained in Chapter 2, the generic term "schema" refers to any constraint model, including DTDs, XML Schema, Relax, etc.

A schema details the content model for an element. Consider Example 3-2, the DTD for Jon Bosak's XML versions of Shakespeare's plays.

Example 3-2. This rather simple DTD constrains the entire body of Shakespeare's works, modeled in XML

```
<!ENTITY amp "&#38;">
<!ELEMENT PLAY      (TITLE, FM, PERSONAE, SCNDESCR, PLAYSUBT, INDUCT?,
                     PROLOGUE?, ACT+, EPILOGUE?)>
```

```
<!ELEMENT TITLE    (#PCDATA)>
<!ELEMENT FM       (P+)>
<!ELEMENT P        (#PCDATA)>
<!ELEMENT PERSONAE (TITLE, (PERSONA | PGROUP)+)>
<!ELEMENT PGROUP   (PERSONA+, GRPDESCR)>
<!ELEMENT PERSONA  (#PCDATA)>
<!ELEMENT GRPDESCR (#PCDATA)>
<!ELEMENT SCNDESCR (#PCDATA)>
<!ELEMENT PLAYSUBT (#PCDATA)>
<!ELEMENT INDUCT   (TITLE, SUBTITLE*, (SCENE+|(SPEECH|STAGEDIR|SUBHEAD)+))>
<!ELEMENT ACT      (TITLE, SUBTITLE*, PROLOGUE?, SCENE+, EPILOGUE?)>
<!ELEMENT SCENE    (TITLE, SUBTITLE*, (SPEECH | STAGEDIR | SUBHEAD)+)>
<!ELEMENT PROLOGUE (TITLE, SUBTITLE*, (STAGEDIR | SPEECH)+)>
<!ELEMENT EPILOGUE (TITLE, SUBTITLE*, (STAGEDIR | SPEECH)+)>
<!ELEMENT SPEECH   (SPEAKER+, (LINE | STAGEDIR | SUBHEAD)+)>
<!ELEMENT SPEAKER  (#PCDATA)>
<!ELEMENT LINE     (#PCDATA | STAGEDIR)*>
<!ELEMENT STAGEDIR (#PCDATA)>
<!ELEMENT SUBTITLE (#PCDATA)>
<!ELEMENT SUBHEAD  (#PCDATA)>
```

As an example, the FM element can only have P elements within it. Any whitespace between the start of the FM element and the start of a P element is therefore ignorable. It doesn't mean anything, because the DTD says not to expect any character data (whitespace or otherwise). The same thing applies for whitespace between the end of an ACT element and the start of another ACT element, as the parent (PLAY) cannot contain character data; therefore, any whitespace can be ignored.

However, *without* a constraint specifying that information to a parser, that whitespace *cannot* be interpreted as meaningless. Without a DTD, these various whitespaces would trigger the characters( ) callback, where previously they triggered the ignorableWhitespace( ) callback. Thus whitespace is never simply ignorable, or nonignorable; it all depends on what (if any) constraints are referenced. Change the constraints, and you might change the meaning of the whitespace.

Let's dive even deeper. In the case where an element can only have other elements within it, things are reasonably clear. Whitespace in between elements is ignorable. However, consider a mixed content model:

```
<!ELEMENT LINE     (#PCDATA | STAGEDIR)*>
```

In this model, there is no whitespace between the starting and ending LINE tags that will ever be reported as ignorable (with or without a DTD or schema reference). That's because it's impossible to distinguish between whitespace used for readability and whitespace that is supposed to be in the document. For example:

```
<SPEAKER>CELIA</SPEAKER>
<LINE>
  <STAGEDIR>Reads</STAGEDIR>
```

```
</LINE>
<LINE>Why should this a desert be?</LINE>
```

In this XHTML fragment, the whitespace between the opening LINE element and the opening STAGEDIR element is not ignorable, and therefore reported through the characters( ) callback. Be prepared to closely monitor both of the character-related callbacks.

Ignorable Whitespace

With all that whitespace discussion done, adding an implementation for the ignorableWhitespace( ) method is a piece of cake. Since the whitespace reported is ignorable, the code does just that—ignores it:

```
public void ignorableWhitespace(char[] ch, int start, int length)
  throws SAXException {

  // This is ignorable, so don't display it
}
```

 Whitespace is reported in the same manner as character data; it can be reported with one callback, or a SAX parser may break up the whitespace and report it over several method invocations. In either case, adhere closely to the precautions about not making assumptions or counting on whitespace as textual data in order to avoid troublesome bugs in your applications.

Entities

Entities often are used to refer to another fragment of XML, as well as special characters like & and >. When your XML document is parsed, those entities that do reference other files are usually expanded and inserted into the document flow. However, nonvalidating parsers are not required to resolve entity references, and instead may skip them; you can also usually configure your parser to intentionally skip entities. In both cases, SAX accounts for this with a callback that is issued when an entity is skipped. The callback gives the name of the entity, which can be included in the viewer's output:

```
public void skippedEntity(String name) throws SAXException {
  DefaultMutableTreeNode skipped =
    new DefaultMutableTreeNode("Skipped Entity: '" + name + "'");
  current.add(skipped);
}
```

You won't see this callback executed often; most established parsers will not skip entities, even if they are not validating. Apache Xerces, for example, never invokes this callback; instead, the entity reference is expanded and the result included in the XML data returned to your application.

The parameter passed to the callback does not include the leading ampersand and trailing semicolon in the entity reference. For &header;, only the name of the entity reference, header, is passed to skippedEntity( ).

The Results

Finally, you need to register the content handler implementation with the XMLReader you've instantiated. This is done with setContentHandler( ):

```
public void buildTree(DefaultTreeModel treeModel,
                      DefaultMutableTreeNode base, String xmlURI)
   throws IOException, SAXException {

   // Create instances needed for parsing
   XMLReader reader =
     XMLReaderFactory.createXMLReader( );
   ContentHandler jTreeHandler =
     new jTreeHandler(treeModel, base);

   // Register content handler
   reader.setContentHandler(jTreeHandler);

   // Register error handler

   // Parse
   InputSource inputSource = new InputSource(xmlURI);
   reader.parse(inputSource);
}
```

Now compile the *SAXTreeViewer.java* source file. Once done, you may run the SAX viewer demonstration on the XML sample file created earlier. Also, make sure that you have added your working directory to the classpath. The complete Java command should read:

```
/usr/local/writing/javaxml3>java javaxml3.SAXTreeViewer as_you.xml
```

Java 5 users, you'll get a warning about unchecked operations when you compile SAXTreeViewer. You can easily fix those with parameterized collections; I chose not to show that, as the code wouldn't compile on pre-Java 5.0 environments.

This should result in a Swing window firing up, loaded with the XML document's content. Your output should look similar to Figure 3-9, depending on what nodes you have expanded.

Now you know how SAX handles a well-formed XML document. You should also have a pretty good understanding of the document callbacks that occur within the parsing process, and how your application uses these callbacks to get information

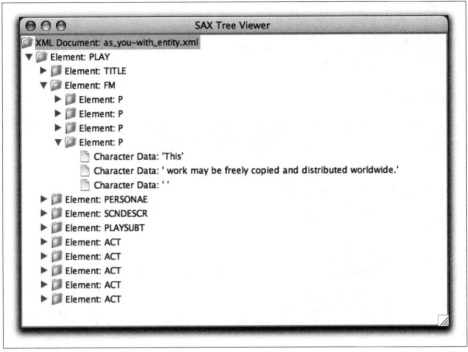

Figure 3-9. *Shakespeare's plays are obviously rather long, but SAX still parsed this file remarkably quickly*

about an XML document as the document is parsed. Before moving on, though, I want to address the issue of what happens when your XML document is not well formed, and the errors that can result from this condition.

Error Handlers

In addition to providing the ContentHandler interface for handling parsing events, SAX provides an ErrorHandler interface that can be implemented to treat various error conditions that may arise during parsing (see Figure 3-10).

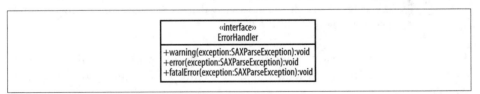

Figure 3-10. *ErrorHandler defines only three methods, but how you implement these methods can have a huge impact on the user experience*

This interface works in the same manner as the document handler already constructed, but defines only three callback methods. Through these three methods, all error conditions are handled and reported by SAX parsers.

Each method receives information about the error or warning that has occurred through a SAXParseException. This object holds the line number where the trouble was encountered, the URI of the document being treated (which could be the parsed document or an external reference within that document), and normal exception details such as a message and a printable stack trace. In addition, each of these methods can throw a SAXException. This may seem a bit odd at first: an exception handler that throws an exception? Keep in mind that each handler receives a parsing exception. This might be a warning that should not cause the parsing process to stop or an error that needs to be resolved for parsing to continue; however, the callback may need to perform system I/O or another operation that can throw another exception, and the method needs to be able to send any problems resulting from these actions up the application chain.

As an example, consider an error handler that receives error notifications and writes those errors to an error log. This callback method needs to be able to either append to or create an error log on the local filesystem. If a warning occurs within the process of parsing an XML document, the warning would be reported to this method. The intent of the warning is to give information to the callback and then continue parsing the document. However, if the error handler cannot write to the logfile, it should notify the parser and application that all parsing should stop. This can be done by catching any I/O exceptions and rethrowing these to the calling application, thus causing any further document parsing to stop. This common scenario is why error handlers must be able to throw exceptions (see Example 3-3).

Example 3-3. Logging a problem in an error handler is a good way to find out what problems might have occurred that don't warrant halting all parsing

```
public void warning(SAXParseException exception)
  throws SAXException {

  try {
    FileWriter fw = new FileWriter("error.log");
    BufferedWriter bw = new BufferedWriter(fw);
    bw.write("Warning: " + exception.getMessage() + "\n");
    bw.flush();
    bw.close();
    fw.close();
  } catch (IOException e) {
    throw new SAXException("Could not write to log file", e);
  }
}
```

It's pretty easy to define the skeleton of an ErrorHandler implementation and register it with the reader implementation in the same way that the content handler was registered. Add another interface to the list that JTreeHandler already implements:

```
class JTreeHandler implements ContentHandler, ErrorHandler {
```

 It's pretty common practice to have one class implement multiple handlers, as shown here.

Next, to actually use the custom error handler you need to register this error handler with your SAX reader. This is done with the setErrorHandler( ) method on the XMLReader instance:

```
public void buildTree(DefaultTreeModel treeModel,
                      DefaultMutableTreeNode base, String xmlURI)
    throws IOException, SAXException {

    // Create instances needed for parsing
    XMLReader reader =
      XMLReaderFactory.createXMLReader( );
    JTreeHandler jTreeHandler =
      new JTreeHandler(treeModel, base);

    // Register content handler
    reader.setContentHandler(jTreeHandler);

    // Register error handler
    reader.setErrorHandler(jTreeHandler);

    // Parse
    InputSource inputSource = new InputSource(xmlURI);
    reader.parse(inputSource);
}
```

Warnings

Any time a warning (as defined by the XML 1.0 specification) occurs, this method is invoked in the registered error handler. There are several conditions that can generate a warning, all related to the DTD and validity of a document. The code in this example writes the warning to a log, and then tries to continue parsing (by not rethrowing a SAXException):

```
public void warning(SAXParseException exception)
    throws SAXException {

    try {
      FileWriter fw = new FileWriter("error.log");
      BufferedWriter bw = new BufferedWriter(fw);
      bw.write("**Warning**\n");
      bw.write("\tLine: ");
```

```
        bw.write(exception.getLineNumber());
        bw.write("\n\tURI: ");
        bw.write(exception.getSystemId());
        bw.write("\n\tMessage: ");
        bw.write(exception.getMessage());
        bw.write("\n\n");
        bw.flush();
        bw.close();
        fw.close();
    } catch (IOException e) {
        throw new SAXException("Could not write to log file", e);
    }
}
```

Nonfatal Errors

Errors that occur within parsing that can be recovered from, but constitute a viola-
tion of some portion of the XML specification, are considered nonfatal errors. An
error handler should always at least log these, as they are typically serious enough to
merit informing the user or administrator of the application, if not so critical as to
cause parsing to cease:

```
public void error(SAXParseException exception)
    throws SAXException {

    try {
        FileWriter fw = new FileWriter("error.log");
        BufferedWriter bw = new BufferedWriter(fw);
        bw.write("**Error**\n");
        bw.write("\tLine: ");
        bw.write(exception.getLineNumber());
        bw.write("\n\tURI: ");
        bw.write(exception.getSystemId());
        bw.write("\n\tMessage: ");
        bw.write(exception.getMessage());
        bw.write("\n\n");
        bw.flush();
        bw.close();
        fw.close();
    } catch (IOException e) {
        throw new SAXException("Could not write to log file", e);
    }
}
```

Fatal Errors

Fatal errors are those that necessitate stopping the parser. These are typically related
to a document not being well formed, and make further parsing either a complete
waste of time or technically impossible. An error handler should almost always
notify the user or application administrator when a fatal error occurs; without inter-
vention, these can bring an application to a shuddering halt. For the example, I'll just

emulate the behavior of the other two callback methods, but then go on to rethrow a SAXException, which will cause all parsing to halt:

```java
public void fatalError(SAXParseException exception)
  throws SAXException {

  try {
    FileWriter fw = new FileWriter("error.log");
    BufferedWriter bw = new BufferedWriter(fw);
    bw.write("**Fatal Error**\n");
    bw.write("\tLine: ");
    bw.write(exception.getLineNumber());
    bw.write("\n\tURI: ");
    bw.write(exception.getSystemId());
    bw.write("\n\tMessage: ");
    bw.write(exception.getMessage());
    bw.write("\n\n");
    bw.flush();
    bw.close();
    fw.close();

    // Bail out
    throw new SAXException("Fatal Error! Check the log!");
  } catch (IOException e) {
    throw new SAXException("Could not write to log file", e);
  }
}
```

With this third error handler coded, you should be able to compile the example source file successfully and run it on the XML document again. Your output should not be any different than it was earlier, as there are no reportable errors in the XML.

Breaking the Data

With some error handlers in place, it is worthwhile to generate some problems and see these handlers in action. To generate a sample error, make the following change to the first line of your XML document:

```xml
<?xml version="1.2"?>
```

Now run the Java SAX viewer program on the modified XML document. Your output should be similar to that shown here (parsing halts, obviously):

```
java javaxml3.SAXTreeViewer as_you.xml
org.xml.sax.SAXException: Fatal Error! Check the log!
        at javaxml3.JTreeHandler.fatalError(SAXTreeViewer.java:289)
        at com.sun.org.apache.xerces.internal.util.ErrorHandlerWrapper.
          fatalError(ErrorHandlerWrapper.java:218)
        at com.sun.org.apache.xerces.internal.impl.XMLErrorReporter.
          reportError(XMLErrorReporter.java:386)
        at com.sun.org.apache.xerces.internal.impl.XMLErrorReporter.
          reportError(XMLErrorReporter.java:316)
        at com.sun.org.apache.xerces.internal.impl.XMLScanner.
```

```
    reportFatalError(XMLScanner.java:1438)
at com.sun.org.apache.xerces.internal.impl.XMLScanner.
    scanXMLDeclOrTextDecl(XMLScanner.java:436)
at com.sun.org.apache.xerces.internal.impl.XMLDocumentFragmentScannerImpl.
    scanXMLDeclOrTextDecl(XMLDocumentFragmentScannerImpl.java:710)
at com.sun.org.apache.xerces.internal.impl.
    XMLDocumentScannerImpl$XMLDeclDispatcher.dispatch(
        XMLDocumentScannerImpl.java:721)
at com.sun.org.apache.xerces.internal.impl.
    XMLDocumentFragmentScannerImpl.scanDocument(
        XMLDocumentFragmentScannerImpl.java:368)
at com.sun.org.apache.xerces.internal.parsers.
    XML11Configuration.parse(XML11Configuration.java:834)
at com.sun.org.apache.xerces.internal.parsers.
    XML11Configuration.parse(XML11Configuration.java:764)
at com.sun.org.apache.xerces.internal.parsers.XMLParser.parse(
    XMLParser.java:148)
at com.sun.org.apache.xerces.internal.parsers.AbstractSAXParser.parse(
    AbstractSAXParser.java:1242)
at javaxml3.SAXTreeViewer.buildTree(SAXTreeViewer.java:72)
at javaxml3.SAXTreeViewer.init(SAXTreeViewer.java:47)
at javaxml3.SAXTreeViewer.main(SAXTreeViewer.java:84)
```

Check the newly created *error.log*, and you should see this entry:

```
**Fatal Error**
        Line: ^A
        URI: file:///Users/bmclaugh/Documents/O'Reilly/Writing/
            Java%20and%20XML%203rd/subs/code/ch03/as_you.xml
        Message: XML version "1.2" is not supported, only XML 1.0 is supported.
```

When an XML parser is operating on a document that reports a version of XML greater than that supported by the parser, a fatal error is reported. This tells an application that newer features expected to be used by the document may not be available within the parser and the version that it supports.

## CHAPTER 4

Advanced SAX

What you've seen regarding SAX so far is essentially the simplest way to process and parse XML. And while SAX is indeed named the Simple API for XML, it offers programmers much more than basic parsing and content handling. There is an array of settings that affect parser behavior, as well as several additional handlers for edge-case scenarios; if you need to specify exactly how strings should be interned, or what behavior should occur when a DTD declares a notation, or even differentiate between CDATA sections and regular text sections, SAX provides. In fact, you can even modify and write out XML using SAX (along with a few additional packages); SAX is a full-featured API, and this chapter will give you the lowdown on features that go beyond simple parsing.

Properties and Features

I glossed over validation in the last chapter, and probably left you with a fair amount of questions. When I cover JAXP in Chapter 7, you'll see that you can use either a method (setValidating( )) or a set of classes (javax.xml.validation) to handle validation; you might expect to call a similar method—setValidation( ) or something similar—to initiate validation in SAX. But then, there's also namespace awareness, dealt with quite a bit in Chapter 2 (and Chapter 3, with respect to Q names and local names—maybe setNamespaceAwareness( )? But what about schema validation? And setting the location of a schema to validate on, if the document doesn't specify one? There's also low-level behavior, like telling the parser what to do with entities (parse them? don't parse them?), how to handle strings, and a lot more. As you can imagine, dealing with each of these could cause real API bloat, adding 20 or 30 methods to SAX's XMLReader class. And, even worse, each time a new setting was needed (perhaps for the next type of constraint model supported? How about setRelaxNGSchema( )?), the SAX API would have to add a method or two, and re-release a new version. Clearly, this isn't a very effective approach to API design.

If this isn't clear to you, check out *Head First Design Patterns*, by Elisabeth and Eric Freeman (O'Reilly). In particular, read up on Chapter 1 (pages 8 and 9), which details why it's critical to *encapsulate what varies*.

To address the ever-changing need to affect parser behavior, *without* causing constant API change, SAX 2 defines a standard mechanism for setting parser behavior: through the use of properties and features.

Setting Properties and Features

In SAX, a *property* is a setting that requires passing in some Object argument for the parser to use; for instance, certain types of handlers are set by specifying a URI and supplying the Object that implements that handler's interface. A *feature* is a setting that is either on (true) or off (false). Several obvious examples come to mind: namespace awareness and validation, for example.

SAX includes the methods needed for setting properties and features in the XMLReader interface. This means you have to change very little of your existing code to request validation, set the namespace separator, and handle other feature and property requests. The methods used for setting these properties and features are outlined in Table 4-1.

Table 4-1. You'll use features almost every time you write a program to parse XML; properties are less commonly used, but still important in your XML programming

Method	Returns	Parameters	Syntax
setProperty( )	void	String propertyID, Object value	parser.setProperty("[Property URI]", propertyValue);
setFeature( )	void	String featureID, boolean state	parser.setFeature("[Feature URI]", featureState);
getProperty( )	Object	String propertyID	Object propertyValue = parser.getProperty("[Property URI]");
getFeature( )	boolean	String featureID	boolean featureState = parser.getFeature("[Feature URI]");

For all of these, the ID of a specific property or feature is a URI. The standard set of features and properties is listed in the Appendix 0. Additionally, most parsers define additional, vendor-specific properties that their parser supports. For example, Apache Xerces defines quite a few additional features and properties, listed online at *http://xml.apache.org/xerces2-j/features.html* and *http://xml.apache.org/xerces2-j/properties.html*.

The most convenient aspect of these methods is that they allow simple addition and modification of properties and features. Although new or updated features will require a parser implementation to add supporting code, the method by which features and properties are accessed remains standard and simple; only a new URI need be defined. Regardless of the complexity (or obscurity) of new XML-related ideas, this robust set of four methods should be sufficient to allow parsers to implement the new ideas.

Error Handling

Invoking the setFeature() and setProperty() methods can result in SAXNotSupportedExceptions and SAXNotRecognizedExceptions.

 Both of these are also in the org.xml.sax package.

The first, SAXNotSupportedException, indicates that the parser "knows" about the feature or property but doesn't support it. This is commonly used when a standard property or feature is not yet coded in (such as in alpha or beta versions of parsers). So invoking setFeature("http://xml.org/sax/features/namespaces") on a parser in development might result in a SAXNotSupportedException. The parser recognizes the feature (and probably plans to support it at some point), but doesn't have the ability to perform the requested processing.

The second exception, SAXNotRecognizedException, commonly occurs when your code uses vendor-specific features and properties, and then you switch out your parser implementations. The new implementation won't know anything about the other vendor's features or properties, and will throw a SAXNotRecognizedException.

You should always explicitly catch these exceptions so you can report them, rather than treating them as just another generic SAXException. Otherwise, you end up losing valuable information about what happened in your code. This means you may have to write a bit of extra code, but thus is the price for good exception handling; here's a slightly updated version of the buildTree() method (detailed originally in Chapter 3) that handles these problems gracefully:

```java
  public void buildTree(DefaultTreeModel treeModel,
                        DefaultMutableTreeNode base, String xmlURI)
    throws IOException, SAXException {

    String featureURI = "";
    XMLReader reader = null;

    try {
      // Create instances needed for parsing
      reader = XMLReaderFactory.createXMLReader();
      JTreeHandler jTreeHandler =
        new JTreeHandler(treeModel, base);

      // Register content handler
      reader.setContentHandler(jTreeHandler);

      // Register error handler
      reader.setErrorHandler(jTreeHandler);

      // Turn on validation
      featureURI = "http://xml.org/sax/features/validation";
      reader.setFeature(featureURI, true);

      // Turn on schema validation, as well
      featureURI = "http://apache.org/xml/features/validation/schema";
      reader.setFeature(featureURI, true);

      // Parse
      InputSource inputSource = new InputSource(xmlURI);
      reader.parse(inputSource);
    } catch (SAXNotRecognizedException e) {
      System.err.println("The parser class " + reader.getClass().getName() +
        " does not recognize the feature URI '" + featureURI + "'");
      System.exit(-1);
    } catch (SAXNotSupportedException e) {
      System.err.println("The parser class " + reader.getClass().getName() +
        " does not support the feature URI '" + featureURI + "'");
      System.exit(-1);
    }
  }
```

Resolving Entities

You've already seen how to interact with content in the XML document you're parsing (using ContentHandler), and how to deal with error conditions (ErrorHandler).
Both of these are concerned specifically with the data in an XML document. What I
haven't talked about is the process by which the parser goes outside of the document
and gets data. For example, consider a simple entity reference in an XML document:

```
<FM>
<P>Text placed in the public domain by Moby Lexical Tools, 1992.</P>
<P>SGML markup by Jon Bosak, 1992-1994.</P>
```

```
<P>XML version by Jon Bosak, 1996-1998.</P>
<P>&usage-terms;</P>
</FM>
```

Your schema then indicates to the parser how to resolve that entity:

```
<!ENTITY usage-terms
    SYSTEM "http://www.newInstance.com/entities/usage-terms.xml">
```

At parse time, the usage-terms entity reference will be expanded (in this case, to "This work may be freely copied and distributed worldwide.", as seen in Figure 4-1).

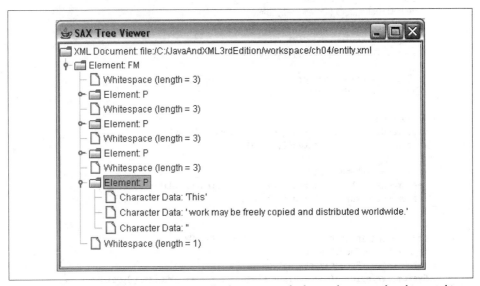

Figure 4-1. The usage-terms entity was resolved to a URI, which was then parsed and inserted into the document

However, there are several cases where you might not want this "default" behavior:

- You don't have network access, so you want the entity to resolve to a local copy of the referenced document (perhaps a version you've downloaded yourself).

- You want to substitute your own content for the content specified in the schema.

You can short-circuit normal entity resolution using org.xml.sax.EntityResolver. This interface does exactly what it says: resolves entities. More important, it allows you to get involved in the entity resolution process. The interface defines only a single method, as shown in Figure 4-2.

To insert your own logic into the resolution process, create an implementation of this interface, and register it with your XMLReader instance through setEntityResolver( ). Once that's done, every time the reader comes across an entity

| «interface» |
| EntityResolver |
| +resolveEntity(publicId : String,systemId : String) : InputSource |

Figure 4-2. There's not much to the EntityResolver class; just a single, albeit useful, method

reference, it passes the public ID and system ID for that entity to the resolveEntity( ) method of your EntityResolver implementation.

Typically, the XML reader resolves the entity through the specified public or system ID. If you want to accept this default behavior in your own EntityResolver implementation, just return null from your version of resolveEntity( ). In fact, you should always make sure that whatever code you add to your resolveEntity( ) implementation, it returns null in the default case. In other words, start with an implementation class that looks like Example 4-1.

Example 4-1. Before coding in special entity resolution, always ensure that any unhandled cases result in a null return value (and therefore normal entity resolution)

```
package javaxml3;

import java.io.IOException;

import org.xml.sax.EntityResolver;
import org.xml.sax.InputSource;
import org.xml.sax.SAXException;

public class SimpleEntityResolver implements EntityResolver {

  public InputSource resolveEntity(String publicID, String systemID)
    throws IOException, SAXException {

    // In the default case, return null
    return null;
  }
}
```

Of course, things are more interesting when you *don't* return null. If you return an InputSource from this method, that InputSource is used in resolution of the entity reference, rather than the public or system ID specified in your schema. In other words, you can specify your own data instead of letting the reader handle resolution on its own. As an example, create a *usage-terms.xml* file on your local machine:

```
Any use of this file could result in your <i>imminent</i> destruction.
Consider yourself warned!
```

Now you can indicate that this file should be used via resolveEntity( ):

```
private static final String USAGE_TERMS_ID =
  "http://www.newInstance.com/entities/usage-terms.xml";
```

```
private static final String USAGE_TERMS_LOCAL_URI =
  "/your/path/to/usage-terms.xml";

public InputSource resolveEntity(String publicID, String systemID)
  throws IOException, SAXException {

  if (systemID.equals(USAGE_TERMS_ID)) {
    return new InputSource(USAGE_TERMS_LOCAL_URI);
  }

  // In the default case, return null
  return null;
}
```

 Be sure to change the USAGE_TERMS_LOCAL_URI to match your own filesystem path.

You can see that instead of allowing resolution to the online resource, an
InputSource that provides access to the local version of *copyright.xml* is returned. If
you recompile your source file and run the tree viewer, you can visually verify that
this local copy is used.

You register this resolver on your XMLReader via the setEntityResolver( ) method, as
shown here (using the SAXTreeViewer example again):

```
// Register content handler
reader.setContentHandler(jTreeHandler);

// Register error handler
reader.setErrorHandler(jTreeHandler);

// Register entity resolver
reader.setEntityResolver(new SimpleEntityResolver( ));

// Turn on validation
featureURI = "http://xml.org/sax/features/validation";
reader.setFeature(featureURI, true);

// Turn on schema validation, as well
featureURI = "http://apache.org/xml/features/validation/schema";
reader.setFeature(featureURI, true);
```

Figure 4-3 shows the usage-terms entity reference expanded, using the local file,
rather than the URI specified in the schema.

In real-world applications, resolveEntity( ) tends to become a lengthy laundry list of
if/then/else blocks, each one handling a specific system or public ID. And this
brings up an important point: try to avoid this method becoming a kitchen sink for
IDs. If you no longer need a specific resolution to occur, remove the if clause for it.

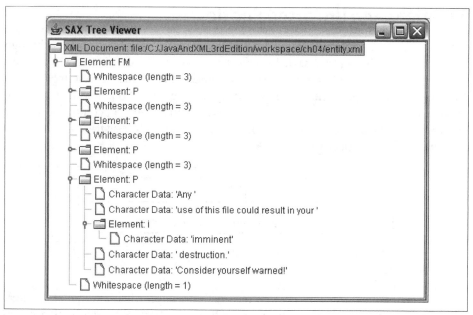

Figure 4-3. This time, the local entity is used (and parsed, as seen by the expanded i element)

Additionally, try to use different `EntityResolver` implementations for different applications, rather than creating one generic implementation for all your applications. Doing this avoids code bloat, and more important, speeds up entity resolution. If you have to wait for your reader to run through 50 `String.equals( )` comparisons, you can really bog down an application. Be sure to put references accessed often at the top of the `if/else` stack, as well, so they are encountered first and result in quicker entity resolution.

Finally, I want to make one more recommendation concerning your `EntityResolver` implementations. You'll notice that I defined my implementation in a separate class file, while the `ErrorHandler`, `ContentHandler`, and (as you'll see in "Notations and Unparsed Entities") `DTDHandler` implementations were in the same source file as parsing occurred in. That wasn't an accident! You'll find that the way you deal with content, errors, and DTDs is fairly static. You write your program, and that's it. When you make changes, you're performing a larger code rewrite, so recompiling your core parsing program is a given. However, you'll make many changes to the way you want your application to resolve entities. Depending on the machine you're on, the type of client you're deploying to, and what (and where) documents are available, you'll often use several different versions of an `EntityResolver` implementation. To allow for rapid changes to this implementation without causing editing or recompilation of your core parsing code, I use a separate source file for `EntityResolver` implementations; I suggest you do the same. And with that, you should know all that you need to know about resolving entities in your applications using SAX.

Notations and Unparsed Entities

After a rather extensive look at EntityResolver, I'm going to cruise through DTDHandler (also in org.xml.sax). In almost nine years of extensive SAX and XML programming, I've used this interface only once—in writing JDOM (covered in Chapter 9)—and even then, it was a rather obscure case. Still, if you work with unparsed entities often, are into parser internals, or just want to get into every nook and cranny of the SAX API, then you need to know about DTDHandler. The interface is shown in all its simplicity in Figure 4-4.

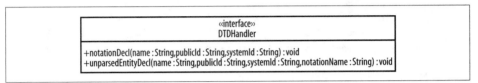

Figure 4-4. *This handler is concerned with the declaration of certain XML types, rather than the actual content of those entities (if and when they are resolved)*

The DTDHandler interface allows you to receive notification when a reader encounters an unparsed entity or notation declaration. Of course, both of these events occur in DTDs, not XML documents, which is why this is called DTDHandler. The two methods listed in Figure 4-4 do exactly what you would expect. The first reports a notation declaration, including its name, public ID, and system ID. Remember the NOTATION structure in DTDs? (Flip back to Chapter 2 if you're unclear.)

```
<!NOTATION jpeg SYSTEM "images/jpeg">
```

The second method provides information about an unparsed entity declaration, which looks as follows:

```
<!ENTITY stars_logo SYSTEM "http://www.nhl.com/img/team/dal38.gif"
                     NDATA jpeg>
```

In both cases, you can take action at these occurrences if you create an implementation of DTDHandler and register it with your reader through the XMLReader's setDTDHandler( ) method. This is generally useful when writing low-level applications that must either reproduce XML content (such as an XML editor), or when you want to build up some Java representation of a DTD's constraints (such as in a data binding implementation). In most other situations, it isn't something you will need very often.

The DefaultHandler Class

Because SAX is interface-driven, you have to do a lot of tedious work to get started with an XML-based application. For example, when you write your ContentHandler implementation, you have to implement each and every method of that interface, even if you aren't inserting behavior into each callback. If you need an ErrorHandler, you add three more method implementations; using DTDHandler? That's a few more. A lot of times, though, you're writing lots of no-operation methods, as you only need to interact with a couple of key callbacks.

Fortunately, org.xml.sax.helpers.DefaultHandler can be a real boon in these situations. This class doesn't define any behavior of its own; however, it does implement ContentHandler, ErrorHandler, EntityResolver, and DTDHandler, and provides empty implementations of each method of each interface. So you can have a single class (call it, for example, MyHandlerClass) that extends DefaultHandler. You then only override the callback methods you're concerned with. You might implement startElement( ), characters( ), endElement( ), and fatalError( ), for example. In any combination of implemented methods, though, you'll save tons of lines of code for methods you don't need to provide action for, and make your code a lot clearer too. Then, the argument to setErrorHandler( ), setContentHandler( ), and setDTDHandler( ) would be the same instance of this MyHandlerClass.

You can pass a DefaultHandler instance to setEntityResolver( ) as well, although (as I've already said) I discourage mixing EntityResolver implementations in with these other handlers.

Extension Interfaces

SAX provides several extension interfaces. These are interfaces that SAX parsers are not required to support; you'll find these interfaces in org.xml.sax.ext. In some cases, you'll have to download these directly from the SAX web site (*http://www.saxproject.org*), although most parsers will include these in the parser download.

 Because parsers aren't required to support these handlers, never write code that absolutely depends on them, unless you're sure you won't be changing parser. If you can provide enhanced features, but fallback to standard SAX, you're in a much better position.

LexicalHandler

The first of these handlers is probably the most useful: `org.xml.sax.ext.LexicalHandler`. This handler provides methods that can receive notification of several lexical events in an XML document, such as comments, entity declarations, DTD declarations, and CDATA sections. In ContentHandler, these lexical events are essentially ignored, and you just get the data and declarations without notification of when or how they were provided.

This is not really a general-use handler, as most applications don't need to know if text was in a CDATA section or not. However, if you are working with an XML editor, serializer, or other component that must know the exact format of the input document—and not just its contents—then the LexicalHandler can really help you out.

To see this guy in action, you first need to add an import statement for `org.xml.sax.ext.LexicalHandler` to your *SAXTreeViewer.java* source file. Once that's done, you can add LexicalHandler to the implements clause in the nonpublic class JTreeContentHandler in that source file:

```
class JTreeHandler implements ContentHandler, ErrorHandler, LexicalHandler {
```

To get started, look at the first lexical event that might happen in processing an XML document: the start and end of a DTD reference or declaration. That triggers the startDTD( ) and endDTD( ) callbacks (I've coded up versions appropriate for SAXTreeViewer here):

```
public void startDTD(String name, String publicID,
                     String systemID)
  throws SAXException {

  DefaultMutableTreeNode dtdReference =
    new DefaultMutableTreeNode("DTD for '" + name + "'");
  if (publicID != null) {
    DefaultMutableTreeNode publicIDNode =
      new DefaultMutableTreeNode("Public ID: '" + publicID + "'");
    dtdReference.add(publicIDNode);
  }
  if (systemID != null) {
    DefaultMutableTreeNode systemIDNode =
      new DefaultMutableTreeNode("System ID: '" + systemID + "'");
    dtdReference.add(systemIDNode);
  }
```

```
  current.add(dtdReference);
}

public void endDTD( ) throws SAXException {
  // No action needed here
}
```

This adds a visual cue when a DTD is encountered, and notes the system ID and public ID of the DTD. Continuing on, there is a pair of similar methods for entity references, startEntity( ) and endEntity( ). These are triggered before and after processing entity references. You can add a visual cue for this event as well:

```
public void startEntity(String name) throws SAXException {
  DefaultMutableTreeNode entity =
    new DefaultMutableTreeNode("Entity: '" + name + "'");
  current.add(entity);
  current = entity;
}

public void endEntity(String name) throws SAXException {
  // Walk back up the tree
  current = (DefaultMutableTreeNode)current.getParent( );
}
```

This ensures that the content of, for example, the usage-terms entity reference is included within an "Entity" tree node. Simple enough.

Next are two events for CDATA sections:

```
public void startCDATA( ) throws SAXException {
  DefaultMutableTreeNode cdata =
    new DefaultMutableTreeNode("CDATA Section");
  current.add(cdata);
  current = cdata;
}

public void endCDATA( ) throws SAXException {
  // Walk back up the tree
  current = (DefaultMutableTreeNode)current.getParent( );
}
```

This is old hat by now; the title element's content now appears as the child of a CDATA node. And with that, only one method is left, which receives comment notification:

```
public void comment(char[] ch, int start, int length)
  throws SAXException {

  String comment = new String(ch, start, length);
  DefaultMutableTreeNode commentNode =
    new DefaultMutableTreeNode("Comment: '" + comment + "'");
  current.add(commentNode);
}
```

This method behaves just like the characters( ) and ignorableWhitespace( ) methods. Keep in mind that only the text of the comment is reported to this method, not the surrounding <!-- and --> delimiters.

Finally, register this handler with your XMLReader. Since the reader isn't required to support LexicalHandler, you can't just call setLexicalHandler( ); instead, use setProperty( ):

```
// Register lexical handler
reader.setProperty("http://xml.org/sax/properties/lexical-handler",
                   jTreeHandler);
```

With these changes in place, you can compile the example program and run it. You should get output similar to that shown in Figure 4-5.

 Be sure you actually have some of these lexical events in your document before trying this out. I've added an entity reference and comment in the as_you-with_entity.xml file, included in the downloadable examples for this book (see http://www.oreilly.com/catalog/9780596101497).

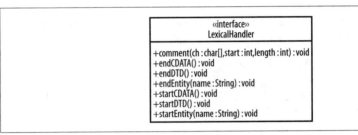

Figure 4-5. The LexicalHandler implementation reports a DTD (in addition to an entity reference for that DTD), as well as a comment and the usage-terms entity

DeclHandler

A lesser used interface, DeclHandler is another of the extended SAX interfaces. This interface defines methods that receive notification of specific events within a DTD, such as element and attribute declarations. This is another item only good for very specific cases; again, XML editors and components that must know the exact lexical structure of documents and their DTDs come to mind. I'm not going to show you an example of using the DeclHandler; at this point you know more than you'll probably ever need to about handling callback methods. Instead, I'll just give you a look at the interface, shown in Figure 4-6.

The DeclHandler interface is fairly self-explanatory. The first two methods handle the <!ELEMENT> and <!ATTLIST> constructs. The third, externalEntityDecl( ), reports entity declarations (through <!ENTITY>) that refer to external resources. The final method, internalEntityDecl( ), reports entities defined inline. That's all there is to it.

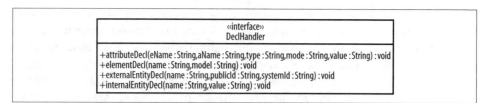

Figure 4-6. The DeclHandler interface isn't used often, but it's a real boon if you need to write code that deals directly with DTDs

Attributes2, Locator2, and EntityResolver2

SAX provides three other interesting interfaces in `org.xml.sax.ext`: `Attributes2`, `Locator2`, and `EntityResolver2`. These all extend their respective core interfaces from `org.xml.sax` (`Attributes`, `Locator`, and `EntityResolver`), and class diagrams are shown for all three in Figure 4-7.

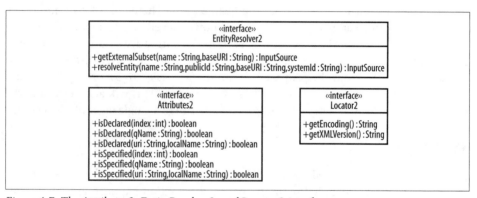

Figure 4-7. The Attributes2, EntityResolver2, and Locator2 interfaces

These interfaces provide additional information for use in parsing, ranging from whether an attribute was specified in a DTD to the encoding of an XML document (pulled from the XML declaration). You can find out if your parser supports and uses these extensions via the `getFeature( )` method:

```
// Check for Attributes2 usage
featureURI = "http://xml.org/sax/features/use-attributes2";
jTreeHandler.setUsingAttributes2(reader.getFeature(featureURI));

// Check for Locator2 usage
featureURI = "http://xml.org/sax/features/use-locator2";
jTreeHandler.setUsingLocator2(reader.getFeature(featureURI));
```

These and all other SAX-standard feature and property URIs are detailed in the Appendix.

Unfortunately, most parsers don't support these extensions, so any sort of detailed coverage of them is infeasible. I could show you how they behave under lesser-used parsers that support them, but that's hardly helpful when you move to more mainstream parsers like Apache Xerces. If you are interested in these extensions, check out the SAX Javadoc at *http://www.saxproject.org/apidoc/org/xml/sax/ext/package-summary.html*, and hope that by the next revision of this book, these will be more commonly supported (and then I'll spend some time on them!).

For those who want the fullest in SAX features, you should check out AElfred2 and the GNU JAXP project, online at *http://www.gnu.org/software/classpathx/jaxp*. I prefer to use Xerces for production work, but your mileage may vary.

Filters and Writers

At this point, I want to diverge from the beaten path. There are a lot of additional features in SAX that can really turn you into a power developer, and take you beyond the confines of "standard" SAX. In this section, I'll introduce you to two of these: SAX filters and writers. Using classes both in the standard SAX distribution and available separately from the SAX web site (*http://www.saxproject.org*), you can add some fairly advanced behavior to your SAX applications. This will also get you in the mindset of using SAX as a pipeline of events, rather than a single layer of processing.

XMLFilters

First on the list is the org.xml.sax.XMLFilter class that comes in the basic SAX download, and should be included with any parser distribution supporting SAX 2. This class extends the XMLReader interface, and adds two new methods to that class, as shown in Figure 4-8.

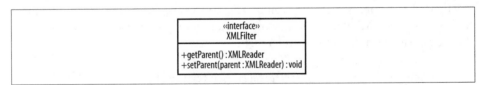

Figure 4-8. Extra methods defined by the XMLFilter interface

It might not seem like there is much to say here; what's the big deal, right? Well, by allowing a hierarchy of XMLReaders through this filtering mechanism, you can build up a processing chain, or *pipeline*, of events. To understand what I mean by a pipeline, you first need to understand the normal flow of a SAX parse:

1. Events in an XML document are passed to the SAX reader.

2. The SAX reader and registered handlers pass events and data to an application.

What developers started realizing, though, is that it is simple to insert one or more additional links into this chain:

1. Events in an XML document are passed to the SAX reader.

2. The SAX reader performs some processing and passes information to another SAX reader.

3. Repeat until all SAX processing is done.

4. Finally, the SAX reader and registered handlers pass events and data to an application.

It's the middle two steps that create a pipeline, where one reader that performed specific processing passes its information on to another reader, repeatedly, instead of having to lump all code into one reader. When this pipeline is set up with multiple readers, modular and efficient programming results. And that's what the XMLFilter class allows for: chaining of XMLReader implementations through filtering. Enhancing this even further is the class org.xml.sax.helpers.XMLFilterImpl, which provides a simple implementation of XMLFilter. It is the convergence of an XMLFilter and the DefaultHandler class: the XMLFilterImpl class implements XMLFilter, ContentHandler, ErrorHandler, EntityResolver, and DTDHandler, providing pass-through versions of each method of each handler. In other words, it sets up a pipeline for all SAX events, allowing your code to override any methods that need to insert processing into the pipeline.

Again, it's best to see these in action. Example 4-2 is a working, ready-to-use filter. You're past the basics, so I'm going to move through this rapidly.

Example 4-2. This simple filter allows for wholesale replacement of a namespace URI with a new URI

```
package javaxml3;

import org.xml.sax.Attributes;
import org.xml.sax.SAXException;
import org.xml.sax.XMLReader;
import org.xml.sax.helpers.XMLFilterImpl;

public class NamespaceFilter extends XMLFilterImpl {

  /** The old URI, to replace */
  private String oldURI;

  /** The new URI, to replace the old URI with */
  private String newURI;

  public NamespaceFilter(XMLReader reader,
                         String oldURI, String newURI) {
    super(reader);
    this.oldURI = oldURI;
    this.newURI = newURI;
```

Example 4-2. This simple filter allows for wholesale replacement of a namespace URI with a new URI (continued)

```
  }

  public void startPrefixMapping(String prefix, String uri)
    throws SAXException {

    // Change URI, if needed
    if (uri.equals(oldURI)) {
      super.startPrefixMapping(prefix, newURI);
    } else {
      super.startPrefixMapping(prefix, uri);
    }
  }

  public void startElement(String uri, String localName,
                           String qName, Attributes attributes)
    throws SAXException {

    // Change URI, if needed
    if (uri.equals(oldURI)) {
      super.startElement(newURI, localName, qName, attributes);
    } else {
      super.startElement(uri, localName, qName, attributes);
    }
  }

  public void endElement(String uri, String localName, String qName)
    throws SAXException {

    // Change URI, if needed
    if (uri.equals(oldURI)) {
      super.endElement(newURI, localName, qName);
    } else {
      super.endElement(uri, localName, qName);
    }
  }
}
```

Start out by extending XMLFilterImpl, so you don't have to worry about any events that you don't want to deal with (like DefaultHandler, you'll get no-op methods "for free"); the XMLFilterImpl class takes care of them by passing on all events unchanged unless a method is overridden. All that's left, in this example, is to change a namespace URI from an old one, to a new one.

 If this example seems trivial, don't underestimate its usefulness. Many times in the last several years, the URI of a namespace for a specification (such as XML Schema or XSLT) has changed. Rather than having to hand-edit all of my XML documents or write code for XML that I receive, this NamespaceFilter takes care of the problem for me.

Passing an XMLReader instance to the constructor sets that reader as its parent, so the parent reader receives any events passed on from the filter (which is all events, by virtue of the XMLFilterImpl class, unless the NamespaceFilter class overrides that behavior). By supplying two URIs—the URI to be replaced, and the URI to replace that old one with—your filter is ready to use. The three overridden methods handle any needed interchanging of that URI. Once you have a filter like this in place, you supply a reader to it, and then operate upon the *filter*, not the *reader*. For example, suppose that the SAXTreeViewer application is used to display XML versions of O'Reilly books, and the O'Reilly namespace URI for these books is universally being changed from http://www.oreilly.com to http://safari.oreilly.com. In that case, you could use the filter like this:

```
public void buildTree(DefaultTreeModel treeModel,
                      DefaultMutableTreeNode base, String xmlURI)
  throws IOException, SAXException {

  String featureURI = "";
  XMLReader reader = null;

  try {
    // Create instances needed for parsing
    reader = XMLReaderFactory.createXMLReader();
    JTreeHandler jTreeHandler =
      new JTreeHandler(treeModel, base);

    NamespaceFilter filter = new NamespaceFilter(reader,
              "http://www.oreilly.com",
              "http://safari.oreilly.com");

    // Register content handler
    filter.setContentHandler(jTreeHandler);

    // Register error handler
    filter.setErrorHandler(jTreeHandler);

    // Register entity resolver
    filter.setEntityResolver(new SimpleEntityResolver());

    // Register lexical handler
    filter.setProperty("http://xml.org/sax/properties/lexical-handler",
                      jTreeHandler);

    // Turn on validation
    featureURI = "http://xml.org/sax/features/validation";
    filter.setFeature(featureURI, true);

    // Turn on schema validation, as well
    featureURI = "http://apache.org/xml/features/validation/schema";
    filter.setFeature(featureURI, true);

    // Parse
```

```
        InputSource inputSource = new InputSource(xmlURI);
        filter.parse(inputSource);
    } catch (SAXNotRecognizedException e) {
        System.err.println("The parser class " + reader.getClass().getName() +
            " does not recognize the feature URI '" + featureURI + "'");
        System.exit(-1);
    } catch (SAXNotSupportedException e) {
        System.err.println("The parser class " + reader.getClass().getName() +
            " does not support the feature URI '" + featureURI + "'");
        System.exit(-1);
    }
}
```

Of course, you can chain these filters together as well, and use them as standard libraries. When I'm dealing with older XML documents, I often create several of these with old XSL and XML Schema URIs and put them in place so I don't have to worry about incorrect URIs:

```
XMLReader reader = XMLReaderFactory.createXMLReader(vendorParserClass);
NamespaceFilter xslFilter = new NamespaceFilter(reader,
                "http://www.w3.org/TR/XSL",
                "http://www.w3.org/1999/XSL/Transform");
NamespaceFilter xsdFilter = new NamespaceFilter(xslFilter,
                "http://www.w3.org/TR/XMLSchema",
                "http://www.w3.org/2001/XMLSchema");
```

Here, I'm building a longer pipeline to ensure that no old namespace URIs sneak by and cause my applications any trouble.

Be careful not to build too long a pipeline; each new link in the chain adds some processing time. All the same, this is a great way to build reusable components for SAX.

XMLWriter

Now that you understand how filters work in SAX, I want to introduce you to a specific filter, XMLWriter. This class, as well its subclass, DataWriter, can be downloaded from David Megginson's site at *http://www.megginson.com/Software*.

David Megginson shepherded SAX through its early days and has now returned to the fold. David is a SAX guru, and even though he no longer actively works on XMLWriter (or DataWriter), he has created some incredibly useful classes, and still hosts them on his personal web site.

XMLWriter extends XMLFilterImpl, and DataWriter extends XMLWriter. Both of these filter classes are used to output XML, which may seem a bit at odds with what you've learned so far about SAX. However, it's not that unusual; you could easily insert statements into a startElement() or characters() callback that fires up a java.io.Writer and outputs to it. In fact, that's awfully close to what XMLWriter and DataWriter do.

I'm not going to spend a lot of time on this class, because it's not really the way you want to be outputting XML in the general sense; it's much better to use DOM, JDOM, or another XML API if you want mutability. However, the XMLWriter class offers a valuable way to inspect what's going on in a SAX pipeline. By inserting it between other filters and readers in your pipeline, it can be used to output a snapshot of your data.

For example, in the case where you're changing namespace URIs, it might be that you want to actually store the XML document with the new namespace URI (be it a modified O'Reilly URI, an updated XSL URI, or whatever other use-case you come up with). This is a piece of cake with the XMLWriter class. Since you've already got SAXTreeViewer using the NamespaceFilter, I'll use that as an example. First, add import statements for java.io.Writer (for output), and the com.megginson.sax. XMLWriter class. Once that's in place, you'll need to insert an instance of XMLWriter between the NamespaceFilter and the XMLReader instances; this means output will occur after namespaces have been changed but before the visual events occur:

```
public void buildTree(DefaultTreeModel treeModel,
                      DefaultMutableTreeNode base, String xmlURI)
    throws IOException, SAXException {

    String featureURI = "";
    XMLReader reader = null;

    try {
        // Create instances needed for parsing
        reader = XMLReaderFactory.createXMLReader();
        JTreeHandler jTreeHandler =
          new JTreeHandler(treeModel, base);

        XMLWriter writer = new XMLWriter(reader, new FileWriter("snapshot.xml"));
        NamespaceFilter filter = new NamespaceFilter(writer,
                    "http://www.oreilly.com",
                    "http://safari.oreilly.com");

        // Register content handler
        filter.setContentHandler(jTreeHandler);

        // Register error handler
        filter.setErrorHandler(jTreeHandler);

        // Register entity resolver
        filter.setEntityResolver(new SimpleEntityResolver());

        // Register lexical handler
        filter.setProperty("http://xml.org/sax/properties/lexical-handler",
                      jTreeHandler);
```

```
      // Turn on validation
      featureURI = "http://xml.org/sax/features/validation";
      filter.setFeature(featureURI, true);

      // Turn on schema validation, as well
      featureURI = "http://apache.org/xml/features/validation/schema";
      filter.setFeature(featureURI, true);

      // Parse
      InputSource inputSource = new InputSource(xmlURI);
      filter.parse(inputSource);
    } catch (SAXNotRecognizedException e) {
      System.err.println("The parser class " + reader.getClass().getName() +
        " does not recognize the feature URI '" + featureURI + "'");
      System.exit(-1);
    } catch (SAXNotSupportedException e) {
      System.err.println("The parser class " + reader.getClass().getName() +
        " does not support the feature URI '" + featureURI + "'");
      System.exit(-1);
    }
  }
```

 Be sure you set the parent of the NamespaceFilter instance to be the XMLWriter, not the XMLReader. Otherwise, no output will actually occur.

Once you've got these changes compiled in, run the example. You should get a *snapshot.xml* file created in the directory from which you're running the example. Both XMLWriter and DataWriter offer a lot more in terms of methods to output XML, both in full and in part, and you should check out the Javadoc included with the downloaded package.

## CHAPTER 5

DOM

SAX is just one of several APIs that allow XML work to be done within Java. This chapter and the next will widen your API knowledge as I introduce the Document Object Model, commonly called the DOM. This API is quite a bit different from SAX, and complements the Simple API for XML in many ways. You'll need both, as well as the other APIs and tools in the rest of this book, to be a competent XML developer.

Because DOM is fundamentally different from SAX, I'll spend a good bit of time discussing the concepts behind DOM, and why it might be used instead of SAX for certain applications. Selecting any XML API involves tradeoffs, and choosing between DOM and SAX is certainly no exception. I'll move on to possibly the most important topic: code. I'll introduce you to a utility class that serializes DOM trees and will provide a pretty good look at the DOM structure and related classes. This will get you ready for some more advanced DOM work.

The Document Object Model

The DOM, unlike SAX, has its origins in the World Wide Web Consortium (W3C; online at *http://www.w3.org*). Whereas SAX is public domain software, developed through long discussions on the XML-dev mailing list, DOM is a standard—just like the actual XML specification. The DOM is designed to represent the content and model of XML documents across all programming languages and tools. On top of that specification, there are several *language bindings*. These bindings exist for Java-Script, Java, CORBA, and other languages, allowing the DOM to be a cross-platform and cross-language specification.

DOM Levels and Modules

In addition to being different from SAX in regard to standardization and language bindings, the DOM is organized into "levels" instead of versions. DOM Level One is an accepted recommendation, and you can view the completed specification at *http://www.w3.org/TR/REC-DOM-Level-1*. Level 1 details the functionality and navigation of content within a document.

A document in the DOM is not just limited to XML, but can be HTML or other content models as well.

DOM Level 2, which was finalized in November of 2000, adds core functionality to DOM Level 1. There are also several additional DOM modules and options aimed at specific content models, such as XML, HTML, and CSS. These less-generic modules begin to "fill in the blanks" left by the more general tools provided in DOM Level 1. You can view the current DOM Level 2 Recommendation at *http://www.w3.org/TR/DOM-Level-2-Core*. This is actually the recommendation for the DOM Core; all the supplemental modules are represented by their own specifications:

DOM Level 2 Views (http://www.w3.org/TR/DOM-Level-2-Views)
> The Views module deals with interaction between an XML document and some type of stylesheet or presentation aspect. For instance, the same XML document could be styled by multiple CSS or XSL stylesheets; each of the resulting documents would be a view. It turns out that this module isn't that useful, as Java tools for document transformation are plentiful; most parsers won't support this module.

DOM Level 2 Events (http://www.w3.org/TR/DOM-Level-2-Events)
> The Events module provides a DOM-centric event model for XML documents. You can register event listeners for specific DOM Nodes (more on the Node class later), and then write code that is triggered when, for example, the data in that Node changes. While some parsers support the complete Events module, many—like Apache Xerces—only provide support for *mutation events*, that is, events that are triggered by the changing of document data. This is plenty for most applications that need event support.

Interestingly, while the Views module is not that helpful in and of itself, the Events module actually depends on it to function correctly.

DOM Level 2 Styles (http://www.w3.org/TR/DOM-Level-2-Style)
> The Styles module provides a DOM-centric model for accessing CSS stylesheets, as well as other DOM stylesheets (called *DOM style sheets* by the specification). Since these are more concerned with HTML and presentation issues, most XML parsers don't support the Styles module.

DOM Level 2 Traversal and Range (http://www.w3.org/TR/DOM-Level-2-Traversal-Range)

The Traversal and Range module is probably of the most interest to Java developers. It allows access and selection of a DOM tree (and subsets of that tree) in ways more interesting and flexible than the core DOM module allows. You can select ranges of Nodes easily and manipulate them as a whole. As you might expect, the more popular XML parsers support this module as a general rule.

DOM Level 2 HTML (http://www.w3.org/TR/DOM-Level-2-HTML)

The HTML module provides a HTML (and XHTML) semantic veneer over DOM. You can access HTML elements as HTMLHead and HTMLLink instead of DOM Elements named head and link; this is incredibly handy if you do lots of HTML work. If you want to use the DOM HTML module, you'll probably want to check out Tidy (*http://tidy.sourceforge.net*), a program specifically aimed at working with HTML.

The most recent entrant on the DOM scene, DOM Level 3 is a recommendation that builds upon the DOM Level 2 core. It's housed online at *http://www.w3.org/TR/DOM-Level-3-Core*, and is mostly concerned with adding support for the XML InfoSet to DOM. However, it also provides a nice bootstrapping implementation, which you'll see in more detail later in this chapter. Support for DOM Level 3 in parsers is a bit sporadic, and you'll often see only portions of the specification implemented (bootstrapping being the most common one).

Apache Xerces, for example, calls its DOM Level 3 implementation experimental.

There are also two new modules introduced by DOM Level 3:

DOM Level 3 Load and Save (http://www.w3.org/TR/DOM-Level-3-LS)

There is no secret about what the Load and Save module does, is there? This adds the much-needed ability to load and serialize XML documents, via DOM, in a vendor-neutral manner. Without this class, you're forced to use parser-specific tools for writing out DOM documents.

DOM Level 3 Validation (http://www.w3.org/TR/DOM-Level-3-Val)

The Validation module allows an in-memory DOM document to be validated. Even more important, you can set up checks to ensure that changes to the document are allowed only if the document remains valid. This is a module that I've rarely seen implemented, as it's pretty tricky to get right. Expect it to be late-coming, but very popular when it finally shows up.

The DOM modules are covered in detail in Chapter 6.

To try and serve the general Java and XML community, I'm largely sticking to DOM Level 2 Core in this chapter; while DOM Level 3 is locked down, parsers have been slow to pick up support for it. That said, I will cover DOM Level 3 bootstrapping, but you'll need to make sure your parser supports the functionality I describe before diving in. For best results, use the latest version of Apache Xerces; when using Xerces directly, I'm using Version 2.6.2, and when using Xerces through JAXP (see Chapters 7 and 8), I'm using the version bundled with Java 5.0, which gives me support for:

- DOM Core Level 1 and 2
- DOM Core Level 3 (in so-called experimental fashion)
- DOM Level 2 Traversal and Range
- DOM Level 2 Mutation Events (the mutation portion of the Events module)
- DOM Level 3 Load and Save (again, in experimental fashion)

DOM Concepts

In addition to fundamentals about the DOM specification, I want to give you a bit of information about the DOM programming structure itself. At the core of DOM is a tree model. Remember that SAX gave you a piece-by-piece view of an XML document, reporting each event in the parsing lifecycle as it happened. DOM is in many ways the converse of this, supplying a complete in-memory representation of the document. The document is supplied to you in a tree format, and all of this is built upon the DOM `org.w3c.dom.Node` interface. Deriving from this interface, DOM provides several XML-specific interfaces, like `Element`, `Document`, `Attr`, and `Text`. So, in a typical XML document, you might get a structure that looks like Figure 5-1.

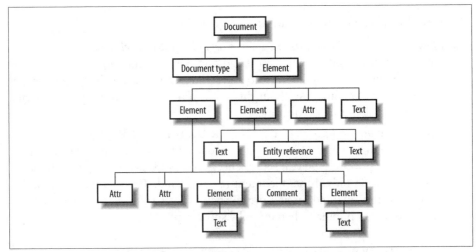

Figure 5-1. DOM documents are often called trees, for reasons obvious from this diagram

A tree model is followed in every sense. This is particularly notable in the case of the Element nodes that have textual values (as in the Title element). Instead of the textual value of the node being available through the Element node (through, for example, a getText( ) method), there is a child node of type Text. So you would get the value of an element from the child Text node, rather than the Element node itself. While this might seem a little odd, it does preserve a very strict tree model in DOM, and allows tasks like walking the tree to be very simple algorithms, without a lot of special cases. Because of this model, all DOM structures can be treated either as their generic type, Node, or as their specific type (Element, Attr, etc.). Many of the navigation methods, like getParent( ) and getChildren( ), operate on that basic Node interface, so you can walk up and down the tree without worrying about the specific structure type.

Another facet of DOM to be aware of is that, like SAX, it defines its own list structures. You'll need to use the NodeList and NamedNodeMap classes when working with DOM lists, rather than Java collections. Depending on your point of view, this isn't a positive or negative, just a fact of life. Figure 5-2 shows a simple UML-style model of the DOM core interfaces and classes, which you can refer to throughout the rest of the chapter.

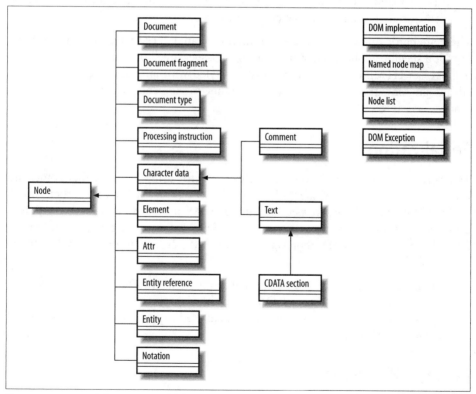

Figure 5-2. Most of the DOM model deals with XML representation; there are also a few exceptions and list classes

When SAX Sucks

There are a lot of times when using DOM isn't a choice, but a requirement. You'd do well to recognize those situations quickly, and not waste time trying to decide which API to use. Here are the times you essentially *must* use DOM:

You need random access to your document
> In SAX, you get information about the XML document as the parser does, and lose that information when the parser does. When the second element in a document comes along, SAX cannot access information in the fourth element, because that fourth element hasn't been parsed yet. When the fourth element *does* come along, SAX can't look back on that second element.

You need access to siblings of an element
> Moving laterally between elements is also difficult with the SAX parsing model. The access provided in SAX is largely hierarchical, as well as sequential. You are going to reach leaf nodes of the first element, then move back up the tree, then down again to leaf nodes of the second element, and so on. At no point is there any clear indication of what level of the hierarchy you are at. There is no concept of a sibling element, or of the next element at the same level, or of which elements are nested within which other elements.

These are hardly indictments of SAX; rather, they are issues that affect what API you use for a specific application. While the above issues are shortcomings for representing, say, an HTML document that must be styled with an XSL stylesheet, they are advantages for extracting data from a 10,000 line catalog entry where you don't need random access to the document.

Serialization

Typically, I'd come up with some clever example for using DOM at this point, and use it to demonstrate how the API works. However, DOM leaves a rather gaping hole, and filling that hole proves to be a good DOM tutorial, as well as having practical value. This hole, of course, is *serialization*. Serialization is the process of taking an XML document in memory, represented as a DOM tree, and writing it to disk (or to a stream).

If you're lucky enough to have a parser that implements the DOM Level 3 Load and Save module, then outputting a DOM tree isn't a problem for you. Most parsers don't provide that support—or slap experimental all over it—and it becomes a real problem for DOM programming.

Getting a DOM Parser

Before you can serialize a DOM tree representing some XML, though, you need to read that XML in the first place. Since you'll usually be reading XML from a file, I'll show you how to do just that. Example 5-1 is a sample class that takes an XML filename, and loads the document into a DOM tree, represented by the org.w3c.dom. Document interface.

Example 5-1. This test class reads in an XML document and loads it into a DOM tree

```java
package javaxml3;

import java.io.File;
import java.io.FileInputStream;
import java.io.FileOutputStream;
import java.io.OutputStream;
import org.xml.sax.InputSource;
import org.w3c.dom.Document;

// Parser import
import org.apache.xerces.parsers.DOMParser;

public class SerializeTester {

  // File to read XML from
  private File inputXML;

  // File to serialize XML to
  private File outputXML;

  public SerializeTester(File inputXML) {
    this.inputXML = inputXML;
  }

  public void test(OutputStream outputStream)
    throws Exception {

    DOMParser parser = new DOMParser();

    // Get the DOM tree as a Document object

    // Serialize
  }

  public static void main(String[] args) {
    if (args.length != 2) {
      System.out.println(
        "Usage: java javaxml3.SerializeTester " +
        "[XML document to read] " +
        "[filename to write output to]");
      return;
    }

    try {
      SerializeTester tester =
        new SerializeTester(new File(args[0]));
      tester.test(new FileOutputStream(new File(args[1])));
```

Example 5-1. This test class reads in an XML document and loads it into a DOM tree (continued)

```
    } catch (Exception e) {
      e.printStackTrace( );
    }
  }
}
```

This example obviously has a couple of pieces missing, represented by the two comments in the test( ) method. I'll supply those in the next two sections, first explaining how to get a DOM tree object, and then detailing the DOMSerializer class, which will do all the heavy lifting.

The DOM Document Object

Remember that in SAX, the focus of interest in the parser was the lifecycle of the process, as all the callback methods provided hooks into the data as it was being parsed. In DOM, the focus of interest lies in the output from the parsing process. Until the entire document is parsed, the XML data is not in a usable state. The output of a parse intended for use with the DOM interface is an org.w3c.dom.Document object. This object acts as a handle to the tree your XML data is in, and in terms of the element hierarchy, it is equivalent to one level above the root element in your XML document. In other words, it owns each and every element in the XML document.

As in SAX, the key method for parsing XML is, unsurprisingly, parse( ); this time the method is on the DOMParser class, though, instead of the SAXParser class. However, DOM requires an additional method to obtain the Document object result from the XML parsing. For DOMParser, this method is named getDocument( ). A simple addition to the SerializeTester class, then, makes reading in XML possible:

```
    public void test(OutputStream outputStream)
      throws Exception {

      DOMParser parser = new DOMParser( );

      // Get the DOM tree as a Document object
      parser.parse(new InputSource(
          new FileInputStream(inputXML)));
      Document doc = parser.getDocument( );

      // Serialize
      }
```

This of course assumes you are using Xerces, as the import statement at the beginning of the source file indicates:

```
    import org.apache.xerces.parsers.DOMParser;
```

If you are using a different parser, you'll need to change this import to your vendor's DOM parser class. Then consult your vendor's documentation to determine which of the parse( ) mechanisms you need to employ to get the DOM result of your parse.

Although there is some variance in getting this result, all the uses of this result that we look at are standard across the DOM specification, so you should not have to worry about any other implementation curveballs in the rest of this chapter.

SAX and DOM at Play

You might have noticed that I supplied the parse( ) method—used for DOM parsing, mind you—a SAX construct, org.xml.sax.InputSource. That might seem surprising, until you realize that DOM parsers often use SAX to handle their parsing! You've already seen that SAX is a fast and efficient method for parsing, so many DOM parsers will actually read in data with SAX, and build up a DOM tree. Even in cases where SAX isn't used wholesale under the covers, the SAX API still offers useful constructs, like InputSource, for representing input and output data.

Serializer Preliminaries

I've been throwing the term "serialization" around quite a bit, and should probably make sure you know what I mean. When I say serialization, I simply mean outputting XML. This could be a file (using a Java File), an OutputStream, or a Writer. There are certainly more output forms available in Java, but these three cover most of the bases (in fact, the latter two do, as a File can be easily converted to a Writer). In this case, the serialization taking place is in an XML format; the DOM tree is converted back to a well-formed XML document in a textual format.

Example 5-2 is the skeleton for the DOMSerializer class. It imports all the needed classes to get the code going, and defines the different entry points (for a File, OutputStream, and Writer) to the class. It also handles setting a few variables that are used in output: the indentation (if any), the encoding, and the line separator (important so that the output works across multiple platforms).

Example 5-2. DOMSerializer handles the preliminary details of DOM output

```
package javaxml3;

import java.io.File;
import java.io.FileWriter;
import java.io.IOException;
import java.io.OutputStream;
import java.io.OutputStreamWriter;
import java.io.Writer;

// DOM imports
import org.w3c.dom.Document;
import org.w3c.dom.DocumentType;
import org.w3c.dom.NamedNodeMap;
import org.w3c.dom.Node;
```

Example 5-2. DOMSerializer handles the preliminary details of DOM output (continued)

```java
import org.w3c.dom.NodeList;

public class DOMSerializer {

  /** Indentation to use (default is no indentation) */
  private String indent = "";

  /** Line separator to use (default is for UNIX) */
  private String lineSeparator = "\n";

  /** Encoding for output (default is UTF-8) */
  private String encoding = "UTF8";

  public void setLineSeparator(String lineSeparator) {
    this.lineSeparator = lineSeparator;
  }

  public void setEncoding(String encoding) {
    this.encoding = encoding;
  }

  public void setIndent(int numSpaces) {
    StringBuffer buffer = new StringBuffer( );
    for (int i=0; i<numSpaces; i++)
      buffer.append(" ");
    this.indent = buffer.toString( );
  }

  public void serialize(Document doc, OutputStream out)
    throws IOException {

    Writer writer = new OutputStreamWriter(out, encoding);
    serialize(doc, writer);
  }

  public void serialize(Document doc, File file)
    throws IOException {

    Writer writer = new FileWriter(file);
    serialize(doc, writer);
  }

  public void serialize(Document doc, Writer writer)
    throws IOException {

    // Serialize document
  }
}
```

One nice facet of DOM is that all of the DOM structures that represent XML (including the Document object) extend the DOM org.w3c.dom.Node interface. This enables the coding of a single method that handles serialization of all DOM node types. Within that method, you can differentiate between node types, but by accepting a Node as input, it enables a very simple way of handling all DOM types. Additionally, it sets up a methodology that allows for recursion, any programmer's best friend. Add the serializeNode( ) method shown here, as well as the initial invocation of that method in the serialize( ) method:

```java
public void serialize(Document doc, Writer writer)
  throws IOException {

  // Start serialization recursion with no indenting
  serializeNode(doc, writer, "");
  writer.flush( );
}

private void serializeNode(Node node, Writer writer,
                           String indentLevel)
  throws IOException {

}
```

In the serializeNode( ) method, an indentLevel variable is used; this sets the method up for recursion. In other words, the serializeNode( ) method can indicate how much the node being worked with should be indented, and when recursion takes place, can add another level of indentation (using the indent member variable). Starting out (within the initial call to serialize( )), there is an empty String for indentation; at the next level, the default is two spaces for indentation, then four spaces at the next level, and so on. Of course, as recursive calls unravel, things head back up to no indentation. All that's left now is to handle the various node types.

Working with Nodes

Once in the serializeNode( ) method, the first task is to determine what type of node has been passed in. Although you could approach this with a Java methodology, using the instanceof keyword and Java reflection, the DOM language bindings for Java make this task much simpler. The Node interface defines a helper method, getNodeType( ), which returns an int value. This value can be compared against a set of constants (also defined within the Node interface), and the type of Node being examined can be quickly and easily determined. This also fits very naturally into the Java switch construct, which can be used to break up serialization into logical sections. The code here covers almost all DOM node types; although there are some additional node types defined (see Figure 5-2), these are the most common, and the concepts here can be applied to the less common node types as well:

```java
private void serializeNode(Node node, Writer writer,
                           String indentLevel)
  throws IOException {

  // Determine action based on node type
  switch (node.getNodeType( )) {
```

```
        case Node.DOCUMENT_NODE:
            break;
        case Node.ELEMENT_NODE:
            break;
      case Node.TEXT_NODE:
            break;
      case Node.CDATA_SECTION_NODE:
            break;
      case Node.COMMENT_NODE:
            break;
      case Node.PROCESSING_INSTRUCTION_NODE:
            break;
      case Node.ENTITY_REFERENCE_NODE:
            break;
      case Node.DOCUMENT_TYPE_NODE:
            break;
    }
  }
```

This code is fairly useless; however, it helps to see all the DOM node types laid out here in a line, rather than mixed in with all the code needed to perform actual serialization. I want to get to that now, though, starting with the first node passed into this method, an instance of the Document interface.

Document nodes

Because the Document interface is an extension of the Node interface, it can be used interchangeably with the other node types. However, it is a special case, as it contains the root element as well as the XML document's DTD and some other special information not within the XML element hierarchy. As a result, you need to extract the root element and pass that back to the serialization method (starting recursion). Additionally, the XML declaration itself is printed out:

```
case Node.DOCUMENT_NODE:
    Document doc = (Document)node;
    writer.write("<?xml version=\"1.0\" encoding=\"UTF-8\"?>");
    writer.write(lineSeparator);
    serializeNode(doc.getDocumentElement( ), writer, "");
    break;
```

Since the code needs to access a Document-specific method (as opposed to one defined in the generic Node interface), the Node implementation must be cast to the Document interface. Then invoke the object's getDocumentElement( ) method to obtain the root element of the XML input document, and in turn, pass that on to the serializeNode( ) method, starting the recursion and traversal of the DOM tree.

Accessing the XML declaration

DOM Level 2 does not provide you access to the XML declaration. That's why the case statement for Document nodes manually outputs a declaration. However, if you're working with a parser that supports DOM Level 3, you get a few additional methods on the Document interface:

```
public String getXmlVersion( );
public void setXmlVersion(String version);

public boolean getXmlStandalone( );
public void setXmlStandalone(boolean standalone);

public String getXmlEncoding( );
```

It is intentional—and correct—that there is no setXmlEncoding( ) option. That attribute of the XML declaration is essentially read-only, as any outgoing encoding is handled by your programming language, and should not be set explicitly by the DOM API.

If you've got access to these methods, make this change to your code:

```
case Node.DOCUMENT_NODE:
    Document doc = (Document)node;
/** DOM Level 2 code
    writer.write("<?xml version=\"1.0\" encoding=\"UTF-8\"?>");
*/
    writer.write("<?xml version=\"");
    writer.write(doc.getXmlVersion( ));
    writer.write("\" encoding=\"UTF-8\" standalone=\"");
    if (doc.getXmlStandalone( ))
        writer.write("yes");
    else
        writer.write("no");
    writer.write("\"");
    writer.write("?>");
    writer.write(lineSeparator);
    serializeNode(doc.getDocumentElement( ), writer, "");
    break;
```

To access DOM Level 3 core functionality in Xerces, either build Xerces from source, using the jars-dom3 target, or download a Xerces distribution built with DOM Level 3 (as I write this, that distribution is in beta release). For more on DOM Level 3 support in Xerces, check out *http://xml.apache.org/xerces2-j/faq-dom.html* and *http://xml.apache.org/xerces2-j/dom3.html*.

Take special note of how getXmlStandalone( ) is used; the method returns either true or false, but the XML declaration defines the standalone attribute as accepting either "yes" or "no". If you're not careful, it's easy to just dump the value of getXmlStandalone( ) into the document, which will cause errors in parsing. You've also got to make sure that the standalone attributes come *after* encoding, or you'll get nasty errors as well.

Something else that should look a little odd to you is the hard-wiring of the encoding (it's set to UTF-8). While it's possible to get the document's encoding through getXmlEncoding( ), it's *not* safe to assume that encoding is being used for writing.

Instead, UTF-8 is applied, making sure that what is written out of Java can be read correctly.

 As an example of this problem, I had a version of DOMSerializer that did output the parsed document's encoding. In one case, the document specified us-ascii as the encoding, and that's what my serializer output. However, when reading back in the serialized document, parsing failed—there were UTF-8 characters, output from my UTF-8 Java Writer, in a document that said it contained only ASCII characters. I learned my lesson, and ensured that the encoding I was outputting in was what was supplied via the XML declaration.

Element nodes

The most common task in serialization is to take a DOM Element and print out its name, attributes, and value, and then serialize its children. First you need to get the name of the XML element, which is available through the getNodeName( ) method on the Node interface. You can then grab the children of the current element and serialize these as well.

A Node's children can be accessed through the getChildNodes( ) method, which returns an instance of a DOM NodeList. It is trivial to obtain the length of this list, and then iterate through the children calling the serializeNode( ) method on each. There's also quite a bit of logic that ensures correct indentation and new lines; these are really just formatting issues, and I won't spend time on them here:

```
case Node.ELEMENT_NODE:
  String name = node.getNodeName( );
  writer.write(indentLevel + "<" + name);
  writer.write(">");

  // recurse on each child
  NodeList children = node.getChildNodes( );
  if (children != null) {
    if ((children.item(0) != null) &&
        (children.item(0).getNodeType( ) ==
        Node.ELEMENT_NODE))
      writer.write(lineSeparator);

    for (int i=0; i<children.getLength( ); i++)
      serializeNode(children.item(i), writer,
                    indentLevel + indent);

    if ((children.item(0) != null) &&
        (children.item(children.getLength( )-1)
              .getNodeType( ) == Node.ELEMENT_NODE))
      writer.write(indentLevel);
  }

  writer.write("</" + name + ">");
  writer.write(lineSeparator);
  break;
```

Of course, astute readers (or DOM experts) will notice that I left out something important: the element's attributes! These are the only pseudoexceptions to the strict tree that DOM builds; attributes are not children (leaf nodes) of elements, but exist as properties of the element. They should be an exception, though, since an attribute is not really a child of an element; it's (sort of) lateral to it. In any case, the attributes of an element are available through the getAttributes() method on the Node interface. This method returns a NamedNodeMap, and that too can be iterated through. Each Node within this list can be polled for its name and value, and suddenly the attributes are handled! Enter the code as shown here to take care of this:

```
case Node.ELEMENT_NODE:
  String name = node.getNodeName();
  writer.write(indentLevel + "<" + name);
  NamedNodeMap attributes = node.getAttributes();
  for (int i=0; i<attributes.getLength(); i++) {
    Node current = attributes.item(i);
    writer.write(" " + current.getNodeName() + "=\"");
    print(writer, current.getNodeValue());
    writer.write("\"");
  }
  writer.write(">");

  // recurse on each child
  NodeList children = node.getChildNodes();
  if (children != null) {
    if ((children.item(0) != null) &&
        (children.item(0).getNodeType() ==
        Node.ELEMENT_NODE))
      writer.write(lineSeparator);

    for (int i=0; i<children.getLength(); i++)
      serializeNode(children.item(i), writer,
                    indentLevel + indent);

    if ((children.item(0) != null) &&
        (children.item(children.getLength()-1)
                .getNodeType() == Node.ELEMENT_NODE))
      writer.write(indentLevel);
  }

  writer.write("</" + name + ">");
  writer.write(lineSeparator);
  break;
```

I've snuck in a new method here: print(). Since there are a lot of special characters in XML (&, <, >, and so forth), those need to be handled differently. That's the job of the utility print() method:

```
private void print(Writer writer, String s)
  throws IOException{

  if (s == null) return;
```

```
for (int i=0, len=s.length(); i<len; i++) {
  char c = s.charAt(i);
  switch(c) {
    case '<':
      writer.write("&lt;");
      break;
    case '>':
      writer.write("&gt;");
      break;
    case '&':
      writer.write("&amp;");
      break;
    case '\r':
      writer.write("&#xD;");
      break;
    default:
      writer.write(c);
  }
}
}
```

You'll see this used in printing out element text as well, which leads us to the next Node type.

Text and CDATA nodes

Next on the list of node types is Text nodes. Output is quite simple, as you only need to use the now-familiar getNodeValue( ) method of the DOM Node interface to get the textual data and print it out; the same is true for CDATA nodes, except that the data within a CDATA section should be enclosed within the CDATA XML semantics (surrounded by <![CDATA[and]]>) and need not use the special character handling in the print() method above. You can add the logic for those two cases now:

```
case Node.TEXT_NODE:
  print(writer, node.getNodeValue( ));
  break;

case Node.CDATA_SECTION_NODE:
  writer.write("<![CDATA[");
  writer.write (node.getNodeValue( ));
  writer.write("]]>");
  break;
```

Comment nodes

Dealing with comments in DOM is about as simple as it gets. The getNodeValue( ) method returns the text within the <!-- and --> XML constructs. That's really all there is to it:

```
case Node.COMMENT_NODE:
  writer.write(indentLevel + "<!-- " +
               node.getNodeValue( ) + " -->");
  writer.write(lineSeparator);
  break;
```

Processing instruction nodes

Moving on to the next DOM node type: the DOM bindings for Java define an interface to handle processing instructions that are within the input XML document, rather obviously called `ProcessingInstruction`. This is useful, as these instructions do not follow the same markup model as XML elements and attributes, but are still important for applications to know about.

The PI node in the DOM is a little bit of a break from what you have seen so far: to fit the syntax into the `Node` interface model, the `getNodeValue( )` method returns all data instructions within a PI in one `String`. This allows quick output of the PI; however, you still need to use `getNodeName( )` to get the name of the PI.

 If you were writing an application that received PIs from an XML document, you might prefer to use the actual `ProcessingInstruction` interface; although it exposes the same data, the method names (`getTarget( )` and `getData( )`) are more in line with a PI's format.

With this understanding, you can add in the code to print out any PIs in supplied XML documents:

```
case Node.PROCESSING_INSTRUCTION_NODE:
   writer.write("<?" + node.getNodeName( ) +
               " " + node.getNodeValue( ) +
               "?>");
   writer.write(lineSeparator);
   break;
```

While the code to deal with PIs is perfectly workable, there is a problem. In the case that handled document nodes, all the serializer did was pull out the document element and recurse. The problem is that this approach ignores any other child nodes of the `Document` object, such as top-level PIs and any `DOCTYPE` declarations. Those node types are actually *lateral* to the document element (root element), and are ignored. Instead of just pulling out the document element, then, the following code serializes *all* child nodes on the supplied `Document` object:

```
case Node.DOCUMENT_NODE:
   Document doc = (Document)node;
   writer.write("<?xml version=\"1.0\" encoding=\"UTF-8\"?>");
   writer.write(lineSeparator);

   // recurse on each top-level node
   NodeList nodes = node.getChildNodes( );
   if (nodes != null)
     for (int i=0; i<nodes.getLength( ); i++)
       serializeNode(nodes.item(i), writer, "");

   // serializeNode(doc.getDocumentElement( ), writer, "");
   break;
```

DocumentType nodes

With this in place, the code can deal with DocumentType nodes, which represent a DOCTYPE declaration. Like PIs, a DTD declaration can be helpful in exposing external information that might be needed in processing an XML document. However, since there can be public and system IDs as well as other DTD-specific data, the code needs to cast the Node instance to the DocumentType interface to access this additional data. Then, use the helper methods to get the name of the Node, which returns the name of the element in the document that is being constrained, the public ID (if it exists), and the system ID of the DTD referenced. It then adds any internal subset information. Using this information, the original DTD can be serialized:

```
case Node.DOCUMENT_TYPE_NODE:
  DocumentType docType = (DocumentType)node;
  String publicId = docType.getPublicId( );
  String systemId = docType.getSystemId( );
  String internalSubset = docType.getInternalSubset( );
  writer.write("<!DOCTYPE " + docType.getName( ));
  if (publicId != null)
    writer.write(" PUBLIC \"" +
                     publicId + "\" ");
  else
    writer.write(" SYSTEM ");
  writer.write("\"" + systemId + "\"");
  if (internalSubset != null)
    writer.write(" [" + internalSubset + "]");
  writer.write(">");
  writer.write(lineSeparator);
  break;
```

Entity Reference nodes

All that's left at this point is handling entities and entity references. In this chapter, I will skim over entities and focus on entity references; more details on entities and notations are in the next chapter. For now, a reference can simply be output with the & and ; characters surrounding it:

```
case Node.ENTITY_REFERENCE_NODE:
  writer.write("&" + node.getNodeName( ) + ";");
  break;
```

There are a few surprises that may trip you up when it comes to the output from a node such as this. The definition of how entity references should be processed within DOM allows a lot of latitude, and also relies heavily on the underlying parser's behavior. In fact, most XML parsers have expanded and processed entity references before the XML document's data ever makes its way into the DOM tree. Often, when expecting to see an entity reference within your DOM structure, you will find the text or values *referenced* rather than the entity reference itself.

And that's it! As I mentioned, there are a few other node types, but covering them isn't worth the trouble at this point; you get the idea about how DOM works.

The Results

With the DOMSerializer class complete, all that's left is to invoke the serializer's serialize() method in the test class. To do this, add the following lines to the SerializeTester class:

```
public void test(OutputStream outputStream)
    throws Exception {

    DOMParser parser = new DOMParser();

    // Get the DOM tree as a Document object
    parser.parse(new InputSource(
        new FileInputStream(inputXML)));
    Document doc = parser.getDocument();

    // Serialize
    DOMSerializer serializer = new DOMSerializer();
    serializer.setIndent(2);
    serializer.serialize(doc, outputStream);
}
```

I ran this program on a couple of files, most notably an XML version of the DOM Level 3 Load and Save module specification *(http://www.w3.org/TR/2004/REC-DOM-Level-3-LS-20040407/xml-source.xml)*. A section of the rather large output is shown here:

```
<?xml version="1.0" encoding="UTF-8" standalone="no"?>
<!-- $Id$ -->
<!DOCTYPE spec PUBLIC "-//W3C//DTD Specification V2.2-Based DOM//EN" "http://www.w3.
org/2002/08/xmlspec-v22-dom.dtd">
<spec role="public" w3c-doctype="rec">
    <!--
    ***************************************************************************
    * FRONT MATTER                                                           *
    ***************************************************************************
    -->

    <!--
    ****************************************************
    | filenames to be used for each section            |
    ****************************************************
    -->

<?command-options --map Copyright-Notice copyright-notice
--map Introduction      introduction
--map TOC expanded-toc
--map Core core
--map Events events
```

```
--map idl idl-definitions
--map ecma-binding ecma-script-binding
--map java-binding java-binding
--map Index def-index
--map Objects object-index
--map References references
--map Errors errors
--map Level-3-AS abstract-schemas
--map Load-Save load-save
...
```

You may notice that there is quite a bit of extra whitespace in the output; that's because the serializer adds some new lines every time `writer.write(lineSeparator)` appears in the code. Of course, the underlying DOM tree has some new lines in it as well, which are reported as Text nodes. The end result in many of these cases is the double line breaks, as seen in the output.

 Let me be very clear that the `DOMSerializer` class shown in this chapter is for example purposes and is not a good production solution. While you are welcome to use the class in your own applications, realize that several important options are left out, like setting advanced options for indentation, new lines, and line wrapping. Additionally, entities are handled only in passing (complete treatment would be twice as long as this chapter already is!). Your parser probably has its own serializer class, if not multiple classes, that perform this task at least as well, if not better, than the example in this chapter. However, you now should understand what's going on under the hood in those classes. As a matter of reference, if you are using Apache Xerces, the classes to look at are in `org.apache.xml.serialize`. Some particularly useful ones are `XMLSerializer`, `XHTMLSerializer`, and `HTMLSerializer`. Check them out—they offer a good solution, until DOM Level 3 support is more common.

Modifying and Creating XML

The biggest limitation when using SAX for dealing with XML is that you cannot change any of the XML structure you encounter, at least not without using filters and writers. Those aren't intended to be used for wholesale document changes anyway, so you'll need to use another API when you want to modify XML. DOM fits the bill nicely, as it provides XML creation and modification facilities.

In working with DOM, the process of creating an XML document is quite different from changing an existing one, so I'll take them one at a time. This section gives you a fairly realistic example to mull over. If you've ever been to an online auction site like eBay, you know that the most important aspects of the auction are the ability to *find* items, and the ability to find *out* about items. These functions depend on a user entering in a description of an item, and the auction using that information. The better auction sites allow users to enter in some basic information as well as actual

HTML descriptions, which means savvy users can bold, italicize, link, and add other formatting to their items' descriptions. This provides a good case for using DOM.

Setting Up an Input Servlet

To get started, a little bit of groundwork is needed. Example 5-3 shows a servlet that displays a simple HTML form that takes basic information about an item to be listed on an auction site. This would obviously be dressed up more for a real site, but you get the idea.

Example 5-3. This servlet-generated form submits the data it collects to itself

```java
package javaxml3;

import java.io.File;
import java.io.IOException;
import java.io.PrintWriter;
import javax.servlet.ServletConfig;
import javax.servlet.ServletException;
import javax.servlet.http.HttpServlet;
import javax.servlet.http.HttpServletRequest;
import javax.servlet.http.HttpServletResponse;

// DOM imports
import org.w3c.dom.Attr;
import org.w3c.dom.Document;
import org.w3c.dom.DOMImplementation;
import org.w3c.dom.Element;
import org.w3c.dom.Text;

// Parser import
import org.apache.xerces.dom.DOMImplementationImpl;

public class UpdateItemServlet extends HttpServlet {

  private String outputDir;

  public void init(ServletConfig config) throws ServletException {
    super.init(config);
    outputDir = config.getInitParameter("OutputDirectory");
    if (outputDir == null) outputDir = "";
  }

  public void doGet(HttpServletRequest req, HttpServletResponse res)
    throws ServletException, IOException {

    // Get output
    PrintWriter out = res.getWriter( );
    res.setContentType("text/html");

    // Output HTML
    out.println("<html>");
```

```
        out.println("  <head><title>Input/Update Item Listing</title></head>");
        out.println("  <body>");
        out.println("   <h1 align='center'>Input/Update Item Listing</h1>");
        out.println("   <p align='center'>");
        out.println("    <form method='POST' action='" + target + "'>");
        out.println("     Item ID (Unique Identifier): <br />");
        out.println("     <input name='id' type='text' maxLength='10' />" +
            "<br /><br />");
        out.println("     Item Name: <br />");
        out.println("     <input name='name' type='text' maxLength='50' />" +
            "<br /><br />");
        out.println("     Item Description: <br />");
        out.println("     <textarea name='description' rows='10' cols='30' " +
            "wrap='wrap' ></textarea><br /><br />");
        out.println("     <input type='reset' value='Reset Form'>  ");
        out.println("     <input type='submit' value='Add/Update Item' />");
        out.println("    </form>");
        out.println("   </p>");
        out.println("  </body>");
        out.println("</html>");
        out.close( );
    }
}
```

Notice that the target of this form submission is actually itself—of course, since the submission is made via POST, the doPost( ) method would be called, instead of this doGet( ) method being invoked over and over. Also note the init( ) method, which grabs an init-param (from your servlet context's *web.xml* file). This parameter is used to specify an output directory where XML files will be written.

If you've never worked with a servlet engine, that probably all seemed like another language. If you want to run this example, and are unfamiliar with servlet basics, pick up Jason Hunter's *Java Servlet Programming*, and throw in a side of Ian Darwin and Jason Brittain's *Tomcat: The Definitive Guide*, both O'Reilly books.

In the doPost( ) method, the request parameters need to be read in, and put into a DOM tree (showcasing DOM's ability to create XML, which is the whole point of this exercise). Then, using the DOMSerializer class, the DOM tree is written out to a file, preserved for other application components to use:

```
public void doPost(HttpServletRequest req, HttpServletResponse res)
    throws ServletException, IOException {

    // Get parameter values
    String id = req.getParameter("id");
    String name = req.getParameter("name");
    String description = req.getParameter("description");
```

```
// Create new DOM tree
DOMImplementation domImpl = new DOMImplementationImpl( );
Document doc = domImpl.createDocument(null, "item", null);
Element root = doc.getDocumentElement( );

// ID of item (as attribute)
root.setAttribute("id", id);

// Name of item
Element nameElement = doc.createElement("name");
Text nameText = doc.createTextNode(name);
nameElement.appendChild(nameText);
root.appendChild(nameElement);

// Description of item
Element descriptionElement = doc.createElement("description");
Text descriptionText = doc.createTextNode(description);
descriptionElement.appendChild(descriptionText);
root.appendChild(descriptionElement);

// Serialize DOM tree
DOMSerializer serializer = new DOMSerializer( );
String filename = outputDir + "item-" + id + ".xml";
File outputFile = new File(filename);
serializer.serialize(doc, outputFile);

// Print confirmation
PrintWriter out = res.getWriter( );
res.setContentType("text/html");
out.println("<HTML><BODY>");
out.println("<p>Thank you for your submission. " +
    "Your item has been processed.</p>");
out.println("<p>Your item was saved as " +
    outputFile.getAbsolutePath( ) + "</p>");
out.println("</BODY></HTML>");
out.close( );
}
```

Make sure the DOMSerializer class is in your servlet's context class-path. In my setup, using Tomcat, my context is called *javaxml3*, in a directory named *javaxml3* under the *webapps* directory. In my *WEB-INF/classes* directory, there is a directory (for the package), and then the *DOMSerializer.class* and *UpdateItemServlet.class* files are within that directory. You should also ensure that a copy of your parser's JAR files (*xercesImpl.jar*, *xml-apis.jar*, and *xmlParserAPIs.jar* in my case) is in the classpath of your engine. In Tomcat, you can simply drop a copy in Tomcat's *common/lib* directory. Then restart Tomcat and everything should work.

Once you've got your servlet in place and the servlet engine started, browse to the servlet and let the GET request your browser generates load the HTML input form. Fill this form out, as I have in Figure 5-3.

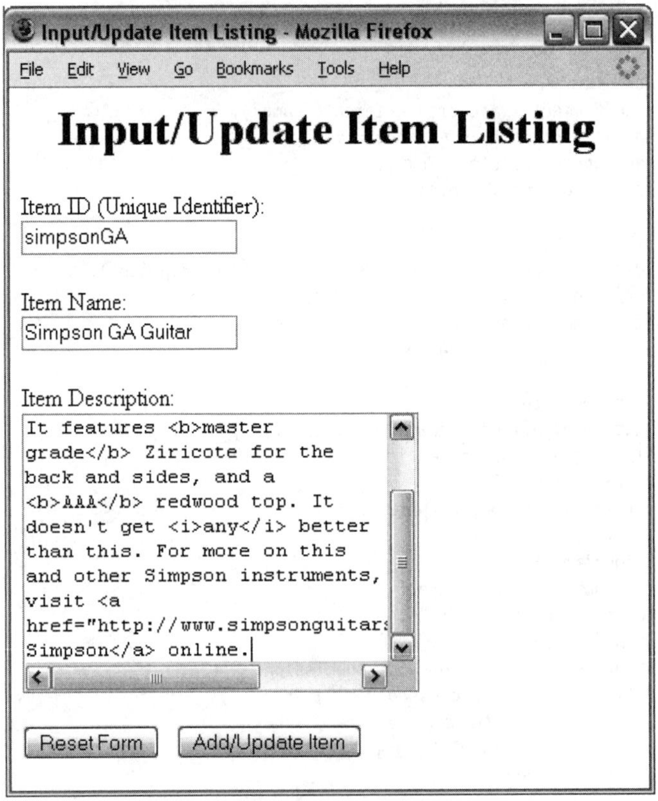

Figure 5-3. Form submission with HTML description

For a better example, enter in HTML for the description; I entered this:

```
This custom-built Simpson GA (<i>Grand Auditorium</i>) is a <b>beautiful</b>
instrument. It features <b>master grade</b> Ziricote for the back and sides, and a
<b>AAA</b> redwood top. It doesn't get <i>any</i> better than this. For more on this
and other Simpson instruments, visit <a href="http://www.simpsonguitars.com">Jason
Simpson</a> online.
```

Creating a New DOM Tree

There are two basic approaches to creating a DOM tree from scratch:

- Create a new instance of the org.w3c.dom.Document class.
- Create a new instance of the org.w3c.dom.DOMImplementation class.

In either case, you're actually going to need to create an instance of an *implementation* of these classes, as both are interfaces. After working with SAX, you should realize that these implementations are what parsers like Xerces provide. For example, Xerces provides the DocumentImpl class to implement Document, and the DOMImplementationImpl class to implement DOMImplementation.

Both of these classes are in the org.apache.xerces.dom package.

So the choice becomes one of functionality. You've already seen what Document provides, and it would seem the obvious choice (why involve another class if you don't need to?). However, DOMImplementation offers you the ability to create a DocType, and therefore set a DOCTYPE declaration on your XML—this alone is worth using DOMImplementation. Further, DOMImplementation provides the hasFeature( ) method, which is critical for working with DOM modules (the focus of Chapter 6).

Once you've got an instance of DOMImplementation, things are pretty simple. Take a look at the relevant code again:

```
// Create new DOM tree
DOMImplementation domImpl = new DOMImplementationImpl( );
Document doc = domImpl.createDocument(null, "item", null);
Element root = doc.getDocumentElement( );

// ID of item (as attribute)
root.setAttribute("id", id);

// Name of item
Element nameElement = doc.createElement("name");
Text nameText = doc.createTextNode(name);
nameElement.appendChild(nameText);
root.appendChild(nameElement);

// Description of item
Element descriptionElement = doc.createElement("description");
Text descriptionText = doc.createTextNode(description);
descriptionElement.appendChild(descriptionText);
root.appendChild(descriptionElement);

// Serialize DOM tree
DOMSerializer serializer = new DOMSerializer( );
String filename = outputDir + "item-" + id + ".xml";
File outputFile = new File(filename);
serializer.serialize(doc, outputFile);
```

First, the createDocument( ) method is used to get a new Document instance. The first argument to this method is the namespace for the document's root element. For simplicity's sake, this is omitted. The second argument is the name of the root element itself, which is simply item. The last argument is an instance of a DocType class, and I again pass in a null value since there isn't one in this particular example.

If you did want a DocType, you could create one with the createDocType( ) method on DOMImplementation.

With a DOM tree to operate upon, it's simple enough to retrieve the new root element. Once you've got that, add an attribute with the ID of the item using setAttribute( ).Things begin to get even simpler now; each type of DOM construct can be created using the Document object as a factory. To create the name and description elements, use createElement. The same approach is used to create textual content for each; since an element has no content but instead has children that are Text nodes, the createTextNode( ) method is the right choice. This method takes in the text for the node, which works out to be the description and item name. You might be tempted to use the createCDATASection( ) method and wrap this text in CDATA tags—there is HTML within this element. However, DOMSerializer handles the HTML characters (like < and &) in its print( ) method, so there's no need to worry about it.

Once you've gotten all of these nodes created, all that's left is to link them together. Use appendChild( ), appending the elements to the root, and the textual content of the elements to the correct parent. Finally, the whole document is passed into the DOMSerializer class from the last chapter and written out to an XML file on disk.

I have assumed that the user is entering well-formed HTML; in other words, XHTML. In a production application, you would probably run this input through JTidy (*http://www.sourceforge.net/projects/jtidy*) to ensure this; for this example, I'll just assume the input is XHTML.

Try this servlet out, and then browse to the directory you specified in *web.xml*. The output from my input is shown in Example 5-4.

Example 5-4. The information is converted to XML and written to a file

```
<?xml version="1.0" encoding="UTF-8" standalone="no"?>
<item id="simpsonGA">
<name>Simpson GA Guitar</name>
<description>This custom-built Simpson GA (&lt;i&gt;Grand Auditorium&lt;/i&gt;) is a
&lt;b&gt;beautiful&lt;/b&gt; instrument. It features &lt;b&gt;master grade&lt;/b&gt;
Ziricote for the back and sides, and a &lt;b&gt;AAA&lt;/b&gt; redwood top. It doesn't get
&lt;i&gt;any&lt;/i&gt; better than this. For more on this and other Simpson instruments,
visit &lt;a href="http://www.simpsonguitars.com"&gt;Jason Simpson&lt;/a&gt; online.</
description>
</item>
```

As I mentioned before, you can see that `DOMSerializer` handled escaping all special characters.

Bootstrapping with DOM Level 3

Those of you who are really into vendor-neutral code, and avoiding being tied to a specific parser product, are probably turned off by working directly with Xerces classes:

```
DOMImplementation domImpl = new org.apache.xerces.dom.DOMImplementationImpl();
```

If this bothers you as much as it does me, then DOM Level 3 should be of great interest to you. The newest version of the DOM specification allows you to use a factory that provides a vendor's implementation of `DOMImplementation` (I know, I know, it's a bit confusing). Vendors can set system properties or provide their own versions of this factory so that it returns the implementation class they want. The resulting code to create DOM trees then looks like this:

```
import org.w3c.dom.Document;
import org.w3c.dom.bootstrap.DOMImplementationRegistry;

// Class declaration and other Java constructs

DOMImplementationRegistry registry =
  DOMImplementationRegistry.newInstance();
DOMImplementation domImpl =
  registry.getDOMImplementation("XML 3.0");
Document doc = domImpl.createDocument();
// And so on...
```

Even though you're requesting an implementation that supports "XML 3.0", you're *not* referring to Version 3.0 of the XML specification; you're requesting Level 3 of the XML module, which is essentially a core DOM Level 3 implementation. This is a rather ill-named feature, but hopefully they'll change that soon.

There are several other classes and interfaces in the `org.w3c.dom`. bootstrap package worth checking out. Until DOM Level 3 is in primetime, though, I'd rather focus on features that you can use immediately.

Modifying a DOM Tree

The process of changing an existing DOM tree is slightly different from the process of creating one; in general, it involves loading the DOM from some source, traversing the tree, and then making changes. These changes are usually either to structure or content. If the change is to structure, it becomes a matter of creation again:

```
// Add a copyright element to the root
Element root = doc.getDocumentElement();
```

```
Element url = doc.createElement("url");
url.appendChild(doc.createTextNode("http://www.simpsonguitars.com"));
root.appendChild(url);
```

The process of changing existing content is a little different, although not overly complex. Example 5-5 is a modified version of the UpdateItemServlet. This version reads the supplied ID and tries to load an existing file if it exists. If so, it doesn't create a new DOM tree, but instead modifies the existing one.

Example 5-5. Modifying a DOM tree involves searching for a particular node and then changing its value

```
package javaxml3;

import java.io.File;
import java.io.IOException;
import java.io.PrintWriter;
import javax.servlet.ServletConfig;
import javax.servlet.ServletException;
import javax.servlet.http.HttpServlet;
import javax.servlet.http.HttpServletRequest;
import javax.servlet.http.HttpServletResponse;

import org.xml.sax.SAXException;

// DOM imports
import org.w3c.dom.Attr;
import org.w3c.dom.Document;
import org.w3c.dom.DOMImplementation;
import org.w3c.dom.Element;
import org.w3c.dom.NodeList;
import org.w3c.dom.Text;

// Parser import
import org.apache.xerces.dom.DOMImplementationImpl;
import org.apache.xerces.parsers.DOMParser;

public class ModifyItemServlet extends HttpServlet {

    // doGet( ) and init( ) methods are unchanged from UpdateItemServlet

  public void doPost(HttpServletRequest req, HttpServletResponse res)
    throws ServletException, IOException {

    // Get parameter values
    String id = req.getParameter("id");
    String name = req.getParameter("name");
    String description = req.getParameter("description");

    // See if this file exists
    Document doc = null;
    String filename = outputDir + "item-" + id + ".xml";
    File outputFile = new File(filename);
```

```
if (!outputFile.exists( )) {
  // Create new DOM tree
  DOMImplementation domImpl = new DOMImplementationImpl( );
  doc = domImpl.createDocument(null, "item", null);
  Element root = doc.getDocumentElement( );

  // ID of item (as attribute)
  root.setAttribute("id", id);

  // Name of item
  Element nameElement = doc.createElement("name");
  Text nameText = doc.createTextNode(name);
  nameElement.appendChild(nameText);
  root.appendChild(nameElement);

  // Description of item
  Element descriptionElement = doc.createElement("description");
  Text descriptionText = doc.createTextNode(description);
  descriptionElement.appendChild(descriptionText);
  root.appendChild(descriptionElement);
} else {
  // Load document
  try {
    DOMParser parser = new DOMParser( );
    parser.parse(outputFile.toURL( ).toString( ));
    doc = parser.getDocument( );
    Element root = doc.getDocumentElement( );

    // Name of item
    NodeList nameElements =
      root.getElementsByTagName("name");
    Element nameElement = (Element)nameElements.item(0);
    Text nameText = (Text)nameElement.getFirstChild( );
    nameText.setData(name);

    // Description of item
    NodeList descriptionElements =
      root.getElementsByTagName("description");
    Element descriptionElement =
      (Element)descriptionElements.item(0);

    // Remove and recreate description
    root.removeChild(descriptionElement);
    descriptionElement = doc.createElement("description");
    Text descriptionText = doc.createTextNode(description);
    descriptionElement.appendChild(descriptionText);
    root.appendChild(descriptionElement);
  } catch (SAXException e) {
    // Print error
    PrintWriter out = res.getWriter( );
    res.setContentType("text/html");
    out.println("<HTML><BODY>Error in reading XML: " +
```

```
            e.getMessage( ) + ".</BODY></HTML>");
        out.close( );
        return;
      }
    }

    // Serialize DOM tree
    DOMSerializer serializer = new DOMSerializer( );
    serializer.serialize(doc, outputFile);

    // Print confirmation
    PrintWriter out = res.getWriter( );
    res.setContentType("text/html");
    out.println("<HTML><BODY>");
    out.println("<p>Thank you for your submission. " +
        "Your item has been processed.</p>");
    out.println("<p>Your item was saved as " +
        outputFile.getAbsolutePath( ) + "</p>");
    out.println("</BODY></HTML>");
    out.close( );
  }
}
```

The changes are fairly simple, nothing that should confuse you. The outputFile is created earlier in the doPost( ) method, so the code can check and see if it already exists. If not, the method behaves just like doPost( ) in UpdateItemServlet, with no changes. If the XML already exists (indicating the item has already been submitted), the XML file is loaded and read into a DOM tree. At that point, some basic tree traversal begins.

Traversing a DOM Tree

The code grabs the root element, and then uses the getElementsByTagName( ) method to locate all elements named name and then all named description. In each case, the returned NodeList will have only one item.

This assumption is safe because we authored the code that creates the XML. In many cases, you can't be sure of things like this, and will have to iterate through the returned NodeList item by item.

You can access this item using the item( ) method on the NodeList, and supplying 0 as the argument (the indexes are all zero-based).

You could have gotten the children of the root through getChildren( ), and peeled off the first and second elements. However, using the element names makes the code much clearer.

The code gets the name element's textual content by invoking getFirstChild( ). Since we know that the name element has a single Text node, you can directly cast this to the appropriate type (Text). Finally, the setData( ) method allows the code to change the existing value for a new name, the updated information the user supplied through the form.

An equally effective, albeit different, approach is used for the description element. Instead of changing its value, the code just replaces the node wholesale. This is mostly for demonstration purposes; however, if you need to replace an element and all of its children, this is a cleaner and quicker approach.

It's no accident that this code is hardwired to the format the XML was written out to. In fact, most DOM modification code relies on at least some understanding of the content to be dealt with. Knowing how the XML is structured is a tremendous advantage. Methods like getFirstChild( ) can be used and the result cast to a specific type, rather than needing lengthy type checking and switch blocks.

For cases when the structure or format is unknown, the DOM Level 2 Traversal module is a better solution; that and other DOM modules are covered in Chapter 6.

Once the creation or modification is complete, the resulting DOM tree is serialized back to XML, and the process can repeat.

Namespaces

So far, I've basically punted on the issue of XML namespaces. Happily, DOM does support namespaces, so let's get into that now. This support is achieved through two methods on the Node interface: getPrefix( ) and getNamespaceURI( ). Additionally, all of the creation methods have namespace-aware versions available. So, instead of calling createElement( ), you call createElementNS( ).

In each of these new namespace-aware methods, the first argument is the namespace URI, and the second is the qualified name of the element, attribute, etc. Note that I said qualified; this means that if you want to use a namespace URI of http://www.ajaxian.com and a prefix of ajax on an element called blog-entry, you would call createElementNS("http://www.ajaxian.com", "ajax:blog-entry"). This is very important, and remembering to use that prefix will save you a lot of time down the road. Calling getPrefix( ) on that new element will return "ajax".

If you want the element in the default namespace (with no prefix), just pass in the element name (the local name), and you're all set. Calling getPrefix( ) on a default-namespaced element returns null, by the way, as it does on an element not in any namespace.

 The prefix tells you very little about whether an element is a namespace. Elements with a default namespace (and no prefix) have the same return value from getPrefix( ) as elements not in *any* namespace.

Rather than simply list all the new namespace-aware methods, let's look at some real code. Here's the bulk of the doPost( ) method from ModifyServlet, using namespaces:

```
// See if this file exists
Document doc = null;
String filename = outputDir + "item-" + id + ".xml";
File outputFile = new File(filename);
String docNS = "http://www.guitarnotes.com";
if (!outputFile.exists( )) {
  // Create new DOM tree
  DOMImplementation domImpl = new DOMImplementationImpl( );
  doc = domImpl.createDocument(docNS, "item", null);
  Element root = doc.getDocumentElement( );

  // ID of item (as attribute)
  root.setAttribute("id", id);

  // Name of item
  Element nameElement = doc.createElementNS(docNS, "name");
  Text nameText = doc.createTextNode(name);
  nameElement.appendChild(nameText);
  root.appendChild(nameElement);

  // Description of item
  Element descriptionElement =
    doc.createElementNS(docNS, "description");
```

```
      Text descriptionText = doc.createTextNode(description);
      descriptionElement.appendChild(descriptionText);
      root.appendChild(descriptionElement);
    } else {
      // Load document
      try {
        DOMParser parser = new DOMParser();
        parser.parse(outputFile.toURL().toString());
        doc = parser.getDocument();
        Element root = doc.getDocumentElement();

        // Name of item
        NodeList nameElements =
          root.getElementsByTagNameNS(docNS, "name");
        Element nameElement = (Element)nameElements.item(0);
        Text nameText = (Text)nameElement.getFirstChild();
        nameText.setData(name);

        // Description of item
        NodeList descriptionElements =
          root.getElementsByTagNameNS(docNS, "description");
        Element descriptionElement =
          (Element)descriptionElements.item(0);

        // Remove and recreate description
        root.removeChild(descriptionElement);
        descriptionElement = doc.createElementNS(docNS, "description");
        Text descriptionText = doc.createTextNode(description);
        descriptionElement.appendChild(descriptionText);
        root.appendChild(descriptionElement);
      } catch (SAXException e) {
        // Error handling
      }
    }
}
```

Using the createElementNS() method to create namespaced elements and searching
for them with getElementsByTagNameNS() is all that's needed to move to namespace-
aware code. The createDocument() method even has a handy place to insert the
namespace URI for the root element. These elements are all put into the default
namespace, and everything looks fine. However, there is a big problem here; look at
the output from running this servlet with no existing XML (this is generated XML,
rather than modified XML):

```
<?xml version="1.0" encoding="UTF-8" standalone="no"?>
<item id="ryanPB">
<name>Ryan Pierre Bensusan Signature Model</name>
<description>This amazing Kevin Ryan guitar is a collaboration between Kevin and
&lt;a href="http://www.pierrebensusan.com"&gt;Pierre Bensusan&lt;/a&gt;. The guitar
has a &lt;b&gt;cedar&lt;/b&gt; top and either rosewood (in Indian, or
&lt;b&gt;Brazilian&lt;/b&gt;!) or Mahogany back and sides. For more, check out the
&lt;a href="http://www.ryanguitars.com/theguitars/Signature/PBS/PBSmain.
htm"&gt;Pierre Bensusan page&lt;/a&gt; at &lt;a href="http://www.ryanguitars.
com"&gt;Ryan Guitars&lt;/a&gt;.</description>
</item>
```

Do you see a problem here? There are no namespace declarations, even though the NS methods were used. The one thing that DOM does not do is add namespace declarations. Instead, you'll need to manually add the xmlns attribute to your DOM tree; otherwise, when reading in the document, the elements won't be placed into a namespace and you will have some problems. One small change takes care of this, though:

```
// Create new DOM tree
DOMImplementation domImpl = new DOMImplementationImpl( );
doc = domImpl.createDocument(docNS, "item", null);
Element root = doc.getDocumentElement( );
root.setAttribute("xmlns", docNS);
```

Now you'll get the namespace declaration that you were probably expecting to show up the first go-round. You can compile these changes and try things out. You won't notice any difference in how the servlet runs; changes are made just as they were before. However, your documents should now have namespaces, both in the reading and writing portions of the servlet application.

A final word on this namespace detail: keep in mind that you could certainly modify the DOMSerializer class to look for namespaces on elements and print out the appropriate xmlns declarations as it walks the tree. This is a perfectly legal change, and would be sort of valuable; in fact, it's what many solutions, like those found within Xerces, already do. In any case, as long as you are aware of this behavior, you are protected from being the victim of it.

## CHAPTER 6

DOM Modules

Chapter 5 introduced and detailed the DOM API, and specifically what is called the *DOM core*. This is the portion of DOM that is most used, as it handles basic XML reading, as well as document creation. However, there are times when basic XML isn't enough—whether you're working with XML, or writing a document editor, or trying to serialize XML using the latest DOM APIs. In these specialized cases, you will often find a DOM module that can help.

I summarized the complete set of DOM specifications, including DOM modules, in Chapter 5. In this chapter, I'll detail each module, and show you how you can use these modules in your applications.

 Since DOM Level 3 is still new and largely unsupported, I've split coverage of these modules depending on the DOM Level they are based on. Most current parsers support at least a few of the DOM Level 2 modules, and a few will support beta versions of the DOM Level 3 modules.

Checking for Module Support

As a brief refresher (and so you're not constantly flipping back to Chapter 5), Table 6-1 lists the DOM modules.

Table 6-1. Each module has a specific name used to query a parser for module support

Specification	Module name	Summary of purpose
DOM Level 2 Core	XML	Extends the DOM Level 1 specification; deals with basic DOM structures like `Element`, `Attr`, `Document`, etc.
DOM Level 2 Views	Views	Provides a model for scripts to dynamically update a DOM structure
DOM Level 2 Events	Events	Defines an event model for programs and scripts to use in working with DOM
DOM Level 2 Style	CSS	Provides a model for CSS based on the DOM Core and DOM Views specifications
DOM Level 2 Traversal and Range	Traversal/Range	Defines extensions to the DOM for traversing a document and identifying the range of content within that document

Specification	Module name	Summary of purpose
DOM Level 2 HTML	HTML	Extends the DOM to provide interfaces for dealing with HTML structures in a DOM format
DOM Level 3 Core	XML	Expands DOM Level 2 to provide bootstrapping of DOM implementations and support for XML InfoSet
DOM Level 3 Load & Save	LS	Defines DOM extensions for loading and writing XML documents to a persistent storage mechanism, like a filesystem, in a vendor-neutral manner
DOM Level 3 Validation	Validation	Allows DOM trees to be validated (in memory) and checked for validity as new Nodes are added to the tree

DOM parsers are not required to implement these modules, so you need to verify that the features you want to use are supported by your XML parser. The DOMImplementation class provides the hasFeature( ) method for just that purpose, as seen in Example 6-1. You will need to change the name of your vendor's DOMImplementation class, but other than that adjustment, it should work for any parser.

Example 6-1. Supply the module name and a version to the hasFeature( ) method to see if a particular DOM parser implementation supports a certain module

```
package javaxml3;

import java.util.HashMap;
import java.util.Iterator;
import java.util.Map;

import org.w3c.dom.DOMImplementation;

public class DOMModuleChecker {

  /** DOM Level 2 Modules */
  private static Map module2Map;

  /** DOM Level 3 Modules */
  private static Map module3Map;

  private static void loadModules( ) {
    module2Map = new HashMap( );
    module3Map = new HashMap( );

    // DOM Level 2
    module2Map.put("XML", "DOM Level 2 Core");
    module2Map.put("Views", "DOM Level 2 Views");
    module2Map.put("Events", "DOM Level 2 Events");
    module2Map.put("CSS", "DOM Level 2 CSS");
    module2Map.put("Traversal", "DOM Level 2 Traversal");
    module2Map.put("Range", "DOM Level 2 Range");
    module2Map.put("HTML", "DOM Level 2 HTML");
```

Example 6-1. Supply the module name and a version to the hasFeature() method to see if a particular DOM parser implementation supports a certain module (continued)

```
    // DOM Level 3
    module3Map.put("XML", "DOM Level 3 Core");
    module3Map.put("LS", "DOM Level 3 Load & Save");
    module3Map.put("Validation", "DOM Level 3 Validation");
  }

  public static void main(String args[]) {
    if (args.length < 1) {
      System.err.println("Usage: java javaxml3.DOMModuleChecker " +
                         "[org.w3c.dom.DOMImplementation impl class]");
      return;
    }

    String vendorImplementationClass = args[0];

    loadModules();
    try {
      DOMImplementation impl =
        (DOMImplementation)Class.forName(vendorImplementationClass)
                           .newInstance( );

      System.out.println("For the DOM implementation class " +
          vendorImplementationClass + "...\n");

      // Check for DOM Level 2 Features
      for (Iterator i=module2Map.keySet().iterator( ); i.hasNext( ); ) {
        String name = (String)i.next( );
        String description = (String)module2Map.get(name);
        System.out.print("The " + description + " module is ");
        if (impl.hasFeature(name, "2.0")) {
          System.out.println("supported.");
        } else {
          System.out.println("not supported.");
        }
      }

      // Check for DOM Level 3 Features
      for (Iterator i=module3Map.keySet().iterator( ); i.hasNext( ); ) {
        String name = (String)i.next( );
        String description = (String)module3Map.get(name);
        System.out.print("The " + description + " module is ");
        if (impl.hasFeature(name, "3.0")) {
          System.out.println("supported.");
        } else {
          System.out.println("not supported.");
        }
      }
    } catch (Exception e) {
          e.printStackTrace( );
    }
  }
}
```

Running this program with Xerces 2.6.2 in my classpath, I got the following output:

```
[bmclaugh:~/code/ch06] java javaxml3.DOMModuleChecker
                       org.apache.xerces.dom.DOMImplementationImpl
For the DOM implementation class
    org.apache.xerces.dom.DOMImplementationImpl...

The DOM Level 2 Range module is supported.
The DOM Level 2 Traversal module is supported.
The DOM Level 2 HTML module is not supported.
The DOM Level 2 Views module is not supported.
The DOM Level 2 Core module is supported.
The DOM Level 2 CSS module is not supported.
The DOM Level 2 Events module is supported.
The DOM Level 3 Validation module is not supported.
The DOM Level 3 Core module is supported.
The DOM Level 3 Load & Save module is supported.
```

These results are fairly typical for a well-featured parser. The only real lack of support is in HTML-related modules (HTML, Views, and CSS), as those are largely the domain of parsers like JTidy; working with HTML using a generic parser like Xerces is a real pain. Also note that Xerces supports several of the DOM Level 3 modules, making Xerces a real boon for cutting- and bleeding-edge development work in XML.

By specifying the DOMImplementation class for your own vendor, you can check the supported modules in your own DOM parser. This will help ensure you don't start coding for features and modules not present in your parser implementation.

Requesting Feature Support in DOM Level 3

In Chapter 5, I discussed using the DOMImplementationRegistry class to bootstrap a DOM implementation:

```
DOMImplementationRegistry registry =
   DOMImplementationRegistry.newInstance( );
DOMImplementation domImpl =
   registry.getDOMImplementation("XML 3.0");
Document doc = domImpl.createDocument( );
```

Note that in the getDOMImplementation( ) method, a feature (XML) and version string (3.0) are passed in. This works hand in hand with the getFeature( ) method, allowing you to request a DOMImplementation that has specific module support. So, you could make a request like this:

```
DOMImplementation domImpl =
   registry.getDOMImplementation("XML 3.0 +Traversal 2.0");
```

Here, you're indicating that you need support for DOM Level 3 core, plus the Traversal Level 2 module. You can also omit the version portion of this string, indicating that you will accept *any* version of support for the specified module:

```
DOMImplementation domImpl =
   registry.getDOMImplementation("XML 3.0 +Events");
```

DOM Level 2 Modules

I'll start with the DOM Level 2 modules. You should expect to find support for most of these (with the repeated exception of HTML-related modules) in most modern DOM-compliant parsers.

Traversal

First up on the list is the DOM Level 2 Traversal module. This module provides tree-walking capability, along with a highly customizable manner. In particular, the DOM Traversal module is useful when you don't know—or aren't sure about—the structure of an XML document you're parsing.

The whole of the traversal module is contained within the org.w3c.dom.traversal package. Just as everything within core DOM begins with a Document interface, everything in DOM Traversal begins with the org.w3c.dom.traversal.DocumentTraversal interface. This interface provides two methods:

```
NodeIterator createNodeIterator(Node root, int whatToShow, NodeFilter filter,
                        boolean expandEntityReferences);
TreeWalker createTreeWalker(Node root, int whatToShow, NodeFilter filter,
                        boolean expandEntityReferences);
```

Most DOM implementations that support traversal choose to have their org.w3c. dom.Document implementation class implement the DocumentTraversal interface as well; in Xerces, you can use the default Document implementation, and you're all set. DocumentTraversal is shown along with the rest of the traversal classes in Figure 6-1.

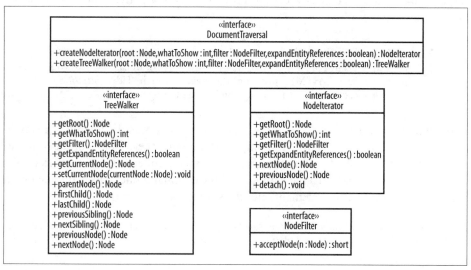

Figure 6-1. DOM Traversal module

There are just three other classes to worry about (all in the org.w3c.dom.traversal package); all focus on selecting certain DOM nodes, and working with the results of that selection. `NodeFilter` does just what it sounds like it does: provides a means of selecting only certain nodes based on filtering criteria. Using a `NodeIterator` provides a list view of the elements iterated over, and the `TreeWalker` class provides a tree view of that same data.

Selecting nodes

One of the more popular applications in today's web-centric world is a spider, or crawler, that searches and indexes web pages. Google has also begun to add more and more power to its search engine (*http://www.google.com*), all in an effort to return the most relevant results for a given set of search terms. Along those same lines, it's a fairly common task to try and parse a given web page, and determine what the subject of that web page is. While sometimes it's enough to simply extract words from the title of the page (within the `title` HTML element), that's not always sufficient. But how else can software make an educated guess at the focus of a site's content?

One rather hackish approach (which, just coincidentally, serves the purposes of this text) is to key in on words formatted in a certain way. For example, you could grab all elements within a document that are in italics (`<i>`) or bold (`<b>`) text, as well as any headings (say, `<h1>`, `<h2>`, and `<h3>`). While this is somewhat crude, you'd be surprised at the number of times this sort of approach yields useful data. The resulting terms and phrases could then be used as a pool of data for a search application.

Of course, reading in HTML line by line and searching for a certain set of tags is a huge pain (and doesn't take advantage of structured markup). What you really want is to parse the HTML into a DOM tree, and then specify a custom traversal—selecting only the nodes that meet a certain criteria. This is a perfect application of the DOM Traversal module.

 I'm making the rather large—and potentially unsafe—assumption that you're dealing with XHTML, well-formed HTML. In cases where you don't have XHTML, just run the page through Tidy (*http://tidy. sourceforge.net*) to clean up tagging before filtering.

Keep in mind that narrowing down the set of Nodes that must be filtered is always a good idea; in the case of HTML, you only need to search the contents of the body element; everything outside of that element is inconsequential for this example. Example 6-2, then, reads in a file supplied on the command line, parses the file into a DOM tree, locates the body element, and does some basic filtering.

Example 6-2. Once you've got a DOM tree, you can set a basicNodeFilter and then traverse over the results of that filtering, using eitherNodeIterator orTreeWalker

```
package javaxml3;

import java.io.File;

// DOM imports
```

```java
import org.w3c.dom.Document;
import org.w3c.dom.Element;
import org.w3c.dom.Node;
import org.w3c.dom.NodeList;
import org.w3c.dom.traversal.DocumentTraversal;
import org.w3c.dom.traversal.NodeFilter;
import org.w3c.dom.traversal.NodeIterator;

// Vendor parser
import org.apache.xerces.parsers.DOMParser;

public class HTMLIndexer {

  public void index(String filename) throws Exception {
    // Parse into a DOM tree
    File file = new File(filename);
    DOMParser parser = new DOMParser();
    parser.parse(file.toURL().toString());
    Document doc = parser.getDocument();

    // Get node to start iterating with
    Element root = doc.getDocumentElement();
    NodeList bodyElementList =
        root.getElementsByTagName("body");
    Element body = (Element)bodyElementList.item(0);

    // Get a NodeIterator
    NodeIterator i = ((DocumentTraversal)doc)
        .createNodeIterator(body, NodeFilter.SHOW_ALL, null, true);

    Node n;
    while ((n = i.nextNode()) != null) {
      if (n.getNodeType() == Node.ELEMENT_NODE) {
        System.out.println("Encountered Element: '" +
            n.getNodeName() + "'");
      } else if (n.getNodeType() == Node.TEXT_NODE) {
        System.out.println("Encountered Text: '" +
            n.getNodeValue() + "'");
      }
    }
  }

  public static void main(String[] args) {
    if (args.length == 0) {
      System.out.println("No HTML files to search through specified.");
      return;
    }

    try {
      HTMLIndexer indexer = new HTMLIndexer();
      for (int i=0; i<args.length; i++) {
        System.out.println("Processing file: " + args[i]);
```

```
        indexer.index(args[i]);
      }
    } catch (Exception e) {
      e.printStackTrace( );
    }
  }
}
```

As you can see, I've created a `NodeIterator`, and supplied it the body element to start with for iteration. The constant value passed as the filter instructs the iterator to show all nodes. You could just as easily provide values like `NodeFilter.SHOW_ELEMENT` and `NodeFilter.SHOW_TEXT`, which would show only elements or textual nodes, respectively. I haven't yet provided a `NodeFilter` implementation (I'll get to that next), and I allowed for entity reference expansion. What is nice about all this is that the iterator, once created, doesn't have just the child nodes of body. Instead, it actually has *all* nodes under body, even when nested multiple levels deep.

 This ability to select child nodes, without knowing their structure, makes the Traversal module handy for dealing with an unknown XML structure—exactly the case when working with HTML.

At this point, you still have *all* the nodes, which is not what you want. I added some code (the last `while` loop) to show you how to print out the element and text node results. You can run the code as is, but it's not really useful; you're going to get every bit of content within the body element. Instead, the code needs to provide a filter, so it only picks up elements with the formatting desired: the text within an i or b tag, or a heading element. You can provide this customized behavior by supplying a custom implementation of the `NodeFilter` interface, which defines only a single method:

```
public short acceptNode(Node n);
```

This method should always return `NodeFilter.FILTER_SKIP`, `NodeFilter.FILTER_REJECT`, or `NodeFilter.FILTER_ACCEPT`. The first skips the examined node but continues to iterate over its children; the second rejects the examined node and its children (only applicable in `TreeWalker`); and the third accepts and passes on the examined node. It behaves a lot like SAX, in that you can intercept nodes as they are being iterated and decide if they should be passed on to the calling method. Add the following nonpublic class to the *HTMLIndexer.java* source file:

```
class ImportantWordsFilter implements NodeFilter {

  public short acceptNode(Node n) {
    if (n.getNodeType( ) == Node.TEXT_NODE) {
      Node parent = n.getParentNode( );
      if ((parent.getNodeName( ).equalsIgnoreCase("b")) ||
          (parent.getNodeName( ).equalsIgnoreCase("i")) ||
          (parent.getNodeName( ).equalsIgnoreCase("h1")) ||
```

```
        (parent.getNodeName( ).equalsIgnoreCase("h2")) ||
        (parent.getNodeName( ).equalsIgnoreCase("h3"))) {
      return FILTER_ACCEPT;
    }
  }
  // If we got here, not interested
  return FILTER_SKIP;
}
}
```

This is basic core DOM code, and shouldn't pose any difficulty to you. First, the code ignores anything but text nodes; the text of the formatted elements is desired, not the elements themselves. Next, the parent is determined, and since it's safe to assume that Text nodes have Element node parents, the code immediately invokes getNodeName( ). If the element name matches one of the "important" elements, the code returns FILTER_ACCEPT. Otherwise, FILTER_SKIP is returned.

All that's left now is a change to the iterator creation call instructing it to use the new filter implementation, and to the output, both in the existing search( ) method of the ItemSearcher class:

```
// Get a NodeIterator
NodeIterator i = ((DocumentTraversal)doc)
    .createNodeIterator(description, NodeFilter.SHOW_ALL,
        new ImportantWordsFilter( ), true);

Node n;
while ((n = i.nextNode( )) != null) {
  System.out.println("Search phrase found: '" + n.getNodeValue( ) + "'");
}
```

 Some astute readers will wonder what happens when a NodeFilter implementation conflicts with the constant supplied to the createNodeIterator( ) method (in this case that constant is NodeFilter.SHOW_ALL). The constant filter is applied first, and then the resulting list of nodes is passed to the filter implementation. If I had supplied the constant NodeFilter.SHOW_ELEMENT, I would not have gotten any search phrases, because my filter would not have received any Text nodes to examine; just Element nodes. Be careful to use the two together in a way that makes sense. In the example, I could have safely used NodeFilter.SHOW_TEXT also.

Now, the class is useful and ready to run. I ran it on the HTML from the front page of Ajaxian.com (*http://www.ajaxian.com*) and got these results:

```
Processing file: Ajaxian-05242005.xhtml
Search phrase found: 'May 24, 2005'
Search phrase found: 'Ajax Slashdotted Again'
Search phrase found: 'JavaScript Threading and Continuations'
Search phrase found: 'Dean Edwards' IE7'
Search phrase found: 'Ajax Usability Mistakes'
Search phrase found: 'Not giving immediate visual cues for clicking
widgets:'
```

```
Search phrase found: 'Breaking the back button:'
Search phrase found: 'Changing state with links (GET requests):'
Search phrase found: 'Blinking and changing parts of the page
unexpectedly:'
Search phrase found: 'Not using links I can pass to friends or bookmark:'
Search phrase found: 'Too much code makes the browser slow:'
Search phrase found: 'Inventing new UI conventions:'
Search phrase found: 'Not cascading local changes to other parts of the
page:'
Search phrase found: 'Asynchronously performing batch operations'
Search phrase found: 'Scrolling the page and making me lose my place:'
Search phrase found: 'May 23, 2005'
Search phrase found: 'Google Maps Platform: ChicagoCrime.org'
Search phrase found: 'Showcase: Lace - Ajaxian Chat Service'
Search phrase found: 'Server to Client callback via mod_pubsub'
Search phrase found: 'May 20, 2005'
Search phrase found: 'Oracle ADF Faces gets Ajaxian, er Partial Page
Rendering'
Search phrase found: 'JavaServer Faces Ajaxian Components'
Search phrase found: 'Thoughts on Rich Clients and Ajax'
Search phrase found: 'May 19, 2005'
Search phrase found: 'XHR Server Validation with DWR'
Search phrase found: 'JavaScript'
Search phrase found: 'Servlet: web.xml'
Search phrase found: 'May 18, 2005'
Search phrase found: 'AjaxPatterns.org'
Search phrase found: 'Example: Live Preview'
Search phrase found: 'Search'
Search phrase found: 'Recent Entries'
Search phrase found: 'Contact Us'
Search phrase found: 'Resources'
Search phrase found: 'Feeds'
Search phrase found: 'Archives'
```

These turn out to be remarkably useful; note how often Ajax, patterns, JavaScript, rich clients, and related terms turn up!

 You could refine this further by setting up a pool of common terms to reject in your NodeFilter implementation. For example, you could return NodeFilter.FILTER_REJECT for terms like "Archives" and "Contact Us", as well as dates, to try and eliminate commonly appearing terms that aren't applicable.

Walking filtered DOM trees

The TreeWalker interface is almost exactly the same as the NodeIterator interface; the only difference is that you get a tree view instead of a list view. This is primarily useful if you want to deal with only a certain type of node within a tree; for instance, you want to see a DOM tree with only elements, or without any comments. By using a constant filter value (such as NodeFilter.SHOW_ELEMENT) and a filter implementation (like one that returns FILTER_SKIP for all comments), you can construct a view of a DOM tree without extraneous information. The TreeWalker interface provides all the basic DOM node operations, such as firstChild( ), parentNode( ), nextSibling( ), and of course getCurrentNode( ).

Range

The DOM Level 2 Range module is one of the least commonly used modules, probably due to a lack of understanding of the module rather than lack of usefulness. This module provides a way to deal with a set of content within a document, en masse. Once you've defined that range of content, you can insert into it, copy it, delete parts of it, and manipulate it in various ways. The most important thing to start with is realizing that "range" in this sense refers to a number of pieces of a DOM tree grouped together. It does *not* refer to a set of allowed values, where a high and low or start and end are defined. Therefore, DOM Range has nothing at all to do with validation of data values.

Like traversal, working with the Range module involves a new DOM package: org. w3c.dom.ranges. There are actually only two interfaces and one exception within this class, so it won't take you long to get your bearings (Figure 6-2 shows the UML for the package).

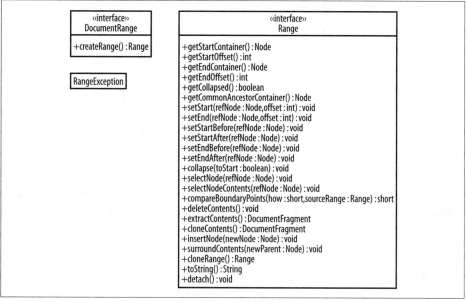

Figure 6-2. DOM Range module

First is the analog to Document (and DocumentTraversal): org.w3c.dom.ranges. DocumentRange. Like the DocumentTraversal interface, DocumentRange is implemented by Xerces's Document implementation class. And also like DocumentTraversal, it has very few interesting methods; in fact, only one:

```
public Range createRange( );
```

All other range operations operate upon the Range class (rather, an implementation of the interface, but you get the idea). Once you've got an instance of the Range interface, you can set the starting and ending points, and edit away.

Just as the Traversal module is ideal for working with documents in which the structure is unknown, so is the Range module. You can set ranges based on starting and ending points, even if you don't know what comes between those two points. For example, it's very easy to clear out all of the contents of an HTML page's body element:

```
// Parse into a DOM tree
File file = new File(filename);
DOMParser parser = new DOMParser();
parser.parse(file.toURL().toString());
Document doc = parser.getDocument();

// Get node to start iterating with
Element root = doc.getDocumentElement();
NodeList bodyElementList =
  root.getElementsByTagName("body");
Element body = (Element)bodyElementList.item(0);

// Nuke everything in the body tag
Range range = ((DocumentRange)doc).createRange();
range.setStartBefore(body.getFirstChild());
range.setEndAfter(body.getLastChild());
range.deleteContents();

// Release contents of the range
range.detach();
```

To remove all the content, I first create a new Range, using the DocumentRange cast.

> You'll need to add import statements for the DocumentRange and Range classes, of course; both in the org.w3c.dom.ranges package.

Once the range is created, set the starting and ending points. Since I want all content within the body element, I start before the first child of that Element node (using setStartBefore()), and end after its last child (using setEndAfter()).

> There are other, similar methods for this task, like setStartAfter() and setEndBefore().

With the range set up, it's simple to call deleteContents(). Just like that, not a bit of content is left. Finally, let the JVM know that it can release any resources associated with the Range by calling detach(). While this step is commonly overlooked, it can really help with lengthy bits of code that use the extra resources.

Another option is to use extractContents( ) instead of deleteContents( ). This method removes content, but returns the content that has been removed. For instance, you might grab a blog entry from an XML feed, and move it from the current listings to an archive section:

```
// Parse into a DOM tree
File file = new File(filename);
DOMParser parser = new DOMParser( );
parser.parse(file.toURL( ).toString( ));
Document doc = parser.getDocument( );

// Get node to start iterating with
Element root = doc.getDocumentElement( );
NodeList blogElementList =
  root.getElementsByTagName("blog");
Element currentBlog = (Element)blogElementList.item(0);

// Nuke everything in the current blog tag
Range range = ((DocumentRange)doc).createRange( );
range.setStartBefore(currentBlog.getFirstChild( ));
range.setEndAfter(currentBlog.getFirstChild( ));
Node entry = range.extractContents( );

// Insert the entry into the archived blogs listings
NodeList archiveBlogList =
  root.getElementsByTagName("archived-blogs");
Element archiveBlog = (Element)archiveBlogList.item(0);

archiveBlog.insertBefore(entry, archiveBlog.getFirstChild( ));

// Release contents of the range
range.detach( );
```

Events, Views, and Style

Aside from the HTML module, which I'll talk about next, there are three other DOM Level 2 modules: Events, Views, and Style. I'm not going to cover these three in depth in this book, largely because I believe that they are more useful for client programming. So far, I've focused on server-side programming, and I'm going to keep in that vein throughout most of the book. These three modules are most often used on client software such as IDEs, web pages, and the like. Still, I want to briefly touch on each so you'll still be on top of the DOM heap at the next alpha-geek soirée.

Events

The Events module provides just what you are probably expecting: a means of "listening" to a DOM document. The relevant classes are in the org.w3c.dom.events package, and the class that gets things going is DocumentEvent. No surprise here; compliant parsers (like Xerces) implement this interface in the same class that implements org.w3c.dom.Document. The interface defines only one method:

```
public Event createEvent(String eventType);
```

The string passed in is the type of event; valid values in DOM Level 2 are UIEvent, MutationEvent, and MouseEvent. Each of these has a corresponding interface: UIEvent, MutationEvent, and MouseEvent. Figure 6-3 provides a visual take on this module. You'll note, in looking at the Xerces Javadoc, that they provide only the MutationEvent interface, the only event type Xerces supports. When an event is "fired" off, it can be handled (or "caught") by an EventListener.

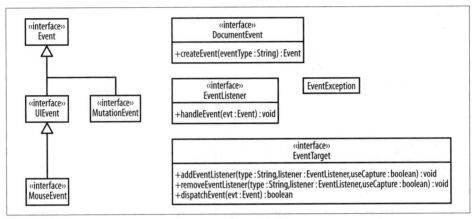

Figure 6-3. DOM Events module

This is where the DOM core support comes in; a parser supporting DOM events should have the org.w3c.dom.Node interface implementing the org.w3c.dom.events. EventTarget interface (see Figure 6-3). So every node can be the target of an event. This means that you have the following method available on any Node, inherited from the EventTarget interface:

```
public void addEventListener(String type, EventListener listener,
                             boolean capture);
```

To use the module, create a new EventListener implementation. You need to implement only a single method:

```
public void handleEvent(Event event);
```

Register that listener on any and all nodes you want to work with. The code in this method typically does some useful task, like emailing users that their information has been changed (in some XML file), revalidating the XML (think XML editors), or asking users if they are sure they want to perform the requested action.

At the same time, you'll want your code to trigger a new Event on certain actions, like the user clicking on a node in an IDE and entering new text, or deleting a selected element. When the Event is triggered, it is passed to the available EventListener instances, starting with the active node and moving up. This is where your listener's code executes, if the event types are the same; if the events don't match up, then the propagation continues. When your code does see a matching event and executes, it can stop the propagation, or continue to bubble the event up the chain—allowing it to be (possibly) handled by other registered listeners.

Views

Next on the list is DOM Level 2 Views. The reason I don't cover Views in much detail is that, really, there is very little to be said. From every reading I can make of the (one-page!) specification, it's simply a basis for future work, perhaps in vertical markets. The specification defines only two interfaces, both in the org.w3c.dom.views package. Here's the first:

```
package org.w3c.dom.views;

public interface AbstractView {
    public DocumentView getDocument( );

}
```

And here's the second:

```
package org.w3c.dom.views;

public interface DocumentView {
    public AbstractView getDefaultView( );

}
```

Figure 6-4 gives you a UML-ish view of these, for the visually inclined.

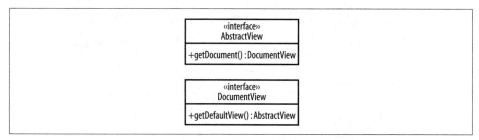

Figure 6-4. DOM Views module

Seems a bit cyclical, doesn't it? A single *source document* (a DOM tree) can have multiple *views* associated with it. In this case, view refers to a presentation, like a styled document (after XSL or CSS has been applied), or perhaps a version with Flash and one without. By implementing the AbstractView interface, you can define your own customized versions of displaying a DOM tree. For example, consider this subinterface:

```
package javaxml3;

import org.w3c.dom.views.AbstractView;

public interface StyledView implements AbstractView {

    public void setStylesheet(String stylesheetURI);

    public String getStylesheetURI( );
}
```

I've left out the method implementations, but you can see how this could be used to provide stylized views of a DOM tree. Additionally, a compliant parser implementation would have the org.w3c.dom.Document implementation implement DocumentView, allowing you to query a document for its default view. It's expected that in a later version of the specification, you will be able to register multiple views for a document, and more closely tie a view or views to a document.

Look for this to be fleshed out more as browsers like Netscape, Mozilla, and Internet Explorer provide these sorts of views of XML.

Style

There is the Style module, referred to as simply CSS. You can check this specification out at *http://www.w3.org/TR/DOM-Level-2-Style*. This module provides a binding for CSS stylesheets to be represented by DOM constructs. Everything of interest is in the org.w3c.dom.stylesheets and org.w3c.dom.css packages (see Figures 6-5 and 6-6). The former contains generic base classes, and the latter provides specific applications to CSS. Both are primarily used for showing a client a styled document.

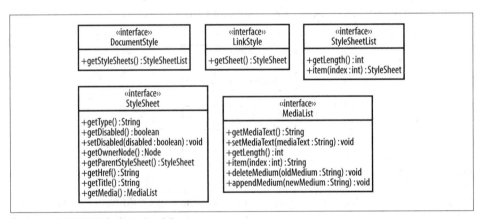

Figure 6-5. DOM Sylesheets module

You use this module exactly like you use the core DOM interfaces: you get a Style-compliant parser, parse a stylesheet, and use the CSS language bindings. This is particularly handy when you want to parse a CSS stylesheet and apply it to a DOM document. You're working from the same basic set of concepts, if that makes sense to you (and it should; when you can do two things with an API instead of one, that's generally good). Again, I only briefly touch on the Style module, because it's accessible with the Javadoc in its entirety. The classes are aptly named (CSSValueList, Rect, CSSDOMImplementation) and are close enough to their XML DOM counterparts that I'm confident you'll have no problem using them if you need to.

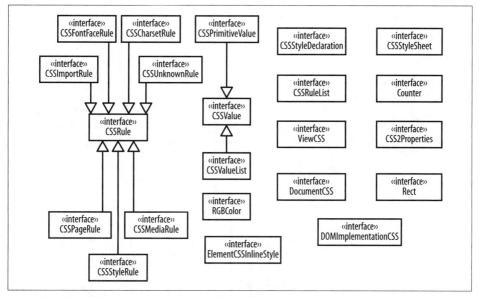

Figure 6-6. DOM Stylesheet implementation for CSS

HTML

For HTML, DOM provides a set of interfaces that model the various HTML elements. For example, you can use the HTMLDocument class, the HTMLAnchorElement, and the HTMLSelectElement (all in the org.w3c.dom.html package) to represent their analog tags in HTML (<HTML>, <A>, and <SELECT> in this case). All of these provide convenience methods like setTitle() (on HTMLDocument), setHref() (on HTMLAnchorElement), and getOptions() (on HTMLSelectElement). Further, these all extend core DOM structures like Document and Element, and so can be used as any other DOM node could.

The HTML package has more than 50 interfaces in it. Figure 6-7 contains the UML for a few of them.

Personally, I find that these classes are a bit cumbersome; for example, I know DOM well enough—and you should by now, too—to prefer calling getFirstChild() or setNodeValue() to remembering all the HTML-specific methods, like setLink() or getEnctype().

The only time I find the HTML module of much practical use is in creating new documents that are to be output as HTML. In these cases, it's sometimes nice to use calls like HTMLFormElement.setAction(), because there's no mistaking what the method does (in this case, it's also a lot nicer than creating an attribute called action, and then setting its value). Unfortunately, there's a rather nasty catch when working with the HTML module: you become tied to a specific implementation very quickly. There is no factory for creating HTML elements, so you have to write code like this:

```
HTMLFormElement form1 = new my.parser.package.HTMLFormElementImpl();
```

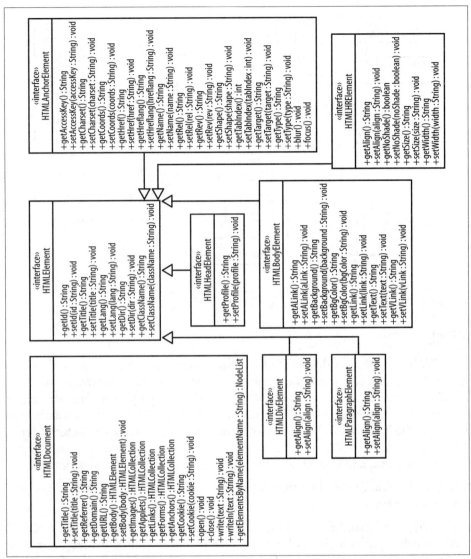

Figure 6-7. Sampling of DOM HTML interfaces

This ties you very quickly to your specific parser, especially when you consider that most HTML documents have hundreds of elements (meaning hundreds of these vendor-specific instantiations). For all of these reasons, I've found the HTML module to be a real pain to work with in general application programming.

All that said, if you've got a closed-box solution, like a piece of software that is packaged and sold, the HTML module might be perfect. You probably don't need to worry much about changing a parser, as your company has invested money into one, and any major rewrite would affect the whole product cycle, anyway. So there are uses of the HTML module that are very legitimate.

DOM Level 3 Modules

DOM Level 3 seems to be the point at which the specification maintainers got very practical about the API. While modules like Traversal, Range, Events, and HTML are nice, they're not the sorts of things you'll find yourself using every day, at least in most programming environments. However, the ability to validate a DOM tree in-memory, as well as writing out XML documents, is something you're more likely to need every *hour*, let alone just once in a while. Fortunately, these key improvements are being adapted fairly quickly, so expect widespread DOM Level 3 support within the next year.

Load and Save

Personally, I'm as excited about the Load and Save module as I am about anything that has come out of DOM since the first edition of this book came out seven years ago. In short, this module allows you to excise the following line from your code, once and for all:

```
import org.apache.xerces.parsers.DOMParser;
```

Now, I'm as much a fan of Xerces as anyone, but I just don't like vendor-specific code in my classes. I'd much rather configure code with system properties, and be able to change parsers, processors, and the like all on the fly. Load and Save (LS) fills this need nicely.

Reading XML documents

There are quite a few classes involved in loading a DOM tree; they're all in the org.w3c.dom.ls package, and shown in Figure 6-8.

I'm not going to cover every nuance of each of these, but instead will focus on what most of you care about: loading a DOM tree without using Xerces (or some other parser) directly.

First, find an instance of org.w3c.bootstrap.DOMImplementationRegistry; this class was covered in the last chapter and is critical for using the LS module:

```
DOMImplementationRegistry registry =
    DOMImplementationRegistry.newInstance( );
```

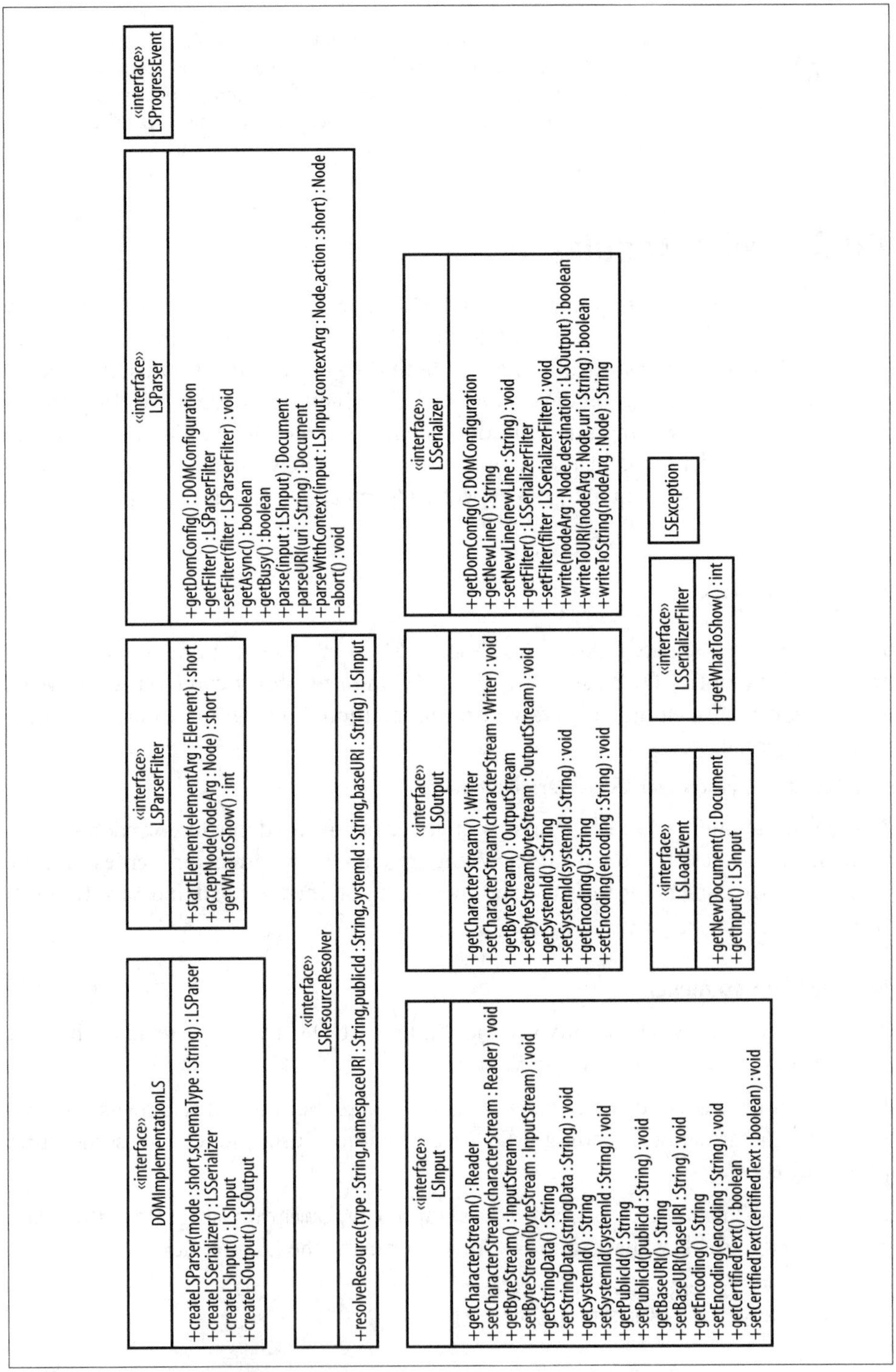

Figure 6-8. DOM Load and Save module

Figure 6-8. DOM Load and Save module

Remember, you can request DOM implementations from this registry via the getDOMImplementation() method; just use the "LS" string to get an LS-capable implementation.

```
DOMImplementationSource impl = registry.getDOMImplementation("LS");
```

You also need to case the returned object (a DOMImplementationSource) to the LS-specific type, org.w3c.dom.ls.DOMImplementationLS, so you can access its methods:

```
DOMImplementationLS lsImpl =
  (DOMImplementationLS)registry.getDOMImplementation("LS");
```

So far, this is easy. Now, though, you need to create a new DOM parser; this is done via the createLSParser() method, available on DOMImplementationLS. You must supply this method with two arguments: a mode (either DOMImplementationLS.MODE_SYNCHRONOUS or DOMImplementationLS.MODE_ASYNCHRONOUS), and a schema type:

```
LSParser parser =
  lsImpl.createLSParser(DOMImplementationLS.MODE_SYNCHRONOUS,
                    null);
```

If you're not sure what type of schema you'll use—or just want a little bit of extra flexibility—use null for this second argument.

Compatibility All Over the Place

Even though Xerces supports the DOM Level 3 core and LS module, it still doesn't provide asynchronous parsing. And, of course, you won't even get this far if your parser isn't DOM3-compatible. Be sure you use the hasFeature() method (detailed in Example 6-1) with "XML" and "3.0" before trying to compile or test any of this code.

Additionally, you can test for asynchronous support in the LS module with "LS-Async" and "3.0".

In SAX parsing (Chapter 3) and JAXP parsing (which we'll discuss in the next chapter), you'd set features and properties to determine how the parser works: should it validate? What about handling errors? In the LS module, though, these options are handled by the org.w3c.dom.DOMConfiguration class (another new DOM 3 class, this one in the core module). Here's the interface definition for this class:

```
package org.w3c.dom;

public interface DOMConfiguration {
  public void setParameter(String name, Object value)
    throws DOMException;
  public Object getParameter(String name)
    throws DOMException;
```

```
    public boolean canSetParameter(String name, Object value);
    public DOMStringList getParameterNames( );
}
```

Pretty simple, right? You can work with this object like this:

```
// Set options on the parser
DOMConfiguration config = parser.getDomConfig( );
config.setParameter("validate", Boolean.TRUE);
```

 The feature is called "validate", not "validation"; you will get a FEATURE_NOT_FOUND exception if you mistype this feature name.

There are a lot more options, ranging from setting an error handler to namespace handling. You can read about the complete list, as defined in the DOM specification, online at *http://www.w3.org/TR/2004/REC-DOM-Level-3-Core-20040407/core. html#DOMConfiguration.*

 The relationships between your validation setting, normalization settings, and the type of schema being used are detailed at *http://www. w3.org/TR/2004/REC-DOM-Level-3-Core-20040407/configuration-settings.html.* This is required reading if you're going to validate using the LS module.

Finally, you can parse XML using the LSParser:

```
Document doc = parser.parseURI(args[0]);
```

When you run this code, you need to specify to your parser and application what DOMImplementationRegistry to use. You can do this in your code:

```
System.setProperty(DOMImplementationRegistry.PROPERTY,
            "org.apache.xerces.dom.DOMXSImplementationSourceImpl");
```

or via a system property:

```
java -Dorg.w3c.dom.DOMImplementationSourceList=
  org.apache.xerces.dom.DOMXSImplementationSourceImpl
  // rest of command line options and class name...
```

 If you use the code version to set this property, make sure it's in some sort of init( ) method, or called before any other DOM Level 3 parsing code.

Using this code to parse the XHTML from Ajaxian.com (mentioned earlier, in the "Traversal" section), you'd get a validated DOM tree. If, however, there are validation errors, they will be reported:

```
[Error] Ajaxian-05242005.xhtml:573:48: Attribute "alt" is required
   and must be specified for element type "img".
[Error] Ajaxian-05242005.xhtml:577:14: Attribute "alt" is required
   and must be specified for element type "img".
```

You can also specify both the type of constraints to use, and the location of those constraints, via the setParameter( ) method on DOMConfiguration:

```
config.setParameter("schema-type", "http://www.w3.org/2001/XMLSchema");
config.setParameter("schema-location", "dw-document-4.0.xsd");
```

 Use a value of "http://www.w3.org/TR/REC-xml" for the schema-type parameter to validate against DTDs.

This should all look a lot like what you used to do with Xerces's DOMParser; now, though, you have untethered your code from that specific parser, which is the whole point of the LS module. You can also use the parse( ) method, which takes as input an LSInput object. LSInput offers a little more flexibility in terms of the types of input you can use for XML:

```
LSInput input = lsImpl.createLSInput();
input.setCharacterStream(new FileReader(new File(args[0])));
Document doc = parser.parse(input);
```

You can also supply LSInput a String (when you have your XML all in one glob) or an InputStream; you can also explicitly set the encoding of LSInput, adding even more flexibility. For simple applications, though, parseURI( ) works just fine.

Writing XML documents

Once you understand how loading documents works, saving them is almost trivial to describe. Here's a code fragment that handles that task:

```
Document doc = parser.parseURI(args[0]);

/* Perform whatever operations on the DOM tree you want */

/* Serialize the document */
LSSerializer serializer = lsImpl.createLSSerializer();

LSOutput output = lsImpl.createLSOutput();
output.setCharacterStream(new FileWriter(new File(args[1])));

serializer.write(doc, output);
```

LSSerializer is the saving equivalent of LSParser, and is obtained the same way: via a factory method on your DOMImplementationLS object. In the same fashion, LSOutput complements LSInput and can accept an OutputStream, Writer, or system ID to which to write. With those two classes in hand, there's not much left to add, other than mentioning some of the options you may want to set for output (again, using the DOMConfiguration object); here are a few samples:

```
/* Serialize the document */
LSSerializer serializer = lsImpl.createLSSerializer();
```

```
// Set output options
config = serializer.getDomConfig( );
// Convert CDATA sections to normal escaped text
config.setParameter("cdata-sections", false);
// Remove any comments
config.setParameter("comments", false);

LSOutput output = lsImpl.createLSOutput( );
output.setCharacterStream(new FileWriter(new File(args[1])));

serializer.write(doc, output);
```

> As mentioned in the section on "Reading XML documents" the complete list of options is online at *http://www.w3.org/TR/2004/REC-DOM-Level-3-Core-20040407/core.html#DOMConfiguration*.

Validation

When it comes to the Validation module, I'm in the unfortunate position of having to demonstrate how it *should* work. Even Xerces, which is about as bleeding edge as parsers get, doesn't provide support for the Validation module as of this writing (Xerces 2.8.0). So, take the instructions and code in this section as guidelines, and realize that some things may change even as this book goes to press.

The classes that make up this module are all stored in the org.w3c.dom.validation package, and are shown in Figure 6-9. There is one exception, and just four additions, so it's not much in terms of additional API to master.

To see if your parser supports validation, use the hasFeature( ) method with the strings "Validation" and "3.0" (or simply run DOMModuleChecker, shown back in Example 6-1).

> Validation depends on the core DOM Level 3 module, and uses some of DOM Level 3's new constructs; that's no big deal, though, as obviously any parser that supports validation will surely support the core of DOM Level 3.

Node types supporting validation

In validation-compatible parsers, the four validation interfaces will be implemented by their corresponding core DOM counterparts:

- org.w3c.dom.validation.NodeEditVAL by org.w3c.dom.Node
- org.w3c.dom.validation.DocumentEditVAL by org.w3c.dom.Document
- org.w3c.dom.validation.ElementEditVAL by org.w3c.dom.Element
- org.w3c.dom.validation.CharacterDataEditVAL by org.w3c.dom.CharacterData

This works much in the same way that the Document interface in DOM might implement DocumentTraversal for traversal support or DocumentView for view support. The

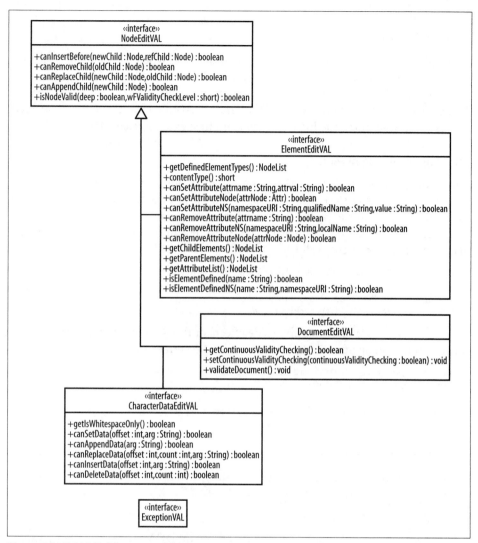

Figure 6-9. DOM Validation module

`CharacterData` interface—which may be unfamiliar to some of you—is extended by the `Text` and `Comment` node types, and then `CDATASection` extends `Text`, so you actually get a three-for-one on support for validation via the `CharacterDataEditVAL` interface. Putting this all together, the following node types all are affected by the Validation module:

- `Node`
- `Document`
- `Element`
- `Text`

- Comment
- CDATASection

Although comments aren't usually something that you worry about with validation, you should see that these other node types make up the whole of what validation concerns itself with (as opposed to, for example, the DocumentType or ProcessingInstruction node types). Of course, even these are tangentially affected, as they extend the core Node interface, which in turn extends NodeEditVAL.

Enforcing validity as you work

The method that most developers will immediately grab for in validation-compliant parsers is setContinuousValidityChecking( ), on the DocumentEditVAL interface (which would make it available on the Document interface in validation-compliant parsers). By turning this feature on, you ensure that nothing can be added to your DOM tree that would make the tree invalid:

```
DocumentEditVAL doc = (DocumentEditVAL) getDocument( );

// Ensure the DOM tree always stays valid
doc.setContinuousValidityChecking(true);
```

You should be aware of some subtle side effects of this setting, though. For example, consider how you might build up a portion of a DOM tree:

```
Element name = doc.createElement("name");
rootElement.appendChild(name);

Element firstName = doc.createElement("firstName");
Element lastName = doc.createElement("lastName");
name.appendChild(firstName);
name.appendChild(lastName);

Text firstNameText = doc.createTextNode("Pete");
Text lastNameText = doc.createTextNode("Huttlinger");
firstName.appendChild(firstNameText);
lastName.appendChild(lastNameText);
```

While this code would work in DOM Level 2—or DOM Level 3 without validation—it would *not* work in cases where continuous validity checking was turned on (and then was any sort of useful schema in place, of course). For example, you would expect a schema to require that a name element have a firstName and lastName; but when the name element is added to the DOM tree, it has no children. The firstName and lastName children are added after name has been inserted into the DOM tree. As a result, you'd get a validity exception (ExceptionVAL) when you tried to execute this line:

```
rootElement.appendChild(name);
```

To avoid this problem, you have to build any fragments you want to add to the tree in their entirety, and then add them to your tree. In this example, that's a fairly trivial change:

```
Element name = doc.createElement("name");
Element firstName = doc.createElement("firstName");
Element lastName = doc.createElement("lastName");
Text firstNameText = doc.createTextNode("Pete");
Text lastNameText = doc.createTextNode("Huttlinger");

firstName.appendChild(firstNameText);
lastName.appendChild(lastNameText);

name.appendChild(firstName);
name.appendChild(lastName);

// Add the completed subtree to the DOM tree last
rootElement.appendChild(name);
```

However, in large documents where an element might have 10, 15, or 20 required children—and each of those children may have several required elements and attributes as well—this can be extremely cumbersome. Be sure that when you turn on continuous validity checking, you're really ready to build your DOM trees in this manner.

Checking for valid operations

Most of the methods on these new interfaces are concerned with checking an operation for validity; in other words, you would use a method to see if an operation is valid *before* actually performing that operation. So, you might want to see if it's legal to set the value of a Text node to "Lady, by yonder blessed moon I vow,//That tips with silver all these fruit-tree tops—":

```
// Get this text node, in whatever fashion your DOM tree provides
Text proseTextNode = getProseTextNode();

String proseText = "Lady, by yonder blessed moon I vow,//" +
    "That tips with silver all these fruit-tree tops-";

// See if entering this data is valid
if (proseTextNode.canSetData(proseText) == NodeEditVAL.VAL_TRUE)
  proseTextNode.setValue(proseText);
```

This is pretty simple code to understand. After two chapters of DOM, you're probably used to having to use constant-based comparisons, rather than Boolean comparisons, so nothing is new there.

 Constant-based comparisons, as well as somewhat silly class names— like NodeEditVAL and ElementEditVAL—are all results of DOM being cross-platform.

In the case of the canXXX( ) methods, though, constant-based comparison is necessary. In some cases, those methods return neither true nor false; it is possible for a DOM parser to return a third value, NodeEditVAL.VAL_UNKNOWN. The specification isn't clear about why this might happen, but I can see several cases where an unknown value is likely:

- There is no schema (DTD, XSD, etc.) available to validate against.
- Dependencies in the schema make validation of the data indefinite or ambiguous.

Also realize that sometimes a value of NodeEditVAL.VAL_FALSE indicates that it's not (just) this data that might be invalid, but other parts of the document. If you don't have the DOM tree constantly enforcing validity, then changes to this particular node can have ripple effects that invalidate other parts of the DOM tree. These get pretty tricky, and the specification isn't at all clear about how to handle these situations.

 Even more concerning, the validation specification isn't clear on what the parser's responsibility is when canXXX( ) is invoked. Is it just to validate the new data with respect to the current node? Is it to validate the entire document? And what happens in cases where the document as a whole is invalid, and *no* data passed to canXXX( ) would return VAL_TRUE? These are all serious—and very complex—issues; I suspect they're also why there aren't any validation-capable parsers yet.

These methods are all pretty self-explanatory; I'll leave it to you, the Java Language Bindings (*http://www.w3.org/TR/2004/REC-DOM-Level-3-Val-20040127/java-binding. html*), and Javadoc to decipher the rest. In most cases, you'll use canInsertBefore( ), canReplaceChild( ), and canAppendChild( )—all on the Node interface—heavily in your applications. ElementEditVAL adds lots of similar methods for attributes (canSetAttribute( ), canRemoveAttribute( ), etc.), and of course CharacterDataEditVAL does the same for text (canAppendData( ), canDeleteData( ), etc.).

 All of these methods, when appropriate, have namespace-capable counterparts. So you can invoke canSetAttribute( ), or in namespace-aware applications, canSetAttributeNS( ).

Checking for state validity

In addition to checking for the validity of an operation—before you undertake that operation—you can also check the validity of a DOM tree at a given moment. This is the in-memory validation that developers have been clamoring about for a while. The easiest way to check a document's validity is with the new validateDocument( ) method, available through the DocumentEditVAL interface:

```
// Get the document in some business-specific manner
DocumentEditVAL doc = (DocumentEditVAL) getDocument( );
if (doc.validateDocument( ) == NodeEditVAL.VAL_TRUE) {
  // Go ahead and serialize the document
} else {
  // Report errors and repeat the cycle
}
```

This is pretty basic, and incredibly useful. In fact, if the validation module offered this functionality alone, developers would be pretty happy, I imagine. It's also particularly useful for the application shown above: ensuring validity before serializing a DOM tree to persistent storage.

What's more interesting—and adds more complexity in, once again—is that the specification defines a similar method on the NodeEditVAL interface:

```
public short nodeValidity(short valType);
```

You can supply four values to this method:

NodeEditVAL.VAL_SCHEMA

Perform what would be considered "normal" validation; check this node and all its children (elements, text, etc.) for validity.

NodeEditVAL.VAL_INCOMPLETE

This is similar to VAL_SCHEMA, but only validates the current node and its immediate children. The children of those children are ignored.

Remember that in DOM, Text nodes are nested within Element nodes. So VAL_INCOMPLETE would ensure that the child elements of the current element are valid, but would *ignore* the textual content of those child elements. If you're not careful, you can get really deceptive results here.

NodeEditVAL.VAL_WF

This simply checks to make sure the current node is well-formed.

NodeEditVAL.VAL_NS_WF

This checks to see if the current node is well-formed and follows namespace rules properly (calling VAL_NS_WF effectively calls VAL_WF as well).

It's in VAL_SCHEMA that things get nasty (as mentioned in the last section). Because constraint models like XML Schema allow for some pretty advanced dependencies, it's possible—and even probable if you're really using XSD to its fullest—that you're going to get VAL_UNKNOWN over and over when trying to validate individual nodes. It's simply a very difficult problem to deal with nodes out of the context of an entire document; if you're unsure about validity, I strongly urge you to simply use validateDocument( ), and not mess with these rather ambiguous node-specific approaches to validation.

CHAPTER 7
JAXP

With SAX and DOM, there aren't a whole lot of XML problems you run into that you can't solve. Loading, reading, and writing XML are all handled by these APIs, and you can even avoid vendor-specific code with the tricks you've already seen in previous chapters. However, Java remains a Sun creation (as much as I'd love to see the language go open source), and as a rule, Sun is going to provide an API for anything it sees as common—the thinking, I suppose, is that if a programmer is going to work with Java, he should be using Sun software as much as possible.

Along those lines, Sun provides JAXP for working with XML. Although initially a very small API that handled only parsing, the latest version of JAXP provides everything you find in SAX and DOM, as well as a few extras, and JAXP makes vendor neutrality much easier than using DOM or SAX directly. In this chapter, I'll walk you through JAXP piece by piece, from parsing to validation to transformations.

More Than an API

Before you get too far into working with JAXP, you need to understand a little bit about exactly what JAXP is. Sun calls it the Java API for XML Processing, although it might better be known as the *Java Abstraction Layer* for XML Processing. JAXP doesn't provide any original functionality, but instead sits on top of existing APIs—most notably SAX and DOM, which of course you're already familiar with, as well as TrAX and a few other APIs which you'll learn about in this chapter.

XML Parsing and Validation

For parsing XML, JAXP allows you to make method calls that affect either SAX parsing or DOM processing. As you'll see shortly, you can either work with SAX and DOM through the JAXP layer, or use JAXP to obtain a SAX or DOM parser and then interact directly with those APIs.

For those of you who think you'll never use SAX or DOM, this should help you change your mind. Anyone who uses JAXP is going to need to have at least passing familiarity with SAX and DOM, and if you want to get the most out of JAXP, you better know these underlying APIs inside and out. JAXP doesn't replace SAX or DOM; it simply supplements them.

In addition to providing a Sun-endorsed means of operating upon XML, recent versions of Sun's JDK and JRE come bundled with JAXP. For example, Java 5.0 includes JAXP 1.3 (the very latest and greatest) alongside other standard Java APIs like Swing, AWT, and Collection classes. Even more important, the servers and systems you deploy on will all have JAXP support as long as they have a recent version of Java running on them. This guarantee makes it a lot simpler to write XML applications, and know they'll run normally on various servers.

In the same vein, JAXP provides a full-featured validation API. Unlike SAX and DOM, though, JAXP breaks out most of its validation functionality into a separate package and set of classes. With this separation comes a lot more flexibility, allowing you to work with DTDs, XML Schema, or even Relax NG schemas, all while staying within the JAXP framework.

XSL Processing

JAXP provides for XML transformations in addition to parsing and validation. You can process XSL stylesheets, apply them to XML documents, and even re-process and validate the output. While you're already familiar with the APIs that underlie JAXP's parsing, the XML transformations API will be new to many of you. Called TrAX—the Transformations API for XML—you can handle all the transformation tasks you'll probably ever run into.

It's also worth noting that TrAX is awfully simple to use. I'm not sure I could fill up even a medium-sized chapter of TrAX details if I tried, at least not without getting into details that you'll use less than two percent of the time in real-world application programming.

XPath

In recent years, XML developers and authors have fallen in love with XPath. It's easy to locate elements that match a certain name, an attribute that has a specific value, or even the third child of the second element beneath the fourth item listing in an XML document, as long as you have XPath available. XPath has been crucial to XSL since its inception, but Java APIs have recently made using XPath simple for us bytecode guys as well.

Parsing XML

XML is pretty much useless unless you can get at the data it represents, so any good API begins with the parsing process. JAXP uses SAX and DOM to get the job done, so this section is largely about how JAXP interacts with those APIs; you should already have the intricacies of SAX and DOM down, and I'll leave out repeated discussions of how these underlying APIs work.

JAXP makes heavy use of the factory model. In general, you'll get a factory for the type of parsing you want to use with a static method on the factory itself. Then, you perform optional configuration on the factory, and obtain a parser. Once you've got the parser, you can set some more options, and then actually parse XML. This is the same process used in both SAX and DOM (as well as TrAX), and it's illustrated by the simple flowchart in Figure 7-1.

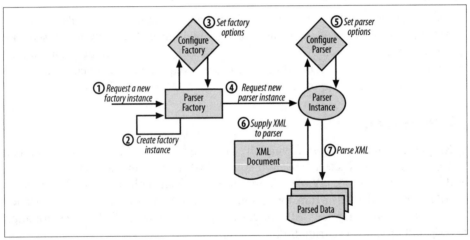

Figure 7-1. The JAXP parsing process is the same for both SAX and DOM

Reading XML with SAX

Working with JAXP and SAX is really just a matter of plugging in the right class and interface names. Along those lines, you need to familiarize yourself with the javax. xml.parsers package.

 By now, I'm assuming you've got a current version of Java and the JDK. As I write this text, Java 5.0 is still somewhat new, but I imagine by the time you're holding this book, it will be fairly commonplace. I recommend moving to Java 5.0 (even if you choose not to take advantage of its new features), simply for JAXP 1.3. That's the version of JAXP covered in this chapter, and throughout the rest of this book. If you can't move to Java 5.0 for any reason, don't worry, JAXP 1.3 is available as a separate download from *https://jaxp.dev.java.net*.

There are only two classes to worry about, as well as an Exception and an Error. It can't get much simpler than that, can it? The UML for these is shown in Figure 7-2.

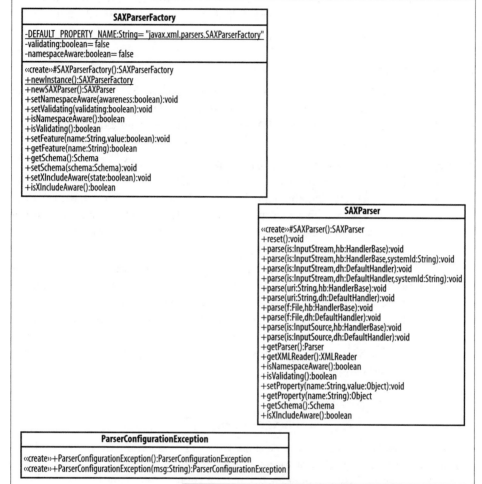

Figure 7-2. The SAX portion of JAXP uses a factory, a parser, an Exception, and an Error, all of which are almost completely self-explanatory

Creating a parser factory

Review Figure 7-1, and it should be obvious that you're going to start with SAXParserFactory. You need to bootstrap an instance of this class, which is done with the newInstance( ) method (this chapter is full of really complex material, isn't it?):

```
SAXParserFactory factory = SAXParserFactory.newInstance( );
```

Configuring the factory

Now you need to set configuration options on the parser. These are options that apply to all parser instances that you obtain from the factory. Each feature has a setXXX( ) method, and a getXXX( ) or isXXX( ) method to determine that feature's current setting on the factory:

Namespace awareness (setNamespaceAware( )/isNamespaceAware( ))

Setting this feature to true ensures that the parser is namespace-aware; in other words, it will see an element named oreilly:book as an element with a local name of book, and a namespace prefix of oreilly. By default, parsers are not namespace-aware; that said, I almost always set this feature to true.

Validation schema (setSchema( )/getSchema( ))

This allows you to specify a javax.xml.validation.Schema object to be used for validating the XML. I'll cover JAXP validation in detail in "XML Validation," so just hold the thought for now. By default, the Schema object is set to null, and won't affect your parsing. It's also worth noting at this point that a Schema is an object type, and doesn't refer to a specific constraint model. You can validate against DTDs, XML Schema, Relax NG schemas, or anything else that implements the Schema interface.

Parser or Factory?

I've run across lots of developers who think you can set options on the parser, or the factory. The thinking is that factory options are "global," while parser options are "local." The fallacy here is in thinking that options configurable on the factory are also configurable directly on the parser, but that's just not so. For instance, you can set validation and namespace awareness on the parser factory, but not on the parser itself. So, if you want to create two parsers—one validating, and one nonvalidating—you have to use setValidating(true) on your SAXParserFactory, get a parser using newSAXParser( ), and then call setValidating(false) on the factory, and get the non-validating parser (again with newSAXParser( )).

JAXP will validate XML documents against a Schema—if one is referenced in the XML document—even if isValidating( ) is set to false.

Validation (setValidating( )/isValidating( ))

This option ensures that all parsers created by the parser factory are validating parsers. In a formal sense, that means validating according to the XML 1.0 specification; in other words, validating parsers validate against DTDs. This option does not affect XML Schema or Relax NG validation, and has nothing to do with the javax.xml.validation package. It's largely still available for backward compatibility with JAXP 1.2, and I'd advise against using it in favor of setSchema( ) and the JAXP 1.3 validation framework. By default, this feature is set to false.

XInclude processing (setXIncludeAware( )/isXIncludeAware( ))

This feature controls whether parsers recognize XInclude markup in parsed XML documents. This feature is set to false by default, and can really affect the time it takes to parse an XML document; it's recommended you only set this feature to true if you're sure you need XInclude information.

Passthrough features (setFeature( )/getFeature( ))

This is the catch-all method that allows you to set features on a parser that aren't explicitly supported by JAXP. This could be a new feature that JAXP hasn't caught up with yet, or a parser-specific feature that doesn't make sense for the JAXP API to add. For example:

```
SAXParserFactory factory = SAXParserFactory.newInstance( );

// Set a Xerces specific feature
factory.setFeature("http://apache.org/xml/features/allow-java-encodings", true);
```

In this case, the code instructs the Apache Xerces parser to allow Java encoding names in addition to ISO-standard encoding names in the XML declaration. If the requested feature isn't supported, the factory will throw an org.xml.sax. SAXNotSupportedException; if the parser doesn't recognize the feature at all, you'll get an org.xml.sax.SAXNotRecognizedException.

That's a mouthful, but turns out to be really simple to use in practice. The following code shows a simple method that creates a parser factory and then sets several configuration options on the factory:

```
// Get SAX Parser Factory
SAXParserFactory factory = SAXParserFactory.newInstance( );

// Turn on validation, and turn off namespaces
factory.setValidating(true);
factory.setNamespaceAware(false);
factory.setXIncludeAware(true);
```

Keep in mind that these features affect all parser instances created by this factory, at least until the features are changed or reset.

Obtaining a parser

Once you've done all your setup and configuration, actually getting a parser is a piece of cake:

```
// Get a new instance of a SAXParser
SAXParser parser = factory.newSAXParser();
```

That's it; if you were expecting something more complicated, I'm sorry to disappoint.

Parsing with JAXP and SAX

SAXParser is the JAXP wrapper for SAX's XMLReader interface. As such, it provides a whole slew of various methods to parse XML, all conveniently called parse( ), as illustrated by Figure 7-3.

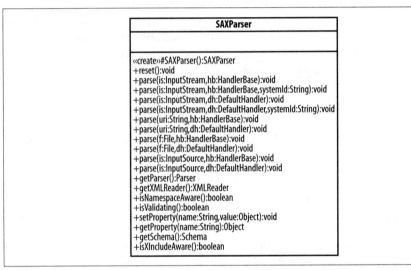

Figure 7-3. SAXParser adds variations on the parse( ) theme, but not much else, to the underlying XMLReader implementation

There's not nearly as much going on here as it may seem; first, there are permutations for accepting the XML as an InputSource, a File, an InputStream, and via a String URI. Then, because JAXP works with both SAX 1.x and 2.x implementations, you'll find that there will be a version—for each type of input—that takes a HandlerBase, as well as a version that accepts a DefaultHandler.

HandlerBase is essentially the SAX 1.x version of SAX 2's DefaultHandler. HandlerBase implements DocumentHandler—replaced in SAX 2 by ContentHandler—as well as EntityResolver, DTDHandler, and ErrorHandler.

Finally, for the versions of parse( ) that accept an InputStream, JAXP allows you to pass in a system ID, to help resolve relative document references within the XML.

Of course, you can bypass this by using an InputSource (which can wrap an InputStream and provide a system ID as well).

Do the math, and this results in a whopping 10 versions of parse( )! Ultimately, all end up in the same place: parsing the XML document. You can also pass through properties to set on the XMLReader using the setProperty( ) method. Essentially, then, SAXParser is just a JAXP-specific stand-in for XMLReader:

```
public static void main(String[] args) {
  try {
    if (args.length != 1) {
      System.err.println ("Usage: java SAXTester [XML filename]");
      System.exit (1);
    }

    // Get SAX Parser Factory
    SAXParserFactory factory = SAXParserFactory.newInstance( );

    // Turn on validation, and turn off namespaces
    factory.setValidating(true);
    factory.setNamespaceAware(false);
    factory.setXIncludeAware(true);

    SAXParser parser = factory.newSAXParser( );
    parser.parse(new File(args[0]), new MyHandler( ));
  } catch (ParserConfigurationException e) {
    System.out.println("The underlying parser does not support " +
                       " the requested features.");
  } catch (FactoryConfigurationError e) {
    System.out.println("Error occurred obtaining SAX Parser Factory.");
  } catch (Exception e) {
    e.printStackTrace( );
  }
}
```

This should look remarkably similar to your SAX code, although you do need to remember to use DefaultHandler as the input, rather than calling setContentHandler( ), setErrorHandler( ), and so forth individually.

This would seem to be at odds with my early admonition to avoid lumping your EntityResolver in with the other SAX handlers. You can't separate out behavior when you only have the one DefaultHandler parameter to pass to parse( ). However, by accessing XMLReader directly, as described in the next section, you can still achieve this functionality; and in fact, that's how I'd urge you to use SAXParser—as an intermediary object, by which you then get access to the underlying XMLReader.

Accessing XMLReader directly

In many cases, you will want to get the SAXParser object and then immediately access the XMLReader object directly. XMLReader offers you direct access to parsing behavior, the ability to register handlers individually, and keeps JAXP doing what JAXP does best: providing vendor-independence for your code (not actual parsing). To get the XMLReader that SAXParser wraps, just call getXMLReader( ):

```
XMLReader reader = parser.getXMLReader( );
```

You can then use methods available on XMLReader that aren't accessible through the JAXP interface:

```
// Get SAX Parser Factory
SAXParserFactory factory = SAXParserFactory.newInstance( );

// Turn on validation, and turn off namespaces
factory.setValidating(true);
factory.setNamespaceAware(false);
factory.setXIncludeAware(true);

SAXParser parser = factory.newSAXParser( );
XMLReader reader = parser.getXMLReader( );

DefaultHandler myHandler = new MyHandler( );
reader.setContentHandler(myHandler);
reader.setErrorHandler(myHandler);

// Set EntityResolver from a separate class
reader.setEntityResolver(new LocalEntityResolver(new File("/usr/local/entities/")));

// Parse
reader.parse(new InputSource(args[0]));
```

Reading and Writing XML with DOM

If you're thinking you need to take a break to gear up for the challenge of DOM, you can save yourself some rest. The process of using DOM with JAXP is nearly identical to that with SAX; all you do is change two class names and a return type, and you are pretty much there. If you understand how SAX works and what DOM is, you won't have any problem.

While SAX consists of an event-based set of callbacks, DOM has an in-memory tree structure. SAX, therefore, does not offer the ability to modify an XML document. DOM provides exactly this type of functionality. Recall that the org.w3c.dom. Document class represents an XML document, and is made up of DOM nodes that represent the elements, attributes, and other XML constructs. So JAXP doesn't have to fire SAX callbacks; it is only responsible for returning a DOM Document object from parsing. Figure 7-4 outlines the DOM-related parsing classes.

DocumentBuilder
«create »#DocumentBuilder():DocumentBuilder +reset():void +parse(is:InputStream):Document +parse(is:InputStream,systemId:String):Document +parse(uri:String):Document +parse(f:File):Document +parse(is:InputSource):Document +isNamespaceAware():boolean +isValidating():boolean +setEntityResolver(er:EntityResolver):void +setErrorHandler(eh:ErrorHandler):void +newDocument():Document +getDOMImplementation():DOMImplementation +getSchema():Schema +isXIncludeAware():boolean

DocumentBuilderFactory
-DEFAULT_PROPERTY_NAME:String= "javax.xml.parsers.DocumentBuilderFactory" -validating:boolean= false -namespaceAware:boolean= false -whitespace:boolean= false -expandEntityRef:boolean= true -ignoreComments:boolean= false -coalescing:boolean= false -canonicalState:boolean= false
«create »#DocumentBuilderFactory():DocumentBuilderFactory +newInstance():DocumentBuilderFactory +newDocumentBuilder():DocumentBuilder +setNamespaceAware(awareness:boolean):void +setValidating(validating:boolean):void +setIgnoringElementContentWhitespace(whitespace:boolean):void +setExpandEntityReferences(expandEntityRef:boolean):void +setIgnoringComments(ignoreComments:boolean):void +setCoalescing(coalescing:boolean):void +isNamespaceAware():boolean +isValidating():boolean +isIgnoringElementContentWhitespace():boolean +isExpandEntityReferences():boolean +isIgnoringComments():boolean +isCoalescing():boolean +setAttribute(name:String,value:Object):void +getAttribute(name:String):Object +setFeature(name:String,value:boolean):void +getFeature(name:String):boolean +getSchema():Schema +setSchema(schema:Schema):void +setXIncludeAware(state:boolean):void +isXIncludeAware():boolean

Figure 7-4. *DocumentBuilderFactory is the analog to SAXParserFactory, and DocumentBuilder replaces SAXParser in the DOM-related portion of JAXP*

From SAXParserFactory to DOMBuilderFactory

With a basic understanding of DOM (which you should have from Chapters 5 and 6), along with what you've already seen about JAXP, there is little else to say. You essentially replace the JAXP SAX classes with their DOM-related counterparts, and obtain a Document object from parse( ); that's all there is to it:

```
// Get DOM Parser Factory
DocumentBuilderFactory factory = DocumentBuilderFactory.newInstance( );

// Turn on validation, and turn off namespaces
factory.setValidating(true);
factory.setNamespaceAware(false);

DocumentBuilder builder = factory.newDocumentBuilder( );
Document doc = builder.parse(new File(args[0]));

// Serialize
DOMSerializer serializer = new DOMSerializer( );
serializer.setIndent(2);
serializer.serialize(doc, System.out);
```

First, a DocumentBuilderFactory is obtained (in the same way that SAXParserFactory was in SAX). Then the factory is configured to handle validation and namespaces (in the same way that it was in SAX). Next, a DocumentBuilder instance—the analog to SAXParser—is retrieved from the factory. Parsing can then occur, and the resultant DOM Document object is handed off to a class that prints the DOM tree.

Two different problems can arise with this code (the same as with SAX-related JAXP parsing): FactoryConfigurationError and ParserConfigurationException. If there's a problem present in the implementation classes, JAXP throws a FactoryConfigurationError; if the parser provided doesn't support the requested features, you'll get a ParserConfigurationException.

DOM factory configuration options

In SAX, even SAXParserFactory had little in the way of configuration. That's largely because SAX developers control quite a bit in terms of what XML events are handled, via the callback implementations in ContentHandler. In DOM, though, DocumentBuilder simply returns to you a parsed and constructed DOM Document object. As a result, DocumentBuilderFactory offers quite a bit more in the way of configuration.

Just as in SAX, options set on the factory affect all instances that the factory creates. The options listed here are in addition to the options already detailed for SAX in "Configuring the factory."

CDATA awareness (setCoalescing( )/isCoalescing( ))

If set to true, the DOM parser will convert CDATA nodes into Text nodes. Additionally, if the CDATA section is next to other Text nodes, the converted Text node will be appended (or prepended, as the case may be) to those adjacent nodes. If you only want character data—and don't care about how that data was represented—then you should set this property to true; otherwise, use the default value of false.

Entity reference expansion (setExpandEntityReferences( )/isExpandEntityReferences( ))

This property determines whether entity references are expanded (which is the default). You might set this to false if you were interested in the lexical content of just the current document, without any data from external sources.

Comment processing (setIgnoringComments( )/isIgnoringComments( ))

By default, comments are not ignored (meaning that the default value of isIgnoringComments( ) is false). However, if you're not interested in comments, then you can set this property to true and ignore them, dropping all Comment nodes from the resulting DOM tree.

Ignorable whitespace (setIgnoringElementContentWhitespace( )/
isIgnoringElementContentWhitespace( ))

This setting tells the DocumentBuilder to drop all ignorable whitespace (discussed in detail in Chapter 3). For elements that may only contain other elements, whitespace is ignored; however, because of a reliance on validation, this option—when set to true—is only actually used when isValidating( ) is also true. The default value is false.

All of these options result in loss of information in the DOM tree produced by parse( ). While it's very easy to perform this processing as an extra layer of filtering after the DOM tree has been produced, it is not possible to get "back" to the original XML document if these features are used before you can access the DOM Document directly. For this reason, I'd recommend you perform any DOM processing yourself, rather than letting JAXP strip information from the DOM tree before your program has access to it.

Changing the Parser Implementation

One of JAXP's core strengths is its abstraction of parser implementation details. Along those lines, it's trivial to change the parser that JAXP uses. Even more important, this change won't affect your code. Just supply the parser class to use to JAXP via the javax.xml.parsers.SAXParserFactory system property (for SAX) and the javax.xml.parsers.DocumentBuilderFactory property (for DOM). This can most easily be done via the command line:

```
java -Djavax.xml.transform.TransformerFactory=org.apache.xerces.parsers.SAXParser
    javaxml3.SAXTester ibm-jaxp-article.xml
```

You might also have a class of constants or initialization code that sets these values; while using that approach will require recompilation if you change the parser, it still keeps you clear of the core of your parsing code.

You can also modify the *lib/jaxp.properties* file in your Java Runtime Environment (JRE), a file in the Java properties file format (name=value pairs). This is dangerous, though, as it's not a portable solution: changes on one JRE will not make it to another JRE, unless you remember to manually update the new properties file.

Processing XSL

Since JAXP 1.1, JAXP has been the Java API for XML Processing; this replaces the 1.0 version, which was the Java API for XML *Parsing*. Much of this change is due to the addition of TrAX (yes, it's an API-happy world). Via TrAX, JAXP offers vendor-neutral XML document transformations. This is a welcome feature, as XSL processors have even greater variance across vendors than their XML parser counterparts.

Thanks to the JAXP expert group—and in particular Scott Boag and Michael Key, two XSL processor gurus—JAXP and TrAX offer a wide array of features and options, and provide complete support for almost all XML transformations. All this is sheltered under the javax.xml.transform package (and a few subpackages); Figure 7-5 shows the complete set of JAXP/TrAX classes and interfaces (omitting subpackage class definitions).

Like the parsing portion of JAXP, performing XML transformations requires just a few basic steps:

1. Obtain a TransformerFactory.

2. Retrieve a Tranformer.

3. Perform transformations on XML documents.

This is summarized in Figure 7-6.

Basic Transformations

For XML transformations, the factory you want is javax.xml.transform. TransformerFactory. This class is analogous to SAXParserFactory and DocumentBuilderFactory, both of which you've already seen. Obtaining a factory instance is a piece of cake:

```
TransformerFactory factory = TransformerFactory.newInstance( );
```

Once you've got the factory, you can set a number of options:

Error listeners (setErrorListener( )/getErrorListener( ))
Defined in the javax.xml.transform package, the ErrorListener interface allows problems in transformations to be caught and handled programmatically.

URI resolvers (setURIResolver( )/getURIResolver( ))
The URIResolver interface (also in javax.xml.transform) works just like an EntityResolver in SAX—it allows you to override normal resolution of URIs (and entities in an XSL stylesheet).

Factory/transformer features (setFeature( )/getFeature( ))
Like features on factories in SAX and DOM, these allow you to request certain options be turned on (true) or off (false), and affect the factory and all of the Transformer instances created by that factory.

Passthrough attributes (setAttribute( )/getAttribute( ))
Attributes in XSL are essentially the same as properties in SAX. They allow you to request specific options not available through JAXP, and are identified by a URI. These are different from features (which accept true/false values, and are either on or off), in that they accept an Object as their value.

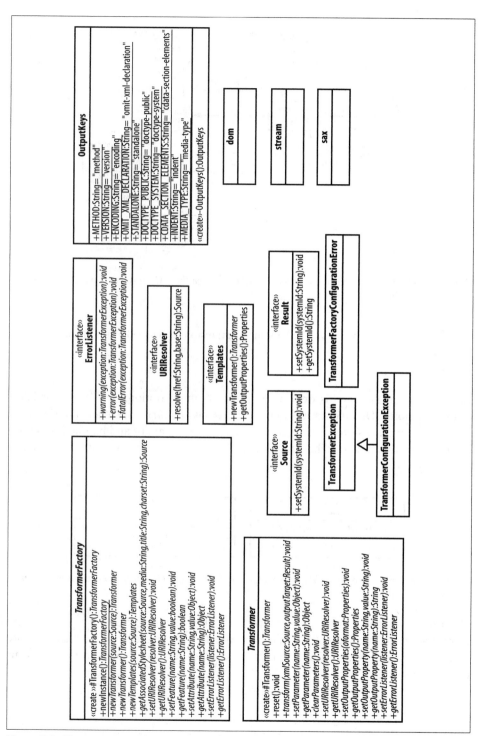

Figure 7-5. There are many classes in TrAX, but you typically use only one or two

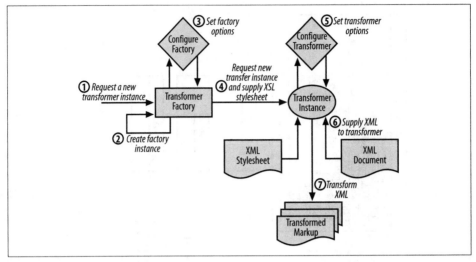

Figure 7-6. *The XML transformation process looks a lot like the SAX and DOM parsing process, involving a transformation factory*

 These options affect all instances of transformers created by the factory.

Setting an ErrorListener is one of the most common options you'll use for XML transformations. Defined in the javax.xml.transform.ErrorListener interface, an ErrorListener allows problems in transformation to be caught and handled programmatically. If this sounds like org.xml.sax.ErrorHandler, it is very similar, as evidenced by Figure 7-7.

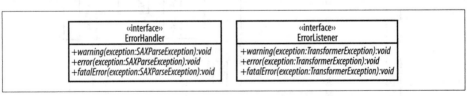

Figure 7-7. *ErrorListener is the TrAX counterpart to SAX's ErrorHandler, and even uses the same three callback methods*

Creating an implementation of this interface, filling the three callback methods, and using the setErrorListener() method on the TransformerFactory instance you are working with sets your transformation code up to deal with any errors that occur during transformation.

In the same vein, a method is provided to set and retrieve the URI resolver for the instances generated by the factory. The interface defined in javax.xml.transform. URIResolver behaves similarly to its SAX counterpart, org.xml.sax.EntityResolver (see Figure 7-8).

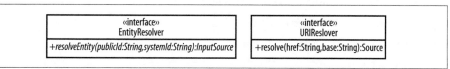

Figure 7-8. Like the relationship between ErrorListener and ErrorHandler, URIResolver mimics the functionality of EntityResolver, albeit with a slightly different method name

This interface, when implemented, allows URIs found in XSL constructs like xsl: import and xsl:include to be handled. Returning a Source (covered next in "Creating a transformer"), you can instruct your transformer to search for the specified document in various locations when a particular URI is encountered. For example, when an include of the URI http://www.headfirstlabs.com/headfirst.xsl is encountered, you might instead return the local document *headfirst-color.xsl*.

Once you set the options of your choice, you can obtain an instance, or instances, of a Transformer through the newTransformer( ) method:

```
// Get the factory
TransformerFactory factory = TransformerFactory.newInstance( );

// Configure the factory
factory.setErrorResolver(myErrorResolver);
factory.setURIResolver(myURIResolver);

// Get a Transformer to work with, with the options specified
Transformer transformer =
    factory.newTransformer(new StreamSource("foundation.xsl"));
```

Creating a transformer

Once you have an instance of a Transformer, you can go about actually performing XML transformations. This consists of two basic steps:

1. Set the XSL stylesheet to use.

2. Perform the transformation, specifying the XML document and result target.

The first step is simple (in fact, you already saw this code in the last code sample): a stylesheet can be supplied when obtaining a Transformer instance from the factory.

```
// Get a Transformer to work with, with the options specified
Transformer transformer =
    factory.newTransformer(new StreamSource("foundation.xsl"));
```

The location of this stylesheet must be specified by providing a javax.xml.transform. Source instance (actually an instance of an implementation of the Source interface) for its location. The Source interface is the means of locating input, be it a stylesheet, document, or other information set. TrAX provides the Source interface and three concrete implementations (all shown in Figure 7-9):

- javax.xml.transform.stream.StreamSource
- javax.xml.transform.dom.DOMSource
- javax.xml.transform.sax.SAXSource

The first of these, StreamSource, reads input from some type of I/O device. Constructors are provided for accepting an InputStream, a Reader, or a String system ID as input. Once created, the StreamSource can be passed to the Transformer for use. This will probably be the Source implementation you use most commonly in programs. It's great for reading a document from a network, input stream, user input, or other static representation of XSL stylesheets.

The next Source implementation, DOMSource, provides for reading from an existing DOM tree. It provides a constructor for taking in a DOM org.w3c.dom.Node, and will read from that Node when used. This is ideal for supplying an existing DOM tree to a transformation, perhaps if parsing has already occurred and an XML document is already in memory as a DOM structure, or if you've built a DOM tree programmatically.

SAXSource provides for reading input from SAX producers. This Source implementation takes either a SAX org.xml.sax.InputSource, or an org.xml.sax.XMLReader as input, and uses the events from these sources. This is ideal for situations in which a SAX content handler is already in use, and callbacks are set up and need to be triggered prior to transformations.

Once you've obtained an instance of a Transformer (by providing the stylesheet to use through an appropriate Source), you're ready to perform a transformation:

```
// Get the factory
TransformerFactory factory = TransformerFactory.newInstance( );

// Configure the factory
factory.setErrorResolver(myErrorResolver);
factory.setURIResolver(myURIResolver);

// Get a Transformer to work with, with the options specified
Transformer transformer =
    factory.newTransformer(new StreamSource("xsl/dw-document-html-4.0.xsl"));

// Perform transformation on myDocument, and print out result
transfomer.transform(new StreamSource("ibm-jaxp-article.xml"),
                     new StreamResult("article.html"));
```

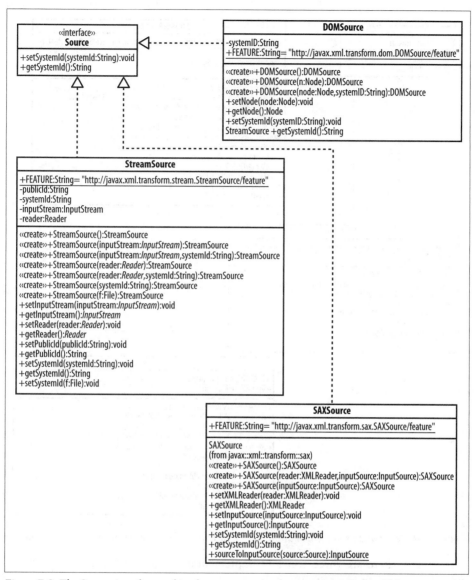

Figure 7-9. The Source interface and its three concrete implementations all provide for input to the TrAX/JAXP engine

The `transform()` method takes two arguments: a `Source` implementation and a `javax.xml.transform.Result` implementation. You should already be seeing the symmetry in how this works and have an idea about the functionality within the `Result` interface. The `Source` provides the XML document to be transformed, and the `Result` provides an output target for the transformation (as seen in Figure 7-10).

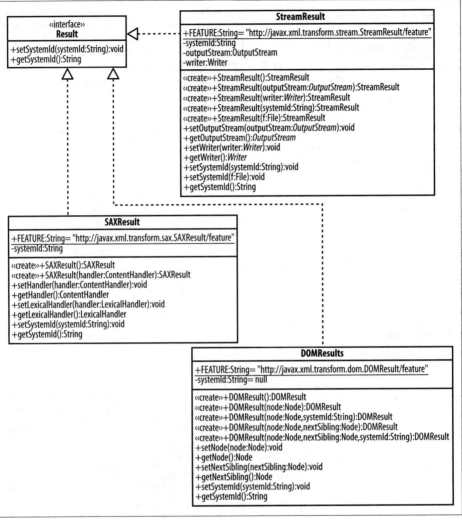

Figure 7-10. Result and its implementations are essentially outbound mirrors of the inbound Source

Like Source, there are three concrete implementations of the Result interface provided with TrAX and JAXP:

- `javax.xml.transform.stream.StreamResult`
- `javax.xml.transform.dom.DOMResult`
- `javax.xml.transform.sax.SAXResult`

The StreamResult class takes an OutputStream, a Java File, a String system ID, or a Writer. DOMResult takes a DOM Node to output the transformation to (presumably as a DOM org.w3c.dom.Document), and SAXResult takes a SAX ContentHandler instance to fire callbacks to, resulting from the transformed XML. All are analogous to their Source counterparts.

While the previous example shows transforming from a stream to a stream, any combination of sources and results is possible. Here are a few examples:

```
// Perform transformation on jordan.xml, and print out result
transformer.transform(new StreamSource("jordan.xml"), new StreamResult(System.out));

// Transform from SAX and output results to a DOM Node
transformer.transform(new SAXSource(new InputSource("http://www.oreilly.com/catalog.
xml")),
                     new DOMResult(DocumentBuilder.newDocument( )));

// Transform from DOM and output to a File
transformer.transform(new DOMSource(domTree),
                     new StreamResult(new FileOutputStream("results.xml")));

// Use a custom source and result (JDOM)
transformer.transform(new org.jdom.transform.JDOMSource(myJdomDocument),
                     new org.jdom.transform.JDOMResult( ));
```

The Identity Transformation

One of the cooler—albeit lesser-known—features of JAXP is the ability to convert easily from one XML format to another, using the Source and Result interfaces. This is known as the *identity transformation*, and is a result of performing a transformation without any stylesheet. A Transformer instance that performs identity transformations is created by calling the newTransformer( ) method of a TransformerFactory with no arguments:

```
Transformer identity = factory.newTransformer( );
```

identity in this example has no associated XSL stylesheet, so the transform( ) method will not change the incoming XML document, at least in terms of its content. However, by providing different Source and Result types, the document will be converted from one format to another:

```
// Convert from a file to a DOM tree
identity.transform(
                new StreamSource("input.xml"),
                new DOMResult(DocumentBuilder.newDocument( )));
```

This is a pretty cool way to quickly convert between different formats. Even more useful, this provides a serialization mechanism:

```
// Convert a DOM tree to a file
identity.transform(new DOMSource(myDocument), new StreamResult("output.xml"));
```

While this is a great way to quickly get a document from memory onto disk, the identity transformation doesn't offer you much in the way of output options. It's best used as a quick solution, rather than a full-fledged serialization technique.

Caching Transformation Instructions

Despite the simplicity of transformations using JAXP, there are two significant disadvantages to using a `Transformer` instance directly from your `TransformerFactory`:

1. The `Transformer` object processes the XSL stylesheet each and every time that `transform( )` is executed.

2. Instances of `Transformer` are not thread-safe—you can't use the same instances across multiple threads.

To understand the root of these problems, realize that a `Transformer` must reprocess the XSL it uses every time it executes a transformation (via the `transform( )` method). Even worse, if this processing is occurring in multiple threads at the same time, you can start to have real problems. And, on top of the threading issues, you've got to pay the processing cost for the XSL stylesheet over and over again.

To solve these problems, JAXP provides the `javax.xml.transform.Templates` object. A `Templates` object represents a stylesheet, but it precompiles the instructions in the supplied XSL stylesheet. This means that while there is a little up-front cost in using a `Templates` object (as it precompiles the XSL), there is no repeat cost in processing. Figure 7-11 shows how the `Templates` object fits into the overall process flow (compare it to Figure 7-6).

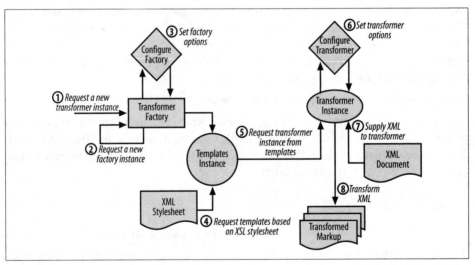

Figure 7-11. Using a Templates object inserts an extra step into the normal JAXP/TrAX workflow process

This is how it translates into actual code:

```
try {
    // Set up input documents
    Source inputXML = new StreamSource(
        new File(args[0]));
```

```
Source inputXSL = new StreamSource(
  new File(args[1]));

// Set up output sink
Result outputXHTML = new StreamResult(
  new File("output.html"));

// Setup a factory for transforms
TransformerFactory factory = TransformerFactory.newInstance();

// Precompile the XSL into a Templates object
Templates templates = factory.newTemplates(inputXSL);

// Get a Transformer from the Templates
Transformer transformer = templates.newTransformer();

// Perform the transformation
transformer.transform(inputXML, outputXHTML);
} catch (TransformerConfigurationException e) {
System.out.println("The underlying XSL processor " +
  "does not support the requested features.");
} catch (TransformerException e) {
System.out.println("Error occurred obtaining " +
  "XSL processor.");
}
```

This just required one additional line of code, and one slightly modified line of code (both are bolded). These are the only changes required to move from direct use of a Transformer to adding precompilation into the process.

So the question becomes when to grab a Transformer directly and when to use Templates objects. When I use XSL, I almost always use the same stylesheet repeatedly. So rather than paying for multiple passes over the XSL, I'd prefer to just precompile the instructions into a Templates object and only pay the cost of processing the XSL instructions once.

That said, there are a few cases where it's better to pull a Transformer straight from your TransformerFactory. If you know that you're only going to perform a single transformation using a specific stylesheet, then it's faster not to precompile the stylesheet into a Templates object. However, that assumes that you're only using the stylesheet a single time; in my own tests, I find that once I've used an XSL twice, it's a wash between using a Templates object as opposed to requesting a Transformer directly, and once you use a stylesheet three times, the Templates approach wins hands down. You also need to be sure you're not going to have any threading issues; that's a simple thing to determine, though, so I'll leave that to you to apply in your programming. As a general rule, it's almost always safer to go with the Templates object.

Changing the Processor Implementation

You've already seen that by using the javax.xml.parsers.SAXParserFactory system property, you can specify your own SAX parser implementation (and the same was true for DOM building). This same principle applies for your XSL processor. JAXP comes prepackaged with Xalan-Java (*http://xml.apache.org/xalan-j*), which is another Apache open source project (and the processing counterpart to Xerces). Xalan-Java is a mature XSL processor and is a good choice for many use-cases. But if you need to use a different XSL processor, JAXP provides a configuration mechanism.

To exercise this option, supply a value for the system property named javax.xml.transform.TransformerFactory. You need to assign this property the name of a class to instantiate; that class should extend javax.xml.transform.TransformerFactory and provide implementations for that interface's abstract methods:

```
java -Djavax.xml.transform.TransformerFactory=net.sf.saxon.TransformerFactoryImpl
         javaxml3.TransformTester ibm-jaxp-article.xml xsl/dw-document-4.0.xsl
```

The name of both the property and the class to extend is javax.xml.transform.TransformerFactory. This isn't meant to be confusing, but to serve as a reminder that the value of the property should extend the class of the same name.

In this example, the Saxon processor (*http://www.saxonica.com*) is specified; Saxon's TransformerFactoryImpl will create Saxon-specific Transformer instances. With this one line, you've effectively moved from Xalan-Java to Saxon. You could also set this property programmatically:

```
private void initTransformer( ) {
  System.setProperty("javax.xml.transform.TransformerFactory",
                   "net.sf.saxon.TransformerFactoryImpl");

  // Perform other Transformer setup tasks
}
```

XPath

With the release of JAXP 1.3, a rich XPath API was added to JAXP. The API was designed to be *object model neutral*, meaning that, assuming the proper classes exist, your code can evaluate XPath expressions on XML objects created by any XML object model as well as return the API-appropriate types for nodes and sets of nodes. In addition to DOM, it is possible to obtain implementations of JAXP XPath interfaces that work with document objects created with JDOM, dom4j, and XOM, among others. (The JDOM and dom4j object models are discussed in Chapters 9 and 10, respectively.) The standard JAXP distribution, however, only includes support for DOM Document objects.

This section is not an exhaustive look at XPath. It specifically discusses the XPath API within JAXP. For more information on XPath, please check out *XPath and XPointer* by John E. Simpson (O'Reilly). As an additional caveat, some of the examples use expressions that are more verbose than necessary for illustrative purposes.

The core interface for the JAXP XPath API is javax.xml.xpath.XPath. This interface defines several methods named evaluate( ) for evaluating an XPath expression against an XML document that has already been parsed into a document object or an instance of org.xml.sax.InputSource in the case that the document has not already been parsed. The XPath interface also supports compiling an expression into an XPathExpression object. This functionality, similar to the Templates objects from TrAX, allows you to avoid the overhead of repeated compilation if you are going to use the same expression repeatedly. Also like Templates objects, XPathExpression objects are thread-safe and can be used by multiple threads simultaneously. Figure 7-12 contains a UML diagram of the JAXP XPath interfaces. I am also including NamespaceContext, which isn't strictly an XPath class (in fact, it's in the javax.xml.namespace package whereas the rest of these interfaces are in the javax.xml.xpath package), but I do discuss it in this section.

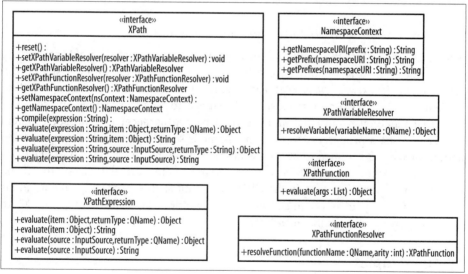

Figure 7-12. JAXP XPath interfaces

Evaluating an XPath expression returns one of five types of responses. JAXP defines Java constants to represent these types; each object model implementation maps these constants to an actual Java type. The requested return type is passed as a javax.xml.namespace.QName object to the evaluate method. If no return type is requested, the STRING type is used. The five return types are listed in Table 7-1 along with the constant from javax.xml.xpath.XPathConstants for that return type and the Java type that is mapped to that XPath type in the DOM implementation.

Table 7-1. SPath return types

Return type	QName constants	Java type
STRING	XPathConstants.STRING	java.lang.String
NUMBER	XPathConstants.NUMBER	java.lang.Double
BOOLEAN	XPathConstants.BOOLEAN	java.lang.Boolean
NODE	XPathConstants.NODE	org.w3c.dom.Node
NODESET	XPathConstants.NODESET	org.w3c.dom.NodeList

Creating an XPath Instance

To obtain an instance of the XPath interface, you must first create an instance of javax.xml.xpath.XPathFactory through one of the static newInstance( ) methods of XPathFactory. To create an XPathFactory instance to work with and return DOM objects, call newInstance( ) without any arguments. To create an XPathFactory instance for a different object model, pass the URI assigned to that object model to newInstance( ). For example, to create an XPathFactory that uses JDOM, write:

```
XPathFactory factory =
    XPathFactory.newInstance("http://jdom.org/jaxp/xpath/jdom");
```

The newInstance( ) method will find the appropriate implementation of XPathFactory in a manner similar to the other JAXP factories. First, it will look for a system property named javax.xml.xpath.XPathFactory:*uri* where *uri* is the URI passed to newInstance( ). If this property exists, it's assumed to be a class name, and the class with that name is instantiated and returned by newInstance( ). If no such system property exists, a property with the same name is searched for in *lib/jaxp.properties* and, if it exists, is assumed to be a class name. Finally, resources named *META-INF/ services/javax.xml.xpath.XPathFactory* are searched for on the classpath. If no resources are found that contain the URI, the default XPathFactory implementation is returned. Once you've obtained an implementation of XPathFactory, an XPath instance is created by a call to newXPath( ).

XPath Examples

I'll be using the XML document in Example 7-1 to demonstrate the basic capabilities of the JAXP XPath API. To simplify the examples, this document is assumed to be in a file named *tds.xml*.

Example 7-1. Document for XPath examples

```xml
<?xml version="1.0" encoding="UTF-8"?>
<schedule name="The Daily Show with Jon Stewart" seriesId="572">
    <show date="06.12.06" weekday="Monday" dayNumber="12">
        <guest>
            <name>Thomas Friedman</name>
            <credit>Author of "The World is Flat"</credit>
        </guest>
    </show>
    <show date="06.13.06" weekday="Tuesday" dayNumber="13">
        <guest>
            <name>Ken Mehlman</name>
            <credit>Chair of the Republican National Committee</credit>
        </guest>
    </show>
    <show date="06.14.06" weekday="Wednesday" dayNumber="14">
        <guest>
            <name>Tim Russert</name>
            <credit>Host of NBC's "Meet the Press"</credit>
        </guest>
    </show>
    <show date="06.15.06" weekday="Thursday" dayNumber="15">
        <guest>
            <name>Louis C.K.</name>
            <credit>Star of HBO series "Lucky Louie"</credit>
        </guest>
    </show>
</schedule>
```

To start, let's write an XPath expression that gets the name attribute of the root schedule element. This can be written as:

```
/schedule/@name
```

Wrapping this expression in some Java code is as simple as creating an XPath instance and calling the evaluate( ) method:

```java
package javaxml3;

import java.io.FileReader;

import javax.xml.xpath.XPath;
import javax.xml.xpath.XPathFactory;

import org.xml.sax.InputSource;

public class GetName {

    public static void main(String[] args) throws Exception {
        XPathFactory factory = XPathFactory.newInstance( );
        XPath xPath = factory.newXPath( );

        String result = xPath.evaluate("/schedule/@name", new InputSource(
```

```
                new FileReader("tds.xml")));
        System.out.println(result);
    }
}
```

Running this code outputs "The Daily Show with Jon Stewart" to the console. Note that because we aren't specifying a result type, the XPath expression returns the value of the attribute as a String. If, instead, we wanted to get a DOM Attr object, we could pass XPathConstants.NODE to evaluate( ):

```
Attr result = (Attr) xPath.evaluate("/schedule/@name", new InputSource(
        new FileReader("tds.xml")), XPathConstants.NODE);
System.out.println(result.getValue());
```

This would enable us to call the methods on the Attr interface to discover information about the attribute other than just the value, such as whether the value of the attribute was specified in the document or is the default from a DTD.

We can also use the NUMBER return type to have JAXP do any numeric conversion for us:

```
Double result = (Double) xPath.evaluate("/schedule/@seriesId",
        new InputSource(new FileReader("tds.xml")),
        XPathConstants.NUMBER);
System.out.println(result.intValue);
```

For the result types STRING, NUMBER, BOOLEAN, and NODE, if there are multiple nodes that match the expression, only the first result is returned. When you want to get a list of nodes, you need to use the NODESET return type. In the DOM implementation, this returns an org.w3c.dom.NodeList object, which can then be looped over. To start, let's get a NodeList containing all of the show elements and output the node count to the console:

```
NodeList shows = (NodeList) xPath.evaluate("/schedule/show",
        new InputSource(new FileReader("tds.xml")),
        XPathConstants.NODESET);
System.out.println("Document has " + shows.getLength() + " shows.");
```

Then we can iterate over the NodeList with a simple for loop. In this case, each of the Node objects within the NodeList are Elements. Since these are DOM objects, we can evaluate other XPath expressions against them. Putting this to use to output a listing of various elements and attribute values looks like:

```
for (int i = 0; i < shows.getLength(); i++) {
    Element show = (Element) shows.item(i);
    String guestName = xPath.evaluate("guest/name/text()", show);
    String guestCredit = xPath.evaluate("guest/credit/text()", show);

    System.out.println(show.getAttribute("weekday") + ", "
            + show.getAttribute("date") + " - " + guestName + " ("
            + guestCredit + ")");
}
```

Namespaces in XPath

XPath allows you to reference elements and attributes that are assigned to a namespace through the same prefix notation as you would within an XML document. If we rewrite the XML document in Example 7-1 such that the schedule and show elements are in a namespace with the URI `uri:comedy:schedule` and the guest, name, and credit elements are in a namespace with the URI `uri:comedy:guest`, it could look like this:

```
<?xml version="1.0" encoding="UTF-8"?>
<schedule name="The Daily Show with Jon Stewart" seriesId="572"
        xmlns="uri:comedy:schedule" xmlns:g="uri:comedy:guest">
    <show date="06.12.06" weekday="Monday" dayNumber="12">
        <g:guest>
            <g:name>Thomas Friedman</g:name>
            <g:credit>Author of "The World is Flat"</g:credit>
        </g:guest>
    </show>
    <show date="06.13.06" weekday="Tuesday" dayNumber="13">
        <g:guest>
            <g:name>Ken Mehlman</g:name>
            <g:credit>Chair of the Republican National Committee</g:credit>
        </g:guest>
    </show>
    <show date="06.14.06" weekday="Wednesday" dayNumber="14">
        <g:guest>
            <g:name>Tim Russert</g:name>
            <g:credit>Host of NBC's "Meet the Press"</g:credit>
        </g:guest>
    </show>
    <show date="06.15.06" weekday="Thursday" dayNumber="15">
        <g:guest>
            <g:name>Louis C.K.</g:name>
            <g:credit>Star of HBO series "Luckie Louie"</g:credit>
        </g:guest>
    </show>
</schedule>
```

To create an XPath expression that evaluates to all the guest elements, you might think you could write an expression such as:

```
/schedule/show/g:guest
```

But this won't work for two reasons. First, although in the XML document the schedule and show elements are in the default namespace, XPath doesn't support a default namespace. The second reason this won't work is that we haven't associated the g prefix with `uri:comedy:guest`—namespace declarations in an XML document do not apply to XPath expressions evaluated against it. There are two solutions for this. The first, and less preferable, is to qualify all elements with the namespace URI, such as:

```
/uri:comedy:schedule:schedule/uri:comedy:schedule:show/uri:comedy:guest:guest
```

Although this leads to ugly expressions, it can be useful if used sparingly. The second solution is to provide an implementation of the javax.xml.namespace. NamespaceContext interface. This interface defines three methods for mapping a single prefix to a URI, a URI to a single prefix, and a URI to multiple prefixes. Example 7-2 contains an implementation of NamespaceContext backed by two HashMaps.

Example 7-2. SimpleNamespaceContext

```
package javaxml3;

import java.util.Collections;
import java.util.HashMap;
import java.util.HashSet;
import java.util.Iterator;
import java.util.Map;
import java.util.Set;

import javax.xml.XMLConstants;
import javax.xml.namespace.NamespaceContext;

public class SimpleNamespaceContext implements NamespaceContext {

    private Map urisByPrefix = new HashMap( );

    private Map prefixesByURI = new HashMap( );

    public SimpleNamespaceContext( ) {
        // prepopulate with xml and xmlns prefixes
        // per JavaDoc of NamespaceContext interface
        addNamespace(XMLConstants.XML_NS_PREFIX, XMLConstants.XML_NS_URI);
        addNamespace(XMLConstants.XMLNS_ATTRIBUTE,
                XMLConstants.XMLNS_ATTRIBUTE_NS_URI);
    }

    public synchronized void addNamespace(String prefix, String namespaceURI) {
        urisByPrefix.put(prefix, namespaceURI);
        if (prefixesByURI.containsKey(namespaceURI)) {
            ((Set) prefixesByURI.get(namespaceURI)).add(prefix);
        } else {
            Set set = new HashSet( );
            set.add(prefix);
            prefixesByURI.put(namespaceURI, set);
        }
    }

    public String getNamespaceURI(String prefix) {
        if (prefix == null)
            throw new IllegalArgumentException("prefix cannot be null");
        if (urisByPrefix.containsKey(prefix))
            return (String) urisByPrefix.get(prefix);
        else
            return XMLConstants.NULL_NS_URI;
    }
```

Example 7-2. SimpleNamespaceContext (continued)

```
    public String getPrefix(String namespaceURI) {
        return (String) getPrefixes(namespaceURI).next( );
    }

    public Iterator getPrefixes(String namespaceURI) {
        if (namespaceURI == null)
            throw new IllegalArgumentException("namespaceURI cannot be null");
        if (prefixesByURI.containsKey(namespaceURI)) {
            return ((Set) prefixesByURI.get(namespaceURI)).iterator( );
        } else {
            return Collections.EMPTY_SET.iterator( );
        }
    }
}
```

We can put this together with the code from the last section to produce:

```
XPathFactory factory = XPathFactory.newInstance( );
XPath xPath = factory.newXPath( );
SimpleNamespaceContext nsContext = new SimpleNamespaceContext( );
xPath.setNamespaceContext(nsContext);
nsContext.addNamespace("s", "uri:comedy:schedule");
nsContext.addNamespace("g", "uri:comedy:guest");

NodeList shows = (NodeList) xPath.evaluate("/s:schedule/s:show",
        new InputSource(new FileReader("tds_ns.xml")),
        XPathConstants.NODESET);
System.out.println("Document has " + shows.getLength( ) + " shows.");
for (int i = 0; i < shows.getLength( ); i++) {
    Element show = (Element) shows.item(i);
    String guestName = xPath.evaluate("g:guest/g:name/text( )", show);
    String guestCredit = xPath.evaluate("g:guest/g:credit/text( )", show);

    System.out.println(show.getAttribute("weekday") + ", "
            + show.getAttribute("date") + " - " + guestName + " ("
            + guestCredit + ")");
}
```

Note that because the namespace prefixes used in the XPath expressions are not connected to the prefixes in the actual document, we didn't have to use g as the prefix for uri:comedy:guest. We could have used anything (other than s).

XPath Variables

XPath expressions can contain variables that are interpolated when the expression is evaluated. These variables are indicated by the use of the dollar sign ($) character. XPath variables can be useful in a variety of ways; for the Java developers, perhaps most so when compiling an XPath expression into an XPathExpression object for repeat use. For example, an expression that would find the appropriate show element for a date might look like:

```
/schedule/show[@date=$date]/guest
```

However, passing this expression to the evaluate( ) method such as in Example 7-3 throws a NullPointerException, because if the XPathExpression or XPath object sees a variable reference, it expects to have an implementation of XPathVariableResolver defined.

Example 7-3. XPathExpression with variable

```
XPathFactory factory = XPathFactory.newInstance( );
XPath xPath = factory.newXPath( );
XPathExpression exp = xPath.compile("/schedule/show[@date=$date]/guest");

// this next line throws a NullPointerException
Element element = (Element) exp.evaluate(inputSource, XPathConstants.NODE);
```

Implementations of XPathVariableResolver resolve variable values based on a javax. xml.namespace.QName object. The resolved variable can be any type, but should really be only one of the XPath return types. Since we only care about the one variable named $date, we can implement a resolver that always returns the same object regardless of the QName value:

```
class StaticVariableResolver implements StaticVariableResolver {

    private Object value = null;

    StaticVariableResolver(Object value) {
        this.value = value;
    }

    public Object resolveVariable(QName name) {
        return value;
    }
}
```

Then we create an instance of this class and pass it to our newly created XPath object:

```
XPathFactory factory = XPathFactory.newInstance( );
XPath xPath = factory.newXPath( );
xPath.setXPathVariableResolver(new StaticVariableResolver("06.12.2006"));

XPathExpression exp = xPath.compile("/schedule/show[@date=$date]/guest");

// this next line throws a NullPointerException
Element element = (Element) exp.evaluate(inputSource, XPathConstants.NODE);
```

This is obviously of limited usefulness as we had to set the value of the variable in advance of the expression compilation, let alone the evaluation. To make a more useful implementation of XPathVariableResolver, we can have the implementation backed by a Map with QName objects as the keys:

```
package javaxml3;

import java.util.HashMap;

import javax.xml.namespace.QName;
import javax.xml.xpath.XPathVariableResolver;

public class MapVariableResolver implements XPathVariableResolver {

    private HashMap variables = new HashMap();

    public void addVariable(String namespaceURI, String localName, Object value) {
        addVariable(new QName(namespaceURI, localName), value);
    }

    public void addVariable(QName name, Object value) {
        variables.put(name, value);
    }

    public Object resolveVariable(QName name) {
        Object retval = variables.get(name);
        return retval;
    }
}
```

Which then allows us to set the value of the variable after the expression has been
compiled, leading us to the full GuestManager class:

```
package javaxml3;

import java.io.File;
import java.io.IOException;
import java.text.SimpleDateFormat;
import java.util.Date;

import javax.xml.parsers.DocumentBuilder;
import javax.xml.parsers.DocumentBuilderFactory;
import javax.xml.parsers.ParserConfigurationException;
import javax.xml.xpath.XPath;
import javax.xml.xpath.XPathConstants;
import javax.xml.xpath.XPathExpression;
import javax.xml.xpath.XPathExpressionException;
import javax.xml.xpath.XPathFactory;

import org.w3c.dom.Document;
import org.w3c.dom.Element;
import org.xml.sax.SAXException;

public class GuestManager {
    private Document document;

    private XPathExpression expression;

    private MapVariableResolver resolver = new MapVariableResolver();
```

```
    private SimpleDateFormat xmlDateFormat = new SimpleDateFormat("MM.dd.yy");

    public GuestManager(String fileName) throws ParserConfigurationException,
            SAXException, IOException, XPathExpressionException {
        DocumentBuilderFactory dbf = DocumentBuilderFactory.newInstance( );
        DocumentBuilder builder = dbf.newDocumentBuilder( );
        document = builder.parse(new File(fileName));

        XPathFactory factory = XPathFactory.newInstance( );
        XPath xPath = factory.newXPath( );
        xPath.setXPathVariableResolver(resolver);
        expression = xPath.compile("/schedule/show[@date=$date]/guest");
    }

    public synchronized Element getGuest(Date guestDate)
            throws XPathExpressionException {
        String formattedDate = xmlDateFormat.format(guestDate);
        resolver.addVariable(null, "date", formattedDate);
        return (Element) expression.evaluate(document, XPathConstants.NODE);
    }
    public static void main(String[] args) throws Exception {
        GuestManager gm = new GuestManager("tds.xml");
        Element guest = gm.getGuest(new Date(2006, 5, 14));
        System.out.println(guest.getElementsByTagName("name").item(0)
                .getTextContent( ));
    }

}
```

 Notice how the getGuest( ) method is synchronized? That's because although the XPathExpression class is thread-safe by itself, our use of XPathVariableResolver is not. If there were multiple threads calling getGuest( ), one thread could execute the addVariable( ) call during an interval between a second thread's call to addVariable( ) and evaluate( ). We could have just synchronized these two lines, locking on the resolver object.

XPath Functions

The XPath specification defines a handful of built-in functions that allow you to access a variety of information about the result of an expression. We've already seen an example of that with the text( ) function, which returns any text content contained within an element. Another commonly seen function is count( ), which counts the number of nodes with a node set. For example, this bit of Java code from previously in this section:

```
    NodeList shows = (NodeList) xPath.evaluate("/schedule/show",
            new InputSource(new FileReader("tds.xml")),
            XPathConstants.NODESET);
    System.out.println("Document has " + shows.getLength( ) + " shows.");
```

Could be rewritten as:

```
Number shows = (Number) xPath.evaluate("count(/schedule/show)",
        new InputSource(new FileReader("tds.xml")),
        XPathConstants.NUMBER);
System.out.println("Document has " + shows.intValue() + " shows.");
```

In addition to the built-in functions, XPath allows for custom functions, and the JAXP XPath API provides interfaces for creating your own custom functions. A custom function is encapsulated in a class that implements the javax.xml.xpath. XPathFunction interface. This interface defines a single method, evaluate( ), which takes a List of arguments and returns an Object. If there are no arguments to a function, the arguments list may be null.

You can't use XPathFunction to override any of the built-in XPath functions. Even if you try, the API will ignore you.

In addition to creating the function class, you must also create an implementation of the XPathFunctionResolver interface. This interface, which is closely related to the XPathVariableResolver interface, defines a method named resolveFunction( ) that accepts a qualified name and an *arity* value and returns the function object. As with XPathVariableResolver and NamespaceContext before it, the implementation of XPathFunctionResolver is set for an XPath object by calling setXPathFunctionResolver( ).

What's Arity?

Arity is a fancy word for the number of arguments a function (or method, if you're talking about Java) accepts. This value can be useful if you want to have separate function classes for two custom functions with the same name that accept a different number of parameters. If you test for the appropriate arity value, you should still check the argument list length in your function class's evaluate( ) method and throw an exception if the incorrect number of arguments has been passed.

Every reference to a custom function must be qualified with a namespace URI or a mapped prefix. Example 7-4 contains a complete example with implementations of XPathFunction and XPathFunctionResolver, as well as the use of an XPath expression that calls this custom function.

Example 7-4. XPathFunction in use

```
package javaxml3;

import java.io.FileReader;
import java.util.List;

import javax.xml.namespace.QName;
import javax.xml.xpath.XPath;
```

Example 7-4. XPathFunction in use (continued)

```java
import javax.xml.xpath.XPathConstants;
import javax.xml.xpath.XPathFactory;
import javax.xml.xpath.XPathFunction;
import javax.xml.xpath.XPathFunctionException;
import javax.xml.xpath.XPathFunctionResolver;

import org.w3c.dom.Element;
import org.w3c.dom.NodeList;
import org.xml.sax.InputSource;

class SampleFunction implements XPathFunction {

    public Object evaluate(List args) throws XPathFunctionException {
        if (args.size( ) != 1)
            throw new XPathFunctionException("I need exactly one argument");

        // args is a single guest node
        NodeList guestNodes = (NodeList) args.get(0);
        Element guest = (Element) guestNodes.item(0);
        NodeList nameNodes = guest.getElementsByTagNameNS("uri:comedy:guest",
                "name");
        NodeList creditNodes = guest.getElementsByTagNameNS("uri:comedy:guest",
                "credit");

        return evaluate(nameNodes, creditNodes);

    }

    private String evaluate(NodeList nameNodes, NodeList creditNodes) {
        return new String("I hope " + nameNodes.item(0).getTextContent( )
                + " makes a good joke about being "
                + creditNodes.item(0).getTextContent( ));
    }

}

class SampleFunctionResolver implements XPathFunctionResolver {

    public XPathFunction resolveFunction(QName functionName, int arity) {
        if ("uri:comedy:guest".equals(functionName.getNamespaceURI( ))
                && "joke".equals(functionName.getLocalPart( )) && (arity == 1)) {
            return new SampleFunction( );
        } else
            return null;
    }

}

public class FunctionExample {

    public static void main(String[] args) throws Exception {
        XPathFactory factory = XPathFactory.newInstance( );
        XPath xPath = factory.newXPath( );
```

Example 7-4. XPathFunction in use (continued)

```
        SimpleNamespaceContext nsContext = new SimpleNamespaceContext();
        xPath.setNamespaceContext(nsContext);
        nsContext.addNamespace("s", "uri:comedy:schedule");
        nsContext.addNamespace("g", "uri:comedy:guest");
        xPath.setXPathFunctionResolver(new SampleFunctionResolver());

        NodeList shows = (NodeList) xPath.evaluate("/s:schedule/s:show",
                new InputSource(new FileReader("tds_ns.xml")),
                XPathConstants.NODESET);
        for (int i = 0; i < shows.getLength(); i++) {
            Element show = (Element) shows.item(i);

            String guestJoke = xPath.evaluate("g:joke(g:guest)", show);
            System.out
                    .println(show.getAttribute("weekday") + " - " + guestJoke);
        }
    }
}
```

XML Validation

Along with XPath support, JAXP 1.3 added an entirely new validation framework. Previously, validation was handled by invoking setValidating() on either a SAXParserFactory or a DocumentBuilderFactory:

```
factory.setValidating(true);
```

This approach, while functional, left a lot to be desired. It relied on the document being parsed to specify the schema to validate against, which can be problematic; it's common for documents to omit a DOCTYPE or schema reference, and yet you still may want to validate that document against a schema you have on hand. Additionally, setValidating() is ambiguous as to the constraint type being used. Is the document to be validated against a DTD? an XML Schema? Can RELAX NG schemas be used? What if the document references both a DTD and XML Schema? These are all questions that prompted the creation of a new JAXP package, javax.xml.validation (shown in Figure 7-13).

Creating a SchemaFactory

This should already start to make some sense; classes like Schema and SchemaFactory look a lot like the SAXParser/SAXParserFactory and DocumentBuilder/DocumentBuilderFactory combinations from SAX and DOM. In fact, you begin—as you do with the other JAXP factory classes—by creating a new SchemaFactory via the newInstance() method:

```
SchemaFactory schemaFactory = SchemaFactory.newInstance(XMLConstants.W3C_XML_SCHEMA_NS_URI);
```

Validator

```
«create»#Validator():Validator
+reset():void
+validate(source:Source):void
+validate(source:Source,result:Result):void
+setErrorHandler(errorHandler:ErrorHandler):void
+getErrorHandler():ErrorHandler
+setResourceResolver(resourceResolver:LSResourceResolver):void
+getResourceResolver():LSResourceResolver
+getFeature(name:String):boolean
+setFeature(name:String,value:boolean):void
+setProperty(name:String,object:Object):void
+getProperty(name:String):Object
```

ValidatorHandler

```
«create»#ValidatorHandler():ValidatorHandler
+setContentHandler(receiver:ContentHandler):void
+getContentHandler():ContentHandler
+setErrorHandler(errorHandler:ErrorHandler):void
+getErrorHandler():ErrorHandler
+setResourceResolver(resourceResolver:LSResourceResolver):void
+getResourceResolver():LSResourceResolver
+getTypeInfoProvider():TypeInfoProvider
+getFeature(name:String):boolean
+setFeature(name:String,value:boolean):void
+setProperty(name:String,object:Object):void
+getProperty(name:String):Object
```

TypeInfoProvider

```
«create»#TypeInfoProvider():TypeInfoProvider
+getElementTypeInfo():TypeInfo
+getAttributeTypeInfo(index:int):TypeInfo
+isIdAttribute(index:int):boolean
+isSpecified(index:int):boolean
```

SchemaFactory

```
«create»#SchemaFactory():SchemaFactory
+newInstance(schemaLanguage:String):SchemaFactory
+isSchemaLanguageSupported(schemaLanguage:String):boolean
+getFeature(name:String):boolean
+setFeature(name:String,value:boolean):void
+setProperty(name:String,object:Object):void
+getProperty(name:String):Object
+setErrorHandler(errorHandler:ErrorHandler):void
+getErrorHandler():ErrorHandler
+setResourceResolver(resourceResolver:LSResourceResolver):void
+getResourceResolver():LSResourceResolver
+newSchema(schema:Source):Schema
+newSchema(schema:File):Schema
+newSchema(schema:URL):Schema
+newSchema(schemas:Source[]):Schema
+newSchema():Schema
```

Schema

```
«create»#Schema():Schema
+newValidator():Validator
+newValidatorHandler():ValidatorHandler
```

SchemaFactoryFinder

```
-debug:boolean=false
-classLoader:ClassLoader
-SERVICE_CLASS:Class= SchemaFactory.class
-SERVICE_ID:String="META-INF/services/"+ SERVICE_CLASS.getName()
«initializer»~  initializer():void
-debugPrintln(msg:String):void
«create»>>+SchemaFactoryFinder(loader:ClassLoader):SchemaFactoryFinder
-debugDisplayClassLoader():void
+newFactory(schemaLanguage:String):SchemaFactory
_newFactory(schemaLanguage:String):SchemaFactory
-createInstance(className:String):SchemaFactory
-loadFromProperty(keyName:String,resourceName:String,in:InputStream):SchemaFactory
-createServiceFileIterator():Iterator
-which(clazz:Class):String
-which(classname:String,loader:ClassLoader):String
```

SchemaFactoryLoader

```
«create»#SchemaFactoryLoader():SchemaFactoryLoader
+newFactory(schemaLanguage:String):SchemaFactory
```

Figure 7-13. Most of the classes in javax.xml.validation are related to internal processing; you'll usually use only SchemaFactory, Schema, and Validator

JAXP hardwires each SchemaFactory instance to a particular type of schema, so you'll need to supply this method with a constant representing the schema variant you want to use. These come from another new JAXP class, javax.xml.XMLConstants; Table 7-2 shows the constants supported for use with validation.

Table 7-2. Constants supported for use with validation

Constant name	Schema language
XMLConstants.RELAXNG_NS_URI	RELAX NG
XMLConstants.W3C_XML_SCHEMA_NS_URI	XML Schema

Where's the DTD?

You'll notice a rather obvious absence: DTDs. If you read through the XML 1.0 specification, there's simply no room for external validation using DTDs. In other words, the specification is adamant that for validation against a DTD to occur, the document must specify that DTD within the document, using a DOCTYPE declaration. So, you're stuck with good old setValidating(true) for DTD validation. But, with the validation API, you can limit that approach to *just* DTD validation, making it a decent solution (and removing ambiguity from your code). For all other validation, use the JAXP validation API.

There are several options on SchemaFactory, although I found that only a few of them were very useful in the "typical" validation process. The most notable of these issetErrorHandler( ), which accepts an org.xml.sax.ErrorHandler implementation. Rather than dealing with errors in parsing an XML document, this handler reports errors in processing a schema loaded via the newSchema( ) method (the subject of the next section, "Representing a Constraint Model in Java"). This is a simple way to deal with schema-loading errors gracefully, via an interface you already should be comfortable with.

Another option you may want to investigate is accessed through the setResourceResolver( ) method. You can pass this method an object to handle resource resolution when parsing schemas; for example, if your schema references other schemas, or external entities, the class handed to this method can intercept resolution requests and redirect them. The downside to this method—and the main reason I tend to use it sparingly—is that the object you must supply to setResourceResolver( ) is an org.w3c.dom.ls.LSResourceResolver: a DOM 3 construct, used in the Load and Save module. Since many parsers are still coming up to speed on DOM Level 3, you may not have an implementation of this interface available to your parsing code.

DOM 3 and the Load and Save module are covered in Chapter 6.

Representing a Constraint Model in Java

Once you've created a SchemaFactory, you can then create a new Schema object, via the newSchema( ) method on your factory. As you might expect, a Schema is a Java representation of a constraint model; therefore, pass the newSchema( ) method the schema it should represent (taking care that the constraint model is in the same schema language as that supported by the SchemaFactory):

```
SchemaFactory schemaFactory = SchemaFactory.newInstance(XMLConstants.W3C_XML_SCHEMA_
NS_URI);
Source schemaSource = new StreamSource(new File(args[1]));
Schema schema = schemaFactory.newSchema(schemaSource);
```

In this example, I've supplied the schema file in the form of a javax.xml.transform. Source implementation, something you should already be familiar with from TrAX (see Figures 7-9 and 7-10 for a refresher). You can also use a File or URL as input.

You can also supply an array of Source implementations (Source[]); the SchemaFactory will combine these into a single Schema object, and return that object from newSchema( ). As you might expect, errors can abound in this situation, so be sure you have an ErrorHandler set to deal with problems that might arise when combining schemas.

Validating XML

With a Schema object created, you just need to call newValidator( ) to get what you want: an object to validate your XML. The Validator class is shown in Figure 7-14.

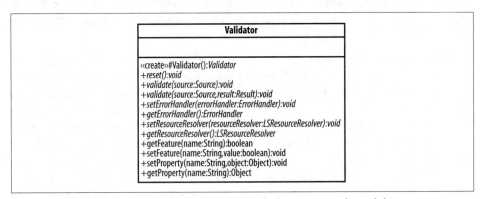

Figure 7-14. Unsurprisingly most of the Validator methods are purposed to validate an XML document

Once you have a Validator, simply call validate( ):

```
// Create the validator
Validator validator = schema.newValidator();

// Validate
validator.validate(new DOMSource(doc));
```

As with SchemaFactory, you can set an ErrorHandler and LSResourceResolver on your Validator to provide some more information from and control over the validation process. In fact, without an ErrorHandler to gracefully handle and report validation errors, this method will simply throw an exception if there are problems—possibly crashing your program! Even with a good try/catch block, there's no substitute for using an ErrorHandler for dealing with potential validation problems.

Fixing errors as they occur

In addition to the version of validate( ) that takes as input a Source, there is another version that takes both a Source and Result. The XML returned in the Result is described as possibly augmented XML; what that means in reality is that you're allowed to change the XML from the Source to produce a valid Result.

For example, there may be some common errors in XML input documents that you are willing to silently "fix," perhaps changing a namespace URI or adding an attribute with a default value. All this is possible through your ErrorHandler implementation, which can actually change the input XML document. That turns out to be a rather clumsy approach to fixing errors, though, as ErrorHandler is really intended to report errors, not fix them. A much better approach is to use the ValidatorHandler class.

Dealing with Files Directly

validate( ) will not accept as input a StreamSource (or a StreamResult for output). Further, you cannot pass in (for example) a DOMSource and a SAXResult; the input and output types must match (DOM for both or SAX for both). If you want to pass in a file, or earlier convert the input to a different type of output, use the identity transformation, detailed in "The Identity Transformation." This frees up Validator to handle validation, and only validation.

Using ValidatorHandler to customize validation processing

If you are interested in really getting to the events that underlie validation processing, you should check out the ValidatorHandler interface, which implements org. xml.sax.ContentHandler (this class is shown in Figure 7-15).

ValidatorHandler
«create»#ValidatorHandler():ValidatorHandler +setContentHandler(receiver:ContentHandler):void +getContentHandler():ContentHandler +setErrorHandler(errorHandler:ErrorHandler):void +getErrorHandler():ErrorHandler +setResourceResolver(resourceResolver:LSResourceResolver):void +getResourceResolver():LSResourceResolver +getTypeInfoProvider():TypeInfoProvider +getFeature(name:String):boolean +setFeature(name:String,value:boolean):void +setProperty(name:String,object:Object):void +getProperty(name:String):Object

Figure 7-15. By implementing ContentHandler, ValidatorHandler allows fine-grained access to the SAX event chain, as parsing and validation occurs

ValidatorHandler, by way of ContentHandler, has access to all the SAX events that occur in parsing, and allows you to (almost) directly deal with XML as it is being processed. You can easily add attributes, change values (perhaps to a new default), and even work with namespace prefixes and URIs.

 ValidatorHandler is also a great way to completely screw up your XML. Be careful how extensively you try and make changes to XML as it is being streamed; you can create errors just as easily as you can fix them.

You get access to a ValidatorHandler via the Schema object's newValidatorHandler( ) method:

```
ValidatorHandler vHandler = schema.newValidatorHandler( );
```

You can then provide a resource resolver (functioning much like an EntityResolver), and of course an ErrorHandler. What you won't find is a validate( ) method, though. When you create a ValidatorHandler, it maintains an association to the Schema it was created by. So, to ensure the handler is invoked, you need to associate the Schema with a SAXParserFactory or DocumentBuilderFactory; both provide a setSchema( ) method for just this purpose:

```
// Load up the document
DocumentBuilderFactory factory = DocumentBuilderFactory.newInstance( );

// Set up an XML Schema validator, using the supplied schema
Source schemaSource = new StreamSource(new File(args[1]));
SchemaFactory schemaFactory = SchemaFactory.newInstance(
  XMLConstants.W3C_XML_SCHEMA_NS_URI);
Schema schema = schemaFactory.newSchema(schemaSource);

// Instead of explicitly validating, assign the Schema to the factory
factory.setSchema(schema);
```

```
// Parsers from this factory will automatically validate against the
// associated schema
DocumentBuilder builder = factory.newDocumentBuilder();
Document doc = builder.parse(new File(args[0]));
```

This may seem a bit odd; you create the ValidatorHandler, and never invoke it directly, or even assign it back to the Schema (that last step—assignment to the Schema—happens implicitly when you create the ValidatorHandler). Then, you assign the Schema to a SAX or DOM factory, and never invoke the Schema directly. But, if you get in a SAX frame of mind, this all makes a lot more sense; you're letting the factories create objects that will call into your Schema (and your ValidatorHandler) as they are needed; it's then that your code has an effect.

A Big Fat Caveat About JAXP Validation

And, the bad news: JAXP validation is, at least as of this writing, buggy and quirky. Validation is new to JAXP—released in JAXP 1.3 and bundled with Java 5.0—and parsers are still adding support (and working out the bugs in that support). Remember that JAXP is largely a set of interfaces that parser vendors have to implement; Sun has the easier part of that deal (they spec out the API, provide a not-for-production reference implementation, and leave the production code to parser vendors). In any case, my tests with the latest versions of Xerces (2.6.3 and 2.7.1) were a bit flaky. Using Validator and validate( ) directly worked fine; assigning a Schema to a SAXParserFactory or DocumentBuilderFactory and initiating parsing sometimes worked well and sometimes bombed.

I suspect that many of these problems will be worked out by the time you read this; just as DOM Level 3 defines validation APIs—and recognizes it as a difficult problem—JAXP defines some pretty cool, albeit complex, interfaces for validation. Try the code samples and your own programs out, and see how they do; just be patient if everything doesn't work right away.

Pull Parsing With StAX

The two APIs we've examined thus far—SAX and DOM—take two different approaches to XML document parsing. A SAX parser notifies your code, through predefined interfaces, of various events as the parser traverses the XML document. DOM creates a tree structure in memory that is then returned to your code as one whole piece.

This chapter looks at an additional API—StAX—that uses yet a third approach for XML parsing commonly referred to as *pull parsing*. Pull parsing is similar to SAX in that your code interacts with the document as it is being read by the parser. The difference lies in how this interaction occurs. As the name implies, when you use a pull parser, your code asks the parser for the next event. Your code need not implement any special interfaces, as is necessary with SAX. As a result, code that uses a pull parser may be more concise and easier to read than the corresponding SAX code.

In addition, StAX provides a set of classes for writing XML documents, something SAX doesn't handle at all. Unlike DOM or any other tree-based parser, the document does not remain in memory while it is being built.

We will also look at an alternative pull parser API—XmlPull—which was the predecessor to StAX but continues to be useful in memory-constrained applications, specifically those that use J2ME.

StAX Basics

StAX is an acronym for Streaming API for XML. It is Java Specification Recommendation (JSR) 173, sponsored by BEA with the goal of standardizing the various pull parser implementations that had been created in the absence of a Java or W3C standard. StAX provides interfaces for parsing XML documents as well as producing them. The JSR should actually be titled "Streaming APIs for XML" because StAX encompasses two distinct APIs. The specification refers to these as the *cursor API* and the *event iterator API*. According to the specification, the objective of the cursor

API is "[t]o allow users to read and write XML as efficiently as possible," whereas for the event iterator API, it's "to be easy to use, event based, easy to extend, and allow easy pipelining." This implies a greater difference between the APIs than actually exists, as we'll see throughout this chapter.

The specific interfaces for the cursor API are XMLStreamReader and XMLStreamWriter. For the event iterator API, these interfaces are XMLEventReader and XMLEventWriter. All of these interfaces are in the package javax.xml.stream.

In the cursor API interfaces, methods on the reader or writer object itself allow the developer to obtain information or add new content to the XML document. This is referred to as the cursor API, as it is similar to how database cursors work. In the event iterator API, you obtain event objects from the reader or add event objects to the writer. This strongly typed event object contains only the methods appropriate for that type of event. In most implementations, the XMLEventReader implementation uses XMLStreamReader under the hood and, likewise, XMLEventWriter uses XMLStreamWriter.

The final release of the StAX specification, API, and JavaDocs can be downloaded from *http://jcp.org/en/jsr/detail?id=173*.

StAX Event Types

Whether using the cursor or event interfaces, StAX defines the same set of events that will occur while traversing the document. As part of the API, each of these is assigned an int. These types are defined in javax.xml.stream.XmlStreamConstants and are listed in Table 8-1.

Table 8-1. StAX event types

Event type ID	Event type name
1	START_ELEMENT
2	END_ELEMENT
3	PROCESSING_INSTRUCTION
4	CHARACTERS
5	COMMENT
6	SPACE
7	START_DOCUMENT
8	END_DOCUMENT
9	ENTITY_REFERENCE
10	ATTRIBUTE
11	DTD
12	CDATA
13	NAMESPACE
14	NOTATION_DECLARATION
15	ENTITY_DECLARATION

After reading the first few chapters of this book, the meaning of these events should be obvious. Table 8-2 contains the correlation between the events and the SAX methods we have already discussed.

Table 8-2. Correlation between StAX events and SAX handler methods

StAX event type name	SAX handler name	SAX handler method
START_ELEMENT	ContentHandler	startElement( )
END_ELEMENT	ContentHandler	endElement( )
PROCESSING_INSTRUCTION	ContentHandler	processingInstruction( )
CHARACTERS	ContentHandler	characters( )
COMMENT	LexicalHandler	comment( )
SPACE	ContentHandler	ignorableWhitespace( )
START_DOCUMENT	ContentHandler	startDocument( )
END_DOCUMENT	ContentHandler	endDocument( )
ENTITY_REFERENCE	ContentHandler	skippedEntity( )
ATTRIBUTE	n/a	n/a
DTD	LexicalHandler	startDTD()/endDTD( )
CDATA	n/a	n/a
NAMESPACE	ContentHandler	startPrefixMapping( )
NOTATION_DECLARATION	DTDHandler	notationDecl( )
ENTITY_DECLARATION	DTDHandler	unparsedEntityDecl( )

Obtaining a StAX Implementation

StAX is simply an API specification, not an implementation. You can write and compile code using only the JAR included with the specification. However, to run the compiled code, you'll need a StAX implementation. As of Java SE 6, a StAX implementation is included. For prior versions of the JRE, you'll need to download an implementation. The reference implementation for StAX is available at *http://stax.codehaus.org*. From this web site, you can download two JAR files. One contains the API interfaces and classes; it is the same JAR available via the JSR web site. The second contains the actual reference implementation. As of the time of this writing, the latest API JAR was *stax-api-1.0.1.jar* and the latest implementation JAR was *stax-1.2.0_rc2-dev.jar*.

For production applications, I strongly recommend the Sun Java Streaming XML Parser (SJSXP) instead of the reference implementation. SJSXP is available either from *https://sjsxp.dev.java.net* or as part of the Java Web Services Developer Pack (JWSDP), downloadable from *http://java.sun.com/webservices/jwsdp*. We'll talk more about JWSDP in Chapter 11.

StAX Factories

To obtain an instance of any of the four primary StAX interfaces mentioned above, you'll use one of two factory classes: javax.xml.stream.XMLInputFactory and javax. xml.stream.XMLOutputFactory. To obtain an instance of the factory class, call the static method newInstance( ) on the abstract class XMLInputFactory.

```
XMLInputFactory inputFactory = XMLInputFactory.newInstance( );
```

The following steps determine which implementation of StAX is returned by the newInstance( ) method:

1. Check the javax.xml.stream.XMLInputFactory system property.

2. Look for a file named *xml.stream.properties* in the *lib* subdirectory of the JRE. This file is in the standard properties file syntax and defines the property javax. xml.stream.XMLInputFactory.

3. Look for a resource named *META-INF/services/javax.xml.stream.XMLInputFactory* in the classpath.

 If these steps look familiar, that's because it's the same process used by JAXP.

In general, an implementation's jar file will provide the *META-INF/services* file. The first two options are useful when you want to provide your own implementation of the interfaces or if you have multiple implementations in your classpath and need to be explicit about which one to use.

Parsing with StAX

Reading a XML document with the two StAX reader interfaces is relatively similar. Both XMLStreamReader and XMLEventReader provide an interface similar to java.util. Iterator. XMLEventReader extends Iterator, whereas XMLStreamReader has methods named hasNext( ) and next( ), just as Iterator does, but the next( ) method returns an int, not an Object. Because of this relation to Iterator, the primary use of either interface looks like one of the event loops in Examples 8-1 and 8-2.

Example 8-1. Basic XMLStreamReader event loop

```
while (streamReader.hasNext( )) {
    int eventTypeID = streamReader.next( );
    // do something
}
```

Example 8-2. Basic XMLEventReader event loop

```
while (eventReader.hasNext( ) {
    XMLEvent event = (XMLEvent) eventReader.next( );
    // do something with event
}
```

Creating a Reader

As described above, `javax.xml.stream.XMLInputFactory` is used to create instances of `XMLStreamReader` and `XMLEventReader`. `XMLInputFactory` has six different overloaded methods named `createXMLStreamReader( )` for creating `XMLStreamReader( )` instances and seven different overloaded methods named `createXMLEventReader( )` for creating `XMLEventReader` instances (the seventh being to create an `XMLEventReader` that wraps an already-created `XMLStreamReader`). The parameters that can be passed to these create methods are:

- A `java.io.InputStream`
- A `java.io.InputStream` and a character encoding
- A `java.io.InputStream` and a system ID to use for resolving relative URIs
- A `java.io.Reader`
- A `java.io.Reader` and a system ID to use for resolving relative URIs
- A `javax.xml.transform.Source`

The last of these, `javax.xml.transform.Source`, is optional. If an implementation does not provide support for `Source` inputs, both `createXMLEventReader( )` and `createXMLStreamReader( )` will throw a `java.lang.UnsupportedOperationException`. One case of an implementation that does not support `Source` inputs is the reference implementation.

If you already have a `String` object in memory containing your XML document, you can use `java.io.StringReader` as follows:

```
// I have the document as a String named documentAsString
StringReader stringReader = new StringReader(documentAsString);
XMLInputFactory inputFactory = XMLInputFactory.newInstance( );
XmlStreamReader reader = inputFactory.createXMLStreamReader(stringReader);
```

By default, `XMLInputFactory` will create `XMLStreamReader` and `XMLEventReader` instances that are nonvalidating and namespace aware. These defaults can be changed by calling the `setProperty( )` method on `XMLInputFactory`. We'll discuss this later in the "Factory Properties" section.

XMLStreamReader

`XMLStreamReader` is the parsing interface from the cursor API. As mentioned above, it does not extend `java.util.Iterator`, but does look like it. Like `Iterator`, you call hasNext( ) to determine if there are more events to process in the document. A UML diagram for the full XMLStreamReader interface is in Figure 8-1.

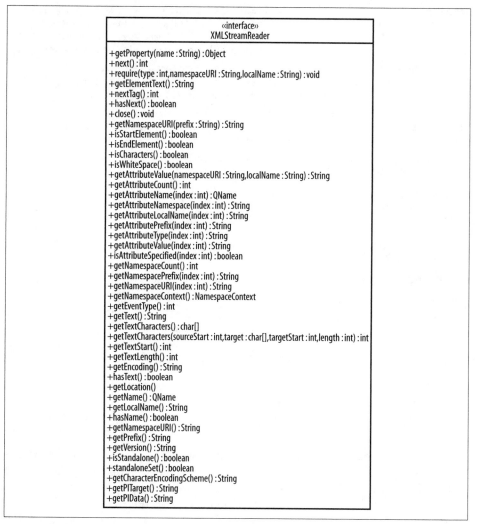

Figure 8-1. The XMLStreamReader interface

That's a lot of methods, but in practice, you'll use relatively few of these. Most important, not all of methods can be called for every event. For example, if you try to call getText( ), which returns the text content of an event on an END_ELEMENT event, a java.lang.IllegalStateException will be thrown because, to put it simply, you are in an illegal state to call getText( ). Table 8-3 lists the available methods for each event type.

Table 8-3. Available XMLStreamReader methods by event type

Event type	Methods available
All event types	getProperty( ),hasNext( ),require( ),close( ), getNamespaceURI( ),isStartElement( ),isEndElement( ), isCharacters( ),isWhiteSpace( ),getNamespaceContext( ), getEventType( ),getLocation( ),hasText( ),hasName( )
START_ELEMENT	next( ),getName( ),getLocalName( ),hasName( ), getPrefix( ),nextTag( ),getAttributeXXX( ), isAttributeSpecified( ),getNamespaceXXX( ), getElementText( )
END_ELEMENT	next( ),getName( ),getLocalName( ),hasName( ), getPrefix( ),nextTag( ),getNamespaceXXX( )
PROCESSING_INSTRUCTION	next( ),getPITarget( ),getPIData( ),nextTag( )
CHARACTERS	next( ),getTextXXX( ),nextTag( )
COMMENT	next( ),getTextXXX( ),nextTag( )
SPACE	next( ),getTextXXX( ),nextTag( )
START_DOCUMENT	next( ),getEncoding( ),getVersion( ),isStandalone( ), standaloneSet( ),getCharacterEncodingScheme( ), nextTag( )
END_DOCUMENT	next( ),getText( ),nextTag( )
ENTITY_REFERENCE	next( ),getLocalName( ),getText( ),nextTag( )
ATTRIBUTE	next( ),nextTag( ),getAttributeXXX( ), isAttributeSpecified( )
DTD	next( ),getText( ),nextTag( )
CDATA	next( ),getTextXXX( ),nextTag( )
NAMESPACE	next( ),nextTag( ),getNamespaceXXX( )
NOTATION_DECLARATION	Not defined
ENTITY_DECLARATION	Not defined

In Chapter 3, we built a Java application that created a tree view of an XML document. We had a class called SAXTreeViewer that extended javax.swing.JFrame and had another class called JTreeHandler that implemented two SAX interfaces ContentHandler and ErrorHandler. SAXTreeViewer created the tree's model, instantiated JTreeHandler and a SAX parser, and then asked the SAX parser to parse a document. Meanwhile, JTreeHandler was responsible for receiving the parser events and creating nodes in the tree model. To do the same thing with the StAX cursor API, let's start by using much of the same boilerplate code from Chapter 3. Example 8-3 contains the boilerplate code that creates the Swing components we'll use to display our tree as well as the code to obtain the XMLStreamReader implementation.

Example 8-3. StAXStreamTreeViewer

```java
package javaxml3;

import java.awt.BorderLayout;
import java.io.File;
import java.io.FileInputStream;
import java.io.FileNotFoundException;

import javax.swing.JFrame;
import javax.swing.JScrollPane;
import javax.swing.JTree;
import javax.swing.tree.DefaultMutableTreeNode;
import javax.swing.tree.DefaultTreeModel;
import javax.xml.stream.XMLInputFactory;
import javax.xml.stream.XMLStreamConstants;
import javax.xml.stream.XMLStreamException;
import javax.xml.stream.XMLStreamReader;

public class StAXStreamTreeViewer extends JFrame {
    /** The base tree to render */
    private JTree jTree;

    /** Tree model to use */
    DefaultTreeModel defaultTreeModel;

    public StAXStreamTreeViewer() {
        // Handle Swing setup
        super("StAX Tree Viewer");
        setSize(600, 450);
    }

    public void init(File file) throws XMLStreamException, FileNotFoundException {
        DefaultMutableTreeNode base = new DefaultMutableTreeNode(
                "XML Document: " + file.getAbsolutePath());

        // Build the tree model
        defaultTreeModel = new DefaultTreeModel(base);
        jTree = new JTree(defaultTreeModel);

        // Construct the tree hierarchy
        buildTree(defaultTreeModel, base, file);

        // Display the results
        getContentPane().add(new JScrollPane(jTree), BorderLayout.CENTER);
    }

    // Swing-related variables and methods, including
    // setting up a JTree and basic content pane

    public static void main(String[] args) {
        try {
            if (args.length != 1) {
                System.out.println("Usage: java javaxml3.StAXStreamTreeViewer "
```

Example 8-3. StAXStreamTreeViewer (continued)

```
                            + "[XML Document]");
                return;
            }
            StAXStreamTreeViewer viewer = new StAXStreamTreeViewer();
            File f = new File(args[0]);

            viewer.init(f);
            viewer.setVisible(true);
        } catch (Exception e) {
            e.printStackTrace();
        }
    }

    public void buildTree(DefaultTreeModel treeModel,
            DefaultMutableTreeNode current, File file)
            throws XMLStreamException, FileNotFoundException {
        FileInputStream inputStream = new FileInputStream(file);
        XMLInputFactory inputFactory = XMLInputFactory.newInstance();
        XMLStreamReader reader = inputFactory
            .createXMLStreamReader(inputStream);


        // parse away!
    }

}
```

The START_DOCUMENT event

When you create an XMLStreamReader instance, the reader positions itself at the start of the document. This is represented by the START_DOCUMENT event. As a result, if we were to insert:

```
        System.out.println(reader.getEventType());
```

at the end of the buildTree( ) method in Example 8-3, the number 7 will be printed to the console, as 7 is the value of XMLStreamConstants.START_DOCUMENT. A quick glance back at Table 8-3 shows that we can get a few interesting bits of information about this document's declaration that weren't available in the SAX version:

```
    public void buildTree(DefaultTreeModel treeModel,
            DefaultMutableTreeNode current, File file)
            throws XMLStreamException, FileNotFoundException {
        FileInputStream inputStream = new FileInputStream(file);
        XMLInputFactory inputFactory = XMLInputFactory.newInstance();
        XMLStreamReader reader = inputFactory
                .createXMLStreamReader(inputStream);

        addStartDocumentNodes(reader, current);

        // parse rest of document
    }
```

```
private void addStartDocumentNodes(XMLStreamReader reader,
        DefaultMutableTreeNode current) {
    DefaultMutableTreeNode version = new DefaultMutableTreeNode(
            "XML Version: " + reader.getVersion());
    current.add(version);

    DefaultMutableTreeNode standalone = new DefaultMutableTreeNode(
            "Standalone? " + reader.isStandalone());
    current.add(standalone);

    DefaultMutableTreeNode standaloneSet = new DefaultMutableTreeNode(
            "Was Standalone Set? " + reader.standaloneSet());
    current.add(standaloneSet);

    DefaultMutableTreeNode encoding = new DefaultMutableTreeNode(
            "Encoding:  " + reader.getEncoding());
    current.add(encoding);

    DefaultMutableTreeNode declaredEncoding = new DefaultMutableTreeNode(
            "Declared Encoding Scheme: "
                    + reader.getCharacterEncodingScheme());
    current.add(declaredEncoding);
}
```

Note that through these methods, you are able to discover the standalone and encoding values from the XML declaration and, in addition, which of these values were in the declaration. You may also run across XML files that do not have a declaration at all. In these cases, the result of getVersion( ) will be null.

If we have an XML document with this declaration:

```
<?xml version="1.0" encoding="ISO-8859-1" standalone="yes" ?>
```

The output of StAXStreamTreeViewer looks like Figure 8-2.

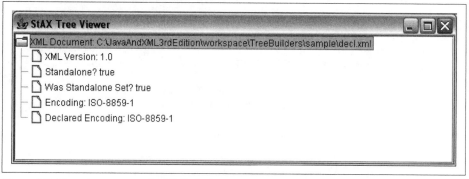

Figure 8-2. Tree viewer output for XML declaration

Parsing the rest of the document

For the purpose of this example, we'll parse the actual document inside a while loop. As long as hasNext( ) returns true, there is more of the document to be parsed. Inside this loop, the document cursor is advanced through the document by calls to the next( ) method. If next( ) is called when the cursor is at the end of the document, an IllegalStateException is thrown. The result of the call to next( ) is the event type ID.

```java
private void parseRestOfDocument(XMLStreamReader reader,
        DefaultMutableTreeNode current) throws XMLStreamException {

    while (reader.hasNext()) {
        int type = reader.next();
        System.out.println(type);
    }
}
```

This method produces a sequence of numbers. The exact sequence depends upon the XML document you are parsing. The simplest document, one containing a single element produces a 1 for the START_ELEMENT event, then a 2 for the END_ELEMENT event, and finally an 8 for the END_DOCUMENT event. For our example application, we want to create a new tree node on START_ELEMENT events. These nodes should contain a sub-node for the namespace, if any, of the element as well as subnodes for each attribute. On an END_ELEMENT event, we need to walk back up the tree so that the parent of the current node is the new current node.

To provide different handling for each event type, we will use the switch construct. Our new parseRestOfDocument( ) method is in Example 8-4.

Example 8-4. New parseRestOfDocument() method

```java
private void parseRestOfDocument(XMLStreamReader reader,
        DefaultMutableTreeNode current) throws XMLStreamException {

    while (reader.hasNext()) {
        int type = reader.next();
        switch (type) {
        case XMLStreamConstants.START_ELEMENT:

            DefaultMutableTreeNode element = new DefaultMutableTreeNode(
                    "Element: " + reader.getLocalName());
            current.add(element);
            current = element;

            // Determine namespace
            if (reader.getNamespaceURI() != null) {
                String prefix = reader.getPrefix();
                if (prefix == null) {
                    prefix = "[None]";
                }
                DefaultMutableTreeNode namespace = new DefaultMutableTreeNode(
                        "Namespace: prefix = '" + prefix + "', URI = '"
```

Example 8-4. New parseRestOfDocument( ) method (continued)

```
                              + reader.getNamespaceURI( ) + "'");
          current.add(namespace);
      }

      if (reader.getAttributeCount( ) > 0) {
          for (int i = 0; i < reader.getAttributeCount( ); i++) {
              DefaultMutableTreeNode attr = new DefaultMutableTreeNode(
                      "Attribute (name = '"
                          + reader.getAttributeLocalName(i)
                          + "', value = '"
                          + reader.getAttributeValue(i) + "')");
              String attURI = reader.getAttributeNamespace(i);
              if (attURI != null) {
                  String attPrefix = reader.getAttributePrefix(i);
                  if (attPrefix == null || attPrefix.equals("")) {
                      attPrefix = "[None]";
                  }
                  DefaultMutableTreeNode attNs = new DefaultMutableTreeNode(
                          "Namespace: prefix = '" + attPrefix
                              + "', URI = '" + attURI + "'");
                  attr.add(attNs);
              }
              current.add(attr);
          }
      }

      break;
  case XMLStreamConstants.END_ELEMENT:
      current = (DefaultMutableTreeNode) current.getParent( );
      break;
  default:
      System.out.println(type);
  }
}
}
```

The node manipulation code is relatively similar to that used in the SAX version from Chapter 3. The main difference is in how the node data is populated. When creating the element node, we set its title to be "Element:" followed by the local name of the element. To get the local name, we call getLocalName( ) on the reader object itself, we call getNamespaceURI( ) to get the namespace URI of the element, and so on. Figure 8-3 shows the result of this newly added code when parsing the default *web.xml* file from the Apache Tomcat servlet container. You will also still see some event IDs being written to the console for events other than START_ELEMENT and END_ELEMENT. At the minimum, this will be an 8 for the END_DOCUMENT event.

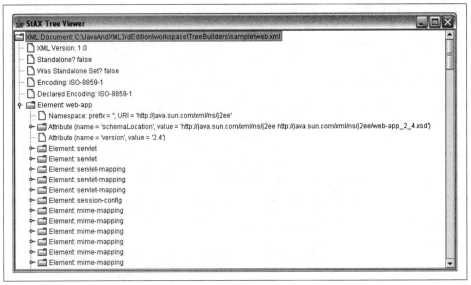

Figure 8-3. Tree viewer output with namespaces

 You may be asking why there are events named NAMESPACE and ATTRIBUTE defined in Table 8-1 since we're able to get the namespace and attribute information from the various getNamespaceXXX( ) and getAttributeXXX( ) methods on the reader object. In fact, when parsing a full document, you'll never run across the NAMESPACE and ATTRIBUTE events. They exist because in some cases, the attribute may be returned directly, outside the context of an element. The only example of this given in the StAX specification is XPath. You also use these events when creating documents with the writer interfaces as discussed in the "Document Output with StAX" section later in this chapter.

Getting character data

The CHARACTERS and CDATA events occur when character data is encountered in the document. Retrieving the character data as a String is done by simply calling getText( ) on the reader. There are also methods for retrieving this data as a character array.

```
case XMLStreamConstants.CHARACTERS:
case XMLStreamConstants.CDATA:
    DefaultMutableTreeNode data = new DefaultMutableTreeNode(
            "Character Data: '" + reader.getText() + "'");
    current.add(data);
    break;
```

Whitespace handling

An event called SPACE occurs when the parser encounters ignorable whitespace in the document. If you do not have a DTD for your XML document, the parser cannot determine which whitespace is ignorable and which is significant. As a result, without a DTD, all whitespace results in CHARACTERS events, but with a DTD, the SPACE event occurs as appropriate. For example, the XML document in Example 8-5, without a DTD, will result in Figure 8-4.

Example 8-5. XML document with whitespace

```
<?xml version="1.0"?>
<person>
  <name>
    <first_name>Alan</first_name>
    <last_name>Turing</last_name>
  </name>
  <profession>computer scientist</profession>
  <profession>mathematician</profession>
  <profession>cryptographer</profession>
</person>
```

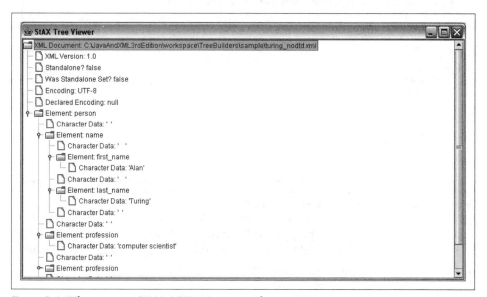

Figure 8-4. Whitespace as CHARACTERS events without a DTD

But when we provide an internal DTD that strictly limits where whitespace is significant (inside the first_name, last_name, and profession elements), as in Example 8-6, we get SPACE events for the ignorable whitespace, leading to the output displayed in Figure 8-5.

Example 8-6. XML document with internal DTD defining ignorable whitespace

```
<?xml version="1.0"?>
<!DOCTYPE person [
  <!ELEMENT first_name (#PCDATA)>
  <!ELEMENT last_name (#PCDATA)>
  <!ELEMENT profession (#PCDATA)>
  <!ELEMENT name (first_name, last_name)>
  <!ELEMENT person (name, profession*)>
]>
<person>
  <name>
    <first_name>Alan</first_name>
    <last_name>Turing</last_name>
  </name>
  <profession>computer scientist</profession>
  <profession>mathematician</profession>
  <profession>cryptographer</profession>
</person>
```

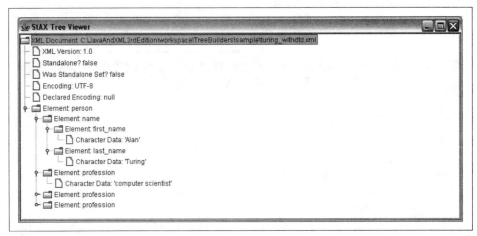

Figure 8-5. Whitespace as SPACE events with a DTD

In addition to the cleaner output, you will see the number 6 (the event ID for SPACE) appear in the console. To get rid of this, we can add a new case for the SPACE event:

```
case XMLStreamConstants.SPACE:
    // let's ignore this
    break;
```

Because there are frequently cases in which no DTD is defined but the document contains a significant amount of whitespace you know you can ignore (even if the XML specification thinks you can't ignore it), StAX provides an easy-to-use mechanism to skip a CHARACTERS element if it contains only whitespace. If we replace the section of parseRestOfDocument( ) that handles the CHARACTERS event with the code in Example 8-7, we will get the same output for Examples 8-5 and 8-6.

Example 8-7. New CHARACTERS handling code

```
case XMLStreamConstants.CHARACTERS:
    if (!reader.isWhiteSpace()) {
        DefaultMutableTreeNode data = new DefaultMutableTreeNode(
                "Character Data: '" + reader.getText() + "'");
        current.add(data);
    }
    break;
```

Two more events

The last two events to mention are COMMENT and DTD. These are relatively self-explanatory. In both cases, you can use the getText( ) method to return the content of the comment or DTD. The content of the DTD will be the full DOCTYPE block. If the document contains a reference to an external DTD, the content will be along the lines of `<!DOCTYPE contacts SYSTEM "name.dtd">`, whereas if the DTD is internal, such as in the example above, the content would be a String containing the following:

```
<!DOCTYPE person [
  <!ELEMENT first_name (#PCDATA)>
  <!ELEMENT last_name (#PCDATA)>
  <!ELEMENT profession (#PCDATA)>
  <!ELEMENT name (first_name, last_name)>
  <!ELEMENT person (name, profession*)>
]>
```

XMLEventReader

XMLEventReader is the parsing interface from the event iterator API. Unlike XMLStreamReader, it does extend java.util.Iterator. The full XMLEventReader interface is contained in Figure 8-6.

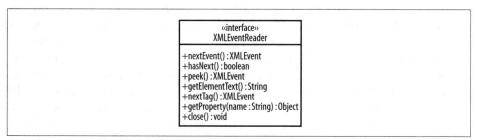

Figure 8-6. The XMLEventReader interface

As you can see, this is a much simpler interface then XMLStreamReader. This is because all of the access methods (getLocalName( ), getAttributeXXX( ), getNamespaceXXX( ), etc.) are encapsulated in the XMLEvent object. There is one cursor-type method—getElementText( )—which, as should be expected, throws an IllegalStateException if the current event isn't a START_ELEMENT event. Other than this, all document access is done through a subclass of XMLEvent. XMLEvent is a base interface from which the StAX API defines 12 interfaces that extend XMLEvent. The correspondence between these interfaces and the event types defined in Table 8-1 are listed in Table 8-4. All interfaces are in the package javax.xml.stream.events.

Table 8-4. Event interfaces

Event type name	Event interface name
START_ELEMENT	StartElement
END_ELEMENT	EndElement
PROCESSING_INSTRUCTION	ProcessingInstruction
CHARACTERS	Characters
COMMENT	Comment
SPACE	Characters
START_DOCUMENT	StartDocument
END_DOCUMENT	EndDocument
ENTITY_REFERENCE	EntityReference
ATTRIBUTE	Attribute
DTD	DTD
CDATA	Characters
NAMESPACE	n/a
NOTATION_DECLARATION	NotationDeclaration
ENTITY_DECLARATION	EntityDeclaration

As you can see, the Characters interface can represent three different events: CHARACTERS, SPACE, and CDATA. To differentiate between them, the Characters interface defines methods called isCData( ) and isIgnorableWhitespace( ).

In general, these interfaces define methods similar to those defined on the XMLStreamReader interface. However, each interface defines only the methods appropriate to the event it represents. As a result, it's nearly impossible to throw an IllegalStateException, because the invalid methods simply don't exist. Other than simple name changes (for example: XMLStreamReader.getPITarget( ) maps to ProcessingInstruction.getTarget( )), the most significant difference between the methods on XMLStreamReader and the methods exposed by the various event interfaces is that you are required to use javax.xml.namespace.QName. As we saw above, XMLStreamReader defined a method called getName( ) that returned the QName for an element and also methods called getLocalName( ), getPrefix( ), and getNamespaceURI( ). In the StartElement interface, only getName( ) is defined and you must call getLocalPart( ), getPrefix( ), and getNamespaceURI( ) on the resulting QName object to read these values.

When you obtain an instance of XMLEvent through a call to XMLEventReader.nextEvent( ), you can determine the type of event through three different mechanisms:

1. Call XMLEvent.getEventType( ) and compare to one of the values from XMLStreamConstants.

2. Call one of the is methods on XMLEvent, such as isStartElement( ).

3. Use the instanceof operator.

For example, these three blocks of code do exactly the same thing:

```
// Block one - using ==
if (event.getEventType( ) == XMLStreamConstant.START_ELEMENT) {
    System.out.println("I'm a start element event!");
}

// Block two - using isStartElement
if (event.isStartElement( )) {
    System.out.println("I'm a start element event!");
}

// Block three - using instanceof
if (event instanceof StartElement) {
    System.out.println("I'm a start element event!");
}
```

These are interchangeable, and which you use is largely a matter of style. The one exception to this is if you want to use the switch construct. In this context, you must use the getEventType( ) method.

Example 8-8 contains the StAX Tree Viewer example application rewritten to use XMLEventReader rather than XMLStreamReader, with the same functionality as the XMLStreamReader version.

Example 8-8. StAXEventTreeViewer

```
package javaxml3;

import java.awt.BorderLayout;
import java.io.File;
import java.io.FileInputStream;
import java.io.FileNotFoundException;
import java.util.Iterator;

import javax.swing.JFrame;
import javax.swing.JScrollPane;
import javax.swing.JTree;
import javax.swing.tree.DefaultMutableTreeNode;
import javax.swing.tree.DefaultTreeModel;
import javax.xml.namespace.QName;
import javax.xml.stream.XMLEventReader;
import javax.xml.stream.XMLInputFactory;
import javax.xml.stream.XMLStreamConstants;
import javax.xml.stream.XMLStreamException;
```

Example 8-8. StAXEventTreeViewer (continued)

```java
import javax.xml.stream.events.Attribute;
import javax.xml.stream.events.Characters;
import javax.xml.stream.events.DTD;
import javax.xml.stream.events.StartDocument;
import javax.xml.stream.events.StartElement;
import javax.xml.stream.events.XMLEvent;

import org.xml.sax.InputSource;

public class StAXEventTreeViewer extends JFrame {
    /** The base tree to render */
    private JTree jTree;

    /** Tree model to use */
    DefaultTreeModel defaultTreeModel;

    public StAXEventTreeViewer() {
        // Handle Swing setup
        super("StAX Tree Viewer");
        setSize(600, 450);
    }

    public void init(File file) throws XMLStreamException,
            FileNotFoundException {
        DefaultMutableTreeNode base = new DefaultMutableTreeNode(
                "XML Document: " + file.getAbsolutePath());

        // Build the tree model
        defaultTreeModel = new DefaultTreeModel(base);
        jTree = new JTree(defaultTreeModel);

        // Construct the tree hierarchy
        buildTree(defaultTreeModel, base, file);

        // Display the results
        getContentPane().add(new JScrollPane(jTree), BorderLayout.CENTER);
    }

    // Swing-related variables and methods, including
    // setting up a JTree and basic content pane

    public static void main(String[] args) {
        try {
            if (args.length != 1) {
                System.out.println("Usage: java javaxml3.StAXEventTreeViewer "
                        + "[XML Document]");
                return;
            }
            StAXEventTreeViewer viewer = new StAXEventTreeViewer();
            File f = new File(args[0]);

            viewer.init(f);
```

Example 8-8. StAXEventTreeViewer (continued)

```
            viewer.setVisible(true);
        } catch (Exception e) {
            e.printStackTrace();
        }
    }

    public void buildTree(DefaultTreeModel treeModel,
            DefaultMutableTreeNode current, File file)
            throws XMLStreamException, FileNotFoundException {

        XMLInputFactory inputFactory = XMLInputFactory.newInstance();
        XMLEventReader reader = inputFactory
                .createXMLEventReader(new FileInputStream(file));
        while (reader.hasNext()) {
            XMLEvent event = reader.nextEvent();
            switch (event.getEventType()) {
            case XMLStreamConstants.START_DOCUMENT:
                StartDocument startDocument = (StartDocument) event;
                DefaultMutableTreeNode version = new DefaultMutableTreeNode(
                        "XML Version: " + startDocument.getVersion());
                current.add(version);

                DefaultMutableTreeNode standalone = new DefaultMutableTreeNode(
                        "Standalone? " + startDocument.isStandalone());
                current.add(standalone);

                DefaultMutableTreeNode standaloneSet = new DefaultMutableTreeNode(
                        "Was Standalone Set? " + startDocument.standaloneSet());
                current.add(standaloneSet);

                DefaultMutableTreeNode encoding = new DefaultMutableTreeNode(
                        "Was Encoding Set? " + startDocument.encodingSet());
                current.add(encoding);

                DefaultMutableTreeNode decEnc = new DefaultMutableTreeNode(
                        "Declared Encoding: "
                                + startDocument.getCharacterEncodingScheme());
                current.add(decEnc);
                break;
            case XMLStreamConstants.START_ELEMENT:
                StartElement startElement = (StartElement) event;
                QName elementName = startElement.getName();

                DefaultMutableTreeNode element = new DefaultMutableTreeNode(
                        "Element: " + elementName.getLocalPart());
                current.add(element);
                current = element;

                if (!elementName.getNamespaceURI().equals("")) {
                    String prefix = elementName.getPrefix();
                    if (prefix.equals("")) {
                        prefix = "[None]";
                    }
```

Example 8-8. StAXEventTreeViewer (continued)

```
                    DefaultMutableTreeNode namespace = new DefaultMutableTreeNode(
                            "Namespace: prefix = '" + prefix + "', URI = '"
                                    + elementName.getNamespaceURI( ) + "'");
                    current.add(namespace);
                }

                for (Iterator it = startElement.getAttributes(); it.hasNext();) {
                    Attribute attr = (Attribute) it.next( );
                    DefaultMutableTreeNode attribute = new DefaultMutableTreeNode(
                            "Attribute (name = '"
                                    + attr.getName().getLocalPart( )
                                    + "', value = '" + attr.getValue() + "')");
                    String attURI = attr.getName().getNamespaceURI( );
                    if (!attURI.equals("")) {
                        String attPrefix = attr.getName().getPrefix( );
                        if (attPrefix.equals("")) {
                            attPrefix = "[None]";
                        }
                        DefaultMutableTreeNode attNs = new DefaultMutableTreeNode(
                                "Namespace: prefix = '" + attPrefix
                                        + "', URI = '" + attURI + "'");
                        attribute.add(attNs);
                    }
                    current.add(attribute);
                }
                break;
            case XMLStreamConstants.END_ELEMENT:
                current = (DefaultMutableTreeNode) current.getParent( );
                break;
            case XMLStreamConstants.CHARACTERS:
                Characters characters = (Characters) event;
                if (!characters.isIgnorableWhiteSpace( )
                        && !characters.isWhiteSpace( )) {
                    String data = characters.getData( );
                    if (data.length( ) != 0) {
                        DefaultMutableTreeNode chars = new DefaultMutableTreeNode(
                                "Character Data: '" + characters.getData( )
                                        + "'");
                        current.add(chars);
                    }
                }
                break;
            case XMLStreamConstants.DTD:
                DTD dtde = (DTD) event;
                DefaultMutableTreeNode dtd = new DefaultMutableTreeNode(
                        "DTD: '" + dtde.getDocumentTypeDeclaration( ) + "'");
                current.add(dtd);
            default:
                System.out.println(event.getClass().getName( ));
            }
        }
    }
}
```

XMLEventReader advantages

The difference between StAXEventTreeViewer and StAXStreamTreeViewer is largely cosmetic. The event iterator API becomes significantly more useful when you want to encapsulate your event processing code. To write code, such as that in Example 8-9, that calls a method to process an event with XMLStreamReader, you have to pass the reader itself to the event processing method.

Example 8-9. Encapsulation problem with XMLStreamReader

```
1 // create an instance of XMLStreamReader and call it reader
2
3 while (reader.hasNext( )) {
4    int eventTypeID = reader.next( );
5    if (eventTypeID == XMLStreamConstants.START_ELEMENT) {
6        if (reader.hasNext( )) {
7            processStartElement(reader);
8            eventTypeID = reader.next( );
9            System.out.println("Event Type ID following START_ELEMENT is "
10                   + eventTypeID);
11               processAfterStartElement(reader);
12        } else {
13               processStartElement(reader);
14        }
15    } else {
16        processOther (reader);
17    }
18}
```

This creates a simple problem—we have no way of ensuring that the processing methods don't change the state of the reader. In Example 8-9, we assume processStartElement( ) won't call next( ) on the XMLStreamReader instance. If it does, then the result of the call to next( ) on line 8 will not be the event type ID for the event following the START_ELEMENT event. What's worse, the processStartElement( ) method could advance the cursor to the end of the document, in which case the call to next( ) on line 8 would throw a java.util.NoSuchElementException. Although this assumption can be documented, it cannot be enforced at compile time.

An implementation of this using XMLEventReader avoids this issue entirely because it passes XMLEvent objects to the event processing methods, as seen in Example 8-10. Since they don't have a reference to the reader object, there is no way for them to change the reader's state.

Example 8-10. Encapsulation with XMLEventReader

```
while (reader.hasNext( )) {
    XMLEvent event = reader.nextEvent( );
    if (event.isStartElement) {
        if (reader.hasNext( )) {
            processStartElement(event);
            event = reader.nextEvent( );
```

Example 8-10. Encapsulation with XMLEventReader (continued)

```
            System.out.println("Event Type ID following START_ELEMENT is "
                + event.getEventType());
            processAfterStartElement(event);
    } else {
        processOther(event)
    }
}
```

Other Traversal Options

In addition to traversing the XML document event by event using the next( ) and nextEvent( ) methods, StAX defines a few additional methods for traversing an XML document. These complement, rather than replace, the next( ) and nextEvent( ) methods. These methods are nextTag( ), require( ), and peek( ).

nextTag( )

The first of these methods, nextTag( ), is defined for both XMLStreamReader and XMLEventReader. For XMLStreamReader, nextTag( ) advances the cursor past any "insignificant" events until it reaches the next START_ELEMENT or END_ELEMENT event. For XMLEventReader, the same advancement occurs, and the new current event is returned. The StAX JavaDocs define insignificant events as SPACE, COMMENT, and PROCESSING_INSTRUCTION events as well as CHARACTERS or CDATA events that are composed only of whitespace. If a CHARACTERS or CDATA event is encountered that contains something other than whitespace, an XMLStreamException is thrown. This is helpful when processing part of an XML document in a linear, as opposed to looping, fashion. To obtain the text within the first_name element from Example 8-11 without using nextTag( ) would look something like Example 8-12.

Example 8-11. Person XML document

```
<?xml version="1.0"?>
<person>
  <name>
    <first_name>Alan</first_name>
    <last_name>Turing</last_name>
  </name>
  <profession>computer scientist</profession>
  <profession>mathematician</profession>
  <profession>cryptographer</profession>
</person>
```

Example 8-12. Person parsingwith next()

```
package javaxml3;

import java.io.File;
import java.io.FileInputStream;
```

Example 8-12. Person parsingwith next() (continued)

```java
import javax.xml.stream.XMLInputFactory;
import javax.xml.stream.XMLStreamReader;

public class NextExample {

    public static void main(String[] args) throws Exception {
        if (args.length != 1) {
            System.out.println("Usage: java javaxml3.NextExample "
                    + "[XML Document]");
            return;
        }
        File file = new File(args[0]);

        XMLInputFactory inputFactory = XMLInputFactory.newInstance();
        XMLStreamReader reader = inputFactory
                .createXMLStreamReader(new FileInputStream(file));

        int eventTypeID = reader.next();

        // skip past any initial whitespace
        while (reader.getEventType() == 6)
            reader.next();

        // the cursor is now at the person start element

        eventTypeID = reader.next();
        // the cursor is now at the whitespace between contact and name

        eventTypeID = reader.next();
        // the cursor is now at the name start element

        eventTypeID = reader.next();
        // the cursor is now at the whitespace between name and first_name

        eventTypeID = reader.next();
        // the cursor is now at the first_name start element

        eventTypeID = reader.next();
        // the cursor should now be at the text within the first_name elemnt
        System.out.println("Hello " + reader.getText());
    }
}
```

There's an inconsistency between various StAX implementations that is being accommodated in Example 8-12: some implementations report a SPACE event for the whitespace between the XML declaration and the start of the document's content, which could be a comment, processing instruction, or (most commonly) an element. The specification is unfortunately vague on this point.

The code is more brittle than it should be. Adding a comment or processing instruction anywhere before the first_name element would result in either the wrong text being output (a newline and four spaces in this case) or a ClassCastException. Clearly we can do better. Using nextTag( ) eliminates some of the calls to next( ) and increases our code's ability to ignore comments and processing instructions. The rewritten class is in Example 8-13.

Example 8-13. Person parsing with nextTag()

```java
package javaxml3;

import java.io.File;
import java.io.FileInputStream;

import javax.xml.stream.XMLInputFactory;
import javax.xml.stream.XMLStreamReader;

public class NextTagExample {

    public static void main(String[] args) throws Exception {
        if (args.length != 1) {
            System.out
                    .println("Usage: java NextTagExample " + "[XML Document]");
            return;
        }
        File file = new File(args[0]);

        XMLInputFactory inputFactory = XMLInputFactory.newInstance();
        XMLStreamReader reader = inputFactory
                .createXMLStreamReader(new FileInputStream(file));

        int eventTypeID = reader.nextTag();
        // the cursor is now at the person start element

        eventTypeID = reader.nextTag();
        // the cursor is now at the name start element

        eventTypeID = reader.nextTag();
        // the cursor is now at the first_name start element

        eventTypeID = reader.next();
        // the cursor should now be at the text within the first_name elemnt
        System.out.println("Hello " + reader.getText());
    }
}
```

This code is still too error-prone. If the order of the first_name and last_name elements were reversed, we would just output the value of the last_name element. All we've done is output the text of the third element in the document. We can use require( ) to ensure that the third element is the correct one.

require( )

XMLStreamReader defines a method named require( ) that compares the cursor's position within the document to a set of expected values. If the cursor's position does not match all of the expected values, a javax.xml.stream.XMLStreamException is thrown. Otherwise, the method returns normally. At the minimum, require( ) compares the current event type ID with an event type ID passed to it. Additionally, you can pass a namespace URI and a local name to require( ). If either of these parameters is null, that comparison is not done. Here are a few sample calls to require( ):

require(START_ELEMENT, null, null)
> Succeeds if the current event type ID is START_ELEMENT

require(END_ELEMENT, "http://www.example.com/ns1", null)
> Succeeds if current event type ID is END_ELEMENT and the current namespace URI is http://www.example.com/ns1

require(START_ELEMENT, null, "name")
> Succeeds if the current event type ID is START_ELEMENT and the current local name is name

require(END_ELEMENT, "http://www.example.com/ns1", "name")
> Succeeds if the current event type ID is END_ELEMENT, the current namespace URI is http://www.example.com/ns1, and the current local name is name

This require( ) method is useful in cases where you have a defined XML syntax, but no DTD is available for validation purposes. In these cases, without some way to verify that the document follows your expectations, your code may throw nonintuitive exceptions like NullPointerException and IllegalStateException. Alternatively, it may just not do what you expect it to do. For example, we could have a document similar to Example 8-11, but with the first_name and last_name elements swapped so that it looks like:

```
<?xml version="1.0"?>
<person>
  <name>
    <last_name>Turing</last_name>
    <first_name>Alan</first_name>
  </name>
  <profession>computer scientist</profession>
  <profession>mathematician</profession>
  <profession>cryptographer</profession>
</person>
```

In this case, the code in Example 8-13 would output "Hello Turing" instead of the expected "Hello Alan." To ensure that we're only outputting the first name, we can add calls to require( ) to produce the code in Example 8-14.

Example 8-14. Person parsing with nextTag() and require()

```java
package javaxml3;

import java.io.File;
import java.io.FileInputStream;

import javax.xml.stream.XMLInputFactory;
import javax.xml.stream.XMLStreamConstants;
import javax.xml.stream.XMLStreamReader;

public class RequireExample {

    public static void main(String[] args) throws Exception {
        if (args.length != 1) {
            System.out
                    .println("Usage: java RequireExample " + "[XML Document]");
            return;
        }
        File file = new File(args[0]);

        XMLInputFactory inputFactory = XMLInputFactory.newInstance();
        XMLStreamReader reader = inputFactory
                .createXMLStreamReader(new FileInputStream(file));

        int eventTypeID = reader.nextTag();
        // the cursor is now at the person start element
        reader.require(XMLStreamConstants.START_ELEMENT, null, "person");

        eventTypeID = reader.nextTag();
        // the cursor is now at the name start element
        reader.require(XMLStreamConstants.START_ELEMENT, null, "name");

        eventTypeID = reader.nextTag();
        // the cursor is now at the first_name start element
        reader.require(XMLStreamConstants.START_ELEMENT, null, "first_name");

        eventTypeID = reader.next();
        // the cursor should now be at the text within the first_name elemnt
        System.out.println("Hello " + reader.getText());
    }
}
```

Because our XML does not have namespaces, we have to pass null as the namespace URI parameter. If we pass the empty string (""), this would match only elements with a namespace such as:

```xml
<name xmlns=""/>
```

Running this class with an XML document where the first_name and last_name elements were swapped so that last_name came first would throw an XMLStreamException with a helpful message such as this:

```
LocalName first_name specified did not match with current local name
```

Don't worry if the exception message you get is worded differently. Different implementations are free to form these messages however they see fit.

You can also use the getLocation( ) method on XMLStreamReader to provide the explicit location within the document where the comparison failed.

```
boolean outputElementText = false;
try {
    reader.require(START_ELEMENT, null, "first_name");
    outputElementText = true;
} catch (XMLStreamException e) {
    System.out.println("Assertion failed. " + e.getMessage( )
            + " at " + reader.getLocation().getLineNumber( ) + ":"
            + reader.getLocation().getColumnNumber( ));
}

if (outputElementText)
    System.out.println(reader.getElementText( ));
```

This outputs:

```
Assertion failed. LocalName first_name specified did not match with current local
name at 4:16
```

The Location Interface

XMLStreamReader and XMLEventReader both have a method named getLocation( ), which returns an instance of javax.xml.stream.Location. Like org.xml.sax.Locator, Location provides the following accessors:

- getLineNumber( )
- getColumnNumber( )
- getPublicId( )
- getSystemId( )

In addition, Location provides a getCharacterOffset( ) method, which returns the current location as expressed in the number of characters from the beginning of the document.

One thing to note about the result of getLocation( ) is that it returns an object representing the position at the end of the current event. If you have a line of XML such as this:

```
<identifier
type="number"
>12345</identifier>
```

When the current event is the START_ELEMENT event for the identifier element, the Location object returned by getLocation( ) will be on the third line of this fragment.

---

peek( )

The peek( ) method of XMLEventReader returns what will be the result of the next invocation of nextEvent( ) or next( ). It does not affect the result of this future invocation. This method is useful for making the processing of the current event conditional on the next event such as in Example 8-15.

Example 8-15. Usage of the peek() method

```
XMLEvent event = reader.nextEvent();
XMLEvent next = reader.peek();
if (next.isStartElement()) {
    processEventWithChild(event);
} else {
    processEvent(event);
}
```

StAX Filters

The StAX API has built-in support for event filtering in both the cursor and event iterator APIs. EventFilter and StreamFilter are separate interfaces for the two APIs, but a filter class will commonly implement both. Both interfaces define a method named accept( ). Each has a single parameter, which is an XMLEvent in the case of EventFilter and an XMLStreamReader in the case of StreamFilter.

Whether using EventFilter or StreamFilter, the accept( ) method is called for each event or change to the cursor positioning—basically when next( ), nextEvent( ), or peek( ) is called. If accept( ) returns true, the event is returned to the caller of next( ) or nextEvent( ). If accept( ) returns false, the cursor position is advanced until accept( ) returns true or the end of the document is reached.

 The StreamFilter interface documentation states that the filter should not change the state of the reader. In other words, do not call next( ), nextTag( ), or close( ). Calling hasNext( ), require( ), or most other methods is acceptable.

Example 8-16 contains a filter that implements both EventFilter and StreamFilter to filter out all events other than START_ELEMENT and END_ELEMENT. It's common to have a single class implement both interfaces, as the acceptance criteria is generally similar, such as in Example 8-16, where both interface methods delegate to acceptInternal( ).

Example 8-16. Example filter implementing EventFilter and StreamFilter

```
package javaxml3;

import javax.xml.stream.EventFilter;
import javax.xml.stream.StreamFilter;
import javax.xml.stream.XMLStreamConstants;
```

Example 8-16. Example filter implementing EventFilter and StreamFilter (continued)

```
import javax.xml.stream.XMLStreamReader;
import javax.xml.stream.events.XMLEvent;

public class ElementOnlyFilter implements EventFilter, StreamFilter {

    /* implementation of EventFilter interface */
    public boolean accept(XMLEvent event) {
        return acceptInternal(event.getEventType( ));
    }

    /* implementation of StreamFilter interface */
    public boolean accept(XMLStreamReader reader) {
        return acceptInternal(reader.getEventType( ));
    }

    /* internal utility method */
    private boolean acceptInternal(int eventType) {
        return eventType == XMLStreamConstants.START_ELEMENT
                || eventType == XMLStreamConstants.END_ELEMENT;
    }

}
```

To create a filtered instance of XMLStreamReader or XMLEventReader, there are two methods on XMLInputFactory named createFilteredReader( ). One of these accepts an instance of XMLStreamReader and an instance of StreamFilter and the other accepts an instance of XMLEventReader and an instance of EventFilter. It's possible to nest filters through repeated calls to createdFilteredReader( ) such as:

```
XMLInputFactory inputFactory = XMLInputFactory.newInstance( );
XMLStreamReader reader = inputFactory
        .createXMLStreamReader(new FileInputStream(file));
reader = inputFactory.createFilteredReader(reader, new ElemenetOnlyFilter( ));
reader = inputFactory.createFilteredReader(reader, new OtherFilter( ));
reader = inputFactory.createFilteredReader(reader. new AnotherFilter( ));
```

Example 8-17 contains a sample class that counts the number of events in a document with an unfiltered reader, then counts the number of events in the same document with a reader filtered using the ElementOnlyFilter class from Example 8-16, and then compares the two counts.

Example 8-17. Filter usage with XMLStreamReader

```
package javaxml3;

import java.io.File;
import java.io.FileInputStream;

import javax.xml.stream.StreamFilter;
import javax.xml.stream.XMLInputFactory;
import javax.xml.stream.XMLStreamException;
import javax.xml.stream.XMLStreamReader;
```

Example 8-17. Filter usage with XMLStreamReader (continued)

```java
public class StreamFilterExample {

    public static void main(String[] args) throws Exception {
        if (args.length != 1) {
            System.out.println("Usage: java javaxml3.StreamFilterExample "
                    + "[XML Document]");
            return;
        }
        File file = new File(args[0]);

        XMLInputFactory inputFactory = XMLInputFactory.newInstance( );
        XMLStreamReader reader = inputFactory
                .createXMLStreamReader(new FileInputStream(file));

        int unfilteredCount = countEvents(reader);
        System.out.println("Unfiltered Count = " + unfilteredCount);

        // reinitialize the reader
        reader = inputFactory.createXMLStreamReader(new FileInputStream(file));

        // create the filter and filtered reader
        StreamFilter filter = new ElementOnlyFilter( );
        reader = inputFactory.createFilteredReader(reader, filter);

        int filteredCount = countEvents(reader);
        System.out.println("Filtered Count = " + filteredCount);

        System.out.println("Filter removed "
                + (unfilteredCount - filteredCount) + " events");
    }

    private static int countEvents(XMLStreamReader reader)
            throws XMLStreamException {
        int counter = 1;
        while (reader.hasNext( )) {
            reader.next( );
            counter++;
        }
        return counter;
    }

}
```

Rewriting the class to use XMLEventReader rather than XMLStreamReader would be as simple as replacing Stream with Event and changing the initial value of counter to 0 (as the first event from an XMLEventReader isn't read until the first call to next( ) or nextEvent( )).

As discussed in "The START_DOCUMENT event" previously in this chapter, when a regular XMLStreamReader is created, the current event is a START_DOCUMENT event. However, if a filter is applied to an XMLStreamReader, this may no longer be the case if the filter doesn't accept the START_DOCUMENT event. Unfortunately, this behavior is not defined in the specification, and some implementations (including the reference implementation) keep the START_DOCUMENT as the first event whereas some implementations (including Sun's SJSXP) advance the cursor until the current event is the first acceptable event. This ambiguity does not exist for EventFilters, as you must call next() or nextEvent() to obtain the first event.

StAX filters are limited to accepting or rejecting events from the reader. Unlike the XMLFilter interface that's part of SAX, there is no way to modify the input document as it's parsed. The NamespaceFilter class from the "Filters and Writers" section of Chapter 4 cannot be implemented as a StAX filter. There is, however, a way of implementing this type of functionality through the XMLEventAllocator interface, as we'll see in the "Factory Properties" section later in this chapter.

Document Output with StAX

The StAX specification states that the first design goal for StAX is to provide "symmetrical APIs for reading and writing XML using a streaming paradigm." This is a significant difference from SAX, which provides an API for reading only. Writing XML documents with StAX solves the fundamental problem with using DOM or any DOM-like API—you do not have to create the entire document in memory before being able to serialize it. Instead, you write events, using the same event vocabulary we've already discussed in this chapter, to a writer object that is attached to an output stream. The writer object will flush the character representation of those events to the output stream as necessary, or when your code requests it by calling the flush() method. As a result, it is possible to create massive documents with StAX with a limited amount of memory, something that isn't possible with DOM.

As with the reading APIs, there are two main interfaces for document output: XMLStreamWriter and XMLEventWriter. Instances of these are created using the static newInstance() method of the abstract class XMLOutputFactory. The concrete implementation of XMLOutputFactory returned by newInstance() is determined using the same process described in the section "StAX Factories" earlier in this chapter. Once you have obtained an instance of XMLOutputFactory, instances of XMLStreamWriter and XMLEventWriter are obtained by invoking methods named createXMLStreamWriter() and createXMLEventWriter(), respectively. As with the createXMLStreamReader() and createXMLEventReader() methods of XMLInputFactory, these writer creation methods have several overloaded versions. There are overloaded methods for each that accept:

- A java.io.Writer
- A java.io.OutputStream

- A `java.io.OutputStream` and a character set encoding
- A `javax.xml.transform.Result`

As with `XMLInputFactory` and `javax.xml.transform.Source`, support by `XMLOutputFactory` for `javax.xml.transform.Result` is optional, and if an implementation does not provide support for `Result` outputs, both `createXMLEventWriter()` and `createXMLStreamWriter()` will throw a `java.lang.UnsupportedOperationException`. To keep things simple, in the examples below, we'll be using the `System.out` `OutputStream`.

XMLStreamWriter

As with `XMLStreamReader`, the `XMLStreamWriter` interface defines quite a few methods. But also like `XMLStreamReader`, it's an easy-to-use interface that allows for lightweight operations without a lot of extra object creation. The full `XMLStreamWriter` interface is diagrammed in Figure 8-7.

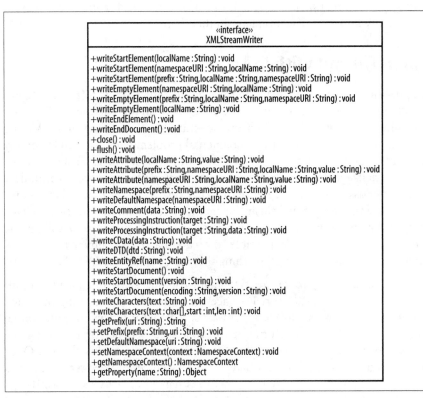

«interface»
XMLStreamWriter

```
+writeStartElement(localName : String) : void
+writeStartElement(namespaceURI : String,localName : String) : void
+writeStartElement(prefix : String,localName : String,namespaceURI : String) : void
+writeEmptyElement(namespaceURI : String,localName : String) : void
+writeEmptyElement(prefix : String,localName : String,namespaceURI : String) : void
+writeEmptyElement(localName : String) : void
+writeEndElement() : void
+writeEndDocument() : void
+close() : void
+flush() : void
+writeAttribute(localName : String,value : String) : void
+writeAttribute(prefix : String,namespaceURI : String,localName : String,value : String) : void
+writeAttribute(namespaceURI : String,localName : String,value : String) : void
+writeNamespace(prefix : String,namespaceURI : String) : void
+writeDefaultNamespace(namespaceURI : String) : void
+writeComment(data : String) : void
+writeProcessingInstruction(target : String) : void
+writeProcessingInstruction(target : String,data : String) : void
+writeCData(data : String) : void
+writeDTD(dtd : String) : void
+writeEntityRef(name : String) : void
+writeStartDocument() : void
+writeStartDocument(version : String) : void
+writeStartDocument(encoding : String,version : String) : void
+writeCharacters(text : String) : void
+writeCharacters(text : char[],start : int,len : int) : void
+getPrefix(uri : String) : String
+setPrefix(prefix : String,uri : String) : void
+setDefaultNamespace(uri : String) : void
+setNamespaceContext(context : NamespaceContext) : void
+getNamespaceContext() : NamespaceContext
+getProperty(name : String) : Object
```

Figure 8-7. The XMLStreamWriter interface

Writing an XML document with `XMLStreamWriter` is simply a matter of creating the writer, calling a series of write methods, and then flushing the writer. A simple example that outputs part of the document in Example 8-5 is contained in Example 8-18.

Example 8-18. Simple XMLStreamWriter example

```
1 package javaxml3;
2
3 import javax.xml.stream.XMLOutputFactory;--
4 import javax.xml.stream.XMLStreamWriter;
5
6 public class SimpleStreamOutput {
7
8     public static void main(String[] args) throws Exception {
9         XMLOutputFactory outputFactory = XMLOutputFactory.newInstance();
10        XMLStreamWriter writer = outputFactory.createXMLStreamWriter(System.out);
11        writer.writeStartDocument("1.0");
12        writer.writeStartElement("person");
13        writer.writeStartElement("name");
14        writer.writeStartElement("first_name");
15        writer.writeCharacters("Alan");
16        writer.writeEndElement();
17        writer.writeEndElement();
18        writer.writeEndElement();
19        writer.writeEndDocument();
20        writer.flush();
21    }
22}
```

When Example 8-18 is run, it produces this on the console (all on one line):

```
<?xml version="1.0"?><person><name><first_name>Alan</first_name></name></person>
```

StAX will not prevent you from creating XML that is not well-formed. If lines 16 through 19 were omitted from Example 8-18, the output would be:

```
<?xml version="1.0"?><person><name><first_name>Alan
```

The one feature XMLStreamWriter has to ensure that a document is well-formed is that writeEndDocument() will close any open elements. As a result, the output of Example 8-18 would be the same if lines 16 through 18 were removed. XMLStreamWriter will also replace the appropriate characters with the entities &, <, and > inside CHARACTERS events and those entities plus " and ' inside ATTRIBUTE events.

Attributes are added with the writeAttribute() methods and are added to the current open element. If there are attributes to be written, they must be written before character data, comments, processing instructions, entity references, and other elements; otherwise, a javax.xml.stream.XMLStreamException will be thrown. Example 8-19 shows the proper sequence of method calls.

What? No Pretty Printing?

If you've used any DOM-style APIs for creating XML documents, you may be surprised that there's no mechanism for *pretty printing*—putting elements on their own lines, using tabs, and so on. If you absolutely need pretty printing, I suggest looking at the JTidy library at *http://jtidy.sourceforge.net*. JTidy is a highly configurable standalone XML pretty printer—you pass it a java.io.InputStream, a DOM Document object, or a DOM Node object along with a java.io.OutputStream and JTidy will output a pretty printed version of your document to the OutputStream. To use JTidy with XMLStreamWriter or XMLEventWriter, you could use a ByteArrayOutputStream with the StAX writer and pass the resulting byte array to JTidy with a ByteArrayInputStream or have StAX write the document to a FileOutputStream and pass JTidy a FileInputStream. Before doing this, be sure you really need pretty printing, as there is a performance hit to using JTidy. Perhaps some future implementations of StAX will provide pretty printing through a vendor-specific property, or it will be added to a future version of the specification.

Example 8-19. Simple XMLStreamWriter example with attribute

```
package javaxml3;

import javax.xml.stream.XMLOutputFactory;
import javax.xml.stream.XMLStreamWriter;

public class AttributeStreamOutput {

    public static void main(String[] args) throws Exception {
        XMLOutputFactory outputFactory = XMLOutputFactory.newInstance();
        XMLStreamWriter writer = outputFactory.createXMLStreamWriter(System.out);
        writer.writeStartDocument("1.0");
        writer.writeStartElement("addresses");
        writer.writeStartElement("address");
        writer.writeAttribute("type", "work");
        writer.writeStartElement("street");
        writer.writeCharacters("1515 Broadway");
        writer.writeComment("in the heart of Times Square");
        writer.writeEndElement();
        writer.writeEndElement();
        writer.writeEndElement();
        writer.writeEndDocument();
        writer.flush();
    }
}
```

XMLStreamWriter also has writeEmptyElement() methods, which create empty XML elements. Empty elements follow the same rules as regular elements as pertains to attributes. If character data, a comment, processing instruction, entity reference, or another element is written, the empty element is closed. Because we can force the XMLStreamWriter to flush its buffer to the output stream with the flush() method, we can write code such as:

```java
package javaxml3;

import javax.xml.stream.XMLOutputFactory;
import javax.xml.stream.XMLStreamWriter;

public class EmptyElement {

    public static void main(String[] args) throws Exception {
        XMLOutputFactory outputFactory = XMLOutputFactory.newInstance();
        XMLStreamWriter writer = outputFactory.createXMLStreamWriter(System.out);
        writer.writeEmptyElement("empty");
        writer.flush(); // write '<empty' to the console
        System.out.println("\n");
        writer.writeAttribute("attribute", "true");
        writer.flush(); // write ' attribute="true"' to the console
        System.out.println("\n");
        writer.writeEndDocument();
        writer.flush(); // write /> to the console
    }
}
```

This shows that the empty element isn't actually closed until the call to writeEndDocument. Note that in this example, if we hadn't called writeEndDocument(), XMLStreamWriter would have never closed the empty element. Always remember that StAX does not try to make your document well formed.

Namespace support

Namespace support is provided by XMLStreamWriter in two separate ways. First, namespace URIs and, optionally, prefixes can be attached to elements and attributes using overloaded versions of the writeStartElement(), writeAttribute(), and writeEmptyElement() methods. Second, the attributes that associate namespace URIs with their prefixes are written to open elements. XMLStreamWriter does not ensure that namespace attributes are written, but it does require that all namespace URIs attached to elements and attributes are associated with a prefix. XMLStreamWriter also supports setting the default namespace for an element.

A call to writeStartElement such as:

```java
writer.writeStartElement("ns1", "sample", "http://www.example.com/ns1");
```

Will result in the following element being written to the output stream:

```xml
<ns1:sample>
```

To write the xmlns attribute, you also need to write a NAMESPACE event using the writeNamespace() method:

```java
writer.writeNamespace("ns1", "http://www.example.com/ns1");
```

These two lines together will output:

```
<ns1:sample xmlns:ns1="http://www.example.com/ns1">
```

Subsequent calls to `writeStartElement()`, `writeEmptyElement()`, and `writeAttribute()` to create elements or attributes in this same namespace need not pass the namespace prefix again, only the namespace URI. When you omit the namespace prefix, `XMLStreamWriter` will use the prefix defined for the namespace URI in the *namespace context*. As you write an XML document with `XMLStreamWriter`, the writer builds a namespace context representing the associations between namespace URIs and prefixes. This context is available as an instance of `javax.xml.namespace.NamespaceContext`, although you'll generally interact with the context using the namespace methods of `XMLStreamWriter`.

Adding a namespace URI and prefix to the namespace context can be done through five `XMLStreamWriter` methods:

`writeStartElement(`*prefix, localName, namespaceURI*`)`
> Write the `START_ELEMENT` event and, in addition, add the prefix and namespace URI to the namespace context.

`writeEmptyElement(`*prefix, localName, namespaceURI*`)`
> Write the `START_ELEMENT` event and, in addition, add the prefix and namespace URI to the namespace context.

`writeAttribute(`*prefix, namespaceURI, localName, value*`)`
> Write the `ATTRIBUTE` event and, in addition, add the prefix and namespace URI to the namespace context.

`writeNamespace(`*prefix, namespaceURI*`)`
> Write the `NAMESPACE` event and, in addition, add the prefix and namespace URI to the namespace context.

`writeDefaultNamespace(`*namespaceURI*`)`
> Writes the default namespace attribute.

`setDefaultNamespace(`*namespaceURI*`)`
> Sets the default namespace to the namespace URI passed to this method.

`setPrefix(`*prefix, namespaceURI*`)`
> Adds a prefix and namespace URI to the namespace context.

Because `writeNamespace()` adds a prefix and namespace URI to the namespace context, you should generally be able to use the methods without a prefix. In fact, it's generally a good idea to use the methods without a prefix, because you'll ensure the namespace attribute for that URI has already been written. For example, the code in Example 8-20 will throw a `javax.xml.stream.XMLStreamException` in the call to `writeEmptyElement` because the namespace URI `http://www.example.com/ns2` has not been bound to a prefix.

Example 8-20. Invalid namespace creation

```
XMLStreamWriter writer = outputFactory.createXMLStreamWriter(System.out);
writer.writeStartElement("ns1", "sample", "http://www.example.com/ns1");
writer.writeNamespace("ns1", "http://www.example.com/ns1");
writer.writeEmptyElement("http://www.example.com/ns2", "inner");
```

If, however, the writeEmptyElement( ) call was:

```
writer.writeEmptyElement("ns2", "inner", "http://www.example.com/ns2");
```

no exception would be thrown, but our output would not have a namespace attribute defining the prefix for the namespace URI http://www.example.com/ns2.

We'll see in the section "Factory Properties" later in the chapter how the StAX writer has an optional mode that does not require namespace prefixes to be specified.

XMLEventWriter

As you can see in Figure 8-8, the XMLEventWriter interface is significantly shorter than XMLStreamWriter.

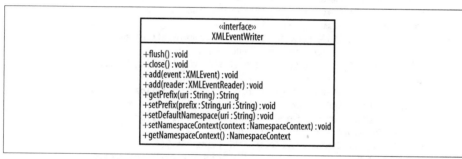

Figure 8-8. The XMLEventWriter interface

XMLEventWriter instances are created using the createXMLEventWriter( ) methods of XMLOutputFactory. To add events to the writer, you use one of the two add( ) methods, passing either a single XMLEvent object or an XMLEventReader object, in which case all of the remaining XMLEvent objects from the XMLEventReader are added to the writer.

To add an XMLEvent object, you must obtain an XMLEvent object class using an implementation of the abstract class XMLEventFactory. Obtaining an implementation of XMLEventFactory is done the same way as XMLOutputFactory and XMLInputFactory: by calling XMLEventFactory.newInstance( ). XMLEventFactory has a series of methods for creating various event objects:

```
public abstract class XMLEventFactory {
    // non-event creation methods omitted
    public abstract Attribute createAttribute(String prefix,
            String namespaceURI, String localName, String value);
```

```
            public abstract Attribute createAttribute(String localName, String value);
            public abstract Attribute createAttribute(QName name, String value);
            public abstract Namespace createNamespace(String namespaceURI);
            public abstract Namespace createNamespace(String prefix, String namespaceUri);
            public abstract StartElement createStartElement(QName name,
                    Iterator attributes, Iterator namespaces);
            public abstract StartElement createStartElement(String prefix,
                    String namespaceUri, String localName);
            public abstract StartElement createStartElement(String prefix,
                    String namespaceUri, String localName, Iterator attributes,
                    Iterator namespaces);
            public abstract StartElement createStartElement(String prefix,
                    String namespaceUri, String localName, Iterator attributes,
                    Iterator namespaces, NamespaceContext context);
            public abstract EndElement createEndElement(QName name, Iterator namespaces);
            public abstract EndElement createEndElement(String prefix,
                    String namespaceUri, String localName);
            public abstract EndElement createEndElement(String prefix,
                    String namespaceUri, String localName, Iterator namespaces);
            public abstract Characters createCharacters(String content);
            public abstract Characters createCData(String content);
            public abstract Characters createSpace(String content);
            public abstract Characters createIgnorableSpace(String content);
            public abstract StartDocument createStartDocument();
            public abstract StartDocument createStartDocument(String encoding,
                    String version, boolean standalone);
            public abstract StartDocument createStartDocument(String encoding,
                    String version);
            public abstract StartDocument createStartDocument(String encoding);
            public abstract EndDocument createEndDocument();
            public abstract EntityReference createEntityReference(String name,
                    EntityDeclaration declaration);
            public abstract Comment createComment(String text);
            public abstract ProcessingInstruction createProcessingInstruction(
                    String target, String data);
            public abstract DTD createDTD(String dtd);
        }
```

As you can see, there are two ways to add attributes, including namespace declarations, to START_ELEMENT events: by passing two java.util.Iterators to the createStartElement() method or by creating Attribute and Namespace event objects and adding them to the XMLEventWriter. As a result, Examples 8-21 and 8-22 write the same text to the output stream.

Example 8-21. Adding Attribute and Namespace objects with an Iterator

```
Namespace ns1 = eventFactory.createNamespace("ns1","http://www.example.com/ns1");
Namespace ns2 = eventFactory.createNamespace("ns2","http://www.example.com/ns2");
List namespaceList = new ArrayList();
namespaceList.add(ns1);
namespaceList.add(ns2);

Attribute attribute = eventFactory.createAttribute("ns2",
```

Example 8-21. Adding Attribute and Namespace objects with an Iterator (continued)

```
  "http://www.example.com/ns2", "attribute", "true");
List attributeList = Collections.singletonList(attribute);
writer.add(eventFactory.createStartElement(ns1.getPrefix(),
  ns1.getNamespaceURI(), "sample", attributeList.iterator(),
  namespaceList.iterator()));
writer.add(eventFactory.createEndElement(("ns1", "http://www.example.com/ns1",
  "sample");
```

Example 8-22. Adding attributes and namespaces one at a time

```
writer.add(eventFactory.createStartElement("ns1",
 "http://www.example.com/ns1", "sample", null, null));
writer.add(eventFactory.createNamespace("ns1", "http://www.example.com/ns1"));
writer.add(eventFactory.createNamespace("ns2", "http://www.example.com/ns2"));
writer.add(eventFactory.createAttribute("ns2", "http://www.example.com/ns2",
  "attribute", "true"));
writer.add(eventFactory.createEndElement(("ns1", "http://www.example.com/ns1",
  "sample");
```

Event objects are reusable; if you wanted to create the same element twice, adding an attribute to the second element, you would only have to create the StartElement and EndElement objects once:

```
    StartElement start = eventFactory.createStartElement(new QName("element"), null,
        null);
    EndElement end = eventFactory.createEndElement(new QName("element"), null,
        null);

    writer.add(start);
    writer.add(end);
    writer.add(start);
    writer.add(eventFactory.createAttribute("attribute", "value"));
    writer.add(end);
```

Namespace support by XMLEventWriter is similar to XMLStreamWriter, but since there's no way to create an event that does not have a defined prefix, XMLEventWriter does not have the same namespace definition checking as XMLStreamWriter. Otherwise, the semantics of namespace handling are the same as in XMLStreamWriter.

Factory Properties

As with SAX and DOM, StAX readers and writers can be configured by changing both settings defined in the specification and any implementation-specific settings that a parser vendor may create for their implementation. In StAX, these settings are referred to as *properties*. Properties are set using the setProperty() method of XMLInputFactory and XMLOutputFactory. Values of properties, which may or may not have been set by your code, can be retrieved using the getProperty() method. This method can be invoked both on factories and the readers and writers they have created. Once set on a factory, properties affect all readers and writers subsequently created by the various create methods.

An interesting difference between SAX and StAX is that, where SAX uses features that get set to true or false as well as properties that get set to a java.lang.Object, StAX only has properties that are set to an Object. As a result, several of the properties defined by the StAX specification are set to a java.lang.Boolean. So where you might use true to set a feature in SAX, you would use Boolean.TRUE in StAX.

If you're using Java 5, you can use the autoboxing language feature to eliminate this difference, as the Java compiler will create the same bytecode from these two method invocations:

```
// works with any version of Java
factory.setProperty("javax.xml.stream.isValidating",
    Boolean.TRUE);
// only with Java 5 or higher
factory.setProperty("javax.xml.stream.isValidating",
    true);
```

Boolean Properties of XMLInputFactory

Table 8-5 contains a list of the properties of XMLInputFactory that are set using java.lang.Boolean values. Most of these have their default values specified in the StAX specification. Support for some of these properties is optional. Like DOM, there is a separate mechanism to test if a property is supported by an implementation through the isPropertySupported() method. If you try to set a property that is not supported, setProperty() will throw a java.lang.IllegalArgumentException indicating that a property is not supported.

Table 8-5. Boolean properties of XMLInputFactory

Feature name	Default	Required?
javax.xml.stream.isValidating	False	No
javax.xml.stream.isCoalescing	False	Yes
javax.xml.stream.isNamespaceAware	True	No
javax.xml.stream.isReplacingEntityReferences	True	Yes
javax.xml.stream.isSupportingExternalEntities	None	Yes

javax.xml.stream.isValidating
    Enable or disable XML validation.

javax.xml.stream.isCoalescing
    Force the parser to combine adjacent CHARACTERS and CDATA events into a single CHARACTERS event.

javax.xml.stream.isNamespaceAware
    Enable or disable namespace support.

javax.xml.stream.isReplacingEntityReferences

If this property is set to true, internal entity references are replaced with their character representation. If it is set to false, these entities result in ENTITY_ REFERENCE events. This does not apply to the five predefined XML entities (<, &, >, ", and '), which are always replaced by their character representation.

javax.xml.stream.isSupportingExternalEntities

Enable or disable resolution of external parsed entities.

Object Properties of XMLInputFactory

XMLInputFactory defines three interfaces that can be implemented to alter the behavior of XMLStreamReader and XMLEventReader instances. Implementations of these interfaces are set on an XMLInputFactory either through calling setProperty( ) with one of the property names from Table 8-6 or by calling the specific setter for each interface.

Table 8-6. Interfaces for object properties of XMLInputFactory

Interface name	Property name	Setter
XMLResolver	javax.xml.stream.resolver	setResolver( )
XMLReporter	javax.xml.stream.reporter	setReporter( )
XMLEventAllocator	javax.xml.stream.allocator	setAllocator( )

XMLResolver

Implementing the javax.xml.stream.XMLResolver interface allows you to override the default resource resolution mechanism for resolving external resources while parsing a document—typically an external DTD. The interface defines one method:

```
public Object resolveEntity(String publicID, String systemID,
        String baseURI, String namespace) throws XMLStreamException;
```

The result of a call to resolveEntity( ) must be a javax.xml.stream.XMLStreamReader, a java.io.InputStream, or a javax.xml.stream.XMLEventReader.

XMLReporter

The java.xml.stream.XMLReporter interface allows you to capture warnings and nonfatal errors that arise while parsing the document. Without setting this property on XMLInputFactory, there is no reporting of warnings or nonfatal errors. The interface defines one method:

```
public void report(String message, String errorType,
        Object relatedInformation, Location location)
        throws XMLStreamException;
```

XMLEventAllocator

An implementation of the `javax.xml.stream.util.XMLEventAllocator` interface is used inside implementations of `XMLEventReader` to create an `XMLEvent` object based on the current state of the underlying `XMLStreamReader`. By contract, an `XMLEventAllocator` should never modify the state of the `XMLStreamReader`. The interface defines three methods:

```
public XMLEventAllocator newInstance();
public XMLEvent allocate(XMLStreamReader reader)
  throws XMLStreamException;
public void allocate(XMLStreamReader reader, XMLEventConsumer consumer)
  throws XMLStreamException;
```

The `newInstance()` method should return a new instance of this `XMLEventAllocator` implementation. This allows `XMLInputFactory` instances to create a new allocator instance per reader. The two allocate methods should read the current state of the `XMLStreamReader` and create the appropriate `XMLEvent` objects. According to the specification, `XMLEventAllocator` instances are not required to use `XMLEventFactory`, but it is recommended. The first version of allocate should return one `XMLEvent` based on the state of the reader. The second passes in an instance of the `XMLEventConsumer` interface (which defines one method—`add()`—that accepts an `XMLEvent` object) to which `XMLEvent` should be passed and, as a result, one call to `allocate()` can result in multiple method calls on the `XMLEventConsumer` object. However, since `XMLEventReader` implementations are free to call either `allocate()` method; you can't count on this multievent behavior. A significant problem with implementing this interface is that there's no way to obtain the default `XMLEventAllocator` implementation for a StAX implementation. This means there is no vendor-independent way to create an implementation of `XMLEventAllocator` that only overrides allocation of only some types of event. If you expect to use `XMLEventAllocator` extensively, you may be best served by standardizing on a StAX implementation so that you can extend its default implementation of `XMLEventAllocator`.

XMLOutputFactory

`XMLOutputFactory` has only one property defined in the StAX specification, `javax.xml.stream.isRepairingNamespaces`. This property allows you to avoid defining a prefix for each namespace URI in your document. Instead, the `XMLStreamWriter` or `XMLEventWriter` implementation will automatically assign a prefix. This can cut down on the amount of namespace handling code you need to write, but with the cost of some potentially very ugly namespace prefixes like `zdef-1428660340`. If your document is going to be read by humans that expect a particular (or short) namespace prefix, using this property may cause you some headaches.

Common Issues with StAX

Here are a couple of errors you might run into:

`Provider com.bea.xml.stream.MXParserFactory not found`
> This indicates that you only have the API JAR in your classpath, not an actual implementation. The default implementation of `javax.xml.stream.XMLInputFactory` is `com.bea.xml.stream.com.bea.xml.stream.MXParserFactory`.

`Current state of the parser is X. But expected state is Y`
> This indicates you are attempting to call a method on `XMLStreamReader` that is not valid for the current event. See Table 8-3 for a list of valid methods for each event.

XmlPull

The XmlPull API was a predecessor to the StAX specification. It defines a simple API similar to the StAX cursor API. Full information about the XmlPull API can be found at *http://www.xmlpull.org*. The advantage the XmlPull API has over StAX is that because it's a much smaller API, it's suitable for memory-constrained environments, such as mobile devices. One implementation of XmlPull is available in a 9 KB JAR file. The API JAR file from the StAX specification is more than 25 KB alone. If you're building a server application, this difference is irrelevant, but if you're developing a game to be run on a mobile phone where the JAR file must be under 100 KB, this is a big difference. Example 8-23 contains a version of the Tree Builder application writing with the XmlPull API.

Example 8-23. XmlPullTreeViewer

```
package javaxml3;

import java.awt.BorderLayout;
import java.io.File;
import java.io.FileInputStream;
import java.io.IOException;

import javax.swing.JFrame;
import javax.swing.JScrollPane;
import javax.swing.JTree;
import javax.swing.tree.DefaultMutableTreeNode;
import javax.swing.tree.DefaultTreeModel;

import org.xmlpull.v1.XmlPullParser;
import org.xmlpull.v1.XmlPullParserException;
import org.xmlpull.v1.XmlPullParserFactory;

public class XmlPullTreeViewer extends JFrame {
    /** The base tree to render */
    private JTree jTree;
```

Example 8-23. XmlPullTreeViewer (continued)

```java
/** Tree model to use */
DefaultTreeModel defaultTreeModel;

public XmlPullTreeViewer( ) {
    // Handle Swing setup
    super("XmlPull Tree Viewer");
    setSize(800, 450);
    // setSize(600, 200);
}

public void init(File file) throws XmlPullParserException, IOException {
    DefaultMutableTreeNode base = new DefaultMutableTreeNode(
            "XML Document: " + file.getAbsolutePath( ));

    // Build the tree model
    defaultTreeModel = new DefaultTreeModel(base);
    jTree = new JTree(defaultTreeModel);

    // Construct the tree hierarchy
    buildTree(defaultTreeModel, base, file);

    // Display the results
    getContentPane( ).add(new JScrollPane(jTree), BorderLayout.CENTER);
}

// Swing-related variables and methods, including
// setting up a JTree and basic content pane

public static void main(String[] args) {
    try {
        if (args.length != 1) {
            System.out.println("Usage: java javaxml3.XmlPullTreeViewer "
                    + "[XML Document]");
            return;
        }
        XmlPullTreeViewer viewer = new XmlPullTreeViewer( );
        File f = new File(args[0]);

        viewer.init(f);
        viewer.setVisible(true);
    } catch (Exception e) {
        e.printStackTrace( );
    }
}

public void buildTree(DefaultTreeModel treeModel,
        DefaultMutableTreeNode current, File file)
        throws XmlPullParserException, IOException {
    FileInputStream inputStream = new FileInputStream(file);
    XmlPullParserFactory factory = XmlPullParserFactory.newInstance( );
    factory.setFeature(XmlPullParser.FEATURE_PROCESS_NAMESPACES, true);
    XmlPullParser parser = factory.newPullParser( );
```

Example 8-23. XmlPullTreeViewer (continued)

```
        parser.setInput(inputStream, null);

        parseRestOfDocument(parser, current);
    }

    private void parseRestOfDocument(XmlPullParser parser,
            DefaultMutableTreeNode current) throws XmlPullParserException,
            IOException {

        int type = parser.getEventType( );
        while (type != XmlPullParser.END_DOCUMENT) {
            switch (type) {
            case XmlPullParser.START_TAG:

                DefaultMutableTreeNode element = new DefaultMutableTreeNode(
                        "Element: " + parser.getName( ));
                current.add(element);
                current = element;

                // Determine namespace
                if (parser.getNamespace( ) != null) {
                    String prefix = parser.getPrefix( );
                    if (!"".equals(prefix)) {
                        prefix = "[None]";
                    }
                    DefaultMutableTreeNode namespace = new DefaultMutableTreeNode(
                            "Namespace: prefix = '" + prefix + "', URI = '"
                                    + parser.getNamespace( ) + "'");
                    current.add(namespace);
                }

                if (parser.getAttributeCount( ) > 0) {
                    for (int i = 0; i < parser.getAttributeCount( ); i++) {
                        DefaultMutableTreeNode attrib = new DefaultMutableTreeNode(
                                "Attribute (name = '"
                                        + parser.getAttributeName(i)
                                        + "', value = '"
                                        + parser.getAttributeValue(i) + "')");
                        String attURI = parser.getAttributeNamespace(i);
                        if (!"".equals(attURI)) {
                            String attPrefix = parser.getAttributePrefix(i);
                            if (attPrefix == null || attPrefix.equals("")) {
                                attPrefix = "[None]";
                            }
                            DefaultMutableTreeNode an = new DefaultMutableTreeNode(
                                    "Namespace: prefix = '" + attPrefix
                                            + "', URI = '" + attURI + "'");
                            attrib.add(an);
                        }
                        current.add(attrib);
                    }
                }
```

Example 8-23. XmlPullTreeViewer (continued)

```
                break;
        case XmlPullParser.END_TAG:
            current = (DefaultMutableTreeNode) current.getParent( );
            break;
        case XmlPullParser.TEXT:
            if (!parser.isWhitespace( )) {
                DefaultMutableTreeNode data = new DefaultMutableTreeNode(
                        "Character Data: '" + parser.getText( ) + "'");
                current.add(data);
            }
            break;
        case XmlPullParser.IGNORABLE_WHITESPACE:
            // let's ignore this
            break;
        case XmlPullParser.COMMENT:
            DefaultMutableTreeNode comment = new DefaultMutableTreeNode(
                    "Comment: '" + parser.getText( ) + "'");
            current.add(comment);
            break;
        default:
            System.out.println(type);
        }
        type = parser.next( );
    }
  }
}
```

As you can see, this is very similar to the StAX cursor API but with far fewer imports. Unlike StAX, implementations of XmlPullParser do not process namespaces by default. As a result, in Example 8-23, we enable the namespace processing feature to best emulate the behavior of the StAX version of this application.

JDOM

JDOM provides a means of accessing an XML document within Java through a tree structure, and in that respect is somewhat similar to the DOM. However, it was built specifically for Java (remember the discussion in Chapter 5 on language bindings for the DOM?), so it is in many ways more intuitive to a Java developer than DOM. I'll describe these aspects of JDOM throughout this chapter; I'll also describe some specific cases in which to use SAX, DOM, or JDOM. And for the complete set of details on JDOM, you should check out the web site at *http://www.jdom.org*.

Additionally, and importantly, JDOM is an open source API. You have the ability to suggest and implement changes yourself. If you find that you like JDOM but are annoyed by one little thing, you can help investigate solutions to your problem.

The Basics

Chapters 5 and 6 should have given you a pretty good understanding of dealing with XML tree representations. So when I say that JDOM also provides a tree-based representation of an XML document, that gives you a starting point for understanding how JDOM behaves. To help you see how the classes in JDOM match up to XML structures, take a look at Figure 9-1, which shows a UML model of JDOM's core classes.

As you can see, the names of the classes tell the story. At the core of the JDOM structure is the Document object, which is both the representation of an XML document, and a container for all the other JDOM structures. Element represents an XML element, Attribute an attribute, Text and CDATA represent character data within Element objects, and so on down the line.

Java Collections Support

Another important item to take note of is that you don't see any list classes like SAX's Attributes class or DOM's NodeList and NamedNodeMap classes. This is a nod to

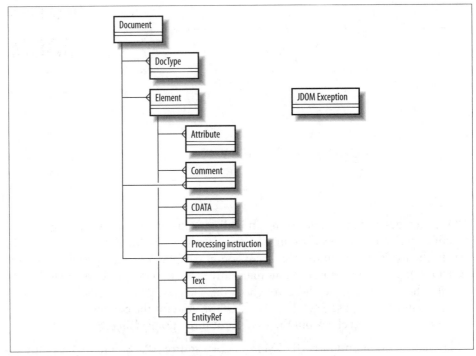

Figure 9-1. UML model of core JDOM classes

Java developers; it was decided that using Java collections (java.util.List, java.util.Map, etc.) would provide a familiar and simple API for XML usage. DOM must serve across languages (remember Java language bindings in Chapter 5?), and can't take advantage of language-specific things like Java collections. For example, when invoking the getAttributes() method on the Element class, you get back a List; you can of course operate upon this List just as you would any other Java List, without looking up new methods or syntax. The List objects returned by JDOM are "live" so that a call such as element.getAttributes.clear() will remove all the attributes from the element object.

Concrete Classes and Factories

Another basic tenet of JDOM that is different from DOM, and not as visible, is that JDOM is an API of concrete classes. In other words, Element, Attribute, ProcessingInstruction, Comment, and the rest are all classes that can be directly instantiated using the new keyword. This generally makes JDOM document construction code much simpler than the corresponding DOM code, since you don't need to create a DocumentBuilderFactory or a DocumentBuilder. Creating a new JDOM document is done like this:

```
Element rootElement = new Element("root");
Document document = new Document(rootElement);
```

It's that simple. On the other hand, not using factories can also be seen as a disadvantage. While you can subclass JDOM classes, you would have to explicitly use those subclasses in your code:

```
element.addContent(new FooterElement("Copyright 2006"));
```

Here, FooterElement is a subclass of org.jdom.Element and does some custom processing (it could, for example, build up several elements that display a page footer). Because it subclasses Element, it can be added to the element variable through the normal means: the addContent( ) method. But since these objects are instantiated with the new keyword, there's no way to instruct JDOM to create FooterElement instances for all elements. For these cases, JDOM does have a factory interface, org.jdom.JDOMFactory, which allows you to specify which subclass should be used. We'll look at JDOMFactory in more detail in the "JDOM and Factories" section later in this chapter.

Useful Return Values

Unlike standard JavaBeans, the setter methods of various JDOM classes return the object on which the setter was called. This allows you to write code that creates a whole XML document with one line of Java code, such as:

```
Document doc = new Document(new Element("root").setAttribute("attribute",
        "value").addContent(new Element("inner")).addContent(
        new Comment("comment text")).addContent("some inline text")
        .addContent(new Element("inner2")));
```

To produce a document like:

```
<?xml version="1.0" encoding="UTF-8"?>
<root attribute="value">
  <inner />
  <!--comment text-->
  some inline text
  <inner2 />
</root>
```

Of course, this should be used judiciously, as the produced code can be so complex as to be unreadable. But you will frequently see cases where an Element is created, given some character data as content, and added to a parent element with one line of code:

```
parent.addContent(new Element("child").setText("text"));
```

Input and Output

A final important aspect of JDOM is its input and output model. First, it is important to understand that JDOM is not a parser; it is an XML document representation in Java. In other words, like DOM and SAX, it is simply a set of classes that can be used to manipulate the data that a parser provides. As a result, JDOM must rely on a parser for reading raw XML. (By default, this is the parser configured through JAXP. See Chapter 7 for more details on JAXP.) It can also accept SAX events or a DOM tree as input, as well as JDBC ResultSet instances and more. To facilitate this, JDOM provides a package specifically for input, org.jdom.input. This package provides *builder* classes; the two you'll use most often are SAXBuilder and DOMBuilder. These build the core JDOM structure, a JDOM Document, from a set of SAX events or a DOM tree. For dealing with input streams, files or documents on disk, or building from existing XML not in a DOM tree, SAXBuilder is the best solution. It's fast and efficient, just like SAX. Using the builder is a piece of cake:

```
SAXBuilder builder = new SAXBuilder( );
Document doc = builder.build(new FileInputStream("contents.xml"));
```

I will detail this further in the code in the chapter, but you can see that it doesn't take much to get access to XML. If you already have your document in a DOM structure, you'll want to use DOMBuilder, which performs a fast conversion from one API to the other:

```
DOMBuilder builder = new DOMBuilder( );
Document doc = builder.build(myDomDocumentObject);
```

It is fairly self-explanatory. This essentially converts from an org.w3c.dom.Document to an org.jdom.Document. The process of converting from a JDOM document back to one of these structures is essentially the same, in reverse; the org.jdom.output package is used for these tasks. To move from JDOM structures to DOM ones, DOMOutputter is used:

```
DOMOutputter outputter = new DOMOutputter( );
org.w3c.dom.Document domDoc = outputter.output(myJDOMDocumentObject);
```

Taking a JDOM Document and firing off SAX events works in the same way:

```
SAXOutputter outputter = new SAXOutputter( );
outputter.setContentHandler(myContentHandler);
outputter.setErrorHandler(myErrorHandler);
outputter.output(myJDOMDocumentObject);
```

This works just like dealing with normal SAX events, where you register content handlers, error handlers, and the rest, and then fire events to those handlers from the JDOM Document object supplied to the output( ) method.

The final outputter, and the one you'll probably work with more than any other, is org.jdom.output.XMLOutputter. This outputs XML to a stream or writer, which wraps a network connection, a file, or any other structure you want to push XML to. This is also effectively a production-ready version of the DOMSerializer class from Chapter 5, except of course it works with JDOM, not DOM. Using the XMLOutputter works like this:

```
XMLOutputter outputter = new XMLOutputter( );
outputter.output(jdomDocumentObject, new FileOutputStream("results.xml"));
```

The format of the output from XMLOutputter is highly configurable through the Format class, as we'll see later in this chapter. By default, XMLOutputter will output without any added newlines or indentation.

So there you have it: the input and output of JDOM all in a few paragraphs. One last thing to note, as illustrated in Figure 9-2: it is very easy to "loop" things because all the input and output of JDOM is actually part of the API. In other words, you can use a file as input, work with it in JDOM, output it to SAX, DOM, or a file, and then consume that as input, restarting the loop. This is particularly helpful in messaging-based applications or in cases where JDOM is used as a component between other XML supplying and consuming components.

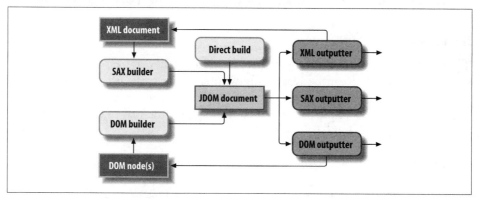

Figure 9-2. Input and output loops in JDOM

The JDOM Distribution

The JDOM 1.0 distribution, downloadable from *http://www.jdom.org*, contains the JDOM JAR file—*jdom.jar*—as well as seven additional JAR files. One of these—*ant.jar*—is used only by the JDOM build process. The rest are JDOM's compile and runtime dependencies. Because JDOM is compatible with all Java versions since Java 1.2, the distribution includes several JAR files that are not required using later versions of the Java runtime. Specifically, if you are using a version of Java after, and including, Java 1.4, the following JAR files are not needed: *xalan.jar*, *xerces.jar*, and *xml-apis.jar*. In addition, the JAR files *jaxen-core.jar*, *jaxen-jdom.jar*, and *saxpath.jar* are needed only if you use JDOM's XPath functionality.

Unlike most open source projects, JDOM doesn't have separate binary and source distributions. The only distribution available includes a prebuilt JAR file, the JDOM sources, all dependencies, and some sample code.

This is not a comprehensive look at JDOM, but it gives you enough information to get started; and I'd rather show you things within the context of working code anyway! So, let's take a look at a utility program that can convert Java properties files to XML.

PropsToXML

To put some real code to the task of learning JDOM, let me introduce the `PropsToXML` class. This class is a utility that takes a standard Java properties file and converts it to an XML equivalent. Many developers out there have requested a means of doing exactly this; it often allows legacy applications using properties files to easily convert to using XML without the overhead of manually converting the configuration files.

Java Properties Files

If you have never worked with Java properties files, they are essentially files with name-value pairs that can be read easily with some Java classes (for instance, the `java.util.Properties` class). These files often look similar to Example 9-1, and in fact, I will use this example properties file throughout the rest of the chapter. Incidentally, it's from the Enhydra application server.

Example 9-1. A typical Java properties file

```
#
# Properties added to System properties
#

# sax parser implementing class
org.xml.sax.parser="org.apache.xerces.parsers.SAXParser"

#
# Properties used to start the server
#

# Class used to start the server
org.enhydra.initialclass=org.enhydra.multiServer.bootstrap.Bootstrap

# initial arguments passed to the server (replace command line args)
org.enhydra.initialargs="./bootstrap.conf"

# Classpath for the parent top enhydra classloader
org.enhydra.classpath="."

# separator for the classpath above
org.enhydra.classpath.separator=":"
```

No big deal here, right? Well, using an instance of the Java `Properties` class, you can load these properties into the object (using the `load(InputStream inputStream)` method) and then deal with them like a `Hashtable`. In fact, the `Properties` class extends the `Hashtable` class in Java; nice, huh? The problem is that many people write these files like the example with names separated by a period (.) to form a sort of hierarchical structure. In the example, you would have a top level (the properties file itself), then the `org` node, and under it the `xml` and `enhydra` nodes, and under the `enhydra` node several nodes, some with values. In other words, you'd expect a structure like the one shown in Figure 9-3.

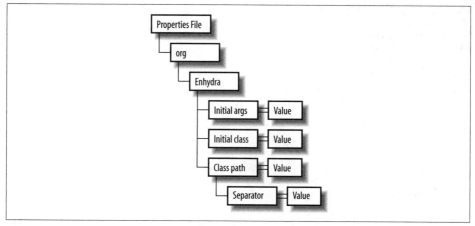

Figure 9-3. *Expected structure of properties shown in Example 9-1*

While this sounds good, Java provides no means of accessing the name-value pairs in this manner. It does not give the period any special value, but instead treats it as just another character. So while you can do this:

```
String classpathValue = Properties.getProperty("org.enhydra.classpath");
```

You cannot do this:

```
List enhydraProperties = Properties.getProperties("org.enhydra");
```

You would expect (or at least I do!) that the latter would work, and provide you all the subproperties with the structure `org.enhydra` (`org.enhydra.classpath`, `org.enhydra.initialargs`, etc.). Unfortunately, that's not part of the `Properties` class. For this reason, many developers have had to write their own little wrapper methods around this object, which of course is nonstandard and a bit of a nuisance. Wouldn't it be nice if this information could be modeled in XML, where operations like the second example are simple? That's exactly what I want to write code to do, and I will use JDOM to demonstrate that API.

Converting to XML

As in previous chapters, it is easiest to start with a skeleton for the class and build out. For the `PropsToXML` class, I want to allow a properties file to be supplied for input, and the name of a file for the XML output. The class reads in the properties file, converts it to an XML document using JDOM, and outputs it to the specified filename. Example 9-2 starts the ball rolling.

Example 9-2. The skeleton of thePropsToXML class

```java
package javaxml3;

import java.io.FileInputStream;
import java.io.FileOutputStream;
import java.io.IOException;
import java.util.Enumeration;
import java.util.Properties;
import org.jdom.Document;
import org.jdom.Element;
import org.jdom.output.Format;
import org.jdom.output.XMLOutputter;

public class PropsToXML {

    /**
     * <p> This will take the supplied properties file, and
     *   convert that file to an XML representation, which is
     *   then output to the supplied XML document filename. </p>
     *
     * @param propertiesFilename file to read in as Java properties.
     * @param xmlFilename file to output XML representation to.
     * @throws <code>IOException</code> - when errors occur.
     */
    public void convert(String propertiesFilename, String xmlFilename)
        throws IOException {

        // Get Java Properties object
        FileInputStream input = new FileInputStream(propertiesFilename);
        Properties props = new Properties();
        props.load(input);

        // Convert to XML
        convertToXML(props, xmlFilename);
    }

    /**
     * <p> This will handle the detail of conversion from a Java
     *   <code>Properties</code> object to an XML document. </p>
     *
     * @param props <code>Properties</code> object to use as input.
     * @param xmlFilename file to output XML to.
     * @throws <code>IOException</code> - when errors occur.
     */
    private void convertToXML(Properties props, String xmlFilename)
        throws IOException {

        // JDOM conversion code goes here
    }

    /**
```

Example 9-2. The skeleton of thePropsToXML class (continued)

```
 * <p> Provide a static entry point for running. </p>
 */
public static void main(String[] args) {
    if (args.length != 2) {
        System.out.println("Usage: java javaxml3.PropsToXML " +
            "[properties file] [XML file for output]");
        System.exit(0);
    }

    try {
        PropsToXML propsToXML = new PropsToXML();
        propsToXML.convert(args[0], args[1]);
    } catch (Exception e) {
        e.printStackTrace();
    }
}
}
```

The only new part of this code is the Java Properties object, which I've mentioned previously. The supplied properties filename is used in the load( ) method, and that object is delegated on to a method that will use JDOM, which I will turn to next.

Creating XML with JDOM

Once the code has the properties in a (more) usable form, it's time to start using JDOM. The first task is to create a JDOM Document object and an Element object for the root element. The root element for a Document can be set either in the constructor or through the setRootElement( ) method. Creating an Element requires only the passing of the element's name. There are alternate versions that take in namespace information, and I will discuss those a little later. For now, it's easiest to use the root element's name, and since this needs to be a top-level, arbitrary name (to contain all the property nestings); I use "properties" in the code. Once this element is created, it's used to create a new JDOM Document.

Then, it's on to dealing with the properties in the supplied file. The list of property names is obtained as a Java Enumeration through the Properties object's propertyNames( ) method. Once that name is available, it can be used to obtain the property value by using the getProperty( ) method. At this point, you've got the root element of the new XML document, the property name to add, and the value for that property. And then, like any other good program, you iterate through all of the other properties until finished. At each step, this information is supplied to a new method, createXMLRepresentation( ). This performs the logic for handling conversion of a single property into a set of XML elements. Add this code, as shown here, to your source file:

```
private void convertToXML(Properties props, String xmlFilename)
    throws IOException {
```

```
    // Create a new JDOM Document with a root element "properties"
    Element root = new Element("properties");
    Document doc = new Document(root);

    // Get the property names
    Enumeration propertyNames = props.propertyNames();
    while (propertyNames.hasMoreElements()) {
        String propertyName = (String)propertyNames.nextElement();
        String propertyValue = props.getProperty(propertyName);
        createXMLRepresentation(root, propertyName, propertyValue);
    }

    // Output document to supplied filename
    Format format = Format.getPrettyFormat();
    XMLOutputter outputter = new XMLOutputter(format);
    FileOutputStream output = new FileOutputStream(xmlFilename);
    outputter.output(doc, output);
}
```

Don't worry about the last few lines that output the JDOM Document yet. I'll deal with this in the next section, but first I want to cover the createXMLRepresentation( ) method, which contains the logic for dealing with a single property, and creating XML from it.

The logical first step to create the XML representation of a property is also the easiest: take the name of the property and create an Element with that name. You've already seen how to do this; simply pass the name of the element to its constructor. Once the element is created, assign the value of the property as the textual content of the element. This can be done easily enough through the setText( ) method, which of course takes a String. Once the element is ready for use, it can be added as a child of the root element through the addContent( ) method. In fact, any legal JDOM construct can be passed to an element's addContent( ) method, as it accepts any object that implements the org.jdom.Content interface. These include DocType, EntityRef, Comment, ProcessingInstruction, and Text. But I'll get to those later; for now, add the following method into your source file:

```
/**
 * <p> This will convert a single property and its value to
 *  an XML element and textual value. </p>
 *
 * @param root JDOM root <code>Element</code> to add children to.
 * @param propertyName name to base element creation on.
 * @param propertyValue value to use for property.
 */
private void createXMLRepresentation(Element root,
                                     String propertyName,
                                     String propertyValue) {

    Element element = new Element(propertyName);
    element.setText(propertyValue);
    root.addContent(element);
}
```

At this point, you can compile the source file, and then use the resulting PropsToXML class. Supply a properties file (you can type in or download the *enhydra.properties* file shown earlier in this chapter), as well as an output filename, as shown here:

```
/javaxml3/build $ java javaxml3.PropsToXML \
                 /javaxml3/ch09/properties/enhydra.properties \
                 enhydraProps.xml
```

This whirs along for a fraction of a second, and then generates an *enhydraProps.xml* file. Open this up; it should look like Example 9-3.

> If you are unfamiliar with *nix, the backslash at the end of each line (\) simply allows for continuation of the command on the next line; Windows users should enter the entire command on one line.

Example 9-3. First version of theenhydraProps.xml document

```
<?xml version="1.0" encoding="UTF-8"?>
<properties>
  <org.enhydra.classpath.separator>":"</org.enhydra.classpath.separator>
  <org.enhydra.initialargs>"./bootstrap.conf"</org.enhydra.initialargs>
  <org.enhydra.initialclass>org.enhydra.multiServer.bootstrap.Bootstrap
</org.enhydra.initialclass>
  <org.enhydra.classpath>"."</org.enhydra.classpath>
  <org.xml.sax.parser>"org.apache.xerces.parsers.SAXParser"
</org.xml.sax.parser>
</properties>
```

> Note that the line wraps in the example are for publishing purposes only; in your document, each property with opening tag, text, and closing tag should be on its own line.

In about 50 lines of code, you've gone from Java properties to XML. However, this XML document isn't much better than the properties file: there is still no way to relate the org.enhydra.initialArgs property to the org.enhydra.classpath property. Our job isn't done yet.

Instead of using the property name as the element name, the code needs to take the property name and split it on the period delimiters. For each of these "subnames," an element needs to be created and added to the element stack. Then the process can repeat. For the property name org.xml.sax, the following XML structure should result:

```
<org>
  <xml>
    <sax>[property Value]</sax>
  </xml>
</org>
```

At each step, using the Element constructor and the addContent( ) method does the trick, and once the name is completely deconstructed, the setText( ) method can be used to set the last element's textual value. The best way is to create a new Element called current and use it as a "pointer" (there aren't any pointers in Java—it's just a term). It will always point at the element that content should be added to. At each step, the code also needs to see if the element to be added already exists. For example, the first property, org.xml.sax, creates an org element. When the next property is added (org.enhydra.classpath), the org element does not need to be created again.

To facilitate this, the getChild( ) method is used. This method takes the name of the child element to retrieve, and is available to all instances of the Element class. If the child specified exists, that element is returned. However, if no child exists, a null value is returned, and it is on this null value that our code can key. In other words, if the return value is an element, that becomes the current element, and no new element needs to be created (it already exists). However, if the return from the getChild( ) call is null, a new element must be created with the current subname, added as content to the current element, and then the current pointer is moved down the tree. Finally, once the iteration is over, the textual value of the property can be added to the leaf element, which turns out to be (nicely) the element that the current pointer references. Add this code to your source file:

```
private void createXMLRepresentation(Element root,
                                     String propertyName,
                                     String propertyValue) {

    /*
    Element element = new Element(propertyName);
    element.setText(propertyValue);
    root.addContent(element);
    */

    int split;
    String name = propertyName;
    Element current = root;
    Element test = null;

    while ((split = name.indexOf(".")) != -1) {
        String subName = name.substring(0, split);
        name = name.substring(split+1);

        // Check for existing element
        if ((test = current.getChild(subName)) == null) {
            Element subElement = new Element(subName);
            current.addContent(subElement);
            current = subElement;
        } else {
            current = test;
        }
    }

    // When out of loop, what's left is the final element's name
    Element last = new Element(name);
    last.setText(propertyValue);
    current.addContent(last);
}
```

With this addition in place, recompile the program and run it again. This time, your output should be a lot nicer, as shown in Example 9-4.

Example 9-4. Updated output fromPropsToXML

```xml
<?xml version="1.0" encoding="UTF-8"?>
<properties>
  <org>
    <enhydra>
      <classpath>
        <separator>":"</separator>
      </classpath>
      <initialargs>"./bootstrap.conf"</initialargs>
      <initialclass>org.enhydra.multiServer.bootstrap.Bootstrap</initialclass>
      <classpath>"."</classpath>
    </enhydra>
    <xml>
      <sax>
        <parser>"org.apache.xerces.parsers.SAXParser"</parser>
      </sax>
    </xml>
  </org>
</properties>
```

And, just as quickly as you've started in on JDOM, you have the hang of it. However, you might notice that the XML document violates one of the rules of thumb for document design introduced in Chapter 2 (in the "DTD Semantics" section, which details usage of elements versus usage of attributes). You see, each property value has a single textual value. That arguably makes the property values suitable as attributes of the last element on the stack, rather than content. Proving that rules are meant to be broken, I prefer them as content in this case.

For demonstration purposes, let's look at converting the property values to attributes rather than textual content. This turns out to be quite easy, and can be done in one of two ways. The first is to create an instance of the JDOM `Attribute` class. The constructor for that class takes the name of the attribute and its value. Then, the resulting instance can be added to the leaf element with that element's `setAttribute( )` method. That approach is shown here:

```java
// When out of loop, what's left is the final element's name
Element last = new Element(name);
/* last.setText(propertyValue); */
Attribute attribute = new Attribute("value", propertyValue);
last.setAttribute(attribute);
current.addContent(last);
```

 If you want to compile the file with these changes, be sure you add an import statement for the `Attribute` class:

```java
import org.jdom.Attribute;
```

A slightly easier way is to use one of the convenience methods that JDOM offers. Since adding attributes is such a common task, the `Element` class provides an overloaded version of `setAttribute()` that takes a name and value, and internally creates an `Attribute` object. In this case, that approach is a little clearer:

```
// When out of loop, what's left is the final element's name
Element last = new Element(name);
/* last.setText(propertyValue); */
last.setAttribute("value", propertyValue);
current.addContent(last);
```

This works just as well and also avoids having to use an extra `import` statement. You can make this change, compile the source file, and run the sample program. The new output should match Example 9-5.

Example 9-5. Output ofPropsToXML using attributes

```
<?xml version="1.0" encoding="UTF-8"?>
<properties>
  <org>
    <enhydra>
      <classpath>
        <separator value="&quot;:&quot;" />
      </classpath>
      <initialargs value="&quot;./bootstrap.conf&quot;" />
      <initialclass value="org.enhydra.multiServer.bootstrap.Bootstrap" />
      <classpath value="&quot;.&quot;" />
    </enhydra>
    <xml>
      <sax>
        <parser value="&quot;org.apache.xerces.parsers.SAXParser&quot;" />
      </sax>
    </xml>
  </org>
</properties>
```

Each property value is now an attribute of the innermost element. Notice that JDOM converts the quotation marks within the attribute values, which are disallowed, to entity references so the document as output is well-formed. However, this makes the output a little less clean, so you may want to switch your code back to using textual data within elements, rather than attributes.

Outputting XML with JDOM

Before we continue, I want to spend a little time on the output portion of the code that I mentioned earlier in the chapter. It's highlighted again here:

```
private void convertToXML(Properties props, String xmlFilename)
    throws IOException {

    // Create a new JDOM Document with a root element "properties"
    Element root = new Element("properties");
    Document doc = new Document(root);
```

```
    // Get the property names
    Enumeration propertyNames = props.propertyNames();
    while (propertyNames.hasMoreElements()) {
        String propertyName = (String)propertyNames.nextElement();
        String propertyValue = props.getProperty(propertyName);
        createXMLRepresentation(root, propertyName, propertyValue);
    }

    // Output document to supplied filename
    Format format = Format.getPrettyFormat();
    XMLOutputter outputter = new XMLOutputter(format);
    FileOutputStream output = new FileOutputStream(xmlFilename);
    outputter.output(doc, output);
}
```

You already know that XMLOutputter is the class to use for handling output to a file, stream, or other static representation. In addition, I supplied a Format object, which instructs the XMLOutputter to use newlines after each element, to indent each level of element nesting with two spaces, and to trim any whitespace before and after character data.

The Format class

JDOM provides three default formatting schemes, available through static methods on the Format class. We've already seen Format.getPrettyFormat(). Format.getRawFormat() returns the default formatting scheme where no extra formatting is done. Format.getCompactFormat() doesn't add indentation or additional newlines, but it does *normalize* the character data in the document, removing leading and trailing whitespace and replacing instances of multiple contiguous whitespace characters into a single space. The Format class allows for customization of any of these Format instances by these properties:

escapeStrategy
> An instance of org.jdom.output.EscapeStrategy that allows you to specify which characters should be escaped for output.

lineSeparator
> Which character or characters should be used when the Format instance adds newlines to the output. This setting applies only to newlines created while outputting.

omitEncoding
> Setting this property to true tells the outputter to skip the outputting of the name of the character encoding scheme in the XML declaration.

omitDeclaration
> Setting this property to true tells the outputter to skip the outputting of the XML declaration entirely.

expandEmptyElements
> This property asks the outputter to never output an empty element such as <name/> and always output <name></name>.

ignoreTrAXEscapingPIs

> TrAX defines processing instructions that indicate to a TrAX Transformer that the standard XML character entities should not be used to escape the output document as is useful when the result of a transformation will not be parsed as XML. JDOM can recognize these processing instructions and apply that behavior to the outputter.

textMode

> Specify a strategy for whitespace handling. The options for textMode are Format. TextMode.PRESERVE, Format.TextMode.TRIM, Format.TextMode.NORMALIZE, and Format.TextMode.TRIM_FULL_WHITE.

indent

> Specify one or more characters to use as the indentation string for each level of element nesting. If indent is non-null, a newline is automatically added before the indentation.

encoding

> Specify a character encoding for the output.

Through setting these properties, you should be able get the output of XMLFormatter to be just as you want it.

Why Don't My Format Customizations Stick?

One frequent area of confusion is why this code doesn't actually change the encoding of the output:

```
outputter.getFormat().setEncoding("ISO-8859-1");
```

The reason is that the getFormat() method actually returns a copy of the Format object. As a result, you need to pass the modified Format object back to the setFormat() method:

```
Format format = outputter.getFormat();
format.setEncoding("ISO-8859-1");
outputter.setFormat(format);
```

Since setEncoding() returns the Format object, you could even write this as:

```
outputter.setFormat(outputter.getFormat()
        .setEncoding("ISO-8859-1"));
```

Other uses of XMLOutputter

There are versions of the output() method (the one used in the example code) that take either an OutputStream or a Writer and an outputString() method that returns a String object. And, although it's generally used to output a Document object, there are versions that take the various JDOM constructs as input, so you could output an entire `Document`, or just an `Element`, `Comment`, `ProcessingInstruction`, or anything else:

```
// Create an outputter with 4 space indentation and new lines
XMLOutputter outputter = new XMLOutputter(Format.getPrettyFormat());

// Output different JDOM constructs
outputter.output(myDocument, myOutputStream);
outputter.output(myElement, myWriter);
outputter.output(myComment, myOutputStream);
// etc...
```

In other words, `XMLOutputter` serves all of your XML output needs. Of course, you can also use `DOMOutputter` and `SAXOutputter`.

XMLProperties

Let's take things to the next logical step and look at reading XML. Continuing with the example of converting a properties file to XML, you are now probably wondering how to access the information in your XML file. Luckily, there's a solution for that, too! In this section, for the sake of explaining how JDOM reads XML, I want to introduce a new utility class, `XMLProperties`. This class is essentially an XML-aware version of the Java `Properties` class; in fact, it extends that class. This class allows access to an XML document through the typical property-access methods like `getProperty()` and `properties()`. In other words, it allows Java-style access (using the `Properties` class) to XML-style storage. In my opinion, this is the best combination you can get.

To accomplish this task, you can start by creating an `XMLProperties` class that extends the `java.util.Properties` class. With this approach, making things work becomes simply a matter of overriding the `load()`, `save()`, and `store()` methods. The first of these, `load()`, reads in an XML document and loads the properties within that document into the superclass object.

 Don't mistake this class for an all-purpose XML-to-properties converter: it will only read in XML that is in the format detailed earlier in this chapter. In other words, properties are elements with either textual or attribute values, but not both. I'll cover both approaches, but you will have to choose one or the other. Don't try to take all your XML documents, read them in, and expect things to work as planned!

The second method, `save()`, is actually deprecated in Java 2, as it doesn't expose any error information; still, it needs to be overridden for Java 1.1 users. To facilitate this, the implementation in `XMLProperties` simply calls `store()`. And `store()` handles the task of writing the properties information out to an XML document. Example 9-6 is a good start at this, and provides a skeleton within which to work.

Example 9-6. The skeleton of theXMLProperties class

```java
package javaxml3;

import java.io.File;
import java.io.FileReader;
import java.io.FileWriter;
import java.io.InputStream;
import java.io.InputStreamReader;
import java.io.IOException;
import java.io.OutputStream;
import java.io.OutputStreamWriter;
import java.io.Reader;
import java.io.Writer;
import java.util.Enumeration;
import java.util.Iterator;
import java.util.List;
import java.util.Properties;

import org.jdom.Attribute;
import org.jdom.Comment;
import org.jdom.Document;
import org.jdom.Element;
import org.jdom.JDOMException;
import org.jdom.input.SAXBuilder;
import org.jdom.output.Format;
import org.jdom.output.XMLOutputter;

public class XMLProperties extends Properties {

    public void load(Reader reader)
        throws IOException {

        // Read XML document into a Properties object
    }

    public void load(InputStream inputStream)
        throws IOException {

        load(new InputStreamReader(inputStream));
    }

    public void load(File xmlDocument)
        throws IOException {

        load(new FileReader(xmlDocument));
    }

    public void save(OutputStream out, String header) {
        try {
            store(out, header);
        } catch (IOException ignored) {
            // Deprecated version doesn't pass errors
        }
    }
```

Example 9-6. The skeleton of theXMLProperties class (continued)

```
public void store(Writer writer, String header)
    throws IOException {

    // Convert properties to XML and output
}

public void store(OutputStream out, String header)
    throws IOException {

    store(new OutputStreamWriter(out), header);
}

public void store(File xmlDocument, String header)
    throws IOException {

    store(new FileWriter(xmlDocument), header);
}
}
```

Please note that I overloaded the load( ) and store( ) methods. While the Properties class only has versions that take an InputStream and OutputStream (respectively), I am a firm believer in providing users with options. The extra versions, which take Files and Readers/Writers, make it easier for users to interact, and add a marginal amount of code to the class. Additionally, these overloaded methods can all delegate to existing methods, which leaves the code ready for loading and storing implementation.

Storing XML

Let's discuss storing XML first, mainly because the code is already written. The logic to take a Properties object and output it as XML is the purpose of the PropsToXML class, and I will simply reuse some of that code here:

```
public void store(Writer writer, String header)
    throws IOException {

    // Create a new JDOM Document with a root element "properties"
    Element root = new Element("properties");
    Document doc = new Document(root);

    // Get the property names
    Enumeration propertyNames = propertyNames( );
    while (propertyNames.hasMoreElements( )) {
        String propertyName = (String)propertyNames.nextElement( );
        String propertyValue = getProperty(propertyName);
        createXMLRepresentation(root, propertyName, propertyValue);
    }

    // Output document to supplied filename
    XMLOutputter outputter = new XMLOutputter(Format.getPrettyFormat( ));
    outputter.output(doc, writer);
}
```

```
            private void createXMLRepresentation(Element root,
                                                  String propertyName,
                                                  String propertyValue) {

        int split;
        String name = propertyName;
        Element current = root;
        Element test = null;

        while ((split = name.indexOf(".")) != -1) {
            String subName = name.substring(0, split);
            name = name.substring(split+1);

            // Check for existing element
            if ((test = current.getChild(subName)) == null) {
                Element subElement = new Element(subName);
                current.addContent(subElement);
                current = subElement;
            } else {
                current = test;
            }
        }

        // When out of loop, what's left is the final element's name
        Element last = new Element(name);
        last.setText(propertyValue);
        /** Uncomment this for Attribute usage */
        /*
        last.setAttribute("value", propertyValue);
        */
        current.addContent(last);
    }
```

Not much needs comment. There are a few lines of code highlighted to illustrate some changes, though. The first two changes ensure that the superclass is used to obtain the property names and values, rather than the Properties object that was passed into the version of this method in PropsToXML. The third change moves from using a string filename to the supplied Writer for output. With those few modifications, you're all set to compile the XMLProperties source file.

There is one item missing, though. Note that the store( ) method allows specification of a header variable; in a standard Java properties file, this is added as a comment to the head of the file. To keep things parallel, the XMLProperties class can be modified to do the same thing. You will need to use the Comment class to do this. The following code additions put this change into effect:

```
        public void store(Writer writer, String header)
            throws IOException {

            // Create a new JDOM Document with a root element "properties"
            Document doc = new Document();
            Element root = new Element("properties");
            doc.setRootElement(root);
```

```
        // Add in header information
        Comment comment = new Comment(header);
        doc.addContent(comment);

        // Get the property names
        Enumeration propertyNames = propertyNames();
        while (propertyNames.hasMoreElements()) {
            String propertyName = (String)propertyNames.nextElement();
            String propertyValue = getProperty(propertyName);
            createXMLRepresentation(root, propertyName, propertyValue);
        }

        // Output document to supplied filename
        Format format = Format.getPrettyFormat();
        XMLOutputter outputter = new XMLOutputter(format);
        outputter.output(doc, writer);
    }
```

The addContent() method of the Document object is overloaded to take both Comment and ProcessingInstruction objects, and appends the content to the file. It is used here to add in the header parameter as a comment to the XML document being written to.

Loading XML

There's not much left to do here. Basically, the class writes out to XML, provides access to XML (through the methods already existing on the Properties class), and now simply needs to read in XML. This is a fairly simple task, which boils down to more recursion. I'll show you the code modifications needed, and then walk you through them. Enter the code shown here into your *XMLProperties.java* source file:

```
    public void load(Reader reader)
        throws IOException {

        try {
            // Load XML into JDOM Document
            SAXBuilder builder = new SAXBuilder();
            Document doc = builder.build(reader);

            // Turn into properties objects
            loadFromElements(doc.getRootElement().getChildren(),
                new StringBuffer(""));

        } catch (JDOMException e) {
            throw new IOException(e.getMessage());
        }
    }

    private void loadFromElements(List elements, StringBuffer baseName) {
        // Iterate through each element
        for (Iterator i = elements.iterator(); i.hasNext(); ) {
            Element current = (Element)i.next();
            String name = current.getName();
            String text = current.getTextNormalize();
```

```
            // Don't add "." if no baseName
            if (baseName.length() > 0) {
                baseName.append(".");
            }
            baseName.append(name);

            // See if we have an element value
            if ((text == null) || (text.equals(""))) {
                // If no text, recurse on children
                loadFromElements(current.getChildren(),
                                 baseName);
            } else {
                // If text, this is a property
                setProperty(baseName.toString(),
                            text);
            }

            // On unwind from recursion, remove last name
            if (baseName.length() == name.length()) {
                baseName.setLength(0);
            } else {
                baseName.setLength(baseName.length() -
                    (name.length() + 1));
            }
        }
    }
}
```

The implementation of the load( ) method (which all overloaded versions delegate to) uses SAXBuilder to read in the supplied XML document.

The name for a property consists of the names of all the elements leading to the property value, with a period separating each name. Here is a sample property in XML:

```
<properties>
  <org>
    <enhydra>
      <classpath>"."</classpath>
    </enhydra>
  </org>
</properties>
```

The property name can be obtained by taking the element names leading to the value (excluding the properties element, which was used as a root-level container): org, enhydra, and classpath. Throw a period between each, and you get org.enhydra. classpath, which is the property name in question. To accomplish this, I coded up the loadFromElements( ) method. This takes in a list of elements, iterates through them, and deals with each element individually. If the element has a textual value, that value is added to the superclass object's properties. If it has child elements instead, then the children are obtained, and recursion begins again on the new list of children. At each step of recursion, the name of the element being dealt with is appended to the baseName variable, which keeps track of the property names. Winding through recursion, baseName would be org, then org.enhydra, then org. enhydra.classpath.

And, as recursion unwinds, the baseName variable is shortened to remove the last element name. Let's look at the JDOM method calls that make it possible.

First, you'll notice several invocations of the getChildren( ) method on instances of the Element class. This method returns all child elements of the current element as a Java List. There are versions of this method that also take in the name of an element to search for, and return either all elements with that name (getChildren(String name)), or just the first child element with that name (getChild(String name)). There are also namespace-aware versions of the method, which will be covered in the next chapter. To start the recursion process, the root element is obtained from the JDOM Document object through the getRootElement( ) method, and then its children are used to seed recursion. Once in the loadFromElements( ) method, standard Java classes are used to move through the list of elements (such as java.util.Iterator). To check for textual content, the getTextNormalize( ) method is used. This method returns the textual content of an element, and returns the element without surrounding whitespace.* Thus, the content " textual content" (note the surrounding whitespace) would be returned as "textual content". While this seems somewhat trivial, consider this more realistic example of XML:

```
<chapter>
  <title>
    Advanced SAX
  </title>
</chapter>
```

The actual textual content of the title element turns out to be several spaces, followed by a line feed, followed by more space, the characters "Advanced SAX," more space, another line feed, and even more space. In other words, probably not what you expected. The returned string data from a call to getTextNormalize( ) would simply be "Advanced SAX," which is what you want in most cases anyway. However, if you do want the complete content (often used for reproducing the input document exactly as it came in), you can use the getText( ) method, which returns the element's content unchanged. If there is no content, the return value from this method is an empty string (""), which makes for an easy comparison, as shown in the example code. And that's about it: a few simple method calls and the code is reading XML with JDOM. Let's see this class in action.

Taking a Test Drive

Once everything is in place in the XMLProperties class, compile it. To test it out, you can enter in or download Example 9-7, which is a class that uses the XMLProperties class to load an XML document, print some information out about it, and then write the properties back out as XML.

---

* It also removes more than one space *between* words. The textual content "lots   of   spaces" would be returned through getTextNormalize( ) as "lots of spaces".

Example 9-7. Testing theXMLProperties class

```
package javaxml3;

import java.io.FileInputStream;
import java.io.FileOutputStream;
import java.util.Enumeration;

public class TestXMLProperties {

    public static void main(String[] args) {
        if (args.length != 2) {
            System.out.println("Usage: java javaxml2.TestXMLProperties " +
                "[XML input document] [XML output document]");
            System.exit(0);
        }

        try {
            // Create and load properties
            System.out.println("Reading XML properties from " + args[0]);
            XMLProperties props = new XMLProperties();
            props.load(new FileInputStream(args[0]));

            // Print out properties and values
            System.out.println("\n\n---- Property Values ----");
            Enumeration names = props.propertyNames();
            while (names.hasMoreElements()) {
                String name = (String)names.nextElement();
                String value = props.getProperty(name);
                System.out.println("Property Name: " + name +
                                " has value " + value);
            }

            // Store properties
            System.out.println("\n\nWriting XML properies to " + args[1]);
            props.store(new FileOutputStream(args[1]),
                "Testing XMLProperties class");
        } catch (Exception e) {
            e.printStackTrace();
        }
    }
}
```

This doesn't do much. It reads in properties, uses them to print out all the property names and values, and then writes those properties back out—but all in XML. You can run this program on the XML file generated by the PropsToXML class I showed you earlier in the chapter.

 The version of XMLProperties used here deals with property values as textual content of elements (the first version of PropsToXML shown), not as attribute values (the second version of PropsToXML). You'll need to use that earlier version of PropsToXML, or back out your changes, if you are going to use it to generate XML for input to the TestXMLProperties class. Otherwise, you won't pick up any property values with this code.

Supply the test program with the XML input file and the name of the output file:

```
C:\javaxml3\build>java javaxml3.TestXMLProperties enhydraProps.xml output.xml
Reading XML properties from enhydraProps.xml


---- Property Values ----
Property Name: org.enhydra.classpath.separator has value ":"
Property Name: org.enhydra.initialargs has value "./bootstrap.conf"
Property Name: org.enhydra.initialclass has value
  org.enhydra.multiServer.bootstrap.Bootstrap
Property Name: org.enhydra.classpath has value "."
Property Name: org.xml.sax.parser has value
  "org.apache.xerces.parsers.SAXParser"


Writing XML properties to output.xml
```

And there you have it: XML data formatting, properties behavior.

Backtracking

Before wrapping up on the code, there are a few items that should be addressed. First, take a look at the XML file generated by TestXMLProperties, the result of invoking store( ) on the properties. It should look similar to Example 9-8 if you used the XML version of *enhydra.properties* detailed earlier in this chapter.

Example 9-8. Output fromTestXMLProperties

```
<?xml version="1.0" encoding="UTF-8"?>
<properties>
  <org>
    <enhydra>
      <classpath>
        <separator>":"</separator>
      </classpath>
      <initialargs>"./bootstrap.conf"</initialargs>
      <initialclass>org.enhydra.multiServer.bootstrap.Bootstrap</initialclass>
      <classpath>"."</classpath>
    </enhydra>
    <xml>
      <sax>
        <parser>"org.apache.xerces.parsers.SAXParser"</parser>
      </sax>
    </xml>
  </org>
</properties>
<!--Testing XMLProperties class-->
```

Notice anything wrong? The header comment is in the wrong place. Take another look at the code that added in that comment, from the store( ) method:

```
// Create a new JDOM Document with a root element "properties"
Document doc = new Document( );
```

```
Element root = new Element("properties");
doc.setRootElement(root);

// Add in header information
Comment comment = new Comment(header);
doc.addContent(comment);
```

The root element appears before the comment because it is added to the Document object first. We could add the comment before calling setRootElement( ), but to demonstrate another feature of JDOM, we'll use a new method, getContent( ). This method returns a List that contains all the content of the Document, including comments, the root element, and processing instructions. Then, you can prepend the comment to this list, as shown here, using methods of the List class:

```
// Add in header information
Comment comment = new Comment(header);
doc.getContent().add(0, comment);
```

With this change in place, your output looks as it should:

```
<?xml version="1.0" encoding="UTF-8"?>
<!--Testing XMLProperties class-->
<properties>
  <org>
    <enhydra>
      <classpath>
        <separator>":"</separator>
      </classpath>
      <initialargs>"./bootstrap.conf"</initialargs>
      <initialclass>org.enhydra.multiServer.bootstrap.Bootstrap</initialclass>
      <classpath>"."</classpath>
    </enhydra>
    <xml>
      <sax>
        <parser>"org.apache.xerces.parsers.SAXParser"</parser>
      </sax>
    </xml>
  </org>
</properties>
```

The getContent( ) method is also available on the Element class, and returns all content of the element, regardless of type (elements, processing instructions, comments, entities, and Text objects for textual content).

Also important are the modifications necessary for XMLProperties to use attributes for property values, instead of element content. You've already seen the code change needed in storage of properties (in fact, the change is commented out in the source code, so you don't need to write anything new). As for loading, the change involves checking for an attribute instead of an element's textual content. This can be done with the getAttributeValue(String name) method, which returns the value of the named attribute, or null if no value exists. The change is shown here:

```
private void loadFromElements(List elements, StringBuffer baseName) {
    // Iterate through each element
```

```
        for (Iterator i = elements.iterator( ); i.hasNext( ); ) {
            Element current = (Element)i.next( );
            String name = current.getName( );
            // String text = current.getTextTrim( );
            String text = current.getAttributeValue("value");

            // Don't add "." if no baseName
            if (baseName.length( ) > 0) {
                baseName.append(".");
            }
            baseName.append(name);

            // See if we have an attribute value
            if ((text == null) || (text.equals("")))) {
                // If no text, recurse on children
                loadFromElements(current.getChildren( ),
                                baseName);
            } else {
                // If text, this is a property
                setProperty(baseName.toString( ),
                            text);
            }

            // On unwind from recursion, remove last name
            if (baseName.length( ) == name.length( )) {
                baseName.setLength(0);
            } else {
                baseName.setLength(baseName.length( ) -
                    (name.length( ) + 1));
            }
        }
    }
}
```

After compiling the changes, you're set to deal with attribute values instead of element content. Leave the code in the state you prefer (as I mentioned earlier, I actually like the values as element content). If you want textual element content, be sure to back out these changes after seeing how they affect output. Whichever you prefer, hopefully you are beginning to know your way around JDOM. And just like SAX, DOM, and StAX, I highly recommend bookmarking the JavaDoc (either locally or online) as a quick reference for those methods you just can't quite remember.

More JDOM Classes

The following sections discuss additional JDOM classes.

The Namespace Class

This section will briefly cover namespace support in JDOM with the Namespace class. This class acts as both an instance variable and a factory within the JDOM architecture. When you need to create a new namespace, either to create a new element or attribute or for searching for existing elements and attributes, you use the static getNamespace( ) methods on this class:

```
// Create namespace with prefix
Namespace schemaNamespace =
    Namespace.getNamespace("xsd", "http://www.w3.org/XMLSchema/2001");

// Create namespace without prefix
Namespace javaxml3Namespace =
    Namespace.getNamespace("http://www.oreilly.com/javaxml3");
```

As you can see, there is a version for creating namespaces with prefixes and one for creating namespaces without prefixes, in which case the namespace URI is set as the default namespace. Either version can be used, with the resulting Namespace object then supplied to the various JDOM methods:

```
// Create element with namespace
Element schema = new Element("schema", schemaNamespace);

// Search for children in the specified namespace
List chapterElements = contentElement.getChildren("chapter", javaxml3Namespace);

// Declare a new namespace on this element
catalogElement.addNamespaceDeclaration(
    Namespace.getNamespace("tng", "http://www.truenorthguitars.com"));
```

These are all fairly self-explanatory. Also, when XML serialization is performed with the various outputters (SAXOutputter, DOMOutputter, and XMLOutputter), the namespace declarations are automatically handled and added to the resulting XML.

One final note: in JDOM, namespace comparison is based solely on URI. That is, two Namespace objects are equal if their URIs are equal, regardless of prefix. This is in keeping with the letter and spirit of the XML Namespace specification, which indicates that two elements are in the same namespace if their URIs are identical, regardless of prefix. Look at this XML document fragment:

```
<guitar xmlns="http://www.truenorthguitars.com">
  <ni:owner xmlns:ni="http://www.newInstance.com">
    <ni:name>Brett McLaughlin</ni:name>
    <tng:model xmlns:tng="http://www.truenorthguitars.com">Model 1</tng:model>
    <backWood>Madagascar Rosewood</backWood>
  </ni:owner>
</guitar>
```

Even though they have varying prefixes, the elements guitar, model, and backWood are all in the same namespace. This holds true in the JDOM Namespace model as well. In fact, the Namespace class's equals( ) method will return equal based solely on URIs, regardless of prefix.

XSL Transformations with JDOM

JDOM includes a simple class for performing XSL transformations called org.jdom. transform.XSLTransformer. Each instance of this class represents one stylesheet and wraps a Templates object from the TrAX API discussed in Chapter 7. You can create an XSLTransformer object by calling the constructor with the stylesheet as a JDOM Document object, a java.io.File, a java.io.InputStream, a java.io.Reader, or a system ID. Example 9-9 transforms an XML document stored as a Document object inputDocument with a stylesheet in the file *stylesheet.xsl*.

Example 9-9. Transformation from Document to Document

```
XSLTransformer transformer = new XSLTransformer(new File("stylesheet.xsl"));
Document outputDocument = transformer.transform(inputDocument);
```

In addition to the basic support provided by the XSLTransformer class, JDOM supplies implementations of the javax.xml.transform.Source and javax.xml.transform. Result interfaces from the TrAX API. These implementations, called org.jdom. transform.JDOMSource and org.jdom.transform.JDOMResult, let you use JDOM Document objects as the source of XSL transformations done using the TrAX API and to save the result of a TrAX transformation in a JDOM Document object. You would use these classes rather than XSLTransformer if you needed to use TrAX directly, such as when you were transforming to or from something other than JDOM, or when you needed to tweak the configuration of the TransformerFactory. Example 9-10 transforms an XML document stored in the file *input.xml* with the stylesheet in the file *stylesheet.xsl* and stores the result in a JDOM Document object.

Example 9-10. Transformation from a file to anorg.jdom.Document object usingTrAX directly

```
TransformerFactory factory = TransformerFactory.newInstance();
Transformer transformer = factory.
     newTransformer(new StreamSource("stylesheet.xsl"));
StreamSource in = new StreamSource("input.xml");
JDOMResult out = new JDOMResult();
transformer.transform(in, out);
Document resultDocument = out.getDocument();
```

In addition to a Document, both JDOMSource and JDOMResult can wrap one or more JDOM Element objects. The XSLTransformer utility class uses JDOMSource and JDOMResult internally and is therefore is a good point of reference for their usage.

XPath and JDOM

JDOM provides support for evaluating XPath expressions on JDOM objects, including Documents and Elements. As with XSLT, JDOM delegates the processing of the XPath expression to a separate library. By default, this library is Jaxen, the JAR files for which are included in the JDOM distribution as described in the earlier section "The JDOM Distribution."

The abstract XPath class, UML for which is in Figure 9-4, has a newInstance() method for creating concrete implementations of the XPath class, along with two utility methods for performing simple XPath expression evaluation with a single method call. The primary advantage of using the newInstance( ) method is the same as using JAXP's XPathExpression class (discussed in Chapter 7)—your expression is precompiled so that you avoid the overhead of expression compilation per evaluation. In addition, compiled XPath instances are the only way to use variables or namespaces in XPath expressions.

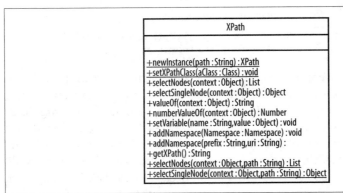

XPath
+newInstance(path : String) : XPath
+setXPathClass(aClass : Class) : void
+selectNodes(context : Object) : List
+selectSingleNode(context : Object) : Object
+valueOf(context : Object) : String
+numberValueOf(context : Object) : Number
+setVariable(name : String,value : Object) : void
+addNamespace(Namespace : Namespace) : void
+addNamespace(prefix : String,uri : String) :
+getXPath() : String
+selectNodes(context : Object,path : String) : List
+selectSingleNode(context : Object,path : String) : Object

Figure 9-4. The JDOM XPath class

 If you compare JDOM's XPath class to JAXP's XPath class, you'll notice that JDOM does not support custom XPath functions. If you need this capability, you should take a look at using the Jaxen library directly (for more on Jaxen, see *http://jaxen.codehaus.org*) or using the Saxon library from *http://www.saxonica.com*. Saxon has the added benefits that it provides support for XPath 2 and plugs into JAXP 1.3 to allow you to use the JAXP XPath API with JDOM documents.

Using the XPath class's static methods couldn't be simpler. First, you need to parse a document or create a Document or Element object.* Once you have this object, you simply pass it to XPath.selectNodes( ) or XPath.selectSingleNode( ) along with your XPath expression:

```
SAXBuilder builder = new SAXBuilder( );
Document doc = builder.build(new File("tds.xml"));
Attribute attr = (Attribute) XPath.selectSingleNode(doc, "/schedule/@name");
```

Compiling this XPath expression to an XPath instance is only slightly different:

```
XPath path = XPath.newInstance("/schedule/@name");
Attribute attr = (Attribute) path.selectSingleNode(doc);
```

And we can also get the result of the expression as a String:

```
String name = path.valueOf(doc);
```

---

* It is possible to evaluate XPath expressions against an Attribute object, but this is an unusual case.

Namespaces and XPath variables are supported through the addNamespace() and setVariable() methods, respectively. The GuestManager class from Chapter 7 can be rewritten with namespace support as:

```java
package javaxml3;

import java.io.File;
import java.io.IOException;
import java.text.SimpleDateFormat;
import java.util.Date;

import org.jdom.Document;
import org.jdom.Element;
import org.jdom.JDOMException;
import org.jdom.Namespace;
import org.jdom.input.SAXBuilder;
import org.jdom.xpath.XPath;

public class JDOMGuestManagerNS {

    private static Namespace NS_GUEST = Namespace.getNamespace("g",
            "uri:comedy:guest");

    private static Namespace NS_SCHEDULE = Namespace.getNamespace("s",
            "uri:comedy:schedule");

    private Document document;

    private SimpleDateFormat xmlDateFormat = new SimpleDateFormat("MM.dd.yy");

    private XPath xPath;

    public JDOMGuestManagerNS(String fileName) throws JDOMException,
            IOException {
        SAXBuilder builder = new SAXBuilder();
        document = builder.build(new File(fileName));

        xPath = XPath.newInstance("/s:schedule/s:show[@date=$date]/g:guest");
        xPath.addNamespace(NS_SCHEDULE);
        xPath.addNamespace(NS_GUEST);
    }

    public synchronized Element getGuest(Date guestDate) throws JDOMException {
        String formattedDate = xmlDateFormat.format(guestDate);
        xPath.setVariable("date", formattedDate);
        return (Element) xPath.selectSingleNode(document);
    }

    public static void main(String[] args) throws Exception {
        JDOMGuestManagerNS gm = new JDOMGuestManagerNS("tds_ns.xml");
        Element guest = gm.getGuest(new Date(2006, 5, 14));
        System.out.println(guest.getChildText("name", NS_GUEST));
    }

}
```

Although this is a reduction in the number of lines of code (mostly because we did not need to write classes to resolve the variable or namespaces), we do lose some of the flexibility that comes with the JAXP XPath API discussed in Chapter 7. In the case of XPath variables, the XPathVariableResolver interface from JAXP allows you to resolve variable values using whatever logic you want. For example, in a servlet context, you could resolve variables based on request parameters or session attributes by writing an implementation of XPathVariableResolver that wraps the Request or Session objects. This is not possible with JDOM's XPath class without a call to setVariable( ) for each parameter or attribute. But in the vast majority of cases, JDOM's XPath support will fit your needs. If it doesn't and more dynamic variables or custom function support are required, you can use the JAXP XPath API instead.

JDOM Filters

The "XMLProperties" section outlined the use of the getContent( ) method of both Document and Element objects. This method is actually defined on the Parent interface, which both Document and Element implement. Parent defines a number of methods in addition to getContent( ):

```
public interface Parent extends Cloneable, Serializable {
    int getContentSize( );
    int indexOf(Content child);
    List cloneContent( );
    Content getContent(int index);
    List getContent( );
    List getContent(Filter filter);
    List removeContent( );
    List removeContent(Filter filter);
    boolean removeContent(Content child);
    Content removeContent(int index);
    Object clone( );
    Iterator getDescendants( );
    Iterator getDescendants(Filter filter);
    Parent getParent( );
    Document getDocument( );
}
```

Most significant are the methods getContent( ), getDescendants( ), and removeContent( ). Each of these has an overloaded version that accepts an instance of the org.jdom.filter.Filter interface.

The Filter performs a similar objective to the filter interfaces and classes we've discussed previously in this book. A call to the no argument getContent( ) method returns a List of the content of the element (which could be empty or could be any combination of Text, Element, Comment, ProcessingInstruction, and EntityRef objects). By creating and passing a Filter object, we can limit the resulting List. Likewise for getDescendants( ), which is a recursive version of getContent( ). The version of removeContent( ) that accepts a `Filter` object will remove only the content that matches that filter.

The `Filter` interface defines one method—match( )—that returns true if the object should be returned and false if it should not. Example 9-11 contains a simple filter that will only pass through `Element` objects.

Example 9-11. Simple JDOM filter

```
package javaxml3;

import org.jdom.Element;
import org.jdom.filter.Filter;

public class ElementOnlyFilter implements Filter {

    public boolean matches(Object obj) {
        return obj instanceof Element;
    }

}
```

This class can be used to perform a variety of functions:

myElement.getContent(new ElementOnlyFilter( ))
: Returns a list of `Element` objects that are children of `myElement`

myElement.getDescendants(new ElementOnlyFilter( ));
: Returns all `Element` objects that are descended from `myElement`

myElement.removeContent(new ElementOnlyFilter( ));
: Removes all elements from the list of child elements of `myElement`

JDOM includes a handful of `Filter` implementations that you should check before writing your own.

ElementFilter

Using its zero-argument constructor, `org.jdom.filter.ElementFilter` provides the same functionality as our `ElementOnlyFilter` class from Example 9-11. However, it goes several steps further and allows you to specify a local name, a `Namespace`, or both to further limit the objects matched by the filter.

ContentFilter

The class `org.jdom.filter.ContentFilter` allows you to filter for any object type or combination of object types. By default, it will accept any valid JDOM object. You can create a customized filter by passing a mask to the constructor of `ContentFilter`. This mask can be constructed by combining constants defined by `ContentFilter` with the | operator. For example, a filter that accepts only `Element` and `Comment` objects could be created with:

```
new ContentFilter(ContentFilter.ELEMENT | ContentFilter.COMMENT);
```

ContentFilter also provides setter methods to selectively enable or disable acceptance of a particular object type:

```
ContentFilter filter = new ContentFilter(); // match( ) now always
                                            // returns true
filter.setCommentVisible(false);
filter.setPIVisible(false);
```

This creates a filter that accepts all objects except for comments and processing instructions. If you want to only enable a few types, this syntax could get wordy; so instead you can pass false to the constructor to get a filter that doesn't accept anything and then selectively enable just the types you want:

```
ContentFilter filter = new ContentFilter(false); // match( ) now always
                                                 // returns false
filter.setElementVisible(true);
filter.setCommentVisible(true);
```

NegateFilter

To reverse the result of a Filter's match( ) method, use org.jdom.filter. NegateFilter. For example, to create a filter that accepts anything *except* Element objects, you could write:

```
Filter filter = new NegateFilter(new ElementOnlyFilter( ));
```

OrFilter and AndFilter

The last of the provided filters, org.jdom.filter.OrFilter and org.jdom.filter. AndFilter allow you to combine other Filter implementations by using the logical OR and AND operations to create complex filtering logic. A filter that accepts comments, elements with the local name "person," and elements in the namespace http://www.oreilly.com/javaxml3 could be created with:

```
Namespace ora = Namespace.getNamespace("http://www.oreilly.com/javaxml3");
Filter filter = new OrFilter(new ContentFilter(ContentFilter.COMMENT),
        new OrFilter(new ElementFilter("person"), new ElementFilter(ora));
```

Note that I am nesting an OrFilter within another OrFilter. This is perfectly legal and appropriate. But please be kind to anyone who might be reading your code in the future by limiting the amount of nesting that occurs in one assignment. The code above is more readable as:

```
Fitler filter = new OrFilter(new ElementFilter("person"), new ElementFilter(ora));
filter = new OrFilter(filter, new ContentFilter(ContentFilter.COMMENT));
```

The EntityRef Class

Next up on the JDOM internals list is the EntityRef class. This is another class that you may not have to use much in common cases, but is helpful to know for special coding needs. This class represents an XML entity reference in JDOM, such as the

OReillyCopyright entity reference in the *contents.xml* document I have been using in examples:

```
<ora:copyright>&OReillyCopyright;</ora:copyright>
```

This class allows for setting and retrieval of a name, public ID, and system ID, just as is possible when defining the reference in an XML DTD or schema. It can appear anywhere in a JDOM content tree, like the Elements and Text nodes. However, like Text nodes, an EntityRef class is often a bit of an irritation in the normal case. For example, in the *contents.xml* document, modeled in JDOM, you are likely to be more interested in the textual value of the reference (the resolved content) rather than the reference itself. In other words, when you invoke getContent( ) on the copyright Element in a JDOM tree, you'd like to get "Copyright O'Reilly, 2007" or whatever other textual value is referred to by the entity reference. This is much more useful (again, in the most common cases) than getting a no-content indicator (an empty string), and then having to check for the existence of an EntityRef. For this reason, by default, all entity references are expanded when using the JDOM builders (SAXBuilder and DOMBuilder) to generate JDOM from existing XML. You will rarely see EntityRefs in this default case, because you don't want to mess with them. However, if you find you need to leave entity references unexpanded and represented by EntityRefs, you can use the setExpandEntities( ) method on the builder classes:

```
// Create new builder
SAXBuilder builder = new SAXBuilder( );

// Do not expand entity references (default is to expand these)
builder.setExpandEnitites(false);

// Build the tree with EntityRef objects (if needed, of course)
Document doc = builder.build(inputStream);
```

In this case, you may have EntityRef instances in the tree (if you were using the *contents.xml* document, for example). And you can always create EntityRefs directly and place them in the JDOM tree:

```
// Create new entity reference
EntityRef ref = new EntityRef("TrueNorthGuitarsTagline");
ref.setSystemID("tngTagline.xml");

// Insert into the tree
tagLineElement.addContent(ref);
```

When serializing this tree, you get XML like this:

```
<guitar>
  <tagLine>&TrueNorthGuitarsTagline;</tagLine>
</guitar>
```

And when reading the document back in using a builder, the resulting JDOM Document would depend on the expandEntities flag. If it is set to false, you'd get the original EntityRef back again with the correct name and system ID. With this value set to false (the default), you'd get the resolved content. A second serialization might result in:

```
<guitar>
  <tagLine>two hands, one heart</tagLine>
</guitar>
```

While this may seem like a lot of fuss over something simple, it's important to realize that whether or not entities are expanded can change the input and output XML you are working with. Always keep track of how the builder flags are set, and what you want your JDOM tree and XML output to look like.

JDOM and Factories

As noted earlier in this chapter, the ability to have some form of factories allows greater flexibility in how your XML is modeled in Java. Take a look at the simple subclass of JDOM's Element class shown in Example 9-12.

Example 9-12. Subclassing the JDOM Element class

```
package javaxml3;

import org.jdom.Element;
import org.jdom.Namespace;

public class ORAElement extends Element {

    private static final Namespace ORA_NAMESPACE =
        Namespace.getNamespace("ora", "http://www.oreilly.com");

    public ORAElement(String name) {
        super(name, ORA_NAMESPACE);
    }

    public ORAElement(String name, Namespace ns) {
        super(name, ORA_NAMESPACE);
    }

    public ORAElement(String name, String uri) {
        super(name, ORA_NAMESPACE);
    }

    public ORAElement(String name, String prefix, String uri) {
        super(name, ORA_NAMESPACE);
    }
}
```

This is about as simple a subclass as you could come up with. It is somewhat similar to the NamespaceFilter class from Chapter 4 in that it disregards whatever namespace is actually supplied to the element (even if there isn't a namespace supplied!), and sets the element's namespace defined by the URI http://www.oreilly.com

with the prefix ora.[*] This is a simple case, but it gives you an idea of what is possible, and serves as a good example for this section.

Creating a Factory

Once you've got a custom subclass, the next step is actually using it. As I already mentioned, JDOM considers having to create all objects with factories a bit over the top. Simple element creation in JDOM works like this:

```
// Create a new Element
Element element = new Element("guitar");
```

Things remain equally simple with a custom subclass:

```
// Create a new Element, typed as an ORAElement
Element oraElement = new ORAElement("guitar");
```

The element is dropped into the O'Reilly namespace because of the custom subclass. Additionally, this method is more self-documenting than using a factory. It is clear at any point exactly what classes are being used to create objects. Compare that to this code fragment:

```
// Create an element: what type is created?
Element someElement = doc.createElement("guitar");
```

It's not clear if the object created is an Element instance, an ORAElement instance, or something else entirely. For these reasons, the custom class approach serves JDOM well. For object creation, you can simply instantiate your custom subclass directly. However, the need for factories arises when you are building a document:

```
// Build from an input source
SAXBuilder builder = new SAXBuilder( );
Document doc = builder.build(someInputStream);
```

Obviously, here you were unable to specify custom classes through the building process. I suppose you could be really bold and modify the SAXBuilder class (and the related org.jdom.input.SAXHandler class), but that's a little ridiculous. So, to facilitate this, the JDOMFactory interface, in the org.jdom package, was introduced. This interface defines methods for every type of object creation. For example, there are four methods for element creation, which match up to the four constructors for the Element class:

```
public Element element(String name);
public Element element(String name, Namespace ns);
public Element element(String name, String uri);
public Element element(String name, String prefix, String uri);
```

You will find similar methods for Document, Attribute, CDATA, and all the rest. By default, JDOM uses the org.jdom.DefaultJDOMFactory, which simply returns all of

---

[*] It is slightly different from NamespaceFilter in that it changes all elements to a new namespace, rather than just those elements with a particular namespace.

the core JDOM classes within these methods. However, you can easily subclass this implementation and provide your own factory methods. Look at Example 9-13, which defines a custom factory.

Example 9-13. A customJDOMFactory implementation

```
package javaxml3;

import org.jdom.DefaultJDOMFactory;
import org.jdom.Element;
import org.jdom.JDOMFactory;
import org.jdom.Namespace;

class CustomJDOMFactory extends DefaultJDOMFactory implements JDOMFactory {

    public Element element(String name) {
        return new ORAElement(name);
    }

    public Element element(String name, Namespace ns) {
        return new ORAElement(name, ns);
    }

    public Element element(String name, String uri) {
        return new ORAElement(name, uri);
    }

    public Element element(String name, String prefix, String uri) {
        return new ORAElement(name, prefix, uri);
    }
}
```

This is a simple implementation; it doesn't need to be very complex. It overrides each of the element() methods and returns an instance of the custom subclass, ORAElement, instead of the default JDOM Element class. At this point, any builder that uses this factory will end up with ORAElement instances in the created JDOM Document object, rather than the default Element instances you would normally see. All that's left is to let the build process know about this custom factory.

Building with Custom Classes

Once you have a valid implementation of JDOMFactory, let your builders know to use it by invoking the setFactory() method and passing in a factory instance. This method is available on both of the current JDOM builders, SAXBuilder and DOMBuilder. To see it in action, check out Example 9-14. This simple class takes in an XML document and builds it using the ORAElement class and CustomJDOMFactory from Examples 9-12 and 9-13. It then writes the document back out to a supplied output filename, so you can see the effect of the custom classes.

Example 9-14. Building with custom classes using a custom factory

```java
package javaxml3;

import java.io.File;
import java.io.FileWriter;
import java.io.IOException;
import org.jdom.Document;
import org.jdom.JDOMException;
import org.jdom.JDOMFactory;
import org.jdom.input.SAXBuilder;
import org.jdom.output.XMLOutputter;

public class ElementChanger {

    public void change(String inputFilename, String outputFilename)
        throws IOException, JDOMException {

        // Create builder and set up factory
        SAXBuilder builder = new SAXBuilder();
        JDOMFactory factory = new CustomJDOMFactory();
        builder.setFactory(factory);

        // Build document
        Document doc = builder.build(inputFilename);

        // Output document
        XMLOutputter outputter = new XMLOutputter();
        outputter.output(doc, new FileWriter(new File(outputFilename)));
    }

    public static void main(String[] args) {
        if (args.length != 2) {
            System.out.println("Usage: javaxml2.ElementChanger " +
                "[XML Input Filename] [XML Output Filename]");
            return;
        }

        try {
            ElementChanger changer = new ElementChanger();
            changer.change(args[0], args[1]);
        } catch (Exception e) {
            e.printStackTrace();
        }
    }
}
```

I ran this on the *contents.xml* file used throughout the first several chapters:

```
bmclaugh@GANDALF
$ java javaxml3.ElementChanger contents.xml newContents.xml
```

This hummed along for a second, and then gave me a new document (*newContents.xml*). A portion of that new document is shown in Example 9-15.

Example 9-15. Output fragment from contents.xml afterElementChanger

```xml
<?xml version="1.0" encoding="UTF-8"?>
<!DOCTYPE book SYSTEM "DTD/JavaXML.dtd">
<!-- Java and XML Contents -->
<ora:book xmlns:ora="http://www.oreilly.com">
  <ora:title ora:series="Java">Java and XML</ora:title>

  <!-- Chapter List -->
  <ora:contents>
    <ora:chapter title="Introduction" label="1">
      <ora:topic name="XML Matters" />
      <ora:topic name="What's Important" />
      <ora:topic name="The Essentials" />
      <ora:topic name="What's Next?" />
    </ora:chapter>
    <ora:chapter title="Nuts and Bolts" label="2">
      <ora:topic name="The Basics" />
      <ora:topic name="Constraints" />
      <ora:topic name="Transformations" />
      <ora:topic name="And More..." />
      <ora:topic name="What's Next?" />
    </ora:chapter>
    <ora:chapter title="SAX" label="3">
      <ora:topic name="Getting Prepared" />
      <ora:topic name="SAX Readers" />
      <ora:topic name="Content Handlers" />
      <ora:topic name="Gotcha!" />
      <ora:topic name="What's Next?" />
    </ora:chapter>
    <ora:chapter title="Advanced SAX" label="4">
      <ora:topic name="Properties and Features" />
      <ora:topic name="More Handlers" />
      <ora:topic name="Filters and Writers" />
      <ora:topic name="Even More Handlers" />
      <ora:topic name="Gotcha!" />
      <ora:topic name="What's Next?" />
    </ora:chapter>
    <!-- Other chapters -->
</ora:book>
```

Each element is now in the O'Reilly namespace, prefixed and referencing the URI specified in the ORAElement class.

Obviously, you can take this subclassing to a much higher degree of complexity. Common examples include adding specific attributes, or even child elements, to every element that comes through. Many developers have existing business interfaces, and define custom JDOM classes that extend the core JDOM classes and also implement these business-specific interfaces. Other developers have built "lightweight" subclasses that discard namespace information and maintain only the bare essentials, keeping documents small (albeit not XML-compliant in some cases). The only limitations are your own ideas in subclassing. Just remember to set up your own factory before building documents, so your new functionality is included.

UncheckedJDOMFactory

JDOM includes an implementation of the `JDOMFactory` interface that warrants some attention: `org.jdom.UncheckedJDOMFactory`. When you create JDOM objects through the default factory or the new keyword, the object constructors do some basic checks to ensure that the objects follow XML standards. For example, trying to create a new `Element` with an invalid name produces an `org.jdom.IllegalNameException`:

```
Element el = new Element("Oname");
```

This is definitely a good thing and worth the extra processing needed to do it, but when parsing a document with a modern parser, it is unnecessary. If you had this element in a file:

```
<book>
    <Oname>Java &amp; XML</Oname>
</book>
```

And tried to parse it, a good SAX parser will throw `org.xml.sax.SAXParseException`. If you are confident your parser will do this, you can skip JDOM's checks by using `UncheckedJDOMFactory`, as in:

```
SAXBuilder builder = new SAXBuilder();
builder.setFactory(new UncheckedJDOMFactory());
// parse away
```

And get your parsing done in about 20 percent less time. `UncheckedJDOMFactory` should definitely be used sparingly and never when creating documents from user input.

Common Issues with JDOM

The following sections discuss some issues you may encounter when working with JDOM.

What Parser Am I Using?

Although I stated it previously, it is worth repeating that JDOM is not an XML parser. It uses an external parser through a builder class. As a result, what frequently appears to be a JDOM issue is actually a problem with the underlying processor. Be sure you understand which parser you are using or specify the parser class directly with the appropriate constructor of `SAXBuilder`.

JDOM Isn't DOM

First and foremost, you should realize that JDOM isn't DOM. It doesn't wrap DOM, and doesn't provide extensions to DOM. In other words, the two have no technical relation to each other. Realizing this basic truth will save you a lot of time and effort; there are many articles out there today that talk about getting the DOM interfaces to use JDOM, or avoiding JDOM because it hides some of DOM's methods. These statements are more likely to confuse than clarify. You don't need to have the DOM interfaces, and DOM calls (like appendChild( ) or createDocument( )) simply won't work on JDOM. Sorry, wrong API!

Null Return Values

Another interesting facet of JDOM, and one that has raised some controversy, is the return values from methods that retrieve element content. For example, the various getChild( ) methods on the Element class may return a null value. I mentioned this, and demonstrated it, in the PropsToXML example code. The gotcha occurs when instead of checking if an element exists (as was the case in the example code), you assume that an element already exists. This is most common when some other application or component sends you XML, and your code expects it to conform to a certain format (be it a DTD, XML Schema, or simply an agreed-upon standard). For example, take a look at the following code:

```
Document doc = otherComponent.getDocument( );
String price = doc.getRootElement( ).getChild("item")
                                    .getChild("price")
                                    .getTextTrim( );
```

The problem in this code is that if there is no item element under the root, or no price element under that, a null value is returned from the getChild( ) method invocations. Suddenly, this innocuous-looking code begins to emit NullPointerExceptions, which are quite painful to track down. You can handle this situation in one of two ways. The first is to check for null values each step of the way:

```
Document doc = otherComponent.getDocument( );
Element root = doc.getRootElement( );
Element item = root.getChild("item");
if (item != null) {
    Element price = item.getChild("price");
    if (price != null) {
        String price = price.getTextTrim( );
    } else {
        // Handle exceptional condition
    }
} else {
    // Handle exceptional condition
}
```

The second option is to wrap the entire code fragment in a try/catch block:

```
Document doc = otherComponent.getDocument( );
try {
    String price = doc.getRootElement( ).getChild("item")
                                        .getChild("price")
                                        .getTextTrim( );
} catch (NullPointerException e) {
    // Handle exceptional condition
}
```

While either approach works, I recommend the first. It allows finer-grained error handling, since it is possible to determine exactly which test failed and therefore determine exactly what problem occurred. The second code fragment informs you only that somewhere a problem occurred. In any case, careful testing of return values can save you some rather annoying `NullPointerExceptions`.

The `Element` class does have a handful of methods that deal with a common `NullPointerException` case: getting the text of a child element. These methods—named `getChildText()`, `getChildTextTrim()`, and `getChildTextNormalize()`—return the text of a child element if the child element exists and `null` if the child element does not. Given the following XML document:

```
<books>
    <book>
        <name>Java &amp; XML</name>
        <pubDate>2006</pubDate>
    </book>
    <book>
        <name>Java In a Nutshell</name>
    </book>
</books>
```

The following code would produce a `NullPointerException`:

```
Iterator it = books.getChildren().iterator();
while (it.hasNext() {
    Element book = (Element) it.next();
    System.out.println(book.getChild("name").getText() +
        " was published in " + book.getChild("pubDate").getText());
}
```

But this code will not:

```
Iterator it = books.getChildren().iterator();
while (it.hasNext() {
    Element book = (Element) it.next();
    System.out.println(book.getChildText("name") +
        " was published in " + book.getChildText("pubDate"));
}
```

Instead of throwing a `NullPointerException`, it outputs:

```
Java & XML was published in 2006
Java In a Nutshell was published in null
```

Nodes Have Only One Parent

In the JDOM object model, node objects can only have at most one parent. This parent could be a `Document` object, in the case of the root element, or an `Element`. When you add a child object to a parent object, the parent object (which could be a `Document` or `Element` object) checks if the child object already has a parent. If it does, an `org.jdom.IllegalAddException` is thrown. This is commonly seen when taking an

`Element` from one document and adding it to another. To remove the relationship between the child object and its parent, you can either pass the child object to the parent's `removeContent( )` method or call the child's `detach( )` method.

More on Subclassing

Since I covered factories and custom classes in this chapter, it is worth pointing out a few important things about subclassing that can be "gotcha" items. When you extend a class, and in particular the JDOM classes, ensure that your custom behavior is going to be activated as you want it. In other words, ensure that there is no path from an application through your subclass and to the superclass that isn't a path you are willing to live with. In almost every case, this involves ensuring that you override each constructor of the superclass. You'll notice that in Example 9-12, the `ORAElement` class, I overrode all four of the `Element` class's constructors. This ensured that any application using `ORAElement` would have to create the object with one of these constructors. While that might seem like a trivial detail, imagine if I had left out the constructor that took in a name and URI for the element. This step effectively reduces the number of ways to construct the object by one. That might seem trivial, but it's not!

Continuing with this hypothetical, you implement a `CustomJDOMFactory` class, like the one shown in Example 9-13, and override the various `element( )` methods. However, you would probably forget to override `element(String name, String uri)`, since you already forgot to override that constructor in your subclass. Suddenly, we have a problem. Every time an element is requested by name and URI (which is quite often in the `SAXBuilder` process), you are going to get a plain, vanilla `Element` instance. However, the other element creation methods all return instances of `ORAElement`. Just like that, because of one lousy constructor, your document is going to have two element implementations, almost certainly not what you wanted. It is crucial to inspect every means of object creation in your subclasses, and generally make sure you override every constructor that is public in the superclass.

Creating Invalid XML

Another tricky problem to watch out for when subclassing is inadvertently creating invalid XML. Using JDOM, it's more or less impossible to create XML that is not well-formed, but consider the `ORAElement` subclass again. This subclass added the ora prefix to every element, which alone could cause it to fail validation. This is probably not a big deal, but you do need to comment out or remove the `DOCTYPE` declaration to avoid problems when reading the document back in.

Even more important, you can get some unexpected results if you aren't careful. Look at this fragment of the XML generated using the `ORAElement` subclass, which only shows the last little bit of the serialized document:

```
<?xml version="1.0" encoding="UTF-8"?>
<!DOCTYPE book SYSTEM "DTD/JavaXML.dtd">
<!-- Java and XML Contents -->
<ora:book xmlns:ora="http://www.oreilly.com">
  <ora:title ora:series="Java">Java and XML</ora:title>

  <!-- Other content -->

  <ora:copyright>

<ora:copyright>
  <ora:year value="2001" />
  <ora:content>All Rights Reserved, O'Reilly &amp; Associates</ora:content>
</ora:copyright>
</ora:copyright>
</ora:book>
```

Notice that there are now *two* ora:copyright elements! What happened is that an existing element was in place in the O'Reilly namespace (the original ora:copyright element). However, the copyright element nested within that, with no namespace, was also assigned the ora prefix and O'Reilly namespace through the ORAElement class. The result is two elements with the same name and namespace, but differing content models. This makes validation very tricky, and is probably not what you intended. These are simple examples, but in more complex documents with more complex subclasses, you will need to watch carefully what results you are generating, particularly with respect to a DTD, XML Schema, or other form of document constraints.

dom4j

Like JDOM, which was explored in the last chapter, dom4j is designed to be a Java-specific alternative to DOM—a *document object model* that is targeted only at Java (thus the repeated use of the letter J) and isn't constrained by language neutrality in the way DOM is. Since dom4j and JDOM share this common goal, portions of the APIs look similar. However, the two APIs do differ on a key design principal in that dom4j is built around a set of core interfaces, whereas JDOM is class-orientated. What this means in practice is that there are various implementations of the core dom4j interfaces that provide different functionality. Through this, dom4j's behavior can be tuned to match the needs of your application.

Also like JDOM, dom4j is an open source project with a vibrant user community that you can join to receive assistance with the API and contribute to the future of dom4j. Full details on dom4j can be found at *http://www.dom4j.org*.

Overview

With that brief introduction to dom4j, let us begin by looking at the interfaces and classes that make up dom4j. We'll start with the core interfaces and then examine some of the special features those interfaces have that set dom4j apart from other similar APIs.

Core dom4j

As I mentioned above, dom4j is built around a set of core interfaces. These interfaces describe the structure and content of an XML document. Figure 10-1 contains a UML model of these core interfaces.

As you can see from the model diagram, dom4j has several levels of interfaces. Every interface ultimately extends the Node interface, which defines common functionality for all components of an XML document and is analogous to org.w3c.dom.Node. The

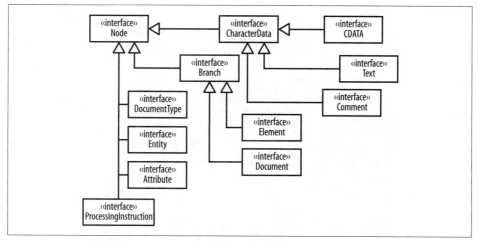

Figure 10-1. UML model of dom4j core interfaces

CharacterData and Branch interfaces similarly define common functionality for nodes that contain text and nodes that contain other nodes, respectively.

Factories

Since the core of dom4j is a set of interfaces, you use a factory object to obtain implementations of these interfaces. The default factory class is org.jdom.DocumentFactory. Figure 10-2 contains the class diagram for DocumentFactory. The various create methods enable you to create instances of the corresponding dom4j interface. Calling createElement() returns an Element instance, createAttribute() returns an Attribute instance, and so on. The createXPath(), createXPathFilter(), and createPattern() methods are slightly different in that they return objects that operate on Node objects; these creation methods will be explored in greater depth later in this chapter.

DocumentFactory returns instances of classes in the org.dom4j.tree package such as DefaultElement and DefaultAttribute. As you'll see later in the "Special-Purpose Factories" section, the dom4j distribution comes with a handful of subclasses of DocumentFactory that create alternate implementations of some of the dom4j interfaces. For example, org.jdom.util.IndexedDocumentFactory creates instances of org.dom4j.util.IndexedElement instead of DefaultElement. IndexedElement builds up maps of the element's attributes and child elements. This results in a slight performance hit on every addition of an attribute or child element, but faster results when looking up attributes and child elements by name. Although it's not always necessary that these alternate factories extend DocumentFactory, in practice a special-purpose factory only needs to override a few create methods and thus extends DocumentFactory.

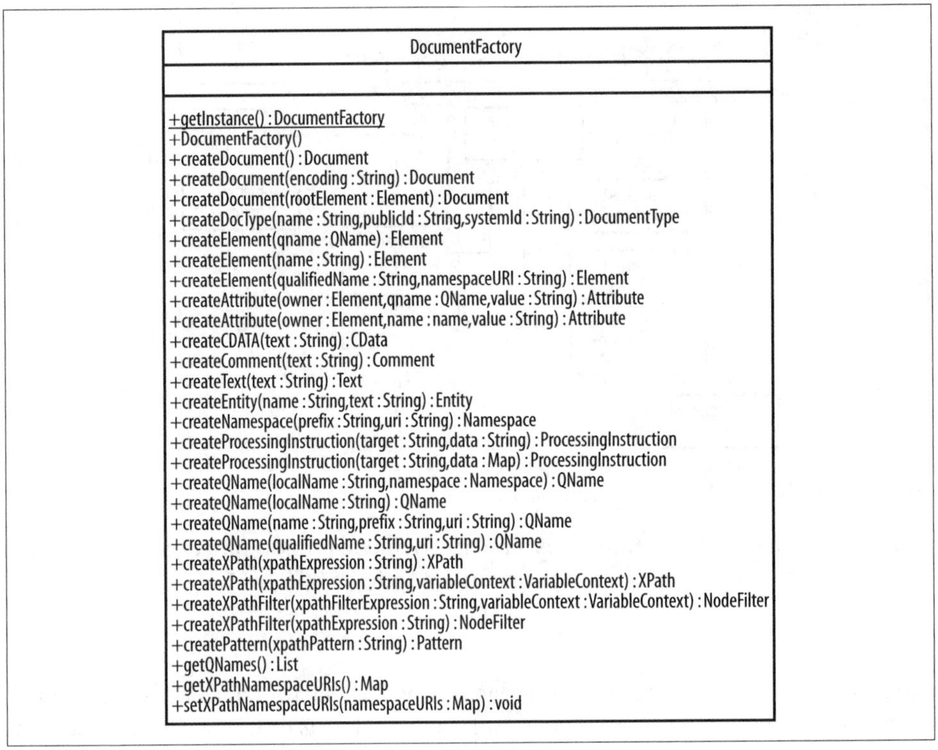

```
                          DocumentFactory

 +getInstance() : DocumentFactory
 +DocumentFactory()
 +createDocument() : Document
 +createDocument(encoding : String) : Document
 +createDocument(rootElement : Element) : Document
 +createDocType(name : String,publicId : String,systemId : String) : DocumentType
 +createElement(qname : QName) : Element
 +createElement(name : String) : Element
 +createElement(qualifiedName : String,namespaceURI : String) : Element
 +createAttribute(owner : Element,qname : QName,value : String) : Attribute
 +createAttribute(owner : Element,name : String,value : String) : Attribute
 +createCDATA(text : String) : CData
 +createComment(text : String) : Comment
 +createText(text : String) : Text
 +createEntity(name : String,text : String) : Entity
 +createNamespace(prefix : String,uri : String) : Namespace
 +createProcessingInstruction(target : String,data : String) : ProcessingInstruction
 +createProcessingInstruction(target : String,data : Map) : ProcessingInstruction
 +createQName(localName : String,namespace : Namespace) : QName
 +createQName(localName : String) : QName
 +createQName(name : String,prefix : String,uri : String) : QName
 +createQName(qualifiedName : String,uri : String) : QName
 +createXPath(xpathExpression : String) : XPath
 +createXPath(xpathExpression : String,variableContext : VariableContext) : XPath
 +createXPathFilter(xpathFilterExpression : String,variableContext : VariableContext) : NodeFilter
 +createXPathFilter(xpathExpression : String) : NodeFilter
 +createPattern(xpathPattern : String) : Pattern
 +getQNames() : List
 +getXPathNamespaceURIs() : Map
 +setXPathNamespaceURIs(namespaceURIs : Map) : void
```

Figure 10-2. DocumentFactory

dom4j Features

In addition to the standard document processing mechanisms that are common to
DOM, JDOM, and dom4j, dom4j has a few unique features that will be explored
later in this chapter.

XPath support

XPath support in dom4j is provided by an XPath class, which allows you to precompile XPath expressions and then evaluate them against some dom4j object, and a
handful of methods on the Node interface. These methods, discussed in the "XPath"
section later on, allow for evaluation of an XPath expression with the Node the
method is called upon as the context for the evaluation.

Support for Visitor Pattern

The Node interface also defines a method named accept( ), which gets passed a
Visitor object. Through this method, Node interfaces implement the *Visitor Pattern*.
The Visitor Pattern separates the logic necessary to traverse an object structure—an
XML document in this case—from the logic one wants to perform on each object

within that structure (i.e., Node objects). In dom4j, passing a Visitor object to the accept( ) method of a Node causes the Node object to pass itself to the Visitor object's visit( ) method. If the Node has children, after passing itself to visit( ), it will pass each of its children to the visit( ) method. I will provide more detail in the "Using the Visitor Pattern" section later in this chapter.

Object-orientated transformation API

In addition to supporting the JAXP TrAX API for XSL transformations, dom4j includes its own transformation API that is entirely object-orientated, called the rule API. Through this API, you create a Stylesheet object, which contains one or more Rule objects. Each Rule object defines an action to be taken and a pattern to determine when that action should be taken. Using this API, it is possible to do many of the tasks you would normally do with XSLT without leaving the comforts of Java. We will explore this later in the "Rule-Based Transformations" section.

The dom4j Distribution

The dom4j distribution is available through *http://www.dom4j.org/download.html*. It's available as both a standalone JAR file, in which case you'll have to provide all of the dependencies, or as a full distribution with all dependencies. As usual, the full distribution is available either as a ZIP file for Windows users or a GZipped TAR file for everyone else, including those using Unix, Linux, and OS X. As with JDOM, the source is included with the full distribution and there is no separate source-only distribution.

In the full distribution, the dom4j JAR file is located in the root directory. JAR files dom4j depends upon are in the *lib* directory. Of the dependency JAR files, only the *jaxen* JAR file is required for any use of dom4j. The other may be required depending on which parts of dom4j you use. For example, if you wanted to use a StAX parser (discussed in Chapter 8 to build dom4j Document objects, you would need the StAX APIs and implementation on your classpath.

You now have a good idea of what dom4j can do. In the next section, we'll look at some basic examples for reading, creating, and outputting XML documents with dom4j.

Reading and Writing with dom4j

Document input and output is probably where JDOM and dom4j are closest. Both define input and output as both being able to read and write XML documents from and to input sources such as files, URLs, and String objects and as a way of interfacing with other XML APIs. Both JDOM and dom4j, for example, have classes (SAXWriter for dom4j and SAXOutputer for JDOM) for firing SAX event method calls based on the structure of a Document object.

One additional, critical thing that JDOM and dom4j have in common is that neither is an XML parser. I mentioned this in the last chapter, but it's worth repeating: both JDOM and dom4j use a parser object provided by some other package. Both can use different parsers (SAX, DOM, StAX, etc.), but most commonly, SAX is used. In the case of SAX and DOM, by default, both JDOM and dom4j will use the SAX or DOM parser retrieved through the JAXP factories as described in Chapter 7. This means that in dom4j, like JDOM, if you run into parsing problems, it's likely that the source of your problem is the underlying SAX parser.

Parsing a Document

As noted above, dom4j is not an XML parser and must use a separate parser to produce Document objects. In general, you will use a SAX parser through the dom4j class org.dom4j.io.SAXReader. A call to one of SAXReader's read( ) methods will create an instance of org.xml.sax.XMLReader and pass it an implementation of the ContentHandler interface that has calls to DocumentFactory to create the dom4j object tree. The code to parse a java.io.File looks something like:

```
// assume we got a path as a command-line argument
File file = new File(args[0];
SAXReader reader = new SAXReader( );
Document doc = reader.read(file);
```

Through various constructor arguments, it's possible to create a SAXReader instance that does validation,* uses an alternate DocumentFactory implementation, or uses a specific SAX implementation. In addition, there are a variety of setter methods (setValidating( ), setDocumentFactory( ), etc.) to set these properties and others on the SAXReader object. See the dom4j Javadocs for a complete listing. The read( ) method is overloaded to accept one of the following inputs:

- A java.io.File object
- A java.net.URL object
- A system ID as a String object (which could be a URL or a filename)
- A java.io.InputStream object
- A java.io.Reader object
- A java.io.InputStream object and a system ID resolving relative URLs
- A java.io.Reader object and a system ID for resolving relative URLs
- An org.xml.sax.InputSource object

If you have a String object that you want to parse as XML, you can either wrap that String in a java.io.StringReader or pass the String to the utility method DocumentHelper.parseText( ). The parseText( ) method determines the proper encoding, parses your String, and returns the resulting Document object.

---

* More precisely, SAXReader asks the underlying SAX parser to validate.

As with JDOM, dom4j includes a class, `org.dom4j.io.DOMReader`, which converts an instance of `org.w3c.dom.Document` to an instance of `org.dom4j.Document`. dom4j also includes reader classes that use the StAX and XMLPull APIs discussed in the last chapter. These classes, `org.dom4j.io.StAXEventReader` and `org.dom4j.io.XPP3Reader`, respectively, require additional JAR files (included with the dom4j distribution) in the classpath. Classpath modifications aside, both classes are similar enough to `SAXReader` that you can easily take either for a test drive.

Creating a Document Object

As discussed above, creation of a `Document` object is done with the `DocumentFactory` class or one of its subclasses. There is also a `DocumentHelper` class that provides static methods for creating `Document`, `Element`, `Attribute`, etc. objects. These static methods call the corresponding method on an instance of `DocumentFactory`. This is simply a shortcut, so that instead of writing:

```
DocumentFactory factory = DocumentFactory.getInstance();
Document doc = factory.createDocument();
```

You can write:

```
Document doc = DocumentHelper.createDocument();
```

Not using the `DocumentFactory` object directly does save us a line of code, but we've lost our ability to use a different factory class, which we'll explore in more depth later in this chapter.

Once you've created your `Document` object, it's easy to add nodes to it by calling one of the methods named `add()`. Based on the XML specification, you can add as many `Comment` and `ProcessingInstruction` objects to a `Document` as you choose, but only one `Element`. In addition to the `add()` methods, the `Branch` interface, which `Document` extends, includes a group of methods named `addElement()`, which accept a `QName` object, a local name, or a local name and a namespace URI. When you call one of the `addElement()` methods, the `createElement()` method on `DocumentFactory` is called and the resulting `Element` object is set as the root element of the `Document` object. As a result, these two blocks of code do the same thing:

```
//block 1 - the long way
Element myElement = factory.createElement("name");
doc.add(myElement);

//block 2 - the short way
doc.addElement("name");
```

The `addElement()` methods return the object that was newly created, which allows you to chain method calls such as:

```
doc.addElement("root").addElement("child").addElement("innerChild");
```

To produce a document that, when serialized to a file, looks like this:

```
<root>
  <child>
    <innerChild/>
  </child>
</root>
```

Similar shortcut methods also exist for creating `Comment` and `ProcessingInstruction` objects as part of the `Document` interface and `Comment`, `ProcessingInstruction`, `Attribute`, `CData`, `Entity`, `Namespace`, and `Text` objects as part of the `Element` interface.

Namespaces and qualified names

In dom4j, as with other XML APIs, the names of elements and attributes are expressed as a triple of a local name, a namespace prefix, and a namespace URI. The namespace prefix and namespace URI are encapsulated in the class `org.dom4j.Namespace`, which is itself encapsulated in the class `org.dom4j.QName`. Instances of both `Namespace` and `QName` are immutable—once instantiated, their properties cannot be modified. And although both provide public constructors, it is recommended that instances be instantiated through the static `get()` methods on both classes. The `get()` methods make use of object caches such that repeated calls to `get()` with the same parameters will return the same object. This leads to lower memory usage, faster object comparisons, and more consistent XML. Figure 10-3 contains diagrams of the `QName` and `Namespace` classes. `Namespace` implements the `Node` interface, and `Namespace` objects can be added to `Element` objects like any other node type. However, for clarity, I have omitted those methods from the diagram. The public constructors are also omitted to discourage their use.

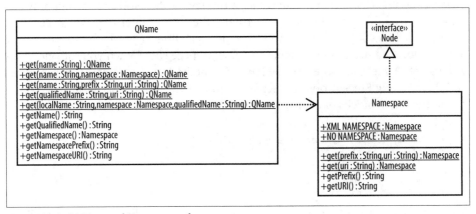

Figure 10-3. QName and Namespace classes

When moving between XML APIs, be sure to not confuse org.dom4j. QName with the JAXP class javax.xml.namespace.QName. The two classes are not related.

Document Output

As with JDOM, document output in dom4j encompasses both XML serialization (writing an XML document or document component as a series of characters (a file, the console, a String object, etc.) and passing dom4j objects to other XML APIs. Of all the APIs covered in this book, dom4j has the simplest mechanism for producing a String from a Document object:

```
String output = doc.asXML();
```

That's it. The asXML() method is part of the Node interface and thus is available on every interface in the dom4j object model. None of the asXML() methods apply any formatting to the output and, other than for Document objects, the character encoding will always be UTF-8. If you want to format your output, you need to use the class org.dom4j.io.XMLWriter. XMLWriter does what its name suggests—writes XML objects to either a java.io.Writer or a java.io.InputStream. When creating an XMLWriter instance, you can pass in an org.dom4j.io.OutputFormat object, which controls how the XML objects are written. dom4j includes three formatting definitions:

Default
   Created by new OutputFormat(). Raw format. No indententation or newlines added. XML declaration with encoding always written with a newline following it.

Pretty Print
   Created by OutputFormat.createPrettyPrint(). Newlines and indentation of two spaces applied between elements. Text is trimmed and normalized.

Compact
   Created by OutputFormat.createCompactFormat(). Default format with text trimming and normalization added.

You can pass an OutputFormat object to the constructor of XMLWriter. However, there is no setOutputFormat() or getOutputFormat() method—once set, you cannot change the format of an XMLWriter. You could create an OutputFormat object, pass it to a constructor of XMLWriter, and then call one of the mutator methods on the OutputFormat instance; but this is not recommended and could lead to inconsistent behavior. Save yourself a headache and configure your OutputFormat object before creating an XMLWriter.

In the current version of dom4j as of the time of writing (Version 1.6.1), there's a bug in the asXML() implementation for Attribute objects—attribute values are not escaped. If you have an element such as:

```
<element name="some &quot;value&quot;"/>
```

The result of calling asXML() on the name attribute will be:

```
name="some "value""
```

To accurately output Attribute objects, use the write() method on XMLWriter.

Formatting options

The OutputFormat object can be customized further beyond the three default formatting definitions. In fact, it's useful to think of those definitions as templates. For example, if you wanted to have indentation and whitespace normalization but exclude the XML declaration, it is simpler to write:

```
OutputFormat format = OutputFormat.createPrettyPrint();
format.setSuppressDeclaration(true);
```

The complete list of customizations is as follows:

lineSeparator
> Which character or characters should be used when the newlines are added to the output. This setting applies only to newlines created while outputting, not to newlines already extant in Text nodes.

newlines
> Indicates whether newlines will be added between elements.

encoding
> What character encoding to use for output. Defaults to UTF-8.

omitEncoding
> If this is true, the encoding is omitted from the XML declaration. Has no effect if the XML declaration isn't written.

suppressDeclaration
> If this is true, the XML declaration is not output.

newLineAfterDeclaration
> If this is false, a newline is output between the XML declaration and first node of the document.

expandEmptyElements
> If this is true, elements without any child nodes are output as <name></name> instead of <name/>.

trimText
> If this is true, leading and trailing whitespace is removed from text nodes and all the interior whitespace is normalized.

padText

> If whitespace is being trimmed, it's possible that word boundaries will disappear. Calling setPadText(true) will partially disable whitespace trimming so that if a text node's content begins or ends with spaces and the node is immediately preceded or followed by an element, a single space is kept between the element and the text. This is helpful when outputting HTML to hello and goodbye rather then helloandgoodbye, for example.

indent

> The String to use for indentation. If this is null (the default), no indentation is done.

XHTML

> Used by the XMLWriter subclass org.dom4j.io.HTMLWriter, which outputs a Document as HTML or XHTML. If this value is true, the output of HTMLWriter will be well-formed XML. Specifically, this means that CDATA sections will be output with the CDATA delimiters. Otherwise, just the text of the CDATA section will be output.

newLineAfterNTags

> Like XHTML, this is used only by HTMLWriter. If this is set to a positive number and newlines is false, then a newline will be output after the set number of close tags. This is useful when trying to output as many tags on one line as possible, but don't want your output all on one line.

attributeQuoteCharacter

> This property allows you to specify whether a single or double quote will be used as the character before and after attribute values. If you try to pass any other value, a java.lang.IllegalArgumentException is thrown.

Outputting to other APIs

In addition to XMLWriter, dom4j comes with three other writer classes that allow you to output a dom4j object to a different XML API. These classes are org.dom4j.DOMWriter, to output to an org.w3c.dom.Document object; org.dom4j.SAXWriter, to output to an org.xml.sax.ContentHandler and (optionally) an org.xml.sax.LexicalHandler; and StAXEventWriter, to output to a javax.xml.stream.XMLEventConsumer. These interfaces have been examined in the prior chapters, so I won't go into too much detail here other than to say that DOMWriter is limited to outputting Document objects whereas SAXWriter and StAXEventWriter can output any Node object.

Document Traversal

After parsing an XML document, you generally need to find some piece of information contained within the document. dom4j provides several different options for moving through the Document object and its children.

Iterator, Lists, and Index-Based Access

Just as in DOM and JDOM, dom4j's Document and Element interfaces have a variety of methods for getting child nodes. In dom4j's case, the basic methods to get child nodes are actually contained within the Branch interface. Figure 10-4 contains a UML diagram containing the Branch, Document, and Element interfaces. For clarity, the methods to add and remove nodes have been removed.

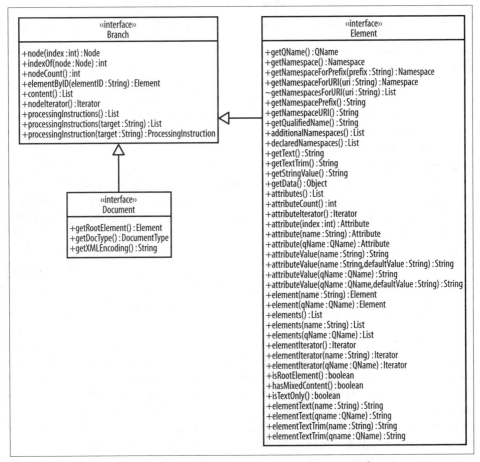

Figure 10-4. Node access methods on Branch, Document, and Element interfaces

After looking at DOM and JDOM, some of these method names may seem a bit unusual: attributes() versus getAttributes(), content() versus getChildNodes() and getContent(), etc. dom4j does *not* consistently follow the JavaBeans method naming conventions. But past these naming differences, these methods are largely the same as what we have already seen in those APIs. Another cosmetic difference is that to access a namespace-qualified element or attribute in dom4j, you create a

QName object encapsulating both the local name and the namespace. Compare this to both DOM and JDOM where getElementsByTagNameNS( ) and getChildren( ) both accept the local name and namespace as two separate parameters.

Using these methods, it is possible to easily write code that, for example, outputs the value of an attribute named location on all of an Element's children:

```
public void outputLocationAttributes(Element parent) {
    for (Iterator it = parent.elementIterator( ); it.hasNext( ); ) {
        Element child = (Element) it.next( );
        String value = child.attributeValue("location");
        if (value == null) {
            System.out.println("No location attribute");
        } else {
            System.out.println("Location attribute value is " + value);
        }
    }
}
```

Note that in this example, I'm using the elementIterator( ) method. This utility method returns a java.util.Iterator for the List returned by elements( ). If you don't want to use the Iterator interface and prefer to use index-based access, the same code could be written using the nodeCount( ) and node( ) methods as:

```
public void outputLocationAttributes2(Element parent) {
    for (int i = 0; i < parent.nodeCount( ); i++) {
        Node node = parent.node(i);
        if (node instanceof Element) {
            Element child = (Element) node;
            String value = child.attributeValue("location");
            if (value == null) {
                System.out.println("No location attribute");
            } else {
                System.out.println("Location attribute value is " + value);
            }
        }
    }
}
```

This is more verbose but will use less memory and could be faster because fewer List and Iterator objects are created. The significance of these optimizations depends upon the size and complexity of your document.

XPath

As mentioned above, dom4j has two different ways of evaluating XPath expressions. dom4j, like JDOM, has an XPath interface, diagrammed in Figure 10-5. Instances of this class are created with the createXPath( ) methods of DocumentFactory listed in Figure 10-2 or the createXPath( ) method on DocumentHelper.

```
                        ┌─────────────────────────────────────────────────────────────┐
                        │                        «interface»                          │
                        │                           XPath                             │
                        ├─────────────────────────────────────────────────────────────┤
                        │ +getText() : String                                         │
                        │ +matches(node : Node) : boolean                             │
                        │ +evaluate(context : Object) : Object                        │
                        │ +selectNodes(context : Object) : List                       │
                        │ +selectNodes(context : Object,sortXPath : XPath) : List      │
                        │ +selectNodes(context : Object,sortXPath : XPath,distinct : boolean) : List │
                        │ +selectSingleNode(context : Object) : Node                  │
                        │ +valueOf(context : Object) : String                         │
                        │ +numberValueOf(context : Object) : Number                   │
                        │ +booleanValueOf(context : Object) : boolean                 │
                        │ +sort(list : List) : void                                   │
                        │ +sort(list : List,distinct : boolean) : void                │
                        │ +getFunctionContext() : FunctionContext                     │
                        │ +setFunctionContext(functionContext : FunctionContext) : void │
                        │ +getNamespaceContext() : NamespaceContext                   │
                        │ +setNamespaceContext(namespaceContext : NamespaceContext) : void │
                        │ +setNamespaceURIs(map : Map) : void                         │
                        │ +getVariableContext() : VariableContext                     │
                        │ +setVariableContext(variableContext : VariableContext) : void │
                        └─────────────────────────────────────────────────────────────┘
```

Figure 10-5. dom4j's XPath interface

 dom4j's XPath support uses the Jaxen library, to which dom4j delegates the actual evaluation of XPath expressions. The `NamespaceContext`, `FunctionContext`, and `VariableContext` interfaces referenced by dom4j's `XPath` interface are Jaxen interfaces in the `org.jaxen` package.

Some of these methods are similar to methods with similar names in JDOM's `XPath` class, specifically `selectNodes()`, `selectSingleNode()`, `valueOf()`, and `numberValueOf()`. What is unique about dom4j's `XPath` interface is the ability to specify an XPath expression for use in sorting either a `List` of `Node` objects (the `sort()` methods) or the result of an expression (the two- and three-argument `selectNodes()` methods). Consider the XML document in Example 10-1.

Example 10-1. XML list of books

```
<?xml version="1.0" encoding="UTF-8"?>
<books>
    <book>
        <title>Java &amp; XML</title>
        <pubDate>2006</pubDate>
    </book>
    <book>
        <title>Learning UML</title>
        <pubDate>2003</pubDate>
    </book>
    <book>
        <title>XML in a Nutshell</title>
        <pubDate>2004</pubDate>
    </book>
```

Example 10-1. XML list of books (continued)

```
    <book>
        <title>Apache Cookbook</title>
        <pubDate>2003</pubDate>
    </book>
</books>
```

If you wanted to get a list of the book titles sorted by publication date, you could do this by creating two separate XPath expressions—one to get the book elements and one to sort them—and then use them like this:

```
package javaxml3;

import java.io.File;
import java.util.Iterator;
import java.util.List;

import org.dom4j.Document;
import org.dom4j.DocumentHelper;
import org.dom4j.Element;
import org.dom4j.XPath;
import org.dom4j.io.SAXReader;

public class SortingXPath {

    public static void main(String[] args) throws Exception {
        Document doc = new SAXReader( ).read(new File("books.xml"));

        XPath bookPath = DocumentHelper.createXPath("//book");
        XPath sortPath = DocumentHelper.createXPath("pubDate");

        List books = bookPath.selectNodes(doc, sortPath);

        for (Iterator it = books.iterator( ); it.hasNext( );) {
            Element book = (Element) it.next( );
            System.out.println(book.elementText("title"));
        }
    }

}
```

This outputs the titles in ascending order, starting with *Learning UML* and ending with *Java & XML*. There's no built-in mechanism to support descending sorting. Instead, you can use the static reverse( ) method of java.util.Collections to reverse the order of the list. The three-argument version of selectNodes( ) removes Node objects with duplicate values from the resulting List.[*] If the call to select nodes in the example above was:

```
List books = bookPath.selectNodes(doc, sortPath, true);
```

---

[*] Assuming the third argument is true. If it's false, then duplicates aren't removed.

Then only three titles would be output. *Apache Cookbook* would be excluded because it has the same publication date as *Learning UML*.

In addition to the XPath class, the Node interface has a handful of methods that allow you to evaluate XPath expressions by simply passing a String to one of these methods. Example 10-2 contains the XPath-specific methods of the Node interface.

Example 10-2. XPath methods in the Node interface

```
public interface Node  {
  // non-XPath methods removed
  List selectNodes(String xpathExpression);
  Object selectObject(String xpathExpression);
  List selectNodes(String xpathExpression, String comparisonXPathExpression);
  List selectNodes(String xpathExpression, String comparisonXPathExpression,
    boolean removeDuplicates);
  Node selectSingleNode(String xpathExpression);
  String valueOf(String xpathExpression);
  Number numberValueOf(String xpathExpression);
  boolean matches(String xpathExpression);
  // non-XPath methods removed
}
```

Behind the scenes, implementations of the Node interface will generally use the XPath class to evaluate the expressions passed to these methods. Because these methods deal with Strings, generally each call will result in the creation of a new XPath object. Thus, if you're going to be repeatedly evaluating the same XPath expression, the XPath class is going to be a better choice as you're expression will get compiled only one time. In addition, these methods can't deal with namespaces, variables, or custom functions, so if those features are necessary, the XPath class is your only choice. But that doesn't mean that these methods are useless; actually they're convenient and result in fewer lines of code.

Before we leave XPath there are a few more methods from the Node interface that warrant mentioning. The methods getPath( ) and getUniquePath( ) return an XPath expression that would evaluate to a List of Nodes containing the current Node. The getUniquePath( ) method goes a step further from getPath( ) and adds indexing to ensure that the resulting XPath expression will evaluate to only this Node. In addition to zero-argument versions, both getPath( ) and getUniquePath( ) are overloaded to accept an Element, in which case, the result will be a relative XPath expression from the passed Element to the current Node. Looking back at the document in Example 10-1, if the object named book is the book element for *Learning UML*, then Table 10-1 contains the results of these methods.

Table 10-1. getPath( ) and getUniquePath( ) results

book.getPath( )	/books/book
book.getUniquePath( )	/books/book[2]
book.getPath(doc.getRootElement( ));	book
book.getUniquePath(doc.getRootElement( ));	book[2]

Using the Visitor Pattern

The final traversal option within dom4j, its support for the Visitor Pattern, is unique among the context of the object-model APIs discussed in this book. If anything, it's most similar to SAX. As described above, the Visitor Pattern in dom4j is used by creating an implementation of the org.dom4j.Visitor interface. As you can see in the UML diagram in Figure 10-6, the Visitor interface defines a visit( ) method for each node type.

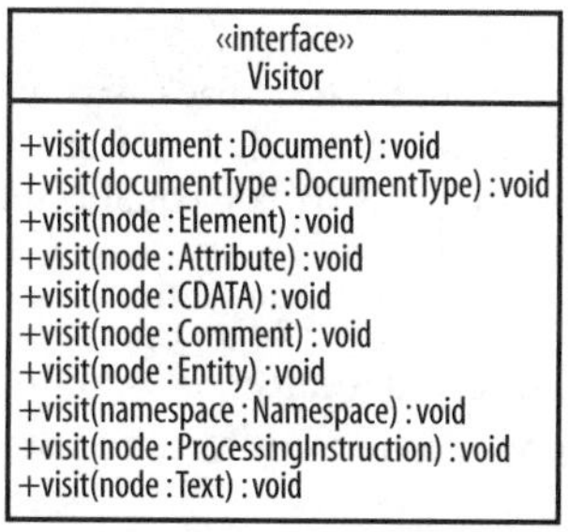

```
                      «interface»
                        Visitor

    +visit(document : Document) : void
    +visit(documentType : DocumentType) : void
    +visit(node : Element) : void
    +visit(node : Attribute) : void
    +visit(node : CDATA) : void
    +visit(node : Comment) : void
    +visit(node : Entity) : void
    +visit(namespace : Namespace) : void
    +visit(node : ProcessingInstruction) : void
    +visit(node : Text) : void
```

Figure 10-6. The Visitor interface

Since you generally only care about a few of these node types, dom4j includes the org.dom4j.VisitorSupport class, which implements all the methods from the Visitor interface with empty method bodies. This lets your classes extend VisitorSupport and only override the methods for the types with which you are concerned.

In prior chapters, we've discussed the common use case of needing to change the namespace of all elements within an XML document. Implementing this with the Visitor interface looks like this:

```
class NamesapceChangingVisitor extends VisitorSupport {

    private Namespace from;
    private Namespace to;

    public NamesapceChangingVisitor(Namespace from, Namespace to) {
        this.from = from;
        this.to = to;
    }

    public void visit(Element node) {
        Namespace ns = node.getNamespace();

        if (ns.getURI().equals(from.getURI())) {
            QName newQName = new QName(node.getName(), to);
            node.setQName(newQName);
        }
```

```
        // we also need to remove the namespace declaration
        ListIterator namespaces = node.additionalNamespaces( ).listIterator( );
        while (namespaces.hasNext( )) {
            Namespace additionalNamespace = (Namespace) namespaces.next( );
            if (additionalNamespace.getURI( ).equals(from.getURI( ))) {
                namespaces.remove( );
            }
        }
    }

}
```

 The equals( ) method of the Namespace class will only return true if the URIs and the prefixes are equal. From an XML standpoint, this is incorrect. Namespaces in XML are equal if their URIs are equal. The prefix is merely a shortcut.

Using our Visitor class is largely a matter of parsing the XML and creating the Namespace objects we need to pass to the constructor of NamespaceChangingVisitor:

```
public class VisitorExample {

    public static void main(String[] args) throws Exception {
        if (args.length != 4) {
            System.err.println(
"Usage: javaxml3.VisitorExample [doc] [old ns] [new prefix] [new ns]");

            System.exit(0);
        }

        Document doc = new SAXReader( ).read(args[0]);
        Namespace oldNs = Namespace.get(args[1]);
        Namespace newNs;
        if (args[2].equals("-")) {
            newNs = Namespace.get(args[3]);
        } else {
            newNs = Namespace.get(args[2], args[3]);
        }

        Visitor visitor = new NamesapceChangingVisitor(oldNs, newNs);
        doc.accept(visitor);
        System.out.println(doc.asXML( ));
    }

}
```

It's also common to implement the `Visitor` interface with an inner class:

```
Visitor visitor = new VisitorSupport( ) {
    public void visit(Element node) {
        System.out.println(node.getName( ));
    }
}
doc.accept(visitor);
```

Transformations

The dom4j has ample support for XML transformations. dom4j objects can be used either with XSL transformations using JAXP or dom4j's rule-based transformation classes. In both cases, you encapsulate the logic used to transform a document and then apply that logic to multiple documents.

TrAX

Document objects created with dom4j can be used as the source or result of transformations done by the TrAX that's part of the JAXP specifications discussed in Chapter 7. This is done with the classes `org.dom4j.io.DocumentSource` and `org.dom4j.io.DocumentResult`. These implement the `javax.xml.transform.Source` and `javax.xml.transform.Result` interfaces, respectively. `DocumentSource` and `DocumentResult` can be used together—where the input and output of a transformation are both dom4j `Document` objects—or independently—for example, a dom4j `Document` as the input and a `String` as the output. Example 10-3 contains sample code transforming the contents of an XML file to a dom4j `Document` object.

Example 10-3. Transformation from a file to an org.dom4j.Document object using TrAX

```
TransformerFactory factory = TransformerFactory.newInstance( );
Transformer transformer = factory.
    newTransformer(new StreamSource("stylesheet.xsl"));
StreamSource in = new StreamSource("input.xml");
JDOMResult out = new DocumentResult( );
transformer.transform(in, out);
Document resultDocument = out.getDocument( );
```

Rule-Based Transformations

dom4j includes an API for defining a transformation entirely with Java. These transformations are written with a series of `org.dom4j.rule.Rule` objects contained within in an `org.dom4j.rule.Stylesheet` object. A `Rule` object is composed of an implementation of the `org.dom4j.rule.Pattern` interface, which governs what nodes a `Rule` applies to, and an implementation of the org.dom4j.rule.Action interface, which performs some action upon the matched nodes. The two implementations of the Pattern interface included with the dom4j distribution are org.dom4j.rule.pattern. NodeTypePattern and org.dom4j.xpath.XPathPattern. These implementations do what their names imply—NodeTypePattern matches nodes based on type and XPathPattern matches nodes based on an XPath expression. XPathPattern instances are created with DocumentFactory's createPattern() method. The Action interface defines a single method called run(), which accepts any Node object as a parameter. Implementations are free to modify the node passed to their run() method.

The easiest way to demonstrate this rule API is to compare a transformation written in XSLT with a transformation written with the rule API. The XSL stylesheet in Example 10-4 takes a child element named pubDate and makes it an attribute. This could be run against a document structured like Example 10-1.

Example 10-4. Sample XSL stylesheet

```
<?xml version="1.0" encoding="UTF-8"?>
<xsl:stylesheet version="1.0" xmlns:xsl="http://www.w3.org/1999/XSL/Transform">
    <xsl:template match="books">
        <books>
            <xsl:apply-templates/>
        </books>
    </xsl:template>
    <xsl:template match="book">
        <book>
            <xsl:attribute name="pubDate">
                <xsl:value-of select="pubDate"/>
            </xsl:attribute>
            <xsl:value-of select="title"/>
        </book>
    </xsl:template>
</xsl:stylesheet>
```

This same transformation could be written with the rule API as:

```
public class RuleExample {

    class BookAction implements Action {

        public void run(Node node) throws Exception {
            if (node instanceof Element) {
                Element element = (Element) node;
                Element newElement = element.createCopy();
                // make pubDate an attribute
                Element pubDateElement = newElement.element("pubDate");

                // remove the pubDate element from the current node
                newElement.remove(pubDateElement);
                Attribute attr = DocumentHelper.createAttribute(newElement,
                        "pubDate", pubDateElement.getTextTrim());
                newElement.add(attr);
```

```
                    // add our new element to the result document's root element
                    rootElement.add(newElement);
                }
            }

        }

        private Element rootElement;

        public Document transform(Document input) throws DocumentException {

            // must be final because we're using it in an inner class
            final Document result = DocumentHelper.createDocument();

            final Stylesheet style = new Stylesheet();

            Rule booksRule = new Rule(DocumentHelper.createPattern("books"),
                    new Action() {
                        public void run(Node node) throws Exception {
                            rootElement = result.addElement("books");
                            style.applyTemplates(node);
                        }
                    });

            Rule bookRule = new Rule(DocumentHelper.createPattern("book"),
                    new BookAction());
            style.addRule(booksRule);
            style.addRule(bookRule);

            try {
                style.run(input);
            } catch (Exception e) {
                System.err.println("Unable to transform: " + e.getMessage());
                e.printStackTrace();
            }
            return result;
        }
    }
```

For purposes of the example, I've created implementations of the Action interface
both as an anonymous inner class and a named inner class. Both are reasonable
options, as is creating a regular public class that implements the Action interface.
Which method is correct in a particular case is largely dependent upon what objects
need to be accessed from the run( ) method.

Always remember that if you need to access any local variables from
an anonymous inner class, those variables must be declared with the
final keyword. Failure to do so will result in a compiler error.

Special-Purpose Factories

In addition to the default DocumentFactory used throughout this chapter, dom4j includes some subclasses of DocumentFactory that both demonstrate the rationale behind dom4j's interface-based design and provide useful functionality. This is not an exhaustive look at all the DocumentFactory classes in the dom4j distribution. For a full list, please take a look at the dom4j Javadocs at *http://www.dom4j.org/apidocs*. In general, these factories can be used when creating new dom4j objects directly or with a builder object. To use a DocumentFactory subclass with a builder, either pass the DocumentFactory to the builder's constructor or its setDocumentFactory( ) method:

```
// create a SAXBuilder with DOMDocumentFactory as it's factory
SAXBuilder builder = new SAXBuilder(DOMDocumentFactory.getInstance());

// parse something

// now switch the factory to BeanDocumentFactory
builder.setDocumentFactory(BeanDocumentFactory.getInstance());
```

DOMDocumentFactory

The factory org.dom4j.dom.DOMDocumentFactory and the classes it produces are perhaps the best case for the interface-based design used by both DOM and dom4j. The instances produced by DOMDocumentFactory implement the corresponding interfaces from both dom4j and W3C DOM—the result of a call to createDocument( ) implements both org.dom4j.Document and org.w3c.dom.Document; createElement( ) returns an object that implements both org.dom4j.Element and org.w3c.dom.Element; and so on.

This is useful when working with classes that use the DOM interfaces such as if you had created a dom4j Element and wanted to pass it to the following interface:

```
public interface ElementProcessor {
    void doSomething(org.w3c.dom.Element element);
}
```

You could use the DOMWriter class to create copies of your objects that implement the DOM interfaces. But using DOMDocumentFactory allows you to simply pass your Element object to the doSomething( ) method, by casting it to the org.w3c.dòm.Element interface:

```
public org.dom4j.Element create(String name, ElementProcessor processor) {
    DocumentFactory factory = DOMDocumentFactory.getInstance();
    Element element = factory.createElement(name);
    processor.doSomething((org.w3c.dom.Element) element);
    return element;
}
```

IndexedDocumentFactory

The factory `org.dom4j.util.IndexedDocumentFactory` creates instances of `org.dom4j.util.IndexedElement`, an implementation of the `Element` interface that has optimized versions of the `attribute(String)`, `attribute(QName)`, `element(String)`, `element(QName)`, `elements(String)`, and `elements(QName)` methods. As child nodes are added to an `IndexedElement`, mappings from name (either as a `String` or `QName`) to child `Elements` and `Attributes` are built. In the default implementation of the `Element` interface, a call to any of these methods actually results in iteration through the list of attributes or elements until a match is found. `IndexedElement` is slower to add new child nodes, due to the need to add entries to the internal `Maps`, but it is definitely advantageous if you do a lot of name-based access.

BeanDocumentFactory

The factory `org.dom4j.bean.BeanDocumentFactory` creates JavaBean objects based on attributes within `Element` objects. These objects are made available through the `getData( )` method of the `Element` interface. The way this works is that when an `Element` is created with an attribute named `class`, a new object is created with that attribute's value as its class name. If no such class exists, a warning is logged to the console. Once the object is created, the other attributes are set as property values on the bean. For example, the following element:

```
<book class="javaxml3.BookBean" pubDate="2004" title="XML in a Nutshell" />
```

if parsed by a builder using `BeanDocumentFactory`, produces an instance of `javaxml3.BookBean`. If they exist, methods called `setPubDate( )` and `setTitle( )` are called with the corresponding attribute value. If no such methods exist, no warning is logged. `BeanDocumentFactory` will not set bean properties based on child elements; this XML would only result in a call to `setPubDate( )`, not `setTitle( )`:

```
<book class="javaxml3.BookBean" pubDate="2003">
    <title>Learning UML</title>
</book>
```

Unlike `DOMDocumentFactory` and `IndexedDocumentFactory`, `BeanDocumentFactory` is really only useful when parsing an XML document. You can use it when building a Document in your code, but the bean objects will not be created.

These three examples of `DocumentFactory` subclasses should give you a good idea of what you can do with a custom `DocumentFactory`. If you come up with a clever `DocumentFactory` subclass, feel free to submit it to the dom4j community via the mailing list. If it is generally useful, it may be included in a future version of dom4j.

This chapter has looked at the broad feature set of dom4j and is the last of the object model XML APIs we discuss in this book. In the next chapter, we will shift gears to discuss a technique for dealing with XML called data binding that removes just about every reference to XML from your code.

## CHAPTER 11

Data Binding with JAXB

As I mentioned at the end of the last chapter, *data binding* is an XML processing technique that eliminates references to XML nodes from your code. Instead of working with elements and attributes, your code uses classes named `Customer` and `PurchaseOrder`. This first means that you have to define the structure of your XML documents using a schema, typically either an XML Schema or a DTD. To bind this schema to specific Java classes, which could include generating those classes from the schema, you'll use a data binding framework. These are generally composed of code-generation tools to build Java classes from a schema and a runtime library that converts an XML document into a tree of Java objects (and vice versa). There are many data binding frameworks available for Java. In this chapter, we'll look specifically at one: the Java Architecture for XML Binding (JAXB).

Data Binding Basics

Before getting into the specifics of JAXB, it will be helpful to take a look at the concepts that underlie data binding in general. Fundamentally, data binding is similar to the document object model APIs we've discussed—DOM, JDOM, and dom4j—in that it defines an association, referred to as a binding, between an XML document and a tree of Java objects. A tree of Java objects can be created from an XML document and vice versa. The difference is that when data binding, the Java objects mapped to the document are instances not of generic interfaces representing elements and attributes (and comments, processing instructions, etc.), but of specific classes that have a meaning beyond the XML document. In part to indicate this difference, with data binding you don't "parse" or "serialize" documents. Instead, you *marshall* XML into Java objects and *unmarshall* Java objects into an XML document. The components that sit between objects and XML documents are called *marshallers* and *unmarshallers*. This relationship is shown in Figure 11-1.

Let's take a look at what we can do with a fictional data binding framework and the XML document in Example 11-1.

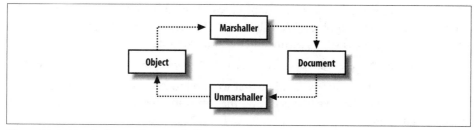

Figure 11-1. Marshallers and unmarshallers

Example 11-1. A person XML document

```
<?xml version="1.0"?>
<person xmlns="http://www.example.com/person">
    <firstName>Lola</firstName>
    <lastName>Arbuckle</firstName>
</person>
```

Using DOM, outputting the first name looks something like:

```
DocumentBuilder documentBuilder = DocumentBuilderFactory.newDocumentBuilder( );
Document doc = documentBuilder.parse(new File("lola.xml"));
Element element = doc.getDocumentElement( );
NodeList firstNames = element.getElementsByTagName("firstName");
Element firstName = (Element) firstName.item(0);
System.out.println(firstName.getTextContent( ));
```

With a data binding framework, we can write much simpler code, as in Example 11-2.

Example 11-2. Unmarshalling to a Person object

```
Unmarshaller unmarshaller = DataBindingFactory.newUnmarshaller( );
Person person = (Person) unmarshaller.unmarshal(new File("lola.xml"));
System.out.println(person.getFirstName( ));
```

This has both fewer lines of code and is much more obvious about what it is doing. The first line uses a factory class in our fictional framework to obtain a new instance of the Unmarshaller interface for this framework. The second line passes a File object for our document to the unmarshaller and returns an instance the Person class. Finally, we call the getFirstName( ) method on this object and output the result to the console.

We can also do the reverse. Producing the XML document in Example 11-1 could be done with the code in Example 11-3.

Example 11-3. Marshalling a Person object

```
Person person = new Person( );
person.setFirstName("Lola");
person.setLastName("Arbuckle");
Marshaller marshaller = DataBindingFactory.newMarshaller( );
marshaller.marshal(person, new FileWriter("lola.xml"));
```

The code above should raise a question: how did the unmarshaller in Example 11-2 know to create a Person object? And how did the marshaller in Example 11-3 know to create that specific XML structure and not, for example:

```
<person xmlns="http://www.example.com/person" firstName="Lola" lastName="Arbuckle"/>
```

The answer to both questions could be that we need to explicitly tell the unmarshaller and marshaller about our Person class and that we want the properties to result in elements, not attributes:

```
// for the unmarshaller
unmarshaller.addMapping(Person.class, "http://www.example.com/person", "person");

// for the marshaller
marshaller.addMapping(Person.class, "http://www.example.com/person", "person");
marshaller.setMarshalPropertiesAsElements(Person.class, true);
```

This is reasonable, and Java's reflection features are good enough that you could write a simple data binding framework using this sort of configuration scheme. However, the more prevalent technique among current data binding frameworks is to put the configuration of the document-to-object mapping in some sort of class-level metadata, as seen in Figure 11-2.

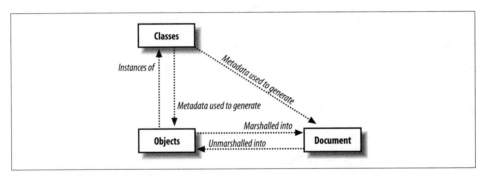

Figure 11-2. Class metadata determines structure

In some frameworks, this metadata is located within the class definition itself, either through static methods and fields or Java annotations. In others, the metadata is contained in an external mapping configuration file (it should come as no surprise that this file is usually XML itself). Some frameworks support multiple configuration methods or combinations of methods.

Data Binding and Schemas

The above description of data binding left out a critical component: a schema. In many applications, the XML documents produced by a marshaller and consumed by an unmarshaller are expected to conform to a schema, whether that be a DTD, an XML Schema, a RELAX NG schema, or some other schema language. For data binding, schemas are used in two distinct ways. The first is that they can be used to validate the result of a marshalling or the input for unmarshalling, as shown in Figure 11-3.

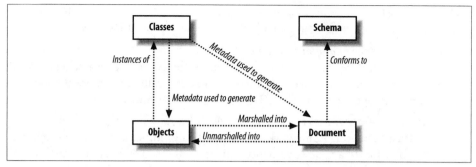

Figure 11-3. Documents conform to a schema

The second area is that many data binding frameworks support generating the Java classes from a schema. This is usually referred to as *compiling* a schema and the application that performs it is called a *schema compiler*. In general, the compiler will have some mechanism for customizing the generated classes.

> If you've used Hibernate or another object-relational mapping framework, you may have used a similar code-generation mechanism to generate Java classes from a database schema.

In addition to generating Java classes from a schema, a few frameworks, including JAXB 2.0, allow for the reverse: a schema definition can be generated from Java classes as seen in Figure 11-4.

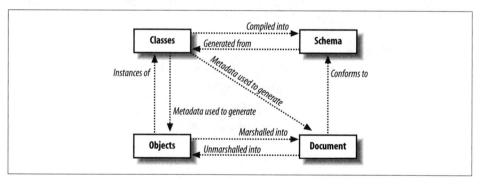

Figure 11-4. JAXB 2.0 includes schema generation

When to (and When Not to) Use Data Binding

Data binding is designed to allow applications to easily move data between a set of Java classes and an XML representation where both the Java classes and the XML representation are defined in some way. When this is the case, data binding can be very useful and, as we've seen, produce significantly more readable source code.

However, if you use data binding when it is not appropriate, you may find yourself spending more time combating the API. Here are some basic guidelines:

If you don't have a schema, don't use data binding
> Although there are data binding frameworks that don't need a schema, XML applications that don't have a defined schema generally need more flexibility in the structure of the produced XML than data binding allows.

If you have a schema that uses mixed content, don't use data binding
> Or at least pick your framework carefully. Data binding, as its name suggested, is designed for data, not documents. Mixed content, like XHTML, just doesn't make sense expressed in a Java interface or class. Some frameworks support partial binding of a schema such that some portion of the object tree is represented by a Node object from DOM or a similar API, but this is not a universal feature.

If you are dealing with large documents, don't use data binding
> Like DOM and its ilk, data binding creates an object tree with at least one Java object per node in the XML document. As a result, the size of a document to be unmarshalled from or marshalled into is dependent upon the amount of memory available.

Introducing JAXB

The Java Architecture for XML Binding has been developed through the Java Community Process (JCP). There are two Java Specification Requests associated with JAXB: JSR 31 and JSR 222 define JAXB 1.0 and JAXB 2.0, respectively. JAXB has a few different web sites associated with it, listed in Table 11-1.

Table 11-1. JAXB web sites

Main site	*http://java.sun.com/webservices/jaxb*
Reference implementation site	*https://jaxb.dev.java.net*
JSR 31	*http://jcp.org/en/jsr/detail?id=31*
JSR 222	*http://jcp.org/en/jsr/detail?id=222*

JAXB 1.0

JAXB 1.0 defines a standardized API for marshalling and unmarshalling as well as a validation API. The specification also defines how a schema compiler binds a schema to its Java representation. However, it does not specify how a schema compiler is invoked. As a result, implementations are free to package their schema compiler in any way, but generally you will see a shell script,[*] an Ant task,[†] or both. Although

---

[*] Or batch file, for Windows users.

[†] Ant is a build tool used extensively for Java applications. More info can be found at *http://ant.apache.org* and in *Ant: The Definitive Guide* by Steve Holzner (O'Reilly).

JAXB 1.0 applications are portable in the sense that the behavior of implementations of the `Marshaller`, `Unmarshaller`, and `Validator` interfaces is defined in the specification, Java classes and interfaces generated by a JAXB 1.0 schema compiler are not portable between JAXB implementations.

JAXB 1.0 requires implementations to support a subset of W3C XML Schemas only. Implementations are free to support additional features of W3C XML Schemas and additional schema languages, including DTDs. The specific features for which support is not required are listed in the JAXB 1.0 specification, available from the JSR 31 web site, listed in Table 11-1.

For each namespace defined in a schema, a JAXB 1.0 schema compiler will produce a package containing a set of Java interfaces, a class named `ObjectFactory`, and, if necessary, classes for any enumerations defined in the schema. The compiler will also produce implementation classes for these interfaces, usually in a separate implementation package. I will detail the interfaces and classes created in the section "Compiling a Schema" later in this chapter. In JAXB 1.0, it is not possible to bind an arbitrary Java class, even one that adheres to JavaBeans naming conventions, to an XML representation. Classes to be marshalled must be generated by the JAXB schema compiler.

The validation features within JAXB 1.0 allow for validation on demand. At any point, an instance of any JAXB-generated class can be validated against the schema constraints compiled into those generated classes. By default, validation occurs during marshalling and unmarshalling, but it is possible to disable validation.

JAXB 2.0

Just a few months after the release of the final JAXB 1.0 specification in the fall of 2003, JSR 222 was created to develop the second version of JAXB. The final specification for JAXB 2.0 was released almost three years later, in May of 2006. JAXB 2.0 is also part of the Java Enterprise Edition 5 specification. Like many of the other specifications that are part of Java EE 5, JAXB 2.0 is dependent upon the new language features introduced with Java 5, most significantly annotations and parameterized types (also known as generics). Thus, if your application must run on Java 1.4 or below, you cannot use JAXB 2.0. JAXB 2.0 adds several significant features to JAXB.

 Although JAXB 2.0 is part of Java EE 5, it is not dependent upon a Java EE container.

Schema compiler generates annotated POJOs

Unlike JAXB 1.0, which produced both public interfaces and private implementation classes for each component of an XML Schema, JAXB 2.0 produces plain Java classes that don't implement any special interfaces or extend any classes. In other words, the generated classes are plain-old Java objects: POJOs. The metadata needed to marshall and unmarshall is contained in Java annotations.

Annotations enable binding arbitrary classes

As a result of the use of annotations, any Java class can be bound to an XML representation simply by adding the appropriate annotations to an existing class.

Schema generation

In addition to the schema compiler specified in JAXB 1.0, JAXB 2.0 includes a schema generator that looks for annotations in Java classes and produces an XML schema. However, if a schema is compiled and then the resulting code is used as the source for schema generation, the compiled schema and the generated schema are not necessarily equivalent.

Portable runtime

Unlike JAXB 1.0, JAXB 2.0 specifies that all interfaces and classes, both those that are part of the API and those generated by the schema compiler, be portable between implementations.

Integration with JAXP validation

Unlike JAXB 1.0, JAXB 2.0 does not include its own validation capabilities. Instead, validation is delegated to the validation features of JAXP 1.3, covered in Chapter 7. Although the javax.xml.bind.Validator class is still part of the API, it is deprecated and optional. This separation of concerns means that it is possible, for example, to have a schema compiler generate classes from a W3C XML Schema, but when validating the marshalled document, use a RELAX NG schema. It also means that enhancements to the JAXP validation features will be usable by JAXB without updating the JAXB API or implementations.

Complete W3C XML Schema support

Whereas JAXB 1.0 did not require complete support for the W3C XML Schema specification, JAXB 2.0 requires support of the complete specification.

Integration with StAX

Implementations of the JAXB 2.0 Marshaller interface can marshall a Java object tree to a javax.xml.stream.XMLStreamWriter or a javax.xml.stream. XMLEventWriter object and Unmarshaller implementations can unmarshall from a javax.xml.stream.XMLStreamReader or a javax.xml.stream.XMLEventReader object. These interfaces were discussed in Chapter 8.

Callback methods

Both Marshaller and Unmarshaller interfaces provide callback mechanisms that allow an object participating in a marshalling or an unmarshalling to be notified before and after the object is marshalled. Additionally, a listener object can be registered with a Marshaller or Unmarshaller instance to receive a notification for each object marshalled or unmarshalled.

 Like JAXB 1.0, JAXB 2.0 only requires support for W3C XML Schema, but does not preclude implementations from including support for additional schema languages.

JAXB Reference Implementations

The reference implementations of both JAXB 1.0 and JAXB 2.0 are included in Sun's Java Web Services Developer Pack. In addition, the reference implementations are open source projects on java.net. The main reference implementation project is located at *https://jaxb.dev.java.net*.

Java WSDP

The Java Web Services Developer Pack (Java WSDP) is a single download that includes a dozen or so XML and web services libraries and applications. It is part of an initiative by Sun to make the XML and web services features of Java more accessible to developers. In addition to libraries and applications, Java WSDP includes documentation and sample code for all of the included components. There's also a tutorial available for download. At the time of writing, the latest version of the Java WSDP is 2.0, released in December of 2005. Java WSDP 2.0 includes the following components:

- JAXP, Version 1.3.1_01
- JAXB Reference Implementation, Version 2.0 EA
- Sun Java Streaming XML Parser, Version 1.0 EA (Early Access)
- Fast Infoset, Version 1.0.1
- XML and Web Services Security, Version 2.0 EA2
- XML Digital Signature, Version 1.0.1
- Java API for XML Registries, Version 1.0.8_01 EA
- Java API for XML Web Services, Version 2.0 EA
- Java API for XML-based RPC, Version 1.1.3_01 EA
- SOAP with Attachments API for Java, Version 1.3 EA
- Apache Ant, Version 1.6

Some of the components of Java WSDP require Java 5 (JAXB 2.0, for example), but most do not (such JAXP 1.3 and SJSXP). The previous version of Java WSDP is 1.6 (released in June 2005). The component list for Java WSDP 1.6 is similar to that of 2.0, just different versions of those components. Version 1.0.5 of the JAXB reference implementation is included in Java WSDP 1.6.

Downloading Java WSDP. The current version of Java WSDP can be downloaded from *http://java.sun.com/webservices/downloads/webservicespack.html*. Sun may ask you to register, but that's not required. Sun does require you to accept the terms of the license agreement before downloading. The available downloads are an *.exe* file for use on Windows and an SH file for use on Linux, Unix, and Mac OS X, as shown in Figure 11-5.

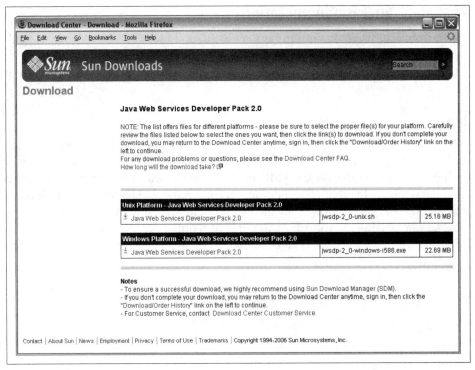

Figure 11-5. Java WSDP download page

Installing Java WSDP can either be done with a graphical wizard-type interface or a console application. The console version has the same prompts as the graphical wizard and is run using the command-line option *-console*:

```
$ ./jwsdp-2_0-unix.sh -console
```

The first step of the installation, regardless of whether you use the graphical or console mode, is accepting the license agreement for Java WSDP. Next, you need to select a JDK for Java 5 or later. The installer will scan your system for an appropriate JDK. If it doesn't find one, or doesn't find the one you want to use, it's possible to select a different JDK, as seen in Figure 11-6.

Next, the installer asks you to select a web container for use with Java WSDP. This is an optional step. Java WSDP 2.0 is compatible with Sun Java System Application Server 8.1 and 9.0 as well as a version of Apache Tomcat customized for use with Java WSDP. The container selection dialog, shown in Figure 11-7, also provides a link to a page on *http://java.sun.com* from which you can download a supported web container. If you're only interested in JAXB or the other applications within Java WSDP that don't require a web container (such as SJSXP), feel free to select the "No Web Container" option. Java WSDP also comes with scripts you can run to integrate Java WSDP with one of these containers after installation.

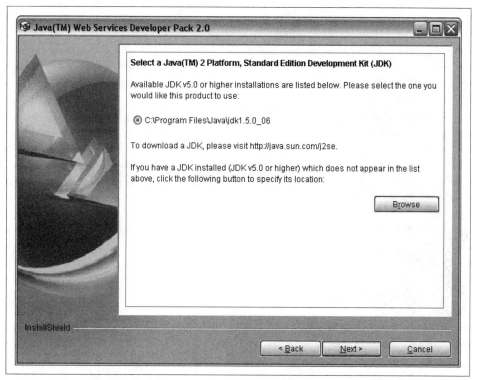

Figure 11-6. JDK selection dialog

The installer will next ask you where you want Java WSDP installed and which components you want installed, as seen in Figure 11-8.

Finally, you'll be asked if you use an HTTP proxy and, if so, what the address and port for your proxy server are. Then, you'll be shown a confirmation screen as seen in Figure 11-9. Once you click the Next button, the files will be copied to your desired destination.

The installer for prior versions of Java WSDP has largely the same dialogs.

Downloading JAXB 2.0 reference implementation

As mentioned above, the JAXB 2.0 reference implementation is an open source project hosted by the Java community site Java.net. As you can see in the screenshot in Figure 11-10, the project page has a prominent link to download the current version of the reference implementation (2.0.1 at the time this screenshot was taken) as well as a link on the left navigation to all downloads, which include previous versions.

The JAR file that you download from java.net is, like the download for Java WSDP, an installer that requires you to accept a license agreement before it installs the contents of the reference implementation.

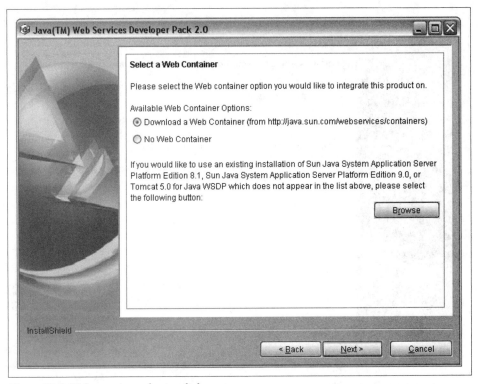

Figure 11-7. Web container selection dialog

Contents

Regardless of how it is downloaded, the JAXB reference implementation contains four directories:

bin

Contains batch and shell scripts for running the schema compiler and generator.

docs

Contains various pieces of documentation, including documentation for the schema compiler, schema generator, and Javadocs for the JAXB API.

lib

Contains the JAR files for both the JAXB API and the reference implementation. The classes for the schema compiler and generator are packaged into a separate JAR file that is not typically necessary at runtime.

samples

Contains various sample applications.

Now that we installed an implementation of JAXB, we can start using it.

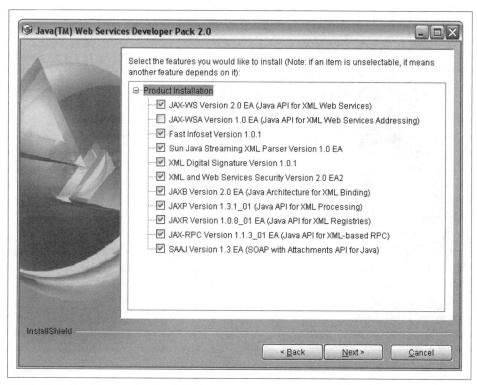

Figure 11-8. Component selection dialog

Using JAXB

The APIs for JAXB 1.0 and JAXB 2.0 are relatively similar even though the implementations are quite different. At the core of both APIs are interfaces called Marshaller and Unmarshaller, both in the javax.xml.bind package. A factory class called JAXBContext (also in javax.xml.bind) exists to create instances of these interfaces. Figure 11-11 contains a UML model for the core JAXB 1.0 API.

The significant changes between the JAXB 1.0 versions of these interfaces and the JAXB 2.0 versions relate to the use of JAXP validation. Specifically, the setValidating( ) and isValidating( ) methods of the Unmarshaller interface are deprecated. Instead, the Marshaller and Unmarshaller interfaces now have methods called setSchema( ) and getSchema( ), which deal with instances of javax.xml.validation.Schema, discussed in Chapter 7. In addition, as mentioned above, both Marshaller and Unmarshaller now have methods that accept the reader and writer interfaces from the StAX API discussed in Chapter 8.

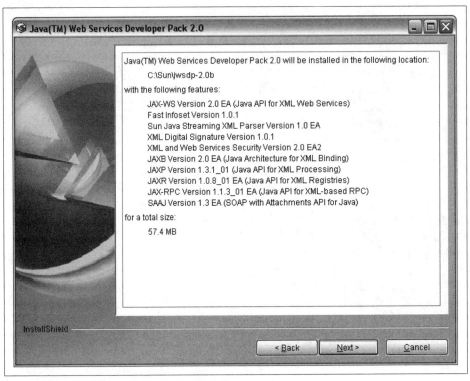

Figure 11-9. Java WSDP installation confirmation

JAXBContext

To obtain an instance of the Marshaller, Unmarshaller, or Validator interfaces, you first need to obtain an instance of JAXBContext. To do so, call one of JAXBContext's static newInstance() methods. In JAXB 1.0, both newInstance() methods accept a colon-separated list of package names. The second newInstance() method also accepts a ClassLoader object that will be used to load the classes in those packages. The newInstance() method searches for classes within these packages to create the *context path*—the list of classes that instances created by the JAXBContext object is able to marshall, unmarshall, and validate. In JAXB 2.0, there are additional newInstance() methods that allow you to pass in a list of Class objects, using the Java 5 varargs language features. When passing one or more classes to newInstance(), the resulting JAXBContext's context path contains both of the classes passed to newInstance() and any dependent classes. Thus, you generally only need to pass one or two top-level classes, and the dependent classes will automatically be added to the context path.

If we had compiled a schema into the package javaxml3.ch11.person1, this line would create the appropriate JAXBContext object in both JAXB 1.0 and JAXB 2.0:

```
JAXBContext context = JAXBContext.newInstance("javaxml3.ch11.person1");
```

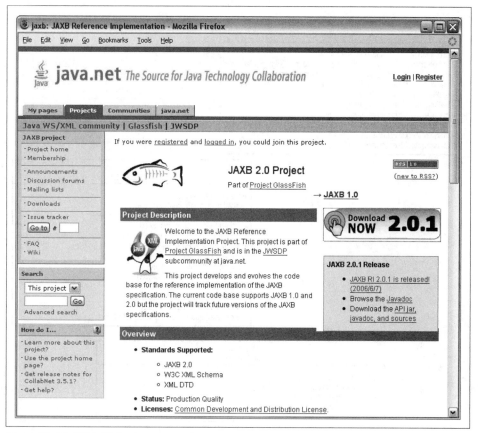

Figure 11-10. JAXB RI Project page at java.net

And in JAXB 2.0, we could also do this, assuming the compiled schema has a root element called Person:

```
JAXBContext context = JAXBContext.newInstance(javaxml3.ch11.person.Person.class);
```

One you have a JAXBContext object, it's easy to create Marshaller, Unmarshaller, and Validator instances:

```
Marshaller marshaller = context.createMarshaller();
Unmarshaller unmarshaller = context.createUnmarshaller();
Validator validator = context.createValidator();
```

But before we use any of those interfaces, we need some classes to work with. So first let's look at compiling a schema.

Compiling a Schema

As noted above, the JAXB specification does not specify how a developer executes a schema compiler, only how the compilation is done. Most implementations provide a command-line application, an Ant task, or both. The reference implementations

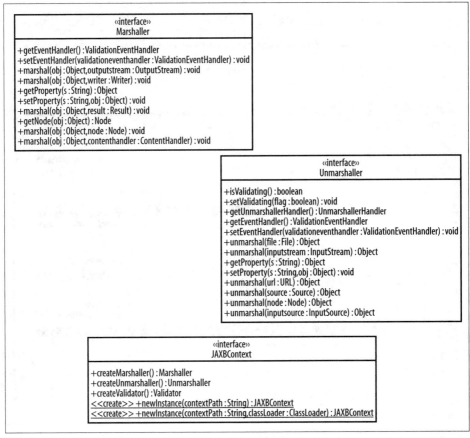

```
                    «interface»
                    Marshaller

+getEventHandler() : ValidationEventHandler
+setEventHandler(validationeventhandler : ValidationEventHandler) : void
+marshal(obj : Object,outputstream : OutputStream) : void
+marshal(obj : Object,writer : Writer) : void
+getProperty(s : String) : Object
+setProperty(s : String,obj : Object) : void
+marshal(obj : Object,result : Result) : void
+getNode(obj : Object) : Node
+marshal(obj : Object,node : Node) : void
+marshal(obj : Object,contenthandler : ContentHandler) : void
```

```
                    «interface»
                    Unmarshaller

+isValidating() : boolean
+setValidating(flag : boolean) : void
+getUnmarshallerHandler() : UnmarshallerHandler
+getEventHandler() : ValidationEventHandler
+setEventHandler(validationeventhandler : ValidationEventHandler) : void
+unmarshal(file : File) : Object
+unmarshal(inputstream : InputStream) : Object
+getProperty(s : String) : Object
+setProperty(s : String,obj : Object) : void
+unmarshal(url : URL) : Object
+unmarshal(source : Source) : Object
+unmarshal(node : Node) : Object
+unmarshal(inputsource : InputSource) : Object
```

```
                    «interface»
                    JAXBContext

+createMarshaller() : Marshaller
+createUnmarshaller() : Unmarshaller
+createValidator() : Validator
<<create>> +newInstance(contextPath : String) : JAXBContext
<<create>> +newInstance(contextPath : String,classLoader : ClassLoader) : JAXBContext
```

Figure 11-11. JAXB 1.0 core API

provide both a command-line application named *xjc* and an Ant task in the class
com.sun.tools.xjc.XJCTask.

> I cover the command-line application below and most of this informa-
> tion also applies to the Ant task. For the details on executing the
> Ant task, check the documentation that comes with your JAXB
> implementation.

Compiling with xjc

The command-line application can be run on Windows systems, using the batch file
xjc.bat, and on Unix-like systems (including Linux and Mac OS X), using the shell
script *xjc.sh*. Both of these files are in the *bin* directory of the JAXB distribution directory. In general, to run either script, you must have the JAVA_HOME environment variable set to the location of your JVM. See your operating system documentation for
more information on how to set environment variables.

The only required parameter to *xjc* is the schema. This could be a local file path or a URL. There are a number of optional parameters that can be included on the command line, listed in Table 11-2.

Table 11-2. xjc command-line options

-nv	Turn off strict validation of the input schema.
-extension	Permit vendor extensions to the JAXB specification.
-b <file/directory>	Specify external bindings file or files. If a directory name is passed, all files with the *xjb* extension will be included. Directories are only supported by JAXB 2.0 RI. Bindings files are discussed later in the section "Schema Compilation Customization."
-d <directory>	Output directory for generated files.
-p <package>	Specify the package for generated classes and interfaces.
-host <proxyHost>	Host name for HTTP proxy, if any. JAXB 1.0 RI only.
-port <proxyPort>	Port number for HTTP proxy, if any. JAXB 1.0 RI only.
-httpproxy <proxy>	HTTP proxy information in the format *[user[:password]@]proxyHost[:proxyPort]*. JAXB 2.0 RI only.
-classpath <classpath>	Additional classpath entries.
-catalog <file>	Catalog files for external entity references.
-readOnly	If specified, generated files will be created in read-only mode.
-use-runtime <package>	Do not generate the impl.runtime package and instead reference these classes in a different package. JAXB 1.0 RI only. See the section "JAXB 1.0 generated files" later in the chapter for more details.
-npa	Suppresses generation of package-level Java annotations. JAXB 2.0 RI only.
-no-header	Suppresses inclusion of a header including the timestamp in all generated files. JAXB 2.0 RI only.
-xmlschema	Forces the treatment of the input file as a W3C XML Schema. This is the default.
-relaxng	Treats the input file as a Relax NG schema. This is an unsupported option.
-relaxng-compact	Treats the input file as a Relax NG compact syntax schema. This is an unsupported option and in JAXB 2.0 RI only.
-dtd	Treats the input file as a DTD. This is an unsupported option.
-wsdl	Treats the input file as a WSDL and searches for schemas within it. This is an unsupported option in JAXB 2.0 RI only.
-verbose	Turns on extra debug logging. JAXB 2.0 RI only.
-quiet	Suppresses compiler output.
-help	Displays a help message containing a list of the command-line options.
-version	Displays version information about the compiler.

By default, the compiler will create a package name for the generated interfaces and classes based on the URI of the target namespace. A namespace URI of *http://www.example.com/person* will result in a package name of com.example.person. If there is no target namespace, such as in Example 11-4, then the package name generated is used. To override this (which I highly recommend), use the *-p* command-line option.

Example 11-4. A schema with no target namespace

```xml
<?xml version="1.0" encoding="UTF-8"?>
<xs:schema xmlns:xs="http://www.w3.org/2001/XMLSchema">
    <xs:element name="person">
        <xs:complexType>
            <xs:sequence>
                <xs:element name="firstName" type="xs:string"/>
                <xs:element name="lastName" type="xs:string"/>
            </xs:sequence>
        </xs:complexType>
    </xs:element>
</xs:schema>
```

To compile the schema in Example 11-4 in a file called *person.xsd* and have the compiled code go in the package com.example.person, run the command:

```
xjc -p com.example.person person.xsd
```

This will create output files in the current directory. To specify the output directory (which must exist already), use the *-d* option:

```
xjc -p com.example.person -d src person.xsd
```

Although the command is the same for both JAXB 1.0 RI and JAXB 2.0 RI (with a few options only available for one or the other), the files generated are dramatically different as you can see by comparing the output of both commands in Figures 11-12 and 11-13.

Before you start counting, I'll save you the trouble: the JAXB 1.0 compiler outputs 38 files compared with JAXB 2.0's two files. Looking more closely at what those files contain explains why this difference is so significant.

JAXB 1.0-generated files

First, let's look at the two interfaces the JAXB 1.0 compiler created in our main package: Person and PersonType. The JAXB 1.0 compiler will create an interface for every element and complex type declared in the schema. If an element contains an anonymous complex type, such as in Example 11-4, the compiler will create one interface to represent the complex type and another to represent the element. If, instead of the anonymous complex type, we had a named complex type, such as in Example 11-5, the PersonType interface would not be created. Instead the interface for the named complex type would be generated. In the case of Example 11-5, this interface's name would be Atype.

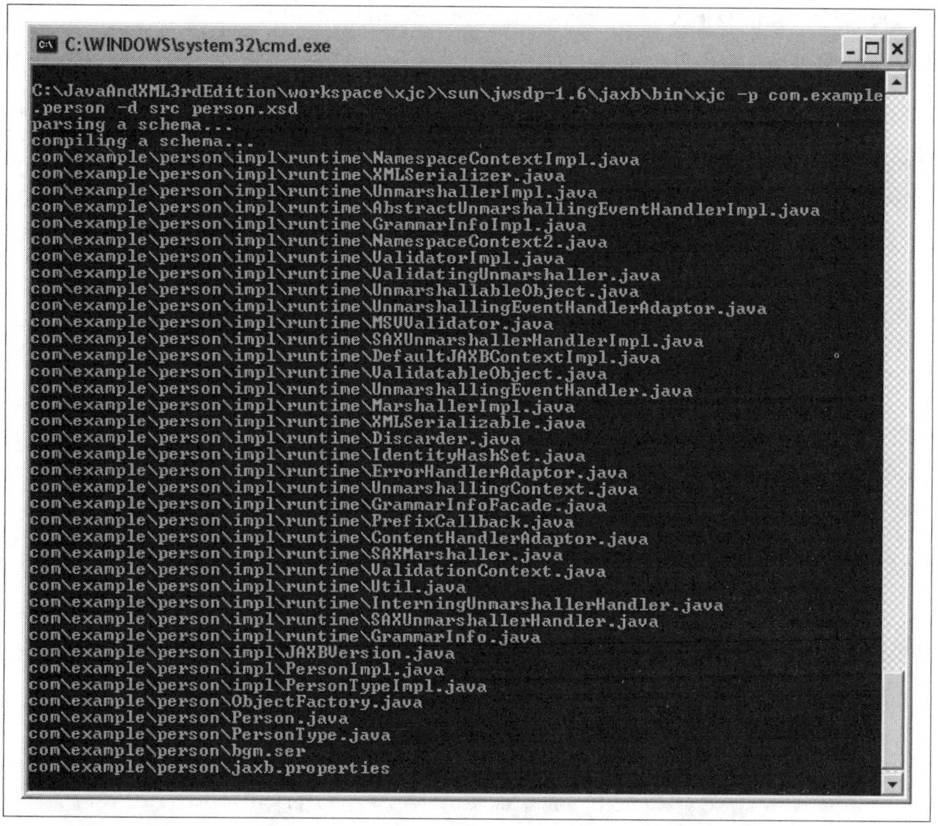

Figure 11-12. JAXB 1.0 compiler output

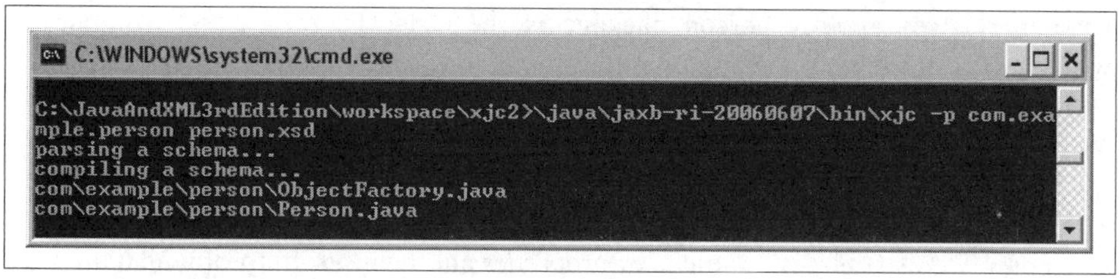

Figure 11-13. JAXB 2.0 compiler output

Example 11-5. Schema without anonymous complex type

```
<?xml version="1.0" encoding="UTF-8"?>
<xs:schema xmlns:xs="http://www.w3.org/2001/XMLSchema">
    <xs:element name="person" type="atype"/>
    <xs:complexType name="atype">
        <xs:sequence>
            <xs:element name="firstName" type="xs:string"/>
            <xs:element name="lastName" type="xs:string"/>
```

Example 11-5. Schema without anonymous complex type (continued)

```
        </xs:sequence>
    </xs:complexType>
</xs:schema>
```

he interfaces themselves are fairly simple. The `PersonType` interface defines getter and setter methods for the `firstName` and `lastName` child elements:

```
package com.example.person;

public interface PersonType {
    java.lang.String getFirstName( );
    void setFirstName(java.lang.String value);
    java.lang.String getLastName( );
    void setLastName(java.lang.String value);

}
```

 The JAXB compiler includes Javadoc comments in the generated code, but those have been removed from these examples.

The `Person` interface merely extends the `PersonType` interface and the `javax.xml.bind.Element` marker interface to mark that this interface represents an element:

```
package com.example.person;

public interface Person
    extends javax.xml.bind.Element, com.example.person.PersonType{

}
```

Also in the `com.example.person` package is the `ObjectFactory` class, instances of which can be used to create implementations of the `Person` and `PersonType` interfaces:

```
ObjectFactory factory = new ObjectFactory( );
Person person = factory.createPerson( );
// or
PersonType personType = factory.createPersonType( );
```

The compiler also creates the file *jaxb.properties* and *bgm.ser*, both of which are used by the `JAXBContext` class to create `Marshaller`, `Unmarshaller`, and `Validator` objects.

Inside `com.example.person`, the JAXB compiler has created an `impl` package containing implementations of the generated `Person` and `PersonType` interfaces. It is instances of these classes (`PersonImpl` and `PersonTypeImpl`) that the `ObjectFactory` class will return. These implementation classes are fairly long—in this case, `PersonImpl` and `PersonTypeImpl` generated by the JAXB 1.0 reference implementation combined come to about 500 lines. Most of the generated code is fairly boilerplate with the exception of the `createRawValidator( )` method, which defines a schema fragment using a byte stream. Clearly if you need to make changes to your schema, you should make them to your schema file and recompile it.

Finally, there's the package com.example.person.impl.runtime. This contains classes and interfaces that are used by the JAXB runtime. If you have multiple packages of JAXB-generated code, you can avoid repeatedly duplicating these files by passing the -use-runtime command-line option with the name of a package that already contains these classes and interfaces.

JAXB 2.0-generated files

Unlike the JAXB 1.0 compiler, the JAXB 2.0 compiler produces a concrete class called Person in our target package. The generated class is an annotated POJO, seen in Example 11-6.

Example 11-6. JAXB 2.0 generated element class

```
package com.example.person;

import javax.xml.bind.annotation.XmlAccessType;
import javax.xml.bind.annotation.XmlAccessorType;
import javax.xml.bind.annotation.XmlElement;
import javax.xml.bind.annotation.XmlRootElement;
import javax.xml.bind.annotation.XmlType;

@XmlAccessorType(XmlAccessType.FIELD)
@XmlType(name = "", propOrder = {
    "firstName",
    "lastName"
})
@XmlRootElement(name = "person")
public class Person {

    @XmlElement(required = true)
    protected String firstName;
    @XmlElement(required = true)
    protected String lastName;

    public String getFirstName() { return firstName; }

    public void setFirstName(String value) { this.firstName = value; }

    public String getLastName() { return lastName; }

    public void setLastName(String value) { this.lastName = value; }
}
```

As you can see, the bulk of this class is basic JavaBean code: two fields named firstName and lastName along with appropriate getters and setters for these fields. All of the metadata JAXB needs to marshall and unmarshall instances of this class are contained within the annotations. And unlike the generated classes from JAXB 1.0, this is actually code you could write yourself. Although you don't need it in this case, the ObjectFactory class is generated and contained in Example 11-7. Instead of using createPerson( ) on an `ObjectFactory` instance, it's generally more natural to use the public constructor of the `Person` class. Having the `ObjectFactory` class is still useful as it enables you to use code written against JAXB 1.0 without modification.

Example 11-7. JAXB 2.0 generated ObjectFactory

```
package com.example.person;

import javax.xml.bind.annotation.XmlRegistry;

@XmlRegistry
public class ObjectFactory {

    public ObjectFactory( ) {
    }

    public Person createPerson( ) {
        return new Person( );
    }

}
```

Let's take a look at what these annotations do and how you can use them directly.

JAXB Annotations

One of the key new features in JAXB 2.0 is the ability to use Java annotations to make any class able to participate in marshalling and unmarshalling. We've already seen some of these annotations in Examples 11-6 and 11-7. These annotations aren't just for classes generated by the schema compiler. It's possible to use them to annotate any class to enable marshalling and unmarshalling of objects of that class.

 If you're not familiar with Java annotations, now would be a good time to stop reading this book and go read *Java in a Nutshell* by David Flanagan (O'Reilly) or *Java 5.0 Tiger: A Developer's Notebook* by David Flanagan and Brett McLaughlin (O'Reilly).

Class-level annotations

Annotations can be attached to a package, a class, a field, or a method. Example 11-6 contains both annotations to both the class and its fields. Again, the class-level annotations in the example were:

```
@XmlAccessorType(XmlAccessType.FIELD)
@XmlType(name = "", propOrder = {
    "firstName",
    "lastName"
})
@XmlRootElement(name = "person")
public class Person {
```

XmlRootElement. The order of annotations is not important, and in this case, the JAXB schema compiler has the most important annotation last. The annotation `javax.xml.bind.annotation.XmlRootElement` declares that the class that it annotates is usable as a root element in a marshalled XML document. In the example above, we set the name member of the annotation to person. This isn't actually necessary, as JAXB would have automatically lowercased the first letter of the class name. Still, it's a good idea to include the name member to ensure the XML element name would survive a renaming of the class. With `XMLRootElement`, you can also specify a namespace URI using the namespace member.

If you were only to specify the `XMLRootElement` annotation, JAXB would include every public JavaBean property of your object as a child element in the marshalled XML. In other words, the simple class in Example 11-8 could produce XML documents such as Example 11-9, with only one annotation.

Example 11-8. A simple Person class

```
package javaxml3;

import javax.xml.bind.annotation.XmlRootElement;

@XmlRootElement( )
public class Person {
    private String firstName;
    private String lastName;

    public String getFirstName( ) { return firstName; }

    public String getLastName( ) { return lastName; }

    public void setFirstName(String s) { firstName = s; }

    public void setLastName(String s) { lastName = s; }

}
```

Example 11-9. Person output XML

```
<?xml version="1.0" encoding="UTF-8"?>
<person>
    <firstName>Burt</firstName>
    <lastName>Arbuckle</lastName>
</person>
```

XmlAccessorType. You can use the `javax.xml.bind.annotation.XmlAccessorType` annotation to specify the default rule for child element marshalling. The member of this annotation is a value from the enumeration class `javax.xml.bind.annotations.XmlAccessType`, which has four possible values:

PUBLIC_MEMBER

This is the default value, whose behavior we saw above. With this value, the marshaller will marshall every public getter and setter pair. To specify that a

JavaBean property should not be included in the marshalled output, either the getter or the setter must be annotated with the `javax.xml.bind.annotation.XmlTransient` annotation.

FIELD

With this value, the marshaller will marshall every nonstatic and nontransient field in the class. As above, if a field should not be marshalled, it must be annotated with `XmlTransient`. Likewise, if a getter/setter pair should be marshalled, it must be explicitly annotated with another JAXB annotation.

PROPERTY

This value is similar to `PUBLIC_MEMBER`, but all getter/setter pairs are marshalled, including those that have private, protected, or package-only access.

NONE

If `NONE` is the value set as the member of `XmlAccessorType`, no child elements will be marshalled automatically. Any fields or properties that need to be marshalled must be explicitly annotated.

XmlType. Last among the class-level annotations from Example 11-6 is `XmlType`. This annotation allows you to specify more detailed information about the schema type that this class represents. In the case of Example 11-6, we have an anonymous complex type (name=""), which is to be expected based on the schema. Like `XmlRootElement`, `XmlType` has a namespace member that can specify the namespace URI for the type. `XmlType` can also, as we saw in Example 11-6, specify the order of children for marshalling. By default, child elements will be marshalled in alphabetical order. If you specify the order using `XmlType`'s `propOrder` member as in Example 11-6, the value of `XmlAccessorType`, if any, is ignored and only those properties listed in `propOrder` are included in the marshalled output.

Field-level annotations

Example 11-6 contained only a single field-level annotation:

```
@XmlElement(required = true)
protected String firstName;
@XmlElement(required = true)
protected String lastName;
```

XmlElement. As with `XmlRootElement`, discussed above, `javax.xml.bind.annotation.XmlElement` declares the existence of an XML element. But whereas `XmlRootElement` annotated classes, `XmlElement` is used to annotate JavaBean properties and fields. `XmlElement` has name and namespace members for overriding the default element name and namespace URI, respectively. It also has several members for declaring constraints on the element. These are:

required

As used above, indicates that the element is required.

nillable

An element that represents a null property will not be output if `nillable` is `false` (the default). However, if `nillable` is true, an empty element will be output with the attribute `xsi:nil` set to `true`.

defaultValue

Sets the default value for an element.

XmlAttribute. The schema in Example 11-4 did not contain any attributes, so our Java class didn't contain any uses of `javax.xml.bind.annotation.XmlAttribute`. `XmlAttribute` can be used in the same ways as `XmlElement`: annotating a field or a JavaBean property. A single field or property can either be marshalled as an element or an attribute, not both. This is illegal:

```
@XmlAttribute(name="valueAttribute")
@XmlElement(name="valueElement")
private String value;
```

However, it is completely legal to have an attribute and element with the same name. The `XmlAttribute` annotation, like `XmlElement`, has `name`, `namespace`, and `required` members.

Package-level annotations

Although it's possible, as I've mentioned, to assign namespace URIs to elements and attributes using the `namespace` member, if you're defining a schema, you need to declare the target namespace. With JAXB annotations, this is done with a package-level annotation called `javax.xml.bind.annotation.XmlSchema`. To create a package-level annotation, create a file called *package-info.java* and add a regular Java package declaration to it. Annotations can then be added to this file and they will apply to the package as a whole. For example, to set the target namespace to *http://www.example.com/person* and set the default element namespace qualification form to qualified, you can use the `XmlSchema` annotation like this:

```
@javax.xml.bind.annotation.XmlSchema(
    namespace = "http://www.example.com/person",
    elementFormDefault = javax.xml.bind.annotation.XmlNsForm.QUALIFIED
)
package javaxml3;
```

You can also use `XmlSchema` to declare namespace prefixes:

```
@javax.xml.bind.annotation.XmlSchema(
    namespace = "http://www.example.com/person",
    elementFormDefault = javax.xml.bind.annotation.XmlNsForm.QUALIFIED,
    xmlns = {
        @javax.xml.bind.annotation.XmlNs(prefix = "p",
            namespaceURI="http://www.example.com/person")
    }
)
package javaxml3;
```

This does not necessarily mean that the prefix specified will be used in the marshalled output. The prefix associations defined with the XmlSchema annotation apply primarily to a schema generated from these classes.

This is only the beginning of what you can do with JAXB 2.0 annotations. There are numerous annotations not covered here. Please see the Javadocs for JAXB 2.0 (included in the distributions) and the JAXB 2.0 specification for more details on these additional annotations.

Schema generation

In JAXB 2.0, XML Schemas can be generated from annotated classes. Like schema compilation, the JAXB specification defines how a schema gets generated but not how a developer triggers the generation process. In the reference implementation, schema generation is done with a command-line application called *schemagen*. Like the *xjc* schema compiler, *schemagen* comes in both a Windows batch file and a Unix shell script. At a minimum, you must pass *schemagen* a list of source files from which to generate the schema. If these source files refer to other classes, the sources for those classes must either be explicitly provided on the command line or in a directory passed to *schemagen* with the *-cp* or *-classpath* command-line options. In general, it's easiest to provide a single source file containing a root element for your schema and pass the directory containing all of your source files as the classpath.

By default, *schemagen* will output the schema and compiled versions of the source files in the current directory. This can be overridden with the *-d* command-line option.

The reference implementation also provides an Ant task for schema generation. Its options are identical to the command-line version. See the JAXB reference implementation documentation for more details.

Marshalling

One you have generated classes from a schema, it is very simple to create and marshall an object:

```
package javaxml3;

import javax.xml.bind.JAXBContext;
import javax.xml.bind.JAXBException;
import javax.xml.bind.Marshaller;

import com.example.person.ObjectFactory;
import com.example.person.Person;

public class PersonMarshaller {

    public static void main(String[] args) throws JAXBException {
        ObjectFactory factory = new ObjectFactory();
```

```
            Person person = factory.createPerson();
            person.setFirstName("Alan");
            person.setLastName("Turing");

            JAXBContext context = JAXBContext.newInstance("com.example.person");
            Marshaller marshaller = context.createMarshaller();
            marshaller.marshal(person, System.out);
        }

    }
```

Running this class produces the following output:

```
<?xml version="1.0" encoding="UTF-8" standalone="yes"?>
<person><firstName>Alan</firstName><lastName>Turing</lastName></person>
```

In addition to the `java.io.OutputStream`-accepting method used in the example above, there are `marshal()` methods that accept the following output mechanisms:

- `org.xml.sax.ContentHandler`
- `org.w3c.dom.Node`
- `javax.xml.transform.Result`
- `javax.io.Writer`

JAXB 2.0 adds two additional options:

- `javax.xml.stream.XMLStreamWriter`
- `javax.xml.stream.XMLEventWriter`

The only one of these that warrants explanation is `org.w3c.dom.Node`. This method will marshall the passed object and create DOM nodes as children of the passed `Node` object. This allows you to add the marshalled output as a fragment inside a preexisting DOM `Document` or `Element` object. As an example, this class:

```
package javaxml3;

import javax.xml.bind.JAXBContext;
import javax.xml.bind.Marshaller;
import javax.xml.parsers.DocumentBuilder;
import javax.xml.parsers.DocumentBuilderFactory;
import javax.xml.transform.TransformerFactory;
import javax.xml.transform.dom.DOMSource;
import javax.xml.transform.stream.StreamResult;

import org.w3c.dom.Document;
import org.w3c.dom.Element;

import com.example.person.ObjectFactory;
import com.example.person.Person;

public class DOMMarshaller {

    public static void main(String[] args) throws Exception {
        DocumentBuilderFactory dbf = DocumentBuilderFactory.newInstance();
```

```
        DocumentBuilder builder = dbf.newDocumentBuilder();
        Document doc = builder.newDocument();
        Element people = doc.createElement("people");
        doc.appendChild(people);

        ObjectFactory factory = new ObjectFactory();
        Person person = factory.createPerson();
        person.setFirstName("Alan");
        person.setLastName("Turing");

        JAXBContext context = JAXBContext.newInstance("com.example.person");
        Marshaller marshaller = context.createMarshaller();
        marshaller.marshal(person, people);

        TransformerFactory tf = TransformerFactory.newInstance();
        tf.newTransformer().transform(new DOMSource(doc),
                new StreamResult(System.out));


    }


}
```

Outputs the following XML document. The highlighted lines contain the elements created by the marshaller.

```
<?xml version="1.0" encoding="UTF-8"?>@XmlAccessorType(XmlAccessType.FIELD)
<people>
    <person>
        <firstName>Alan</firstName>
        <lastName>Turing</lastName>
    </person>
</people>
```

 I have reformatted the output. The identity transform used to output the document puts all the content on one line.

Bidirectional DOM support

Both JAXB 1.0 and 2.0 define an optional method named getNode() for the Marshaller interface. The purpose of this method is to return a DOM Node object that provides access to the object tree through the DOM interfaces. Unlike the marshal() method, getNode() does not create a copy of your objects. Instead, the DOM Node interface is a façade on top of your object tree. Changes made to the DOM tree are made directly to your object tree, where if you modify the result of a call to marshal(), you would need to unmarshall the changed DOM Node back into an object tree.

If a JAXB implementation chooses to not provide a full implementation of this method, it will throw a java.lang.UnsupportedOperationException. Unfortunately, neither reference implementation supports this method.

Marshaller properties

As seen in Figure 11-11, the `Marshaller` interface includes `getProperty()` and `setProperty()` methods for setting various options on the output. The JAXB specification defines several properties that all implementations are required to support. Implementations are free to support additional properties. The standard properties for JAXB 1.0 and 2.0 are:

`jaxb.encoding`
> Specifies the output encoding as a `java.lang.String`. Defaults to `UTF-8`.

`jaxb.formatted.output`
> A `java.lang.Boolean` value that, if true, adds linebreaks and indentation to the XML output. Defaults to `false`.

`jaxb.schemaLocation`
> This property, a `java.lang.String`, instructs the marshaller to include an `xsi:schemaLocation` attribute to the XML output. If not specified, no attribute is included.

`jaxb.noNamespaceSchemaLocation`
> This property, a `java.lang.String`, instructs the marshaller to include an `xsi:noNamespaceSchemaLocation` attribute to the XML output. If not specified, no attribute is included.

In addition, JAXB 2.0 added a new property:

`jaxb.fragment`
> This property, a `java.lang.Boolean`, tells the marshaller to treat the result of the marshalling as a fragment, not a full XML document. The default value is `false`. The effect of this property depends on where the marshaller output is destined.
>
> `org.xml.sax.ContentHandler`
>> The `Marshaller` will not call the `startDocument()` event on the `ContentHandler` object.
>
> `org.w3c.dom.Node`
>> No impact.
>
> `java.io.OutputStream` *or* `java.io.Writer`
>> XML declaration is not generated.
>
> `javax.xml.stream.XMLEventWriter` *and* `javax.xml.stream.XMLStreamWriter`
>> `START_DOCUMENT` and `END_DOCUMENT` events will not be generated.

The impact on the marshal() method that accepts a javax.xml.transform.Result depends on the type of Result object passed and will generally follow one of the rules above.

Unmarshalling

Unmarshalling an XML document to a tree of Java objects is fairly similar to marshalling to an XML document.

If we had this document in a file called *james.xml*:

```
<?xml version="1.0" encoding="UTF-8"?>
<person>
    <firstName>James</firstName>
    <lastName>Gosling</lastName>
</person>
```

Then this code will output Mr. Gosling's first name:

```
package javaxml3;

import java.io.File;

import javax.xml.bind.JAXBContext;
import javax.xml.bind.JAXBException;
import javax.xml.bind.Unmarshaller;

import com.example.person.Person;

public class PersonUnmarshaller {

    public static void main(String[] args) throws JAXBException {
        JAXBContext context = JAXBContext.newInstance("com.example.person");
        Unmarshaller unmarshaller = context.createUnmarshaller();
        Person person = (Person) unmarshaller.unmarshal(new File("james.xml"));
        System.out.println(person.getFirstName());

    }

}
```

Like the `Marshaller` interface's `marshal()` method, there are a handful of different input options for the `unmarshal()` method, in addition to the `java.io.File` used in the example above:

- `org.xml.sax.InputSource`
- `java.io.InputStream`
- `org.w3c.dom.Node`
- `javax.xml.transform.Source`
- `java.net.URL`

JAXB 2.0 adds these additional input options:

- `java.io.Reader`
- `javax.xml.stream.XMLStreamReader`
- `javax.xml.stream.XMLEventReader`

With the `Node`, `Source`, `XMLStreamReader`, and `XMLEventReader` inputs, there are also overloaded versions that accept both the input mechanism and a `Class`. These methods return an instance of `javax.xml.bind.JAXBElement` parameterized with the `Class` passed to the method. These methods allow you to specify into which type the input XML will be unmarshalled, regardless of the mapping between the root element of the input XML and a JAXB type. For example, let's say we wanted to tolerate misspellings of the root element like:

```
<?xml version="1.0" encoding="UTF-8"?>
<perso>
    <firstName>James</firstName>
    <lastName>Gosling</lastName>
</perso>
```

This could be accomplished by using JAXB 2.0 with one of the parameterized methods:

```
package javaxml3;

import javax.xml.bind.JAXBContext;
import javax.xml.bind.JAXBElement;
import javax.xml.bind.JAXBException;
import javax.xml.bind.Unmarshaller;
import javax.xml.transform.stream.StreamSource;

import com.example.person.Person;

public class MisspelledPersonUnmarshaller {

    public static void main(String[] args) throws JAXBException {
        JAXBContext context = JAXBContext.newInstance("com.example.person");
        Unmarshaller unmarshaller = context.createUnmarshaller();

        JAXBElement<Person> element = unmarshaller.unmarshal(new StreamSource(
                "james_misspelled.xml"), Person.class);
        Person person = element.getValue();
        System.out.println(person.getFirstName());

    }
}
```

Unmarshall-time validation

The `Unmarshaller` interface defines methods `setValidating()` and `isValidating()` to turn on and off JAXB validation of input documents. By default, `Unmarshaller` instances do not validate. These methods have been deprecated in JAXB 2.0, something we'll discuss later in the "Validation" section.

Unmarshaller properties

Like `Marshaller`, `Unmarshaller` defines `getProperty()` and `setProperty()` methods for setting options. However, neither JAXB specifications define any standard properties for `Unmarshaller` instances.

Validation

JAXB 1.0 contained a `Validator` interface in the `javax.xml.bind` package that performed on-demand validation of a tree of JAXB objects. Instances of this interface used the metadata stored within the generated classes to perform the validation. In JAXB 2.0, the Validator interface has been deprecated and implementations are not required to implement it. The JAXB 2.0 reference implementation, for one, throws a java.lang.UnsupportedOperationException if you attempt to create a Validator object.

Instead of a JAXB-specific validation mechanism, JAXB 2.0 is dependent upon the JAXP validation mechanism discussed in Chapter 7. As part of this, on-demand validation was replaced with marshall-time validation. This seems like a bigger change than it actually is, as you can easily simulate on-demand validation by performing a marshall with validation enabled and just not use the result of the marshalling.

To use JAXP validation within either a marshall or an unmarshall operation, create an instance of javax.xml.validation.Schema and pass it to the setSchema( ) method of either an Unmarshaller or Marshaller instance. In Example 11-10, we create an incomplete person object (there's no last name specified). Without validation enabled, the marshaller's output would not be valid according to the schema. But because we enable schema validation, an exception is thrown.

Example 11-10. Schema validation when marshalling

```
package javaxml3;

import java.io.File;

import javax.xml.XMLConstants;
import javax.xml.bind.JAXBContext;
import javax.xml.bind.Marshaller;
import javax.xml.validation.Schema;
import javax.xml.validation.SchemaFactory;

import com.example.person.Person;

public class MarshalValidation {

    public static void main(String[] args) throws Exception {
        // create an incomplete Person object
        Person p = new Person();
        p.setFirstName("Burt");

        // create our marshaller
        JAXBContext context = JAXBContext.newInstance(Person.class);
        Marshaller marshaller = context.createMarshaller();

        // create a schema
        SchemaFactory sf = SchemaFactory
                .newInstance(XMLConstants.W3C_XML_SCHEMA_NS_URI);
        Schema schema = sf.newSchema(new File("person.xsd"));

        // assign the schema to the marshaller
        marshaller.setSchema(schema);

        // this will throw a javax.xml.bind.MarshalException
```

Example 11-10. Schema validation when marshalling (continued)

```
        marshaller.marshal(p, System.out);
    }

}
```

This same logic can be applied to unmarshalling: create a `SchemaFactory`, then a Schema, and finally pass the `Schema` object to the `setSchema()` method of your `Unmarshaller` instance.

Validation events

By default, any validation error will result in an immediate failure of the marshall or unmarshall operation with an appropriate exception (either `MarshalException` or `UnmarshalException`) thrown. For finer control over this behavior, the JAXB API includes a series of interfaces that allow you to intercept validation errors as they occur. These interfaces are shown in Figure 11-14. These interfaces are the same in both JAXB 1.0 and JAXB 2.0.

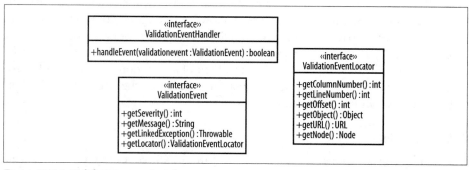

Figure 11-14. Validation event interfaces

To use these interfaces, create an implementation of the `ValidationEventHandler` interface and pass it to the `setEventHandler()` method of a `Marshaller` or `Unmarshaller` instance. As validation problems occur while marshalling or unmarshalling, your handler's `handleEvent()` method is called with a `ValidationEvent` object. This object informs you of the severity of the problem, a related exception (if available), and a human-readable message. The event object also contains an implementation of the `ValidationEventLocator` interface, which allows you to pinpoint where in your object tree or input XML the problem has occurred. The `ValidationEvent` interface defines three levels of severity: warning, error, and fatal error. There are constants within the `ValdiationEvent` interface that allow you to write code such as:

```
    if (event.getServerity() == ValidationEvent.WARNING) {
        System.out.println("Warning received. Ignoring it.");
    } else {
        System.out.println("Error or Fatal Error received. Uh Oh.");
    }
```

The handleEvent( ) method returns a boolean value that determines whether or not the marshall or unmarshall operation in the process will proceed. If the method returns false or the method throws an unchecked exception, the current operation is halted immediately and an exception is thrown. If the method returns true, the operation proceeds.

 If the marshall or unmarshall validation succeeds, your handler's handleEvent( ) method will never be called.

Schema Compilation Customization

JAXB 1.0 and 2.0 provide extensive capabilities for customizing the behavior of the schema compiler through a *binding declaration*. These declarations can be in within your schema file, an external binding file, or both. Regardless of what file they're located in, the customizations take more or less the same form: elements within the namespace *http://java.sun.com/xml/ns/jaxb*. One way to think about these elements is as the mirror images of the annotations added in JAXB 2.0. For example, the XmlSchema annotation previously discussed allows you to specify the namespace URI for classes within a package. With the binding declaration package, you can do the opposite: specify the package name for the target namespace of a schema. In fact, thinking about the binding declarations as a kind of annotation makes a lot of sense, since to include them in an XML Schema file, you place the declaration elements within the xs:annotation element.

Inline declarations

To use inline declarations, you must first add the JAXB namespace to your schema document along with a version property indicating which version of JAXB the declarations are targeted. Then, for each schema component you want to add a declaration to, add an xs:annotation element containing an xs:appinfo element. Inside the xs:appinfo element, add your declarations. Example 11-11 contains a simple schema annotated with JAXB binding declarations.

Example 11-11. A simple annotated schema

```
<?xml version="1.0" encoding="UTF-8"?>
<xs:schema xmlns:xs="http://www.w3.org/2001/XMLSchema"
  xmlns:jaxb="http://java.sun.com/xml/ns/jaxb" jaxb:version="2.0">
    <xs:annotation>
        <xs:appinfo>
            <jaxb:schemaBindings>
                <jaxb:package name="com.example.artist"/>
            </jaxb:schemaBindings>
        </xs:appinfo>
    </xs:annotation>
```

Example 11-11. A simple annotated schema (continued)

```
<xs:element name="artist">
    <xs:annotation>
        <xs:appinfo>
            <jaxb:class name="MyArtist"/>
        </xs:appinfo>
    </xs:annotation>
    <xs:complexType>
        <xs:sequence>
            <xs:element name="name" type="xs:string"/>
            <xs:element name="nameForSorting" type="xs:string" minOccurs="0">
                <xs:annotation>
                    <xs:appinfo>
                        <jaxb:property name="keyName"/>
                    </xs:appinfo>
                </xs:annotation>
            </xs:element>
        </xs:sequence>
    </xs:complexType>
</xs:element>
</xs:schema>
```

 The reason for needing both xs:annotation and xs:appinfo is that xs:annotation can also contain the xs:documentation element, which allows you to provide documentation for each element within a schema. Do yourself a favor and use xs:documentation, not comments, to document your XML Schema files.

External declaration

By convention, an external binding declaration file is given the extension *xjb*. This isn't strictly required unless you want to pass in a directory name to the schema compiler and have all of the files within that directory used as external declarations files as mentioned in Table 11-2. An external binding declaration file is an XML document with the root element bindings (in the *http://java.sun.com/xml/ns/jaxb* namespace). A binding declaration file can contain declarations for one or more schema documents. If the file only applies to a single schema, then the root bindings element will have a schemaLocation attribute whose value is the URI of the schema document as in Example 11-12. If the file applies to multiple schemas, the root bindings element will contain multiple child bindings elements, each with their own schemaLocation element, as seen in Example 11-13.

Example 11-12. Binding declaration file applied to a single schema

```
<?xml version="1.0" encoding="UTF-8"?>
<jaxb:bindings version="2.0" xmlns:jaxb="http://java.sun.com/xml/ns/jaxb"
  xmlns:xs="http://www.w3.org/2001/XMLSchema" schemaLocation="schema.xsd">
    <!-- declaractions go here -->
</jaxb:binding>
```

Example 11-13. Binding declaration file applied to a multiple schemas

```
<?xml version="1.0" encoding="UTF-8"?>
<jaxb:bindings version="2.0" xmlns:jaxb="http://java.sun.com/xml/ns/jaxb"
  xmlns:xs="http://www.w3.org/2001/XMLSchema">
    <jaxb:bindings schemaLocation="schema1.xsd">
        <!-- declaractions go here -->
    </jaxb:bindings>

    <jaxb:bindings schemaLocation="schema2.xsd">
        <!-- declaractions go here -->
    </jaxb:bindings>

</jaxb:bindings>
```

Within bindings elements with a schemaLocation attribute, there are one or more child bindings elements with a node attribute. This attribute contains an XPath expression used to find the schema component the contained declarations are applied to. Since bindings elements can be nested, the XPath expressions can be relative expressions based on the current node. Putting these pieces together allows us to extract the binding declarations from Example 11-11 into an external file:

```
<?xml version="1.0" encoding="UTF-8"?>
<jaxb:bindings version="2.0" xmlns:jaxb="http://java.sun.com/xml/ns/jaxb"
  xmlns:xs="http://www.w3.org/2001/XMLSchema">
    <jaxb:bindings schemaLocation="artist.xsd">
        <jaxb:bindings node="/xs:schema">
            <jaxb:schemaBindings>
                <jaxb:package name="com.example.artist"/>
            </jaxb:schemaBindings>
            <jaxb:bindings node="./xs:element[@name='artist']">
                <jaxb:class name="MyArtist"/>
                <jaxb:bindings node=".//xs:element[@name='nameForSorting']">
                    <jaxb:property name="keyName"/>
                </jaxb:bindings>
            </jaxb:bindings>
        </jaxb:bindings>
    </jaxb:bindings>
</jaxb:bindings>
```

Binding declarations

JAXB 1.0 defined seven binding declarations for use inside jaxb:bindings or xs: appinfo elements. JAXB 2.0 added three additional declarations:

globalBindings

Since JAXB 1.0. Sets various options that affect the schema compilation as a whole such as which Java type is used for collections and whether or not to generate methods to determine if a property has been set explicitly. This declaration can only exist at the schema level. It can contain javaType declarations, described below.

schemaBindings

Since JAXB 1.0. Sets the package name for the schema as well as specifying prefixes and suffixes for generated classes. For example, you can specify that all the names of classes generated from xs:elements will start with My and end with Element. This declaration can only exist at the schema level. The package child element, which defines the package name, see above, can contain a javadoc declaration, described below.

class

Since JAXB 1.0. This declaration sets the name of the generated class for the associated schema component. It can contain a javadoc declaration.

property

Since JAXB 1.0. This declaration customizes the generation of a Java property including the name, as we saw above. It can contain a javadoc declaration, which if provided, is used to generate the Javadoc for both the getter and setter method for the generated property.

javaType

Since JAXB 1.0. This declaration specifies a mapping between an XML type and a Java class or primitive. This declaration can exist inside globalBindings or schemaBindings declarations, in which case the XML type must be specified and the mapping will apply globally or schema-wide, respectively. It can also annotate a schema type component directly, in which case the XML type is not specified. The declaration also allows you to specify methods for reading and writing to a String. If the mapped Java type is a class, not a primitive, the read method is optional if the class defines a constructor with a single String argument.

typesafeEnum

Since JAXB 1.0. This declaration customizes how the schema compiler generates typesafe enumeration classes.

javadoc

Since JAXB 1.0. This declaration allows you to insert custom text into the generated class's Javadoc. It must be specified inside one of the declarations defined above.

dom

Since JAXB 2.0. When this declaration is included, the annotated schema component will be represented in the generated Java classes as an object in a document object model library rather than JAXB types. This is very useful when working with mixed content for which JAXB (and data binding in general) is ill-suited. Although support is only for W3C DOM, implementations are free to support other libraries.

inlineBinaryData

Since JAXB 2.0. This declaration provides control of the binary data optimizations in JAXB 2.0.

factoryMethod

Since JAXB 2.0. This declaration defines the name of the factory method for a type in the generated ObjectFactory class.

For details on these declarations, see the JAXB specifications. You can also download the XML Schemas for the binding declarations from *http://java.sun.com/xml/ns/jaxb/bindingschema_1_0.xsd* and *http://java.sun.com/xml/ns/jaxb/bindingschema_2_0.xsd*.

JAXB Callbacks

With JAXB 2.0, callback mechanisms were added to Marshaller and Unmarshaller. The callback mechanism allows objects to be notified throughout the marshalling or unmarshalling process. This mechanism has two facets to it: class-defined and external listener.

Class-defined callbacks

A class bound with JAXB can implement methods to be notified before or after it is marshalled or unmarshalled. These methods are:

```
private void beforeUnmarshal(Unmarshaller unmarshaller, Object parent)
private void afterUnmarshal(Unmarshaller unmarshaller, Object parent)
private void beforeMarhshal(Marshaller marshaller)
private void afterMarhsal(Marshaller marshaller)
```

In the case of the before methods, the object is free to modify itself or perform other additional processing.

 Note that these methods are not described in an interface. They're discovered by the JAXB implementation by reflection.

External listener

Both Marshaller and Unmarshaller interfaces include an abstract inner class named Listener. By extending this class and passing it to the setListener() method of the appropriate class, an external object can be notified before and after each object is marshalled or unmarshalled. Unmarshaller.Listener defines methods named beforeUnmarshal() and afterUnmarshal():

```
public static abstract class Listener {
    public void beforeUnmarshal(Object target, Object parent) { }
    public void afterUnmarshal(Object target, Object parent) { }
}
```

And Marshaller.Listener defines methods named beforeMarshal() and afterMarshal():

```
public static abstract class Listener {
    public void beforeMarshal(Object source) { }
    public void afterMarshal(Object source) { }
}
```

 These are abstract classes, not interfaces, specifically so that you only need to override one method. You can, of course, override both. But you don't need to as you would if Listener was an interface.

Other Binding Frameworks

Despite the standardization effort around JAXB, there are numerous other Java-XML data binding frameworks available, including many under some sort of open source license. Before leaving data binding behind and moving on to the next chapter, I want to touch on a two of these non-JAXB frameworks, albeit briefly.

XMLBeans

XMLBeans was originally written by BEA, but is now a project of the Apache Software Foundation. The web site for XMLBeans is *http://xmlbeans.apache.org*. XMLBeans is under active development, with the most recent version (2.2.0) released in June of 2006. XMLBeans is fairly unique among Java-XML data binding frameworks in that it stores the full XML infoset. This allows you to perform round-tripping of XML: unmarshall a document and then marshall the resulting object and know that the input and output will be identical, including things like processing instructions and comments. However, XMLBeans (unlike JAXB 2.0) requires that all bound classes be created with their schema compiler.

Castor

Castor is one of the oldest Java-XML data binding frameworks that are still in active development. Its web site is *http://www.castor.org*. The latest version (1.0.1) was released in July 2006. Castor actually does much more than Java-XML data binding, including a full implementation of Java Data Objects (JDO). The Castor developers are currently hard at work implementing the new Java Persistence API (JPA). Although it is not done with annotations and is more limited than JAXB 2.0, Castor does support binding classes that were not created by its schema compiler.

## CHAPTER 12

Content Syndication with RSS

The next few chapters of this book will discuss some specific XML applications rather than the generalized toolkits for processing XML documents examined in previous chapters. The first such application is content syndication. Traditional content syndication, by companies, such as the Associated Press and Reuters for news, King World and DiC Entertainment for entertainment, and King Features Syndicate and United Feature Syndicate for editorial columns and comic strips, is a business-to-business enterprise. Many distributors—newspapers, radio stations, television stations, etc.—do not have the resources to pay the salary of an Oprah Winfrey or a Scott Adams, so they license this content from a content syndicator for a fraction of the overall cost.

With the advent of the Web, content syndication changed in four dramatic ways:

- The Web empowered thousands, if not millions, of content providers—basically anyone with a web site.

- Electronic distribution of content in the form of content feeds all but eliminated the barrier to entry for new content syndicators and enabled content providers to become their own syndicators.

- Thousands of new distribution outlets were opened, many in need of some level of syndicated content.

- Unlike newspapers or television and radio stations, these new distribution outlets are not limited by geography and thus are able to compete with one another. Because the barriers to becoming a distribution outlet are so low, some syndicators began direct-to-consumer distribution, competing with their commercial customers.

So what does this have to do with Java and XML? Well, although there are a variety of means for syndicating content on the Web, the vast majority use XML. And as a Java developer, you may need to create a syndication feed and/or ingest one or more feeds. This ingesting could occur with a single feed to display syndicated content on a web site; or you may need to write an application to ingest several feeds to produce an aggregated view of those feeds' content. In recent years, web content syndication has consolidated around a family of XML formats referred to under the umbrella name of RSS.

What Is RSS?

RSS is an application of XML that defines a sequenced list of content. RSS calls this list a *channel*. Within the channel are one or more *items*. These items are usually located at a URL. The feed also contains metadata about the channel and each item; the feed can specify an image to be used as the logo of the channel, a description of each item, and so on. RSS was originally created by Netscape for use on its My Netscape portal. Users needed to be able to add channels of content to their portals, and Netscape wanted a consistent way to represent those channels. Thus, the first version of RSS was born as Version 0.9 in March of 1999. In this initial specification, the letters RSS stood for RDF Site Summary. Since then, RSS has been used as an acronym for two additional terms:

- Rich Site Summary
- Really Simple Syndication

In addition, some people involved with the development of RSS now claim that it is not an acronym at all.

Blogs and Podcasting

Two popular uses for RSS are *blogs* and *podcasting*. A blog is generally a web site containing a series of entries. Although it's not strictly required to have a site be called a blog, the majority of blogs have an RSS feed available and many blogging applications are built on RSS.

Podcasting, on the other hand, is very much tied to RSS. Podcasting is the distribution of multimedia content through a syndication feed, generally using the enclosure element within RSS 2.0. A podcatcher (an application that reads podcast feeds) downloads the media files referenced by a podcast feed. Most podcatchers are designed to put downloaded files in a specific location on a user's computer from which they will be copied to a portable audio or video player.

RSS Variants

Nine different specifications have been released under the name RSS. These can be separated into those that are based on the Resource Description Framework (RDF) and those that aren't, as seen in Table 12-1.

Table 12-1. RSS variants

Based on RDF	Not based on RDF
RSS 0.9	RSS 0.91 (both Netscape and Userland versions)
RSS 1.0	RSS 0.92 through RSS 0.94
	RSS 2.0

This chapter will focus on RSS 1.0 and RSS 2.0, the two current versions. For comparison, Examples 12-1 and 12-2 contain excerpts from RSS 1.0 and 2.0 feeds respectively.

> The evolution of RSS has been fairly controversial. There are many online resources describing the events that led to a situation where "RSS" refers to two different, incompatible, specifications. I suggest starting with the Wikipedia page: *http://en.wikipedia.org/wiki/RSS_%28file_format%29* and browsing from there. In addition, a blog entry titled "The myth of RSS compatibility" at *http://diveintomark.org/archives/2004/02/04/incompatible-rss* is worth a look, especially if you're writing an application that ingests RSS feeds. The author, Mark Pilgrim, has been involved with a number of open source feed validators and parsers.

Example 12-1. Example RSS 1.0 feed

```
<?xml version="1.0" encoding="UTF-8"?>
<rdf:RDF xmlns:rdf="http://www.w3.org/1999/02/22-rdf-syntax-ns#"
  xmlns="http://purl.org/rss/1.0/">
  <channel>
    <title>Example RSS 1.0 Feed</title>
    <link>http://www.example.org</link>
    <description>the Example Organization web site</description>
    <image rdf:about="http://www.example.org/images/logo.gif">
      <title>Example</title>
      <url>http://www.example.org/images/logo.gif</url>
      <link>http://www.example.org</link>
    </image>
    <items>
      <rdf:Seq>
        <rdf:li resource="http://www.example.org/item1/"/>
        <rdf:li resource="http://www.example.org/item2/"/>
      </rdf:Seq>
    </items>
  </channel>
  <item rdf:about="http://www.example.org/item1/">
    <title>New Status Updates</title>
    <link>http://www.example.org/item1/</link>
    <description>News about the Example project</description>
  </item>
  <item rdf:about="http://www.example.org/item2/">
    <title>Another New Status Updates</title>
    <link>http://www.example.org/item2/</link>
    <description>More news about the Example project</description>
```

Example 12-1. Example RSS 1.0 feed (continued)

```
  </item>
  <textinput rdf:about="http://www.example.org/search/">
    <title>Search example.org</title>
    <description>Search the website www.example.org</description>
    <name>searchterm</name>
    <link>http://www.example.org/search/</link>
  </textinput>
</rdf:RDF>
```

Example 12-2. Example RSS 2.0 feed

```
<?xml version="1.0" encoding="UTF-8"?>
<rss version="2.0">
  <channel>
    <title>Example RSS 2.0 Feed</title>
    <link>http://www.example.org</link>
    <description>The Example Organization web site</description>
    <image>
      <title>Example</title>
      <url>http://www.example.org/images/logo.gif</url>
      <link>http://www.example.org</link>
    </image>
    <textInput>
      <title>Search this site:</title>
      <description>Find:</description>
      <name>q</name>
      <link>http://example.com/search</link>
    </textInput>
    <item>
      <title>New Status Updates</title>
      <link>http://www.example.org/item1/</link>
      <guid isPermaLink="true">http://www.example.org/item1/</guid>
      <description>News about the Example project</description>
    </item>
    <item>
      <title>Another New Status Updates</title>
      <link>http://www.example.org/item2/</link>
      <guid isPermaLink="true">http://www.example.org/item2/</guid>
      <description>More news about the Example project</description>
    </item>
  </channel>
</rss>
```

As you can see from these examples, although the vocabulary—channel, item, and so on—is the same, these documents have important syntactical differences. Most significantly, the root elements and namespaces are different. In RSS 1.0, the root element is named RDF in the namespace *http://www.w3.org/1999/02/22-rdf-syntax-ns#* and the RSS 1.0 elements are in the namespace *http://purl.org/rss/1.0*. In RSS 2.0, the root element is named rss; it and all the other RSS 2.0 elements are in no namespace.

In RSS 2.0, the description element can contain HTML markup. The HTML elements must be either XML-escaped or within a CDATA block. The descriptions in Example 12-2 could be enhanced with:

```
<description>News about the &lt;b&gt;Example&lt;/b&gt; project</description>
```

Or with CDATA:

```
<description>
<![CDATA[<i>More</i> news about the <b>Example</b> project]]>
</description>
```

In addition to the elements shows in Example 12-2, RSS 2.0 has many optional elements available at both the channel and item levels. Table 12-2 lists these additional elements.

Table 12-2. Additional RSS 2.0 elements

channel subelements	item subelements
language	author
copyright	category
managingEditor	comments
webmaster	enclosure
pubDate	pubDate
lastBuildDate	source
generator	
docs	
cloud	
ttl	
rating	
skipHours	
skipDays	

Some of these will be examined later in this chapter. For full definitions of all of the RSS 2.0 elements, please refer to the specification at *http://www.rssboard.org/rss-specification.*

RSS Modules

Both RSS 1.0 and 2.0 are extensible through the use of *RSS modules*. An RSS module is simply a set of elements in a namespace other than the namespace of the host RSS document. RSS modules are widely used in both RSS 1.0 and 2.0 documents. Although some modules are specified for a particular version of RSS, most will work with either. The RSS 1.0 specification defines three modules: Dublin Core, Syndication, and Content.

Dublin Core

The Dublin Core Metadata Initiative (DCMI) is an organization dedicated to creating standardized metadata vocabularies. Dublin Core allows metadata to be expressed using the same terms in a variety of formats. Dublin Core elements are commonly seen in HTML/XHTML, RDF (including RSS 1.0), and XML (including RSS 2.0) documents. More information about Dublin Core can be found at *http://purl.org/dc*.

Dublin Core Simple, the basic set of Dublin Core metadata, contains 15 elements in the namespace *http://purl.org/dc/elements/1.1*:

- title
- creator
- subject
- description
- publisher
- contributor
- date
- type
- format
- identifier
- source
- language
- relation
- coverage
- rights

As you can see, some of these elements can be used to bring some of the extra elements from RSS 2.0 into RSS 1.0: Dublin Core elements date, language, and rights can hold the same data as the RSS 2.0 elements pubDate, language, and copyright.

 However, the Dublin Core date element is in ISO 8601 format (2006-07-29T09:25:37.421+00:00) whereas RSS 2.0 pubDate and lastBuildDate elements are in RFC 822 format (Sat 29 Jul 2006 09:25:37 GMT).

Syndication

The RSS 1.0 Syndication module in the namespace *http://purl.org/rss/1.0/modules/syndication* adds elements describing how often the feed is updated. It defines elements updatePeriod and updateFrequency that let you define pretty much any consistent update schedule. For example, to declare that a feed is updated twice hourly, you could add the following to your feed:

```
<sy:updatePeriod>hourly</sy:updatePeriod>
<sy:updateFrequency>2</sy:updateFrequency>
```

This same schedule could be expressed with the RSS 2.0 ttl element:

```
<ttl>30</ttl>
```

Content

The RSS 1.0 Content module in the namespace *http://purl.org/rss/1.0/modules/content* enables the embedding of HTML content as an RSS 1.0 item's description. A formatted version of the description in Example 12-1 could be included as:

```
<content:encoded><![CDATA[<i>More</i> news about the Example project]]>
</content:encoded>
```

Embedding HTML in RSS 1.0 with the Content module is actually superior to embedding HTML in RSS 2.0, because there's no way to indicate whether the content of an RSS 2.0 description element should be treated as HTML. As a result, there is no way to distinguish between these two descriptions:

- *More* news about Example project
- <i>More</i> news about Example project

This may not seem like a problem, but if you have a feed about HTML markup, it can be important.

CommentAPI

The CommentAPI defines an interface for blogs to accept comments without requiring the user to fill out a form on a web site. Instead, comments can be accepted directly from an RSS aggregator. Comments are posted as RSS 2.0 items. In order to discover the URL to post the comment XML to, the CommentAPI module using the namespace *http://wellformedweb.org/CommentAPI* defines a comment element to contain the URL. More information about the CommentAPI module is available at that URL.

iTunes

When Apple Computer's iTunes Music Store added support for podcasting in mid-2005, it introduced an RSS module that added additional elements to RSS 2.0 to support the podcast directory within the iTunes Music Store. This module uses the namespace *http://www.itunes.com/dtds/podcast-1.0.dtd* and is fully documented at *http://www.apple.com/itunes/podcasts/techspecs.html*. To have your podcast listed within the iTunes podcast directory, it must use this module.

Atom

The Atom Syndication Format was created in an attempt to merge the simplicity of RSS 2.0 (like RSS, Atom doesn't use RDF) with the more structured aspects of RSS 1.0 (for one thing, all Atom elements are within a namespace). The feed in Examples 12-1 and 12-2 can be written in Atom as Example 12-3.

Example 12-3. Example Atom feed

```
<?xml version="1.0" encoding="utf-8"?>
<feed xmlns="http://www.w3.org/2005/Atom">
  <title>Example Atom Feed</title>
  <subtitle>The Example Organization web site</subtitle>
  <link href="http://www.example.org/"/>
  <id>urn:uuid:68063c50-1f77-11db-a98b-0800200c9a66</id>
  <entry>
    <title>New Status Updates</title>
    <link href="http://www.example.org/item1/"/>
    <id>urn:uuid:68063c51-1f77-11db-a98b-0800200c9a66</id>
    <summary>News about the Example project</summary>
  </entry>
  <entry>
    <title>More New Status Updates</title>
    <link href="http://www.example.org/item2/"/>
    <id>urn:uuid:975ceb20-1f77-11db-a98b-0800200c9a66</id>
    <summary type="html"><![CDATA[<i>More</i> news about the Example
project]]></summary>
  </entry>
</feed>
```

In addition, there is a related Atom Publishing Protocol that defines a standard API for creating and editing entries on a blog. Both Atom specifications are developed by the AtomPub Working Group, part of the Internet Engineering Task Force (IETF). Although Atom is an interesting set of technologies, we will not be looking extensively at Atom here. For more details on Atom, see the Working Group's web site: *http://www.ietf.org/html.charters/atompub-charter.html*.

Creating an RSS Feed

Based on the examples and information above, you should be able to create RSS documents using the tools explored earlier in this book. DOM, JDOM, dom4j, and StAX can all be used to create XML documents and thus can be used to create RSS documents. You don't even need to use an XML library. For example, the Java blogging application blojsom (available from *http://www.blojsom.com*) generates its RSS feeds using the Velocity scripting language. If you find yourself creating multiple different RSS feeds, you may find it helpful to use an RSS library that contains an RSS data model so that you deal with classes named Channel and Item instead of Document and Element. Because feeds are represented in this data model, an RSS library can be used to output or input feeds targeting a variety of RSS formats with a consistent data model. One open source RSS library is ROME: **R**SS and A**tom** Utilities.

Introducing ROME

ROME is an RSS library supporting the full range of RSS and Atom formats:

- RSS 0.9
- RSS 0.91 Netscape
- RSS 0.91 Userland
- RSS 0.92
- RSS 0.93
- RSS 0.94
- RSS 1.0
- RSS 2.0
- Atom 0.3
- Atom 1.0

ROME supports parsing and generating feeds as well as converting between one format and another. ROME is downloadable from its project web site, *https://rome.dev.java.net/*. As of the time of writing, the current version of ROME is 0.8 beta. ROME uses the JDOM library we examined in Chapter 9, and you will need to include the JDOM JAR file, along with the ROME JAR file, in your classpath.

ROME data models

ROME includes three different data models: an RSS data model in the package com.sun.syndication.feed.rss, an Atom data model in the package com.sun.syndication.feed.atom, and a format-independent data model in the package com.sun.syndication.feed.synd. Figure 12-1 contains a UML diagram of the interfaces in the format-independent model.

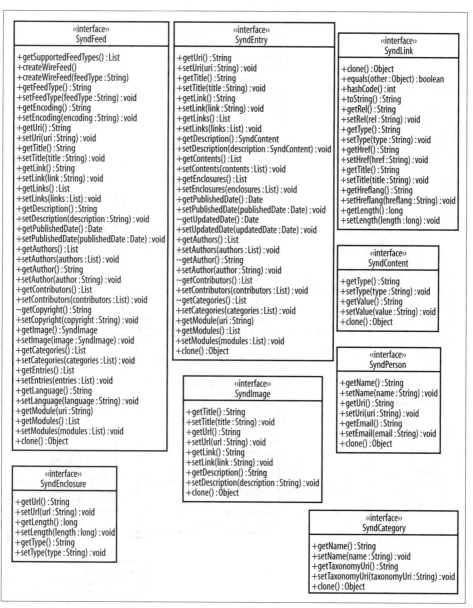

Figure 12-1. ROME format-independent data model

For each of these interfaces, ROME includes an implementation class: `SyndFeedImpl` for the `SyndFeed` interface, `SyndEntryImpl` for the `SyndEntry` interface, and so on. As you can see, this format-independent model is based on a superset of features from RSS and Atom. Likewise, the RSS data model, diagrammed in Figure 12-2, contains the superset of the features from all the various RSS versions; the Atom data model, diagrammed in Figure 12-3, supports all the features in both released versions of the Atom specification: 0.3 and 1.0.

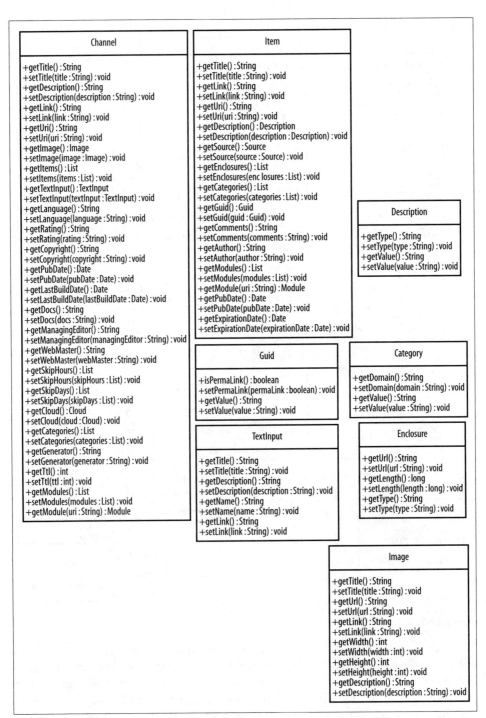

Figure 12-2. ROME RSS data model

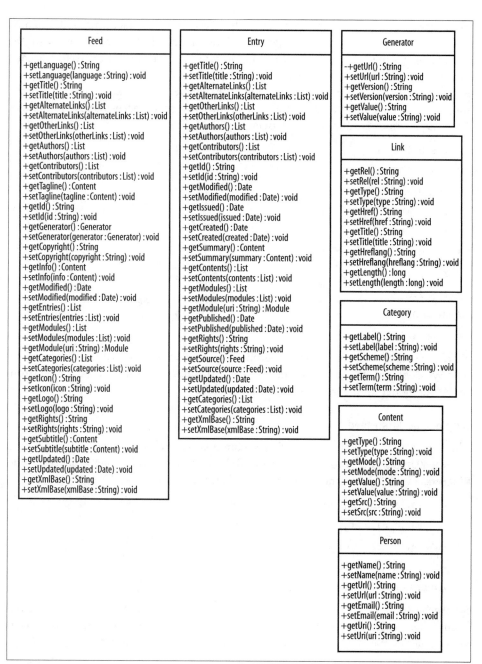

Feed

+getLanguage() : String
+setLanguage(language : String) : void
+getTitle() : String
+setTitle(title : String) : void
+getAlternateLinks() : List
+setAlternateLinks(alternateLinks : List) : void
+getOtherLinks() : List
+setOtherLinks(otherLinks : List) : void
+getAuthors() : List
+setAuthors(authors : List) : void
+getContributors() : List
+setContributors(contributors : List) : void
+getTagline() : Content
+setTagline(tagline : Content) : void
+getId() : String
+setId(id : String) : void
+getGenerator() : Generator
+setGenerator(generator : Generator) : void
+getCopyright() : String
+setCopyright(copyright : String) : void
+getInfo() : Content
+setInfo(info : Content) : void
+getModified() : Date
+setModified(modified : Date) : void
+getEntries() : List
+setEntries(entries : List) : void
+getModules() : List
+setModules(modules : List) : void
+getModule(uri : String) : Module
+getCategories() : List
+setCategories(categories : List) : void
+getIcon() : String
+setIcon(icon : String) : void
+getLogo() : String
+setLogo(logo : String) : void
+getRights() : String
+setRights(rights : String) : void
+getSubtitle() : Content
+setSubtitle(subtitle : Content) : void
+getUpdated() : Date
+setUpdated(updated : Date) : void
+getXmlBase() : String
+setXmlBase(xmlBase : String) : void

Entry

+getTitle() : String
+setTitle(title : String) : void
+getAlternateLinks() : List
+setAlternateLinks(alternateLinks : List) : void
+getOtherLinks() : List
+setOtherLinks(otherLinks : List) : void
+getAuthors() : List
+setAuthors(authors : List) : void
+getContributors() : List
+setContributors(contributors : List) : void
+getId() : String
+setId(id : String) : void
+getModified() : Date
+setModified(modified : Date) : void
+getIssued() : Date
+setIssued(issued : Date) : void
+getCreated() : Date
+setCreated(created : Date) : void
+getSummary() : Content
+setSummary(summary : Content) : void
+getContents() : List
+setContents(contents : List) : void
+getModules() : List
+setModules(modules : List) : void
+getModule(uri : String) : Module
+getPublished() : Date
+setPublished(published : Date) : void
+getRights() : String
+setRights(rights : String) : void
+getSource() : Feed
+setSource(source : Feed) : void
+getUpdated() : Date
+setUpdated(updated : Date) : void
+getCategories() : List
+setCategories(categories : List) : void
+getXmlBase() : String
+setXmlBase(xmlBase : String) : void

Generator

-+getUrl() : String
+setUrl(url : String) : void
+getVersion() : String
+setVersion(version : String) : void
+getValue() : String
+setValue(value : String) : void

Link

+getRel() : String
+setRel(rel : String) : void
+getType() : String
+setType(type : String) : void
+getHref() : String
+setHref(href : String) : void
+getTitle() : String
+setTitle(title : String) : void
+getHreflang() : String
+setHreflang(hreflang : String) : void
+getLength() : long
+setLength(length : long) : void

Category

+getLabel() : String
+setLabel(label : String) : void
+getScheme() : String
+setScheme(scheme : String) : void
+getTerm() : String
+setTerm(term : String) : void

Content

+getType() : String
+setType(type : String) : void
+getMode() : String
+setMode(mode : String) : void
+getValue() : String
+setValue(value : String) : void
+getSrc() : String
+setSrc(src : String) : void

Person

+getName() : String
+setName(name : String) : void
+getUrl() : String
+setUrl(url : String) : void
+getEmail() : String
+setEmail(email : String) : void
+getUri() : String
+setUri(uri : String) : void

Figure 12-3. ROME Atom data model

ROME refers to feeds in one of the format-specific models as *wire feeds* and both the
`Channel` and `Feed` objects extend the abstract class `com.sun.syndication.feed.`
`WireFeed`. To convert from an instance of the format-independent `SyndFeed` interface

to a specific wire feed format, use the SyndFeed interface methods named createWireFeed(). A SyndFeed object can have a default feed type, set with the setFeedType() method, in which case the no-argument version of createWireFeed() can be used. There is also an overloaded createWireFeed() method that accepts a String parameter to determine the format of the created wire feed. To get a list of the supported values for this parameter, call the getSupportedFeedTypes() method. These type strings are supported by default in ROME:

- rss_0.9
- rss_0.91N
- rss_0.91U
- rss_0.92
- rss_0.93
- rss_0.94
- rss_1.0
- rss_2.0
- atom_0.3
- atom_1.0

To do the reverse—create a SyndFeed object from a wire feed—you can construct a new SyndFeedImpl object by passing a Channel (from the RSS model) or a Feed (from the Atom model) to the SyndFeedImpl constructor.

Outputting a ROME feed

The com.sun.syndication.io package contains the classes SyndFeedOutput and WireFeedOutput to handle outputting ROME feeds. Both SyndFeedOutput and WireFeedOutput have methods to output feeds to:

- A java.lang.String object
- A java.io.File object
- A java.io.Writer object
- An org.w3c.dom.Document object
- An org.jdom.Document object

SyndFeedOutput can be used only if the SyndFeed object's setFeedType() method has been called to set the default wire feed format. Otherwise, you'll need to convert your SyndFeed object to a WireFeed object and then use WireFeedOutput.

Creating a Feed with ROME

Example 12-4 contains a class that generates a generic example feed as a SyndFeed object and then outputs it in the format specified on the command line.

Example 12-4. Outputting an example feed with ROME

```
package javaxml3;

import java.io.IOException;
import java.io.OutputStreamWriter;
import java.util.Collections;
import java.util.List;

import com.sun.syndication.feed.WireFeed;
import com.sun.syndication.feed.synd.SyndContent;
import com.sun.syndication.feed.synd.SyndContentImpl;
import com.sun.syndication.feed.synd.SyndEntry;
import com.sun.syndication.feed.synd.SyndEntryImpl;
import com.sun.syndication.feed.synd.SyndFeed;
import com.sun.syndication.feed.synd.SyndFeedImpl;
import com.sun.syndication.feed.synd.SyndPerson;
import com.sun.syndication.feed.synd.SyndPersonImpl;
import com.sun.syndication.io.FeedException;
import com.sun.syndication.io.WireFeedOutput;

public class ExampleRomeOutput {

    public static void main(String[] args) {
        if (args.length != 1) {
            System.err
                    .println("Usage: java javaxml3.ExampleRomeOutput [feedtype]");
            return;
        }

        SyndPerson author = new SyndPersonImpl();
        author.setEmail("editor@example.org");
        author.setName("Example Person");

        SyndFeed feed = new SyndFeedImpl();
        feed.setTitle("Example Feed Output from ROME");
        feed.setDescription("The Example Organization web site");
        feed.setAuthors(Collections.singletonList(author));
        feed.setLink("http://www.example.org/");
        feed.setPublishedDate(new Date());

        SyndEntry entry = new SyndEntryImpl();
        entry.setTitle("First Entry Title");
        entry.setLink("http://www.example.org/item1");
        SyndContent description = new SyndContentImpl();
        description.setValue("News about the Example project");
        description.setType("text");
        entry.setDescription(description);
```

Example 12-4. Outputting an example feed with ROME (continued)

```
            entry.setAuthors(Collections.singletonList(author));
            feed.getEntries( ).add(entry);

            entry = new SyndEntryImpl( );
            entry.setTitle("Second Entry Title");
            entry.setLink("http://www.example.org/item2");
            description = new SyndContentImpl( );
            description.setValue("<i>More</i> news about the Example project");
            description.setType("html");
            entry.setDescription(description);
            entry.setAuthors(Collections.singletonList(author));
            feed.getEntries( ).add(entry);

            List supportedTypes = feed.getSupportedFeedTypes( );
            String feedType = args[0];
            if (!supportedTypes.contains(feedType)) {
                System.err.println("Feed Type is not supported.");
                System.err.println("Supported feed types are: "
                        + supportedTypes.toString( ));
                return;
            }

            WireFeed rssFeed = feed.createWireFeed(feedType);

            WireFeedOutput output = new WireFeedOutput( );
            try {
                output.output(rssFeed, new OutputStreamWriter(System.out));
            } catch (IOException e) {
                System.err.println("Unable to output feed: " + e.getMessage( ));
                e.printStackTrace( );
            } catch (FeedException e) {
                System.err.println("Unable to generate feed: " + e.getMessage( ));
                e.printStackTrace( );
            }
        }

}
```

 ROME 0.8 has a nasty bug where if the type of an item/entry description isn't set with the setType( ) method, a NullPointerException is thrown when outputting RSS 2.0. The problem is that RSS 2.0 doesn't support typed descriptions, so if you're targeting a feed to RSS 2.0, you may not think to call the setType( ) method. Both to avoid this bug and to enable you to support feed formats that do support typed description, you should always call setType( ).

This class can be used to generate an RSS 2.0 feed by running:

```
    java javaxml3.ExampleRomeOutput rss_2.0
```

This will produce:

```
<?xml version="1.0" encoding="UTF-8"?>
<rss xmlns:taxo="http://purl.org/rss/1.0/modules/taxonomy/"
xmlns:rdf="http://www.w3.org/1999/02/22-rdf-syntax-ns#"
xmlns:dc="http://purl.org/dc/elements/1.1/" version="2.0">
  <channel>
    <title>Example Feed Output from ROME</title>
    <link>http://www.example.org/</link>
    <description>The Example Organization web site</description>
    <pubDate>Thu, 03 Aug 2006 02:49:20 GMT</pubDate>
    <managingEditor>Example Person</managingEditor>
    <dc:date>2006-08-03T02:49:20Z</dc:date>
    <item>
      <title>First Entry Title</title>
      <link>http://www.example.org/item1</link>
      <description>News about the Example project</description>
      <author>editor@example.org</author>
      <guid>http://www.example.org/item1</guid>
    </item>
    <item>
      <title>Second Entry Title</title>
      <link>http://www.example.org/item2</link>
      <description>&lt;i&gt;More&lt;/i&gt; news about the Example
project</description>
      <author>editor@example.org</author>
      <guid>http://www.example.org/item2</guid>
    </item>
  </channel>
</rss>
```

This same feed can be output as RSS 1.0 by running:

```
java javaxml3.ExampleRomeOutput rss_1.0
```

producing:

```
<?xml version="1.0" encoding="UTF-8"?>
<rdf:RDF xmlns:rdf="http://www.w3.org/1999/02/22-rdf-syntax-ns#"
xmlns="http://purl.org/rss/1.0/"
xmlns:taxo="http://purl.org/rss/1.0/modules/taxonomy/"
xmlns:sy="http://purl.org/rss/1.0/modules/syndication/"
xmlns:dc="http://purl.org/dc/elements/1.1/">
  <channel rdf:about="http://www.example.org/">
    <title>Example Feed Output from ROME</title>
    <link>http://www.example.org/</link>
    <description>The Example Organization web site</description>
    <items>
      <rdf:Seq>
        <rdf:li resource="http://www.example.org/item1" />
        <rdf:li resource="http://www.example.org/item2" />
      </rdf:Seq>
    </items>
    <dc:date>2006-08-03T02:51:45Z</dc:date>
  </channel>
  <item rdf:about="http://www.example.org/item1">
    <title>First Entry Title</title>
    <link>http://www.example.org/item1</link>
```

```
      <description>News about the Example project</description>
    </item>
    <item rdf:about="http://www.example.org/item2">
      <title>Second Entry Title</title>
      <link>http://www.example.org/item2</link>
      <description>&lt;i&gt;More&lt;/i&gt; news about the Example
project</description>
    </item>
  </rdf:RDF>
```

And finally, output as Atom 1.0 by running:

```
java javaxml3.ExampleRomeOutput atom_1.0
```

which produces:

```
<?xml version="1.0" encoding="UTF-8"?>
<feed xmlns="http://www.w3.org/2005/Atom"
xmlns:taxo="http://purl.org/rss/1.0/modules/taxonomy/"
xmlns:rdf="http://www.w3.org/1999/02/22-rdf-syntax-ns#"
xmlns:sy="http://purl.org/rss/1.0/modules/syndication/"
xmlns:dc="http://purl.org/dc/elements/1.1/">
  <title>Example Feed Output from ROME</title>
  <link rel="alternate" href="http://www.example.org/" />
  <author>
    <name>Example Person</name>
    <email>editor@example.org</email>
  </author>
  <subtitle>The Example Organization web site</subtitle>
  <updated>2006-08-03T02:50:02Z</updated>
  <dc:date>2006-08-03T02:50:02Z</dc:date>
  <entry>
    <title>First Entry Title</title>
    <link rel="alternate" href="http://www.example.org/item1" />
    <author>
      <name>Example Person</name>
      <email>editor@example.org</email>
    </author>
    <summary type="text">News about the Example project</summary>
  </entry>
  <entry>
    <title>Second Entry Title</title>
    <link rel="alternate" href="http://www.example.org/item2" />
    <author>
      <name>Example Person</name>
      <email>editor@example.org</email>
    </author>
    <summary type="html">&lt;i&gt;More&lt;/i&gt; news about the Example
project</summary>
  </entry>
</feed>
```

 As you can see from these sample outputs, ROME tends to create namespace declarations when they aren't required. You can safely ignore these. We'll see why this happens in the section "Creating a ROME Module" later in this chapter.

Reading an RSS Feed

Because RSS is an XML application, any XML library from SAX through dom4j is capable of parsing RSS documents. However, due to the sheer number of RSS versions, an RSS library can be especially useful if you need to parse RSS feeds. (For this same reason, data binding is a poor technique to use with RSS.)

Feed Input with ROME

Just as there are `SyndFeedOutput` and `WireFeedOutput` classes to output syndicated feeds, ROME includes classes called `SyndFeedInput` and `WireFeedInput` to input feeds. These input classes can read feeds from a variety of sources:

- A `java.io.File` object
- A `java.io.Reader` object
- An `org.xml.sax.InputSource` object
- An `org.w3c.dom.Document` object
- An `org.jdom.Document` object

When parsing a feed, `WireFeedInput` determines what type of feed it is by looking at elements, attributes, and namespaces defined in the feed. `SyndFeedInput` delegates parsing to `WireFeedInput` and then converts the resulting `WireFeed` object to a `SyndFeed` object.

Building a Simple Aggregator

To demonstrate these feed reading capabilities, let's build a simple command-line RSS and Atom aggregator. Our aggregator will be passed a list of feed URLs on the command line and output the entries in those feeds in a single list. The user can then select a single entry from the list to see the title, description, and link for that entry. Because we want this aggregator to support both RSS and Atom, we'll use `SyndFeedInput` and the classes in the `com.sun.syndication.feeds.synd` package. Example 12-5 contains the skeleton code for our `SimpleAggregator` class.

Example 12-5. Framework aggregator code

```
package javaxml3;

import java.util.List;

import com.sun.syndication.feed.synd.SyndEntry;
import com.sun.syndication.io.SyndFeedInput;

public class SimpleAggregator {

    private SyndFeedInput feedInput;
```

Example 12-5. Framework aggregator code (continued)

```java
    public SimpleAggregator( ) {
        feedInput = new SyndFeedInput( );
    }

    private void run(String[] args) {
        System.out.println("Welcome to the Simple Aggregator.");

        List allEntries = loadFeeds(args);

        System.out.println("Done loading feeds.");
        System.out.println( );

        System.out.println("Please choose an entry below:");

        outputMenu(allEntries);

        int choice = acceptUserChoice(allEntries.size( ));
        if (choice > 0) {
            System.out.println("You chose entry #:" + choice);
            SyndEntry entry = (SyndEntry) allEntries.get(choice);
            outputEntry(entry);
        }

    }

    public static void main(String[] args) {
        if (args.length == 0) {
            System.err.println("Usage: java javaxml3.SimpleAggregator [URLs]");
            return;
        }

        SimpleAggregator aggregator = new SimpleAggregator( );
        aggregator.run(args);

    }

}
```

To load the feeds, we'll loop through the command-line arguments and build a SyndFeed object for each URL. To keep our output simple, we're only going to add five items from each feed to our entry menu.

```java
    private List loadFeeds(String[] feedURLs) {
        List allEntries = new ArrayList( );
        for (int i = 0; i < feedURLs.length; i++) {
            String feedURL = feedURLs[i];
            System.out.println("Loading feed from: " + feedURL + ".....");
            SyndFeed feed = null;
            try {
                feed = feedInput.build(new InputSource(feedURL));
            } catch (IllegalArgumentException e) {
                System.err.println("Unable to parse feed from: " + feedURL);
                e.printStackTrace( );
```

```
        } catch (FeedException e) {
            System.err.println("Unable to parse feed from: " + feedURL);
            e.printStackTrace();
        }
        System.out.println("Found a feed of type " + feed.getFeedType());
        System.out.println("Feed title: " + feed.getTitle());

        List entryList = feed.getEntries();
        if (!entryList.isEmpty()) {
            int entryListLength = Math.min(entryList.size(), 5);
            entryList = entryList.subList(0, entryListLength);
            allEntries.addAll(entryList);
        }
    }
    return allEntries;
}
```

Our menu contains an index and the title for each feed entry:

```
private void outputMenu(List allEntries) {
    for (int i = 0; i < allEntries.size(); i++) {
        SyndEntry entry = (SyndEntry) allEntries.get(i);
        System.out.println("#" + (i + 1) + ": " + entry.getTitle());
    }
}
```

Finally, the methods to accept the user's selection and output are fairly simple:

```
private int acceptUserChoice(int menuLength) {
    BufferedReader reader = new BufferedReader(new InputStreamReader(
            System.in));
    System.out.print(">");
    String choice = null;
    try {
        choice = reader.readLine();
    } catch (IOException e) {
        System.err.println("Could not read choice.");
        return 0;
    }
    try {
        int choiceInt = Integer.parseInt(choice);
        if (choiceInt > menuLength)
            return 0;
        else
            return choiceInt;
    } catch (NumberFormatException e) {
            return 0;
    }
}
private void outputEntry(SyndEntry entry) {
    System.out.println("Title: " + entry.getTitle());
    System.out.println("Description: " + entry.getDescription().getValue());
    System.out.println("Link: " + entry.getLink());
}
```

Here's the output of this class when I passed the URLs for Slashdot's RSS feed and an RSS feed from BBC News.

```
Welcome to the Simple Aggregator.
Loading feed from: http://rss.slashdot.org/Slashdot/slashdot.....
Found a feed of type rss_1.0
Feed title: Slashdot
Loading feed from:
http://news.bbc.co.uk/rss/newsonline_world_edition/front_page/rss091.xml.....
Found a feed of type rss_2.0
Feed title: BBC News | News Front Page | World Edition
Done loading feeds.

Please choose an entry below:
#1: Stem Cells - The Hope and the Hype
#2: 50th Anniversary of the First Hard Drive
#3: Knock Some Commands Into Your Laptop
#4: The End of E3?
#5: Fun Things To Do With Your Honeypot System
#6: Israel halts fire for Qana probe
#7: Polls close in Congo elections
#8: Rally challenges Mexico poll
#9: Bosnia Muslim sentence contested
#10: Seychelles head wins re-election
>2
You chose entry #:2
Title: 50th Anniversary of the First Hard Drive
Description: ennuiner writes "Over at Newsweek Steven Levy has a column
commemorating IBM's introduction of the first hard drive 50 years ago.
Link: http://rss.slashdot.org/~r/Slashdot/slashdot/~3/7395897/article.pl
```

As you can see, the menu output isn't quite right. We want our aggregator's menu to combine entries from both feeds in date order, not all the Slashdot entries followed by the BBC News entries. To sort the entries, we use an implementation of the java. util.Comparator interface to compare entries based on the result of the getPublishedDate( ) method. We have to be careful to deal with cases where getPublishedDate( ) returns null:

```java
private void sort(List entryList) {
    Collections.sort(entryList, new Comparator( ) {

        public int compare(Object arg0, Object arg1) {
            SyndEntry entry0 = (SyndEntry) arg0;
            SyndEntry entry1 = (SyndEntry) arg1;
            if (entry0.getPublishedDate( ) == null)
                return -1;
            if (entry1.getPublishedDate( ) == null)
                return 1;

            return entry1.getPublishedDate( ).compareTo(
                    entry0.getPublishedDate( ));
        }
    });
}
```

With this code in place, our aggregator actually produces an aggregated menu:

```
Welcome to the Simple Aggregator.
Loading feed from: http://rss.slashdot.org/Slashdot/slashdot.....
Found a feed of type rss_1.0
Feed title: Slashdot
Loading feed from:
http://news.bbc.co.uk/rss/newsonline_world_edition/front_page/rss091.xml.....
Found a feed of type rss_2.0
Feed title: BBC News | News Front Page | World Edition
Done loading feeds.

Please choose an entry below:
#1: Israel halts fire for Qana probe
#2: Seychelles head wins re-election
#3: Stem Cells - The Hope and the Hype
#4: Bosnia Muslim sentence contested
#5: 50th Anniversary of the First Hard Drive
#6: Knock Some Commands Into Your Laptop
#7: Rally challenges Mexico poll
#8: The End of E3?
#9: Fun Things To Do With Your Honeypot System
#10: Polls close in Congo elections
>2
You chose entry #:2
Title: Seychelles head wins re-election
Description: The incumbent president of Seychelles, James Michel, wins another five
years in office in presidential elections.
Link: http://news.bbc.co.uk/go/rss/-/2/hi/africa/5230012.stm
```

Modules with ROME

Just as RSS is extensible through modules, ROME supports an extension mechanism called modules. ROME modules are used to represent any element outside of the base set of elements defined for the SyndFeed, SyndEntry, Feed, Channel, Entry, and Item objects. We actually already used one of the modules that are included with the ROME distribution: Dublin Core. Because RSS 1.0 does not support any sort of date element either within a channel or item, the RSS 1.0 feed produced by our example feed generator contained the Dublin Core date element to define the date for the feed:

```
<dc:date>2006-08-03T02:51:45Z</dc:date>
```

When our SyndFeed object was converted to an RSS 1.0 Channel object, the Dublin Core module was used to store this date value. And when WireFeedOutput was given this Channel object, it saw that the Dublin Core module was present and had the Dublin Core module add this additional element to the output XML document.

In addition to the Dublin Core and RSS 1.0 Syndication modules included with the ROME distribution, there are many useful modules available listed on the ROME

Wiki, located at *http://wiki.java.net/bin/view/Javawsxml/Rome*. Currently these include ROME modules support these RSS modules:

- RSS 1.0 Content
- iTunes
- Slashcode
- Google Base
- Creative Commons
- MediaRSS
- GeoRSS
- Apple iPhoto Photocast
- A9 Open Search

ROME modules are packaged in regular JAR files. By simply adding the JAR file to your classpath, the module discovery mechanism used by the feed parser will be able to find it. We'll see how this happens later in the section "Creating a ROME Module." When creating a feed or entry object, it's necessary to add an instance of a module object. A module can be applied to a feed-level object (SyndFeed, Feed, and Channel), an entry-level object (SyndEntry, Entry, and Item), or both.

Each ROME module includes one or two module interfaces and implementations of those classes. The module interface extends com.sun.syndication.feed.module.Module and the implementation class extends com.sun.syndication.feed.module.ModuleImpl. Modules can also include auxiliary classes to be used with the module interface.

As you can see in Figures 12-1, 12-2, and 12-3, each of the SyndFeed, SyndEntry, Feed, Channel, Entry and Item classes have three module-related methods:

getModules( )
> Returns a List of module objects

setModules(List list)
> Replaces the current list of module objects

getModule(String uri)
> Returns the module object associated with a particular namespace URI

To demonstrate the use of a ROME module, we'll create a podcast for submission to the iTunes Music Store using the ROME iTunes module. The iTunes module is one of the more complex ROME modules, so even if you aren't interested in creating a podcast, you'll be able to apply the concepts in this example to your use of other modules.

Creating a Podcast RSS Feed

As I mentioned in the "Blogs and Podcasting" sidebar earlier in this chapter, a podcast feed is an RSS feed that contains references to a multimedia file. Podcasting began with the use of the enclosure RSS 2.0 element, although there is now an RSS 1.0 module to support enclosures in RSS 1.0 documents (for more details, see *http://www.xs4all.nl/~foz/mod_enclosure.html*) For the purposes of our example, we'll create a RSS 2.0 feed. The RSS 2.0 enclosure element has three required attributes:

url
> The URL of the referenced media file

length
> The length of the media file in bytes

type
> The MIME type of the media file

ROME includes an Enclosure class in the RSS data model (seen in Figure 12-2) and a SyndEnclosure interface in the format-independent data model (seen in Figure 12-1). Both have getters and setters for properties representing these attributes.

Creating a simple podcast is just a matter of creating an RSS 2.0 channel where the items have enclosure elements, as seen in Example 12-6.

Example 12-6. Generating a simplepodcast feed

```
package javaxml3;

import java.io.IOException;
import java.io.OutputStreamWriter;
import java.util.Collections;

import com.sun.syndication.feed.rss.Channel;
import com.sun.syndication.feed.rss.Description;
import com.sun.syndication.feed.rss.Enclosure;
import com.sun.syndication.feed.rss.Item;
import com.sun.syndication.io.FeedException;
import com.sun.syndication.io.WireFeedOutput;

public class PodcastExample throws Exception {

    public static void main(String[] args) {
        Channel channel = new Channel("rss_2.0");
        channel.setTitle("Example Podcast Feed");
        channel.setDescription("Example podcast description.");
        channel.setLink("http://www.example.org");

        Item item = new Item();
        item.setTitle("My First Podcast");

        Description description = new Description();
        description.setType("text");
```

Example 12-6. Generating a simplepodcast feed (continued)

```
        description.setValue("My first attempt at a podcast.");
        item.setDescription(description);

        Enclosure enclosure = new Enclosure( );
        enclosure.setUrl("http://www.example.org/podcast/ep1.mp3");
        enclosure.setType("audio/mpeg");
        enclosure.setLength(4182295);
        item.getEnclosures( ).add(enclosure);

        channel.getItems( ).add(item);

        WireFeedOutput outputter = new WireFeedOutput( );
        outputter.output(channel, new OutputStreamWriter(System.out));
    }

}
```

The output of this class is:

```
<?xml version="1.0" encoding="UTF-8"?>
<rss xmlns:taxo="http://purl.org/rss/1.0/modules/taxonomy/"
xmlns:rdf="http://www.w3.org/1999/02/22-rdf-syntax-ns#"
xmlns:dc="http://purl.org/dc/elements/1.1/" version="2.0">
  <channel>
    <title>Example Podcast Feed</title>
    <link>http://www.example.org</link>
    <description>Example podcast description.</description>
    <item>
      <title>My First Podcast</title>
      <description>My first attempt at a podcast.</description>
      <enclosure url="http://www.example.org/podcast/ep1.mp3" length="4182295"
type="audio/mpeg" />
    </item>
  </channel>
</rss>
```

Loading this feed into a podcatcher will have the podcatcher download the MP3 file from *http://www.example.org/podcast/ep1.mp3*. You can post a link to this RSS feed on your web site and your visitors can subscribe to it in their podcatcher. However, to reach a wider audience, you should submit your podcast feed to one or more podcast directories.

A podcast directory is a categorized listing of podcast feeds. Popular podcast directories include Podcast Alley (*http://www.podcastalley.com/*), Odeo.com, Yahoo! (*http://podcasts.yahoo.com/*), and the iTunes Music Store. A podcast directory will use the description and categorization information contained within your RSS feed, but some directories, most significantly the iTunes Music Store, have additional requirements to add your feed to the directory. In the case of iTunes, Apple has created an RSS module, described at *http://www.apple.com/itunes/podcasts/techspecs.html*, to support the needs of the iTunes directory. This module includes elements to be included inside both channel and item elements. You must include support for this module to have your feed listed in the iTunes directory. The elements defined by the iTunes module are contained in Table 12-3.

Table 12-3. Elements defined by the iTunes module

Element name	Channel	Item	Required
author	Y	Y	N
block	Y	Y	N
category	Y	N	Y
image	Y	N	N
duration	N	Y	N
explicit	Y	Y	Y (for channel)
keywords	Y	Y	N
new-feed-url	Y	N	N
owner	Y	N	N
subtitle	Y	Y	N
summary	Y	Y	N

The namespace URI for these elements is *http://www.itunes.com/dtds/podcast-1.0.dtd*.

A ROME module that supports these elements is available from the ROME Wiki. The module includes two different interfaces: FeedInformation and EntryInformation to represent the elements within the iTunes RSS module. Both interfaces extend the ITunes interface, which defines the elements included at both levels of the feed. These interfaces and their associated implementation classes are in the com.sun. syndication.feed.module.itunes package, diagrammed in Figure 12-4.

We can use this module to add the new elements to our sample podcast feed. To start, we create an instance of the FeedInformationImpl class and add it to the list of modules for our Channel object:

```
FeedInformation feedInfo = new FeedInformationImpl();
channel.getModules().add(feedInfo);
```

Adding this to the code in Example 12-6 immediately changes the output:

```
<?xml version="1.0" encoding="UTF-8"?>
<rss xmlns:taxo="http://purl.org/rss/1.0/modules/taxonomy/"
xmlns:rdf="http://www.w3.org/1999/02/22-rdf-syntax-ns#"
xmlns:itunes="http://www.itunes.com/dtds/podcast-1.0.dtd"
xmlns:dc="http://purl.org/dc/elements/1.1/" version="2.0">
  <channel>
    <title>Example Podcast Feed</title>
    <link>http://www.example.org</link>
    <description>Example podcast description.</description>
    <itunes:owner>
      <itunes:email />
      <itunes:name />
```

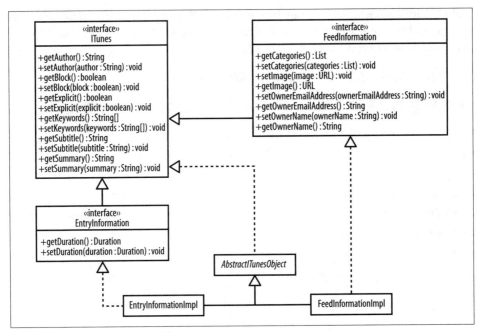

Figure 12-4. ROME iTunes module

```
      </itunes:owner>
      <itunes:explicit>no</itunes:explicit>
      <itunes:keywords />
      <item>
        <title>My First Podcast</title>
        <description>My first attempt at a podcast.</description>
        <enclosure url="http://www.example.org/podcast/ep1.mp3" length="4182295"
type="audio/mpeg" />
      </item>
    </channel>
</rss>
```

Similarly, if we add the `EntryInformationImpl` module class to our `Item` object's module list, the output of that item includes some new elements:

```
      <item>
        <title>My First Podcast</title>
        <description>My first attempt at a podcast.</description>
        <enclosure url="http://www.example.org/podcast/ep1.mp3" length="4182295"
type="audio/mpeg" />
        <itunes:explicit>no</itunes:explicit>
        <itunes:keywords />
      </item>
```

Then, using the getters and setters shown in Figure 12-4, we can set the specific element values for our channel:

```
feedInfo.setKeywords(new String[] { "Example", "Java", "XML" });
feedInfo.setOwnerEmailAddress("podcasts@example.org");
feedInfo.setOwnerName("Podcast Owner");
```

And also to our item:

```
entryInfo.setKeywords(new String[] { "Education" });
entryInfo.setAuthor("learning@example.org");
```

But before we can submit our updated feed to iTunes, we must add category information.

iTunes categories

The iTunes podcast directory is organized into a two-level hierarchy of categories. In other words, a sports-related podcast could be categorized in the Professional subcategory of the Sports category. The RSS 2.0 category element is just a string and Apple could have encoded the categories in a single element such as:

```
<category>Sports\Professional</category>
```

Instead, it choses to use a category element within the iTunes namespace that could be nested so that a feed could be categorized like this:

```
<itunes:category text="Sports">
    <itunes:category text="Professional" />
</itunes:category>
```

Alternatively, no subcategories are available for some top-level categories:

```
<itunes:category text="Comedy"/>
```

To represent this, the ROME iTunes module contains classes named Category and Subcategory in the com.sun.syndication.feed.module.itunes.types package. A Category can contain a Subcategory, and a FeedInformation object can contain multiple Category objects. Putting all of our modifications in place gives us:

```
public static void main(String[] args) throws Exception {
    Channel channel = new Channel("rss_2.0");
    channel.setTitle("Example Podcast Feed");
    channel.setDescription("Example podcast description.");
    channel.setLink("http://www.example.org");

    FeedInformation feedInfo = new FeedInformationImpl();
    channel.getModules().add(feedInfo);
    feedInfo.setKeywords(new String[] { "Example", "Java", "XML" });
    feedInfo.setOwnerEmailAddress("podcasts@example.org");
    feedInfo.setOwnerName("Podcast Owner");

    Category category = new Category("Technology");
    category.setSubcategory(new Subcategory("Podcasting"));
    feedInfo.getCategories().add(category);
    feedInfo.getCategories().add(new Category("Comedy"));

    Item item = new Item();
    item.setTitle("My First Podcast");

    Description description = new Description();
    description.setType("text");
```

```java
        description.setValue("My first attempt at a podcast.");
        item.setDescription(description);

        Enclosure enclosure = new Enclosure( );
        enclosure.setUrl("http://www.example.org/podcast/ep1.mp3");
        enclosure.setType("audio/mpeg");
        enclosure.setLength(4182295);
        item.getEnclosures( ).add(enclosure);

        EntryInformation entryInfo = new EntryInformationImpl( );
        entryInfo.setKeywords(new String[] { "Education" });
        entryInfo.setAuthor("learning@example.org");
        item.getModules( ).add(entryInfo);

        channel.getItems( ).add(item);

        WireFeedOutput outputter = new WireFeedOutput( );
        outputter.output(channel, new OutputStreamWriter(System.out));
    }
}
```

This updated class outputs:

```xml
<?xml version="1.0" encoding="UTF-8"?>
<rss xmlns:taxo="http://purl.org/rss/1.0/modules/taxonomy/"
xmlns:rdf="http://www.w3.org/1999/02/22-rdf-syntax-ns#"
xmlns:itunes="http://www.itunes.com/dtds/podcast-1.0.dtd"
xmlns:dc="http://purl.org/dc/elements/1.1/" version="2.0">
  <channel>
    <title>Example Podcast Feed</title>
    <link>http://www.example.org</link>
    <description>Example podcast description.</description>
    <itunes:owner>
      <itunes:email>podcasts@example.org</itunes:email>
      <itunes:name>Podcast Owner</itunes:name>
    </itunes:owner>
    <itunes:category text="Technology">
      <itunes:category text="Podcasting" />
    </itunes:category>
    <itunes:category text="Comedy" />
    <itunes:explicit>no</itunes:explicit>
    <itunes:keywords>Example, Java, XML</itunes:keywords>
    <item>
      <title>My First Podcast</title>
      <description>My first attempt at a podcast.</description>
      <enclosure url="http://www.example.org/podcast/ep1.mp3" length="4182295"
type="audio/mpeg" />
      <itunes:author>learning@example.org</itunes:author>
      <itunes:explicit>no</itunes:explicit>
      <itunes:keywords>Education</itunes:keywords>
    </item>
  </channel>
</rss>
```

This is ready to be submitted to Apple, leading you to fame and fortune in the world of podcasting.

You can also use the iTunes module to access the iTunes elements in a feed you've parsed with ROME. For example, to retrieve the feed owner's email address, you would determine if the iTunes module was included in the feed and, if it was, call the getOwnerEmailAddress() method of the FeedInformation object, as seen in Example 12-7.

Example 12-7. Using the iTunes module with input

```
package javaxml3;

import org.xml.sax.InputSource;

import com.sun.syndication.feed.WireFeed;
import com.sun.syndication.feed.module.itunes.FeedInformation;
import com.sun.syndication.feed.module.itunes.ITunes;
import com.sun.syndication.io.FeedException;
import com.sun.syndication.io.WireFeedInput;

public class OutputOwnerEmail {

    public static void main(String[] args) throws FeedException {
        if (args.length != 1) {
            System.err.println("Usage: java javaxml3.OutputOwnerEmail [url]");
            return;
        }

        WireFeedInput input = new WireFeedInput();

        // first, parse the feed
        WireFeed feed = input.build(new InputSource(args[0]));

        // second, get the module for the iTunes URI
        FeedInformation feedInfo = (FeedInformation) feed.getModule(ITunes.URI);
        if (feedInfo != null)
            System.out.println(feedInfo.getOwnerEmailAddress());
        else
            System.out.println("No iTunes module available");
    }

}
```

Creating a ROME Module

ROME makes it very simple to create your own module. As noted above, the core of a module is an interface that encapsulates the metadata contained within the module elements. This interface must extend com.sun.syndication.feed.module.Module. As we saw with the iTunes module, some RSS modules are complex enough to need a different interface for feed-level elements and another for entry-level elements. In addition to this interface and an implementation of it, a module needs to define a class to output the module elements and a class to parse the module elements. To enable this input and output of module elements, ROME defines two interfaces: com. sun.syndication.io.ModuleGenerator and com.sun.syndication.io.ModuleParser. The Module, ModuleGenerator, and ModuleParser interfaces are diagrammed in Figure 12-5.

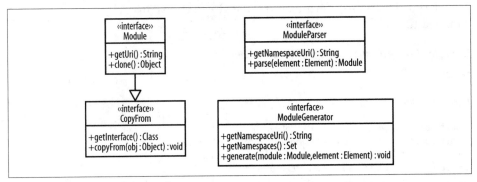

Figure 12-5. ROME module interfaces

Beyond simply containing these interfaces and classes, your module needs to be discoverable by ROME. When a WireFeedInput or WireFeedOutput object is created, the constructor looks for files named rome.properties in the classpath. These files use the standard properties file syntax. The keys are constructed like:

```
<feedtype>.<feed or item>.<ModuleGenerator or ModuleParser>.classes
```

The values for these properties are one or more fully qualified class name(s). If there is more than one class, the class names can be separated with commas or spaces. For example, the rome.properties file from the iTunes module includes these lines to register the class that outputs the iTunes module elements:

```
rss_2.0.feed.ModuleGenerator.classes=\
    com.sun.syndication.feed.module.itunes.io.ITunesGenerator
rss_2.0.item.ModuleGenerator.classes=\
    com.sun.syndication.feed.module.itunes.io.ITunesGenerator
```

And these lines to register the classes that parse feeds:

```
rss_2.0.feed.ModuleParser.classes=\
    com.sun.syndication.feed.module.itunes.io.ITunesParser \
    com.sun.syndication.feed.module.itunes.io.ITunesParserOldNamespace
rss_2.0.item.ModuleParser.classes=\
    com.sun.syndication.feed.module.itunes.io.ITunesParser \
    com.sun.syndication.feed.module.itunes.io.ITunesParserOldNamespace
```

Because instances of the parser and generator classes are created by the ROME framework, it is necessary that they both have zero-argument, public constructors.

The iTunes module includes a second parser class because a single parser or generator class can only be associated with a single namespace. As earlier versions of the iTunes RSS module used a different namespace, the authors of the ROME iTunes module needed to create a second class whose getNamespaceURI( ) method returns the old namespace.

Once this properties file is populated with the correct properties, ROME will able to discover the generator and parsers associated with your module. To demonstrate module development, let's create a simple ROME module to store the location of a feed entry.

The ICBM module

The ICBM RSS module, documented at *http://postneo.com/icbm*, includes elements to store the latitude and longitude of a feed entry. For example, a blog entry could look like:

```
<item>
    <!-- some item element -->
    <icbm:latitude>26.03226</icbm:latitude>
    <icbm:longtitude>-80.307344</icbm:longtitude>
    <!-- other item elements -->
</item>
```

To create a ROME module to represent these elements, we first create a module interface. In addition to getters and setters for the two element values, we'll also include constants to store this module's namespace URI and preferred namespace prefix:

```
package javaxml3.icbm;

import com.sun.syndication.feed.module.Module;

public interface ICBMModule extends Module {

    public static final String PREFIX = "icbm";

    public static final String URI = "http://postneo.com/icbm/";

    public void setLatitude(float latitude);

    public void setLongitude(float longitude);

    public float getLatitude( );

    public float getLongitude( );

}
```

Next, we create our implementation class. In addition to implementing the interface methods from ICBMModule, we must also implement methods from the Module and CopyFrom interfaces:

```
package javaxml3.icbm;

public class ICBMModuleImpl implements ICBMModule {

    private float latitude;

    private float longitude;

    // ICBMModule interface methods
    public float getLatitude() {
        return latitude;
    }

    public float getLongitude() {
        return longitude;
    }

    public void setLatitude(float latitude) {
        this.latitude = latitude;
    }

    public void setLongitude(float longtitude) {
        this.longitude = longtitude;
    }

    // Module interface methods
    public Object clone() {
        ICBMModuleImpl clone = new ICBMModuleImpl();
        clone.copyFrom(this);
        return clone;
    }

    public String getUri() {
        return URI;
    }

    // CopyFrom interface methods
    public void copyFrom(Object obj) {
        ICBMModuleImpl icbm = (ICBMModuleImpl) obj;
        latitude = icbm.latitude;
        longitude = icbm.longitude;
    }

    public Class getInterface() {
        return ICBMModule.class;
    }

}
```

To implement the ModuleParser interface, it's necessary to create a method named parse( ) that accepts a JDOM Element object as input and returns a module object. If the module object cannot be created, the parse( ) method should return null. In the case of the ICBM module, we want to ensure that both latitude and longitude are specified, so we only return an instance of ICBMModuleImpl if both elements are included:

```
package javaxml3.icbm.io;

import javaxml3.icbm.ICBMModule;
import javaxml3.icbm.ICBMModuleImpl;

import org.jdom.Element;
import org.jdom.Namespace;

import com.sun.syndication.feed.module.Module;
import com.sun.syndication.io.ModuleParser;

public class ICBMParser implements ModuleParser {

    private static final Namespace NS = Namespace.getNamespace(ICBMModule.URI);

    public String getNamespaceUri( ) {
        return ICBMModule.URI;
    }

    public Module parse(Element element) {
        boolean foundSomething = false;
        ICBMModuleImpl icbm = new ICBMModuleImpl( );

        Element e = element.getChild("latitude", NS);
        if (e != null) {
            try {
                icbm.setLatitude(Float.parseFloat(e.getText( )));
                foundSomething = true;
            } catch (NumberFormatException ex) {
                // do nothing
            }
        }

        if (foundSomething) {
            e = element.getChild("longitude", NS);
            if (e != null) {
                try {
                    icbm.setLongitude(Float.parseFloat(e.getText( )));
                } catch (NumberFormatException ex) {
                    // can't have a latitude without a longtitude
                    foundSomething = false;
                }
            } else {
                // can't have a latitude without a longtitude
                foundSomething = false;
```

```
            }
        }

        return (foundSomething) ? icbm : null;
    }

}
```

Our generator class is responsible for adding appropriate elements to a JDOM Element object. In addition, the getNamespaces( ) method can return a Set of JDOM Namespace objects to be added to the output document's root element.

```
package javaxml3.icbm.io;

import java.util.Collections;
import java.util.Set;

import javaxml3.icbm.ICBMModule;

import org.jdom.Element;
import org.jdom.Namespace;

import com.sun.syndication.feed.module.Module;
import com.sun.syndication.io.ModuleGenerator;

public class ICBMGenerator implements ModuleGenerator {

    private static final Namespace ICBM_NS = Namespace.getNamespace(
            ICBMModule.PREFIX, ICBMModule.URI);

    private static final Set NS_SET = Collections.singleton(ICBM_NS);

    public void generate(Module module, Element element) {
        ICBMModule icbm = (ICBMModule) mm odule;

        Element latitude = new Element("latitude", ICBM_NS);
        latitude.setText(Float.toString(icbm.getLatitude( )));
        element.addContent(latitude);

        Element longitude = new Element("longitude", ICBM_NS);
        longitude.setText(Float.toString(icbm.getLongitude( )));
        element.addContent(longitude);
    }

    public Set getNamespaces( ) {
        return NS_SET;
    }

    public String getNamespaceUri( ) {
        return ICBMModule.URI;
    }

}
```

Finally, we need a *rome.properties* file to register our parser and generator. We'll tell ROME that the module is usable with RSS 1.0 and RSS 2.0:

```
rss_2.0.item.ModuleParser.classes=javaxml3.icbm.io.ICBMParser
rss_1.0.item.ModuleParser.classes=javaxml3.icbm.io.ICBMParser

rss_2.0.item.ModuleGenerator.classes=javaxml3.icbm.io.ICBMGenerator
rss_1.0.item.ModuleGenerator.classes=javaxml3.icbm.io.ICBMGenerator
```

From here, all that needs to be done is to create a JAR file containing these classes and properties file. I'll leave that up to you to create (or you can just download it from this book's web site at *http://www.oreilly.com/catalog/9780596101497*). With that JAR file, our module is complete and ROME will be able to create instances of `ICBMParser` and `ICBMGenerator`, invoke the `getNamespaceUri()` method to discover the namespace these classes apply to, and then class the appropriate interface method when necessary. I'll leave it up to you to package these classes and the properties file in a JAR file. Keep in mind that the *rome.properties* file must be in the root directory of the JAR file.

The extensibility of ROME and its extensive support for the various flavors of RSS (which is a by-product of the library's extensibility) make it a compelling choice if you need to write Java code that reads and/or writes RSS and Atom feeds. It is not alone. Informa, available at *http://informa.sourceforge.net*, is another popular library and there are many others. Although RSS is simple enough that you could just use a generic XML library such as SAX or DOM, the wide availability of these RSS-specific libraries should inspire you to check out one or two others before writing your own RSS parsing or generating code.

## CHAPTER 13

XML As Presentation

So far, we've primarily looked at XML as a low-level enabling technology—end users won't know if you're using regular properties files or the XML properties files shown in Chapter 9. And when the XML documents we discussed are meant to be shared between applications, those applications are generally data-centric server applications. The last chapter explored examples in which XML was used in a client-server context: RSS and Atom feeds are delivered directly to clients, in those cases RSS and Atom aggregators. (Of course, there are server-based RSS aggregators like News-Gator (*http://www.newsgator.com*) and My Yahoo! (*http://my.yahoo.com*).) But that is a limited case tied to the specific vocabularies of RSS and Atom. In this chapter, we'll look at more generic cases of using XML as part of the presentation technology in a web application.

I need to make a few assumptions here. First, I'm going to assume you have read the prior chapters. As with the ROME library used in the last chapter, we're going to be using some of the libraries used prior in this chapter, most significantly, DOM. Second, that you have some familiarity with various web technologies such as HTML, JavaScript, Java servlets, and JavaServer Pages (JSP). Along the same lines, I'm assuming you know how to set up a Java servlet container (such as Apache Tomcat) or can get someone's help to do so. If you want to learn how to write a Java web application, this chapter won't help. So, if you're not at least a little familiar with the above technologies, I'd highly recommend putting this book down, picking up a different one, and coming back here when you're ready. Great books on Java web technology include *Java Servlet Programming* by Jason Hunter (O'Reilly) and *JavaServer Pages* by Hans Bergsten (O'Reilly).

XML and the Model-View-Controller Pattern

When I refer to XML as a presentation technology, I am referring primarily to the view in an application using a Model-View-Controller (MVC) architecture. Model-View-Controller is a software architecture originally documented as a pattern for traditional client applications (like those created with Swing) but has been widely adopted as an architecture for web applications. In short, an MVC application separates an application into three main areas:

Model
> The raw data and business rules of an application

View
> The user-visible rendition of the model

Controller
> Functionality that receives requests from users, interprets those requests, interacts with the model, and provides the view with any necessary model objects

In more concrete terms, an MVC web application written with Java servlets and JSPs could processes a request in four steps:

1. A servlet (the controller) receives the request and parses it.
2. The servlet calls some methods on a data access object (the model).
3. The servlet passes model data objects to a JSP page for rendering.
4. The JSP page outputs an HTML page including data from the model objects.

There are a number of Java web MVC frameworks available that provide much of the base code necessary in any web application. Popular examples include Apache Struts (*http://struts.apache.org*), Spring MVC (*http://www.springframework.org*), JavaServer Faces (*http://java.sun.com/javaee/javaserverfaces*), and Tapestry (*http://tapestry.apache.org*).

XML in MVC Web Applications

XML can be used in several places in an MVC web application. Most MVC frameworks make heavy use of XML for internal configuration. More interesting for our purposes is where XML is used to contain the data passed between the view and the controller. Instead of the controller passing one or more model objects to the view, the controller constructs an XML representation of the model objects and passes the XML document to the view. In some cases, your application is responsible for delivering XML; the "view" is simply serializing the XML document as the HTTP response. In others, the view is some form of server-side transformation from the controller-supplied XML to a different XML syntax or to HTML. In addition, the use of XML to transfer model data between the controller and the view allows us to move any necessary transformations from the server to users' client applications (usually web browsers).

To start, let's simply create a servlet that produces an XML document. Example 13-1 contains a simple servlet that creates an XML document containing a list of books. Our model is a List of Map objects. Once it has created a DOM Document object, the servlet outputs the document using the identity transformation technique discussed in Chapter 7.

Example 13-1. Servlet generating XML document

```
package javaxml3.ch13;

import java.io.IOException;
import java.util.ArrayList;
import java.util.Collections;
import java.util.HashMap;
import java.util.Iterator;
import java.util.List;
import java.util.Map;

import javax.servlet.ServletException;
import javax.servlet.http.HttpServlet;
import javax.servlet.http.HttpServletRequest;
import javax.servlet.http.HttpServletResponse;
import javax.xml.parsers.DocumentBuilder;
import javax.xml.parsers.DocumentBuilderFactory;
import javax.xml.parsers.ParserConfigurationException;
import javax.xml.transform.Result;
import javax.xml.transform.Transformer;
import javax.xml.transform.TransformerException;
import javax.xml.transform.TransformerFactory;
import javax.xml.transform.dom.DOMSource;
import javax.xml.transform.stream.StreamResult;

import org.w3c.dom.Document;
import org.w3c.dom.Element;
import org.w3c.dom.Text;

public class BookListXMLServlet extends HttpServlet {

    private DocumentBuilderFactory documentBuilderFactory;

    private TransformerFactory transformerFactory;

    public void init() {
        documentBuilderFactory = DocumentBuilderFactory.newInstance();
        transformerFactory = TransformerFactory.newInstance();
    }

    private Element newElementFromMap(Map map, String key, Document doc) {
        String text = (String) map.get(key);
        Text textNode = doc.createTextNode(text);
        Element element = doc.createElement(key);
        element.appendChild(textNode);
        return element;
    }

    protected void renderDocument(Document doc, HttpServletRequest request,
            HttpServletResponse response) throws IOException, ServletException {

        // tell the browser we're sending XML
        response.setContentType("text/xml");
```

Example 13-1. Servlet generating XML document (continued)

```
        // now do the identity transformation
        try {
            Transformer identity = transformerFactory.newTransformer();

            // our Result object is a StreamResult wrapping the
            // ServletOutputStream
            Result result = new StreamResult(response.getOutputStream());
            identity.transform(new DOMSource(doc), result);
        } catch (TransformerException e) {
            throw new ServletException(
                    "Unable to perform identity transformation", e);
        }
    }

    protected void service(HttpServletRequest request,
            HttpServletResponse response) throws ServletException, IOException {
        List bookList = BookListFactory.INSTANCE;

        DocumentBuilder docBuilder = null;
        try {
            docBuilder = documentBuilderFactory.newDocumentBuilder();
        } catch (ParserConfigurationException e) {
            throw new ServletException(
                    "Unable to create DocumentBuilderFactory", e);
        }

        // create the DOM document
        Document doc = docBuilder.newDocument();
        Element books = doc.createElement("books");
        doc.appendChild(books);
        for (Iterator it = bookList.iterator(); it.hasNext();) {
            Map bookMap = (Map) it.next();
            Element book = doc.createElement("book");
            books.appendChild(book);
            book.appendChild(newElementFromMap(bookMap,
                    BookListConstants.TITLE, doc));
            book.appendChild(newElementFromMap(bookMap,
                    BookListConstants.AUTHOR, doc));
            book.appendChild(newElementFromMap(bookMap,
                    BookListConstants.PUBDATE, doc));
        }

        renderDocument(doc, request, response);
    }
}

class BookListConstants {

    public static final String AUTHOR = "author";

    public static final String PUBDATE = "pubdate";

    public static final String TITLE = "title";
}
```

Example 13-1. Servlet generating XML document (continued)

```
class BookListFactory {

    public static final List INSTANCE;

    static {
        List templist = new ArrayList();
        Map m = new HashMap();
        m.put(BookListConstants.TITLE, "Ajax Hacks");
        m.put(BookListConstants.AUTHOR, "Bruce W. Perry");
        m.put(BookListConstants.PUBDATE, "March 2006");
        templist.add(m);

        m = new HashMap();
        m.put(BookListConstants.TITLE, "LDAP System Administration");
        m.put(BookListConstants.AUTHOR, "Gerald Carter");
        m.put(BookListConstants.PUBDATE, "March 2003");
        templist.add(m);

        m = new HashMap();
        m.put(BookListConstants.TITLE, "Java Servlet Programming");
        m.put(BookListConstants.AUTHOR, "Jason Hunter");
        m.put(BookListConstants.PUBDATE, "April 2001");
        templist.add(m);

        INSTANCE = Collections.unmodifiableList(templist);
    }

    private BookListFactory() {
    }

}
```

Example 13-2 contains a *web.xml* servlet configuration file that maps this servlet to the path */booklist-xml*.

Example 13-2. Simple web.xml file

```
<?xml version="1.0" encoding="UTF-8"?>
<web-app id="ch13-servlet" version="2.4"
    xmlns="http://java.sun.com/xml/ns/j2ee"
    xmlns:xsi="http://www.w3.org/2001/XMLSchema-instance">
    <display-name>ch13-servlet</display-name>
    <servlet>
        <servlet-name>BookListXMLServlet</servlet-name>
        <servlet-class>javaxml3.ch13.BookListXMLServlet</servlet-class>
    </servlet>
    <servlet-mapping>
        <servlet-name>BookListXMLServlet</servlet-name>
        <url-pattern>/booklist-xml</url-pattern>
    </servlet-mapping>
</web-app>
```

Once we've created a web application containing this servlet class and configuration file, we can view the results in a browser, as seen in Figure 13-1.

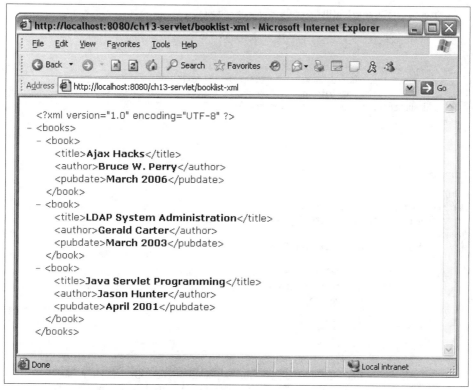

Figure 13-1. XML output from a servlet

We didn't have to use a servlet to build this document. A page using JSP or another template language (such as Velocity) could build the same document. Instead of the servlet from Example 13-1, we could have a much simpler servlet such as Example 13-3 and then do the XML creation in a JSP such as the one seen in Example 13-4.

Example 13-3. Much simpler book list servlet

```
package javaxml3.ch13;

import java.io.IOException;
import java.util.List;

import javax.servlet.RequestDispatcher;
import javax.servlet.ServletException;
import javax.servlet.http.HttpServlet;
import javax.servlet.http.HttpServletRequest;
import javax.servlet.http.HttpServletResponse;
```

Example 13-3. Much simpler book list servlet (continued)

```java
public class BookListXMLJSPServlet extends HttpServlet {

    protected void service(HttpServletRequest request,
            HttpServletResponse response) throws ServletException, IOException {
        List bookList = BookListFactory.INSTANCE;

        request.setAttribute("bookList", bookList);
        RequestDispatcher dispatcher = getServletContext()
                .getRequestDispatcher("/booklist1.jsp");
        dispatcher.include(request, response);
    }

}
```

Example 13-4. Rendering XML with JSP tags

```xml
<?xml version="1.0" encoding="UTF-8" ?>
<%@ page contentType="text/xml"%>
<%@ taglib prefix="c" uri="http://java.sun.com/jsp/jstl/core"%>
<books>
<c:forEach items="${bookList}" var="book">
    <book>
        <title>${book.title}</title>
        <author>${book.author}</author>
        <pubdate>${book.pubdate}</pubdate>
    </book>
</c:forEach>
</books>
```

 Note that the XML declaration is placed at the top of the JSP page, above the directives. This is because the XML declaration must be the first thing in an XML document.

However, when we generate XML with a JSP such as Example 13-4, we are now able to produce an XML document that is not well-formed. Because the servlet in Example 13-2 creates its document with DOM, there's no way a document that's not well-formed would be produced (except in case of a bug in the XML libraries). But with this method of creating a document with JSP, there is nothing to prevent you from accidentally creating a document with mismatched end tags such as:

```xml
<?xml version="1.0" encoding="UTF-8" ?>
<books>
    <book>
        <title>Ajax Hacks</title>
        <author>Bruce W. Perry</pubdate>
        <pubdate>March 2006</author>
    </book>
</books>
```

Or any of a variety of other well-formedness issues. Nevertheless, creating the document this way with JSP is bound to be faster and consume far less memory, since intermediate DOM objects are not created.

Transforming to HTML with JSP

If, instead of XML, the expected responses from our web application are HTML documents, we have a number of options for transforming an XML representation of model objects to HTML. Although basic JSP does not have any special XML capabilities, the Java Standard Tag Library (JSTL) contains several custom tags for working with XML documents. With these tags, we can transform XML to HTML with either XPath or XSLT. In addition, JSTL includes a tag to parse an XML document into a DOM object, to which the other tags can then be applied.

JSTL XML Tags

The JSTL is a collection of JSP custom tags meant to address a variety of basic needs when writing JSP pages. It includes an XML tag library that contains a series of tags used for processing XML documents within JSP pages:

out
>   Evaluates an XPath expression and outputs the result

parse
>   Parses a string into a DOM Document object

set
>   Evaluates an XPath expression and saves the result as a local JSP variable

if
>   Executes the tag's body if an XPath expression returns the Boolean value true

choose/when/otherwise
>   Provides functionality similar to the Java switch/case/default language construct using XPath expressions

forEach
>   Iterates over a list of DOM nodes

transform
>   Performs an XSLT transformation

Because all of these tags (with the exception of parse) accept a DOM node as a starting point, we can modify the renderBooks( ) method from Example 13-1 to save the DOM Document object as a request attribute and dispatch to a file named *booklist2.jsp*:

```
private void renderBooks(Document doc, HttpServletRequest request,
        HttpServletResponse response) throws IOException, ServletException {

    request.setAttribute("xml", doc);
```

```
        RequestDispatcher dispatcher = getServletContext()
                .getRequestDispatcher("/booklist2.jsp");
        dispatcher.include(request, response);
    }
```

Example 13-5 contains the *booklist.jsp* page. Note that the request attribute xml is available as an XPath variable. In addition to request attributes, session attributes, application attributes, request parameters, HTTP headers, cookies, and servlet init parameters can all be utilized within these XPath expressions.

Example 13-5. Ouputting a list of books with JSTL

```
<%@ taglib prefix="x" uri="http://java.sun.com/jsp/jstl/xml"%>
<!DOCTYPE HTML PUBLIC "-//W3C//DTD HTML 4.01 Transitional//EN">
<html>
<head>
<title>Book List</title>
</head>
<body>
<h1>Book List</h1>
<table border="1">
    <tbody>
        <tr>
            <th>Title</th>
            <th>Author</th>
            <th>Publication Date</th>
        </tr>
        <x:forEach select="$xml/books/book" var="book">
            <tr>
                <td><x:out select="$book/title" /></td>
                <td><x:out select="$book/author" /></td>
                <td><x:out select="$book/pubdate" /></td>
            </tr>
        </x:forEach>
    </tbody>
</table>
</body>
</html>
```

With the updated servlet code and JSP page, our HTML output now looks more like we'd expect, as seen in Figure 13-2.

As I mentioned above, there's a transform tag in JSTL for performing XSL transformations. Let's look at using XSL transformations next.

Using XSLT

As seen in prior chapters, XSLT is a powerful tool for transforming an XML document from one XML syntax to another as well as transforming from XML to HTML. One interesting option enabled by the use of XSLT is offloading the transformation processing onto client applications, as most modern web browsers support XSLT.

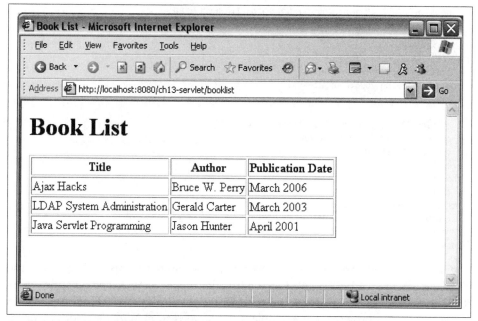

Figure 13-2. HTML output of book list from JSP page

However, there are definite downsides to this offloading. Unless you're building applications for a limited and controlled audience, you will have little to no control as to how fast your users' client applications run. As a result, different users could have widely different experiences. Of course, this is also somewhat true with regular HTML. That being said, client-side transformations are a useful addition to any XML developer's toolbox.

Performing Client-Side Transformations

There are two main methods for performing a client-side transformation: processing instructions and client-side scripting.

Using processing instructions

The simplest way requesting an XSL transformation is to include an `xml-stylesheet` processing instruction between the XML declaration and the document's root element. For example, if a web browser receives a document such as in Example 13-6, it will make a request for *http://www.example.com/books.xsl* and use that stylesheet to transform this document for display.

Example 13-6. XML document with reference to stylesheet

```
<?xml version="1.0" encoding="UTF-8"?>
<?xml-stylesheet type="text/xsl" href="http://www.example.com/books.xsl"?>
```

Example 13-6. XML document with reference to stylesheet (continued)

```
<books>
  <book>
    <title>Ajax Hacks</title>
    <author>Bruce W. Perry</author>
    <pubDate>March 2006</pubDate>
  </book>
  <book>
    <title>LDAP System Administration</title>
    <author>Gerald Carter</author>
    <pubDate>March 2003</pubDate>
  </book>
  <book>
    <title>Java Servlet Programming</title>
    <author>Jason Hunter</author>
    <pubDate>April 2001</pubDate>
  </book>
</books>
```

The xml-stylesheet processing instruction can be limited to apply only when the XML document is to be displayed on a particular type of device. For example, many RSS feeds now use this processing instruction to display an HTML page when viewed through a browser. For example, the RSS feed from *Wired* includes this processing instruction:

```
<?xml-stylesheet href="http://feeds.wired.com/~d/styles/rss2full.xsl"
    type="text/xsl" media="screen"?>
```

As a result, when I view the feed (*http://feeds.wired.com/wired/topheadlines*) in a web browser (which is visible on my screen), I see the feed content as well as a variety of links to subscribe to the feed in my RSS aggregator of choice, as seen in Figure 13-3.

When an RSS aggregator loads this same document, it knows to ignore the transformation because of the media portion of the processing instruction.

Transforming with JavaScript

In addition to using processing instructions for triggering a client-side transformation, Mozilla Firefox and Internet Explorer both support performing XSL transformations from JavaScript. This capability is explored further in the "Using XSLT with Ajax" section later in this chapter.

Performing Server-Side Transformations

As I mentioned above, there are some disadvantages to relying on client-side transformations. In addition to the performance issue, there is the simple fact that not all browsers support transformations. One option is to use client-side transformations on clients that support them and provide a server-side transformation otherwise.

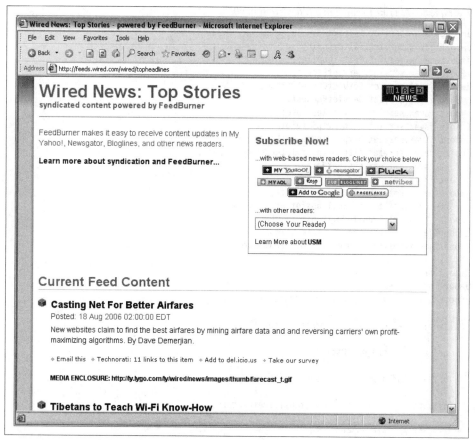

Figure 13-3. Media-specific transformation

Transforming in a filter

Using a Java servlet filter, it is possible to catch requests for XML documents from browsers that don't support client-side transformations and, if the document includes an xml-stylesheet processing instruction, perform the transformation on the server. Such a filter, which performs server-side transformations to support the Lynx text-mode browser, is contained in Example 13-7.

Example 13-7. Transforming in a filter

```
package javaxml3.ch13;

import java.io.CharArrayWriter;
import java.io.IOException;
import java.io.PrintWriter;
import java.io.StringReader;
import java.util.regex.Matcher;
import java.util.regex.Pattern;
```

Example 13-7. Transforming in a filter (continued)

```java
import javax.servlet.Filter;
import javax.servlet.FilterChain;
import javax.servlet.FilterConfig;
import javax.servlet.ServletException;
import javax.servlet.ServletOutputStream;
import javax.servlet.ServletRequest;
import javax.servlet.ServletResponse;
import javax.servlet.http.HttpServletRequest;
import javax.servlet.http.HttpServletResponse;
import javax.servlet.http.HttpServletResponseWrapper;
import javax.xml.parsers.SAXParser;
import javax.xml.parsers.SAXParserFactory;
import javax.xml.transform.Transformer;
import javax.xml.transform.TransformerException;
import javax.xml.transform.TransformerFactory;
import javax.xml.transform.stream.StreamResult;
import javax.xml.transform.stream.StreamSource;

import org.xml.sax.InputSource;
import org.xml.sax.SAXException;
import org.xml.sax.helpers.DefaultHandler;

public class XSLFilter implements Filter {

    private Pattern hrefPattern;

    private SAXParserFactory saxParserFactory;

    private TransformerFactory transformerFactory;

    private Pattern typePattern;

    public void destroy() {
    }

    public void doFilter(ServletRequest request, ServletResponse response,
            FilterChain chain) throws IOException, ServletException {
        if (request instanceof HttpServletRequest) {
            if (isLynxRequest((HttpServletRequest) request)) {
                CharResponseWrapper wrapper = new CharResponseWrapper(
                        (HttpServletResponse) response);
                chain.doFilter(request, wrapper);
                String xml = wrapper.toString();

                // only parse XML responses
                if ("text/xml".equals(wrapper.getContentType())) {
                    String stylesheetHref = getStylesheetHref(xml);
                    if (stylesheetHref != null) {
                        response.setContentType("text/html");
                        transformResponse(response, xml, stylesheetHref);
                    } else {
                        response.getWriter().print(xml);
```

Example 13-7. Transforming in a filter (continued)

```
                }
            } else {
                response.getWriter( ).print(xml);
            }
        } else {
            chain.doFilter(request, response);
        }
    } else {
        chain.doFilter(request, response);
    }
}

private String getStylesheetHref(String xml) {
    StylesheetPIHandler handler = new StylesheetPIHandler( );
    try {
        SAXParser parser = saxParserFactory.newSAXParser( );
        InputSource input = new InputSource(new StringReader(xml));
        parser.parse(input, handler);

        return handler.getHref( );
    } catch (Exception e) {
        return null;
    }
}

public void init(FilterConfig config) throws ServletException {
    saxParserFactory = SAXParserFactory.newInstance( );
    transformerFactory = TransformerFactory.newInstance( );
    typePattern = Pattern.compile(".*type\\s*=\\s*\"(\\S*)\".*");
    hrefPattern = Pattern.compile(".*href\\s*=\\s*\"(\\S*)\".*");
}

private boolean isLynxRequest(HttpServletRequest request) {
    String userAgent = request.getHeader("User-Agent");
    return (userAgent.indexOf("Lynx") >= 0);
}

private void transformResponse(ServletResponse response, String xml,
        String stylesheetHref) throws IOException, ServletException {
    StreamSource sheetSource = new StreamSource(stylesheetHref);
    StreamSource xmlSource = new StreamSource(new StringReader(xml));
    StreamResult result = new StreamResult(response.getWriter( ));
    try {
        Transformer trans = transformerFactory.newTransformer(sheetSource);
        trans.transform(xmlSource, result);
    } catch (TransformerException e) {
        throw new ServletException("Unable to transform", e);
    }
}

class CharResponseWrapper extends HttpServletResponseWrapper {
    private CharArrayWriter output;
```

Example 13-7. Transforming in a filter (continued)

```
    public CharResponseWrapper(HttpServletResponse response) {
        super(response);
        output = new CharArrayWriter();
    }

    public ServletOutputStream getOutputStream() throws IOException {
        return new ServletOutputStream() {

            public void write(int b) throws IOException {
                output.write(b);
            }

        };
    }

    public PrintWriter getWriter() {
        return new PrintWriter(output);
    }

    public String toString() {
        return output.toString();
    }
}

class StylesheetPIHandler extends DefaultHandler {

    private String href = null;

    public String getHref() {
        return href;
    }

    public void processingInstruction(String target, String data)
            throws SAXException {
        if ("xml-stylesheet".equals(target)) {
            Matcher typeMatcher = typePattern.matcher(data);
            if (typeMatcher.matches()
                    && "text/xsl".equals(typeMatcher.group(1))) {
                Matcher hrefMatcher = hrefPattern.matcher(data);
                if (hrefMatcher.matches())
                    href = hrefMatcher.group(1);
            }
        }
    }
}
}
```

As you can see, this filter intercepts requests; if it's possible that the response will
need to be transformed, it replaces the current HttpServletResponse object with a
wrapper object that buffers the response output. Once the response has been generated, a SAX parser is used to find processing instructions, and then two regular
expressions are used to discover the appropriate stylesheet URI.

With this filter in place, a request for *books.xml* will return HTML to Lynx and XML to other browsers. The outputs, seen in Figures 13-4 and 13-5, contain renderings of the same HTML in Lynx and Internet Explorer, respectively. The only difference is where that HTML was generated.

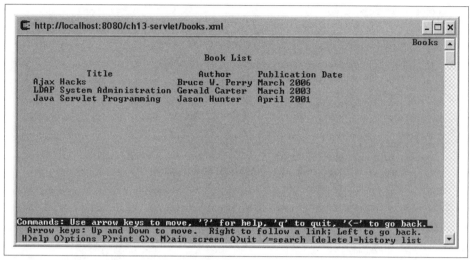

Figure 13-4. Result of server-side transformation in Lynx

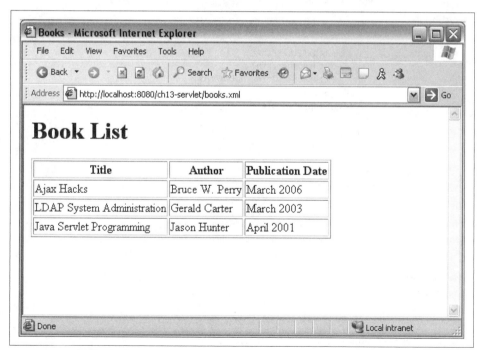

Figure 13-5. Result of client-side transformation in Internet Explorer

Transforming with JSTL

As noted above, JSTL includes a transform custom tag that allows you to perform transformations of XML documents. It needs both an XML document and a stylesheet document. These documents can be defined in the page:

```
<c:set var="doc">
    <books>
        <book>
            <title>Ajax Hacks</title>
            <author>Bruce W. Perry</author>
            <pubdate>March 2006</pubdate>
        </book>
        <!-- add more books here -->
    </books>
</c:set>
<c:set var="xsl">
    <xsl:stylesheet version="1.0"
        xmlns:xsl="http://www.w3.org/1999/XSL/Transform">
        <xsl:output method="html" />
        <xsl:template match="books">
            <html>
            <head>
            <title>Books</title>
            </head>
            <body>
            <h1>Book List</h1>
            <table border="1">
                <tbody>
                    <tr>
                        <th>Title</th>
                        <th>Author</th>
                        <th>Publication Date</th>
                    </tr>
                    <xsl:apply-templates select="book" />
                </tbody>
            </table>
            </body>
            </html>
        </xsl:template>
        <xsl:template match="book">
            <tr>
                <td><xsl:value-of select="title" /></td>
                <td><xsl:value-of select="author" /></td>
                <td><xsl:value-of select="pubdate" /></td>
            </tr>
        </xsl:template>
    </xsl:stylesheet>
</c:set>

<x:transform doc="${doc}" xslt="${xsl}" />
```

The documents can also be loaded from URLs:

```
<%@ taglib prefix="x" uri="http://java.sun.com/jsp/jstl/xml"%>
<%@ taglib prefix="c" uri="http://java.sun.com/jsp/jstl/core"%>
```

```
<c:import var="doc" url="http://localhost:8080/ch13-servlet/books.xml"/>
<c:import var="xsl" url="http://localhost:8080/ch13-servlet/books.xsl"/>

<x:transform doc="${doc}" xslt="${xsl}" />
```

The XML can also be provided as the body of the transform tag:

```
<%@ taglib prefix="x" uri="http://java.sun.com/jsp/jstl/xml"%>
<%@ taglib prefix="c" uri="http://java.sun.com/jsp/jstl/core"%>

<c:import var="xsl" url="http://localhost:8080/ch13-servlet/books.xsl"/>

<x:transform xslt="${xsl}">
    <books>
        <book>
            <title>Ajax Hacks</title>
            <author>Bruce W. Perry</author>
            <pubdate>March 2006</pubdate>
        </book>
        <!-- add more books here -->
    </books>
</x:transform>
```

Finally, the result of the transformation can be saved as a DOM object against which XPath expressions can be evaluated:

```
<%@ taglib prefix="x" uri="http://java.sun.com/jsp/jstl/xml"%>
<%@ taglib prefix="c" uri="http://java.sun.com/jsp/jstl/core"%>

<c:import var="xsl" url="http://localhost:8080/ch13-servlet/books.xsl"/>

<x:transform xslt="${xsl}" var="result">
    <books>
        <book>
            <title>Ajax Hacks</title>
            <author>Bruce W. Perry</author>
            <pubdate>March 2006</pubdate>
        </book>
        <!-- add more books here -->
    </books>
</x:transform>

<x:out select="$result//h1"/>
```

Ajax

Ajax is a name for a group of related web development patterns used to create interactive web applications. In a traditional, non-Ajax web application, users browse through the application page by page: each user action results in a request from the web browser for a new page. However, in an Ajax application, user actions result in the updating of a portion of the page based on a small amount of data transferred between the browser and the web server asynchronously. As a result, the application appears much more responsive and consumes far less bandwidth. Although the term Ajax was coined in 2005,* similar techniques have been in use since frames were introduced to HTML in the mid-1990s. In those early applications, hidden frames and the IFRAME tag, in Internet Explorer, were used to load HTML documents using JavaScript. These HTML documents contained JavaScript that changed the appearance of the page. In addition, similar functionality could be achieved using Java Applets and browser plug-ins.

Although asynchronous capabilities existed with frames, these capabilities were fairly error-prone. For example, if the user clicked the browser's back button, the application could be put into an invalid state. Alternatives to using frames such as Java Applets or browser plug-ins had their own browser compatibility and security issues. As a result, Ajax applications were not common and, where they did exist, were designed for specific user bases or platforms. This all changed when Microsoft introduced the XMLHttpRequest object in Internet Explorer 5 in 2000.

Is Ajax an Acronym?

Strictly speaking, Ajax is defined as an acronym for Asynchronous JavaScript and XML. However, the convention is to only uppercase the A—i.e., Ajax not AJAX. Furthermore, as Ajax patterns have gained wider usage among developers, techniques have arisen to accomplish the goals of Ajax without using XML. For example, Google's Ajax applications (Gmail, Google Maps, Google Spreadsheets, etc.) use relatively little XML. It is therefore increasingly clear that Ajax shouldn't be considered an acronym. Or, if it is to be considered an acronym, it's for Asynchronous JavaScript and the XMLHttpRequest object.

XMLHttpRequest

The XMLHttpRequest object is an object used by a scripting language within the browser (usually JavaScript, but it's not limited to JavaScript) to make an HTTP request. As its name suggests, this object was created to make a request for an XML document. However, there's nothing XML-specific about the object's behavior. XMLHttpRequest is not currently standardized, although current implementations have more or less the same capabilities. There is an effort underway by the W3C to standardize the object's interface and functionality. A working draft of the standard is available at *http://www.w3.org/TR/XMLHttpRequest*.

In Internet Explorer versions prior to 7, XMLHttpRequest is an ActiveX control instantiated like:

```
var req = new ActiveXObject("Microsoft.XMLHTTP");
```

---

* See *http://www.adaptivepath.com/publications/essays/archives/000385.php*.

In IE 7 and other browsers, it is a JavaScript object instantiated with the new keyword:

```
var req = new XMLHttpRequest();
```

As a result, you'll generally use an if-else construct to create the appropriate object based on the browser:

```
var req;
if (window.XMLHttpRequest) {
  req = new XMLHttpRequest();
} else if (window.ActiveXObject) {
  req = new ActiveXObject("Microsoft.XMLHTTP");
}
```

XMLHttpRequest can operate in either synchronous mode, in which the script waits for the response to be returned by the server, or asynchronous mode, in which the script is contained to execute after sending the request and a callback method is invoked when the response has been returned. Example 13-8 contains a page that requests an XML document and outputs it as the value of a form field within the body of the HTML page.

Example 13-8. Synchronous use of XMLHttpRequest

```
<html>
<body>
<form id="form"><textarea rows="20" cols="80" id="xmlarea"></textarea>
</form>
<script language="JavaScript">
var req;
var xmlarea = document.forms['form'].elements['xmlarea']
if (window.XMLHttpRequest) {
    req = new XMLHttpRequest();
} else if (window.ActiveXObject) {
    req = new ActiveXObject("Microsoft.XMLHTTP");
}

if (req == undefined) {
    xmlarea.value = "XMLHttpRequest object not available.";
} else {
    req.open("GET", "/ch13-servlet/booklist-xml", false);
    // third param = false means use synchronous mode
    req.send(null);
    // check the status
    if (req.status == 200)
        xmlarea.value = req.responseText;
    else
        xmlarea.value = "Got Response Code: " + req.status;
}
</script>
</body>
</html>
```

Example 13-9 does the same thing, but in asynchronous mode.

Example 13-9. Asynchronous use of XMLHttpRequest

```
<html>
<body>
<form id="form"><textarea rows="20" cols="80" id="xmlarea"></textarea>
</form>
<script language="JavaScript">
var xmlarea = document.forms['form'].elements['xmlarea'];
var req;
if (window.XMLHttpRequest) {
    req = new XMLHttpRequest( );
} else if (window.ActiveXObject) {
    req = new ActiveXObject("Microsoft.XMLHTTP");
}

if (req == undefined) {
    xmlarea.value = "XMLHttpRequest object not available.";
} else {
    req.open("GET", "/ch13-servlet/booklist-xml", true);
    // third param = true means use asynchronous mode
    req.onreadystatechange = docLoaded;
    req.send(null);
}

function docLoaded( ) {
    if (req.readyState == 2) {
        xmlarea.value = "Waiting...";
    }

    if (req.readyState == 4) {
        xmlarea.value = "Got Response...";
        // just for effect, update the textarea after waiting a second
        setTimeout("updateTextArea( )",1000);
    }
}

function updateTextArea( ) {
    if (req.status == 200)
        xmlarea.value = req.responseText;
    else
        xmlarea.value = "Got Response Code: " + req.status;
}
</script>
</body>
</html>
```

In asynchronous mode, the XMLHttpRequest object needs to have a callback function set using the onreadystatechange property. When this function is called, it checks the readyState property to determine what the current state of the request is. Possible values for this property are contained in Table 13-1. Note that the callback function may not be called for each of these states.

Table 13-1. Possible values for XMLHttpRequest's readyState property

Value	Meaning
0	Uninitialized
1	Open
2	Sent
3	Receiving
4	Loaded

 In general, an XMLHttpRequest cannot make requests to a server other than the server the containing page was loaded from.

These examples simply include the contents of an XML document into the page when it's first loaded. Example 13-10 goes a step further and allows the user to switch between two documents without reloading the page.

Example 13-10. Requesting different documents based on user actions

```
<html>
<body>
<form id="form"><textarea rows="20" cols="80" id="xmlarea">No Books.</textarea>
</form>
<script language="JavaScript">
var xmlarea = document.forms['form'].elements['xmlarea'];
var req;
if (window.XMLHttpRequest) {
    req = new XMLHttpRequest();
} else if (window.ActiveXObject) {
    req = new ActiveXObject("Microsoft.XMLHTTP");
}

function loadBooks(filename) {
    if (req == undefined) {
        xmlarea.value = "XMLHttpRequest object not available.";
    } else {
        xmlarea.value = "Waiting...";
        req.open("GET", "/ch13-servlet/"+filename, true);
        req.onreadystatechange = docLoaded;
        req.send(null);
    }
}

    if (req.readyState == 4) {
        if (req.status == 200)
            xmlarea.value = req.responseText;
        else
            xmlarea.value = "Got Response Code: " + req.status;
    }
</script>
```

```
<a href="javascript:loadBooks('books.xml')">Load Books</a><br/>
<a href="javascript:loadBooks('morebooks.xml')">Load More Books</a><br/>
</body>
</html>
```

When this page is first loaded, the textarea contains the string "No Books." The user can then click on one of the links to populate the textarea. Figures 13-6 and 13-7 show the page upon load and after clicking the "Load More Books" link, respectively.

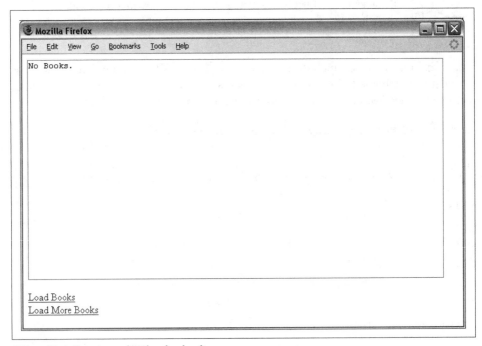

Figure 13-6. Page immediately after loading

Using DOM with Ajax

In addition to the responseText property containing the response as a string, XMLHttpRequest has a responseXML property that contains the response as a DOM object. We can use the DOM API to extract values from this object instead of just dumping the XML into the page, as we'd done above. The HTML page in Example 13-11 contains a div tag whose content is populated with the title and authors of each book in an XML file. When one of the file selection links is chosen, the default text is overwritten with the book list by using the innerHTML property. We use the getElementsByTagName( ) DOM method as well as various DOM properties.

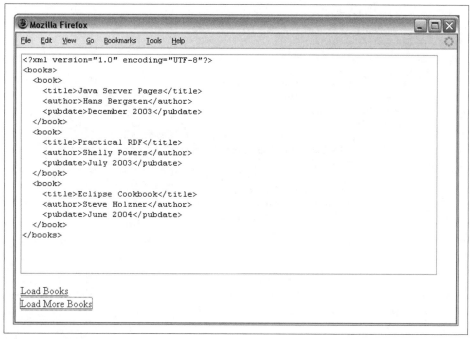

Figure 13-7. Page after clicking Load More Books

Example 13-11. DOM document access in JavaScript

```
<html>
<body>
<div id="xmlarea">
No Books Loaded.
</div>
<hr/>
<script language="JavaScript">
var xmlarea = document.getElementById('xmlarea');
var req;
if (window.XMLHttpRequest) {
    req = new XMLHttpRequest();
} else if (window.ActiveXObject) {
    req = new ActiveXObject("Microsoft.XMLHTTP");
}

function loadBooks(filename) {
    if (req == undefined) {
        xmlarea.innerHTML = "XMLHttpRequest object not available.";
    } else {
        xmlarea.innerHTML = "Waiting...";
        req.open("GET", "/ch13-servlet/"+filename, true);
        req.onreadystatechange = docLoaded;
        req.send(null);
    }
}
```

Example 13-11. DOM document access in JavaScript (continued)

```
function docLoaded( ) {
    if (req.readyState == 4) {
        doc = req.responseXML;
        newValue = "Books:<br/>\n";
        books = doc.getElementsByTagName("book");
        for (i = 0; i < books.length; i++) {
            book = books.item(i);
            var title;
            var author;
            for (j = 0; j < book.childNodes.length; j++) {
                node = book.childNodes[j];
                if (node.nodeName == "title") {
                    title = node.firstChild.nodeValue;
                } else if (node.nodeName == "author") {
                    author = node.firstChild.nodeValue;
                }
            }

            newValue = newValue + (i+1) + ") " + title +
                " by " + author + "<br/>\n";
        }
        xmlarea.innerHTML = newValue;
    }
}
</script>
Choose a file list:<br/>
<a href="javascript:loadBooks('books.xml')">books.xml</a><br/>
<a href="javascript:loadBooks('morebooks.xml')">morebooks.xml</a><br/>

</body>
</html>
```

Figure 13-8 shows the page as it displays when initially loaded. The page after selecting *books.xml* can be seen in Figure 13-9. Note that the div element is resized automatically and, as a result, the links are pushed down.

If you have a solid understanding of the DOM API in Java, you should be able to apply this knowledge to using DOM in JavaScript. The DOM language bindings for ECMAScript (the standard scripting language of which JavaScript is a derivative) are defined by the W3C at *http://www.w3.org/TR/DOM-Level-3-Core/ecma-script-binding.html*. For additional details on the JavaScript DOM API, please consult *Java-Script: The Definitive Guide* by David Flanagan (O'Reilly).

Using XSLT with Ajax

Internet Explorer and Mozilla Firefox both support XSL transformations through JavaScript. Unfortunately, as with the XMLHttpRequest object, the transformation support is accessed in a different way in each browser. In IE Internet Explorer, DOM

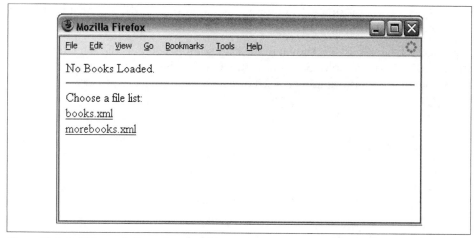

Figure 13-8. DOM page before selecting a file

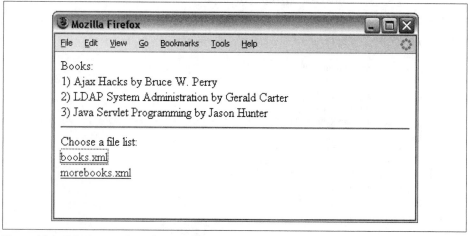

Figure 13-9. DOM page after selecting a file

objects have a method named `transformNode()`, which is passed a DOM `Document` object containing the stylesheet:

```
transformOutput = element.transformNode(xslDocument);
```

The output of a transformation can be a string, as above, or a DOM object.

In Firefox, there is a JavaScript object called `XSLTProcessor` to which stylesheet documents are added before a transformation is done:

```
xsltProcessor = new XSLTProcessor();
xsltProcessor.importStylesheet(xslDocument);
transformOutputDoc = xsltProcessor.transformToFragment(element, document);
```

The output of a transformation in Firefox can either be a DOM fragment or a DOM document.

The page in Example 13-12, shown in the next section, contains the same functionality using XSLT as Example 13-11 did with DOM. In this example, you can see how the output of the transformation is used differently in Internet Explorer and Firefox.

```
<html>
<body>
<div id="xmlarea">
No Books Loaded.
</div>
<hr/>
<script language="JavaScript">
var xmlarea = document.getElementById('xmlarea');
var req;
if (window.XMLHttpRequest) {
    req = new XMLHttpRequest();
} else if (window.ActiveXObject) {
    req = new ActiveXObject("Microsoft.XMLHTTP");
}

req.open("GET", "/ch13-ajax/authortitle.xsl", false);
req.send(null);
var xsldoc = req.responseXML;

function loadBooks(filename) {
    if (req == undefined) {
        xmlarea.innerHTML = "XMLHttpRequest object not available.";
    } else {
        xmlarea.innerHTML = "Waiting...";
        req.open("GET", "/ch13-servlet/"+filename, true);
        req.onreadystatechange = docLoaded;
        req.send(null);
    }
}

function docLoaded() {
    if (req.readyState == 4 && req.status == 200) {
        xmldoc = req.responseXML;
        if (window.ActiveXObject) {
            xmlarea.innerHTML = xmldoc.transformNode(xsldoc);
        } else if (window.XSLTProcessor) {
            processor = new XSLTProcessor();
            processor.importStylesheet(xsldoc);
            xmloutput = processor.transformToFragment(xmldoc, document);
            xmlarea.innerHTML = "";
            xmlarea.appendChild(xmloutput);
        } else {
            xmlarea.innerHTML = "XSLT not available in your browser.";
        }
    }
}
```

```
</script>
Choose a file list:<br/>
<a href="javascript:loadBooks('books.xml')">books.xml</a><br/>
<a href="javascript:loadBooks('morebooks.xml')">morebooks.xml</a><br/>

</body>
</html>
```

Posting XML to the Server

In the examples above, the requests made with XMLHttpRequest have all been basic
URLs. We can easily add simple parameters to these requests using the query string,
such as *http://www.example.com/servlets/stock?s=IBM*. For more complex parameters, XMLHttpRequest supports posting content as the body of the request, using the
HTTP POST method. One use for this capability is to post XML documents to an
application running on the server. To do this, you should set the Content-Type
header of the request to be text/xml and pass the XML document, either as a string
or a DOM object, to the XMLHttpRequest object's send( ) method.

Creating an XML document in JavaScript

To generate the XML document for the request, you could use simple string concatenation such as:

```
req.send("<search><name>" + document.getElementById("name").value +
    "</name><year>" + document.getElementById("year").value +
    "</year></search>");
```

The JavaScript necessary to construct a document with concatenation can quickly
become confusing and error-prone as nothing stops you from generating ill-formed
documents. To ensure that well-formed documents are produced, you should use the
DOM capabilities in JavaScript.

As with XMLHttpRequest, DOM Document objects are created as ActiveX objects in
Internet Explorer and through a native JavaScript API in other browsers. To create a
DOM Document in Internet Explorer, you first create the empty document and then
the root element:

```
doc = new ActiveXObject("Microsoft.XMLDOM");
doc.appendChild(doc.createElement("search"));
```

And in Firefox and other browsers, the document is created already populated with a
root element:

```
doc = document.implementation.createDocument(null, "search", null);
```

The createDocument( ) method accepts a namespace URI and a DTD in addition to
the root element name.

Submitting the XML document

Once you have built the document, either as a string or a DOM object, it gets passed to the send( ) method of XMLHttpRequest. Example 13-12 contains a simple HTML form whose submit button results in posting the form fields as an XML document.

Example 13-12. Submitting form data as XML

```html
<html>
<body>
<h1>Book Search</h1>
<form id="form" onsubmit="search( ); return false;">
    Name: <input type="text" id="name"/><br/>
    Year (optional): <select id="year">
        <option value="notselected">...select one...</option>
        <option value="2001">2001</option>
        <option value="2002">2002</option>
        <option value="2003">2003</option>
        <option value="2004">2004</option>
        <option value="2005">2005</option>
    </select><br/>
    <input type="submit" />
    <hr/>
    Search Results:<br/>
    <textarea rows="3" cols="50" id="results" readonly="true"></textarea>
</form>
<script language="JavaScript">
function search( ) {
    var req;
    var form = document.forms['form'];
    if (window.XMLHttpRequest) {
        req = new XMLHttpRequest( );
    } else if (window.ActiveXObject) {
        req = new ActiveXObject("Microsoft.XMLHTTP");
    }

    if (req == undefined) {
        document.getElementById("results").value =
            "XMLHttpRequest object not available.";
    } else {
        req.open("POST", "/ch13-ajax/post", false);
        req.setRequestHeader("Content-Type", "text/xml");

        postDoc = makePostData( );

        req.send(postDoc);
        // check the status
        if (req.status == 200)
            document.getElementById("results").value = req.responseText;
        else
            document.getElementById("results").value = "Got Response Code: " +
                req.status;
    }
}
```

Example 13-12. Submitting form data as XML (continued)

```
function makePostData( ) {
    var doc;
    if (window.ActiveXObject) {
        doc = new ActiveXObject("Microsoft.XMLDOM");
        doc.appendChild(doc.createElement("search"));
    } else {
        doc = document.implementation.createDocument(null, "search", null);
    }
    nameElement = doc.createElement("name");
    nameText = doc.createTextNode(document.getElementById("name").value);
    nameElement.appendChild(nameText);
    doc.documentElement.appendChild(nameElement);

    yearElement = doc.createElement("year");
    yearText = doc.createTextNode(document.getElementById("year").value);
    yearElement.appendChild(yearText);
    doc.documentElement.appendChild(yearElement);

    return doc;
}
</script>
</body>
</html>
```

> In a real application, you will want to perform some validation in Java-
> Script before submitting the request. One significant advantage of
> Ajax applications as compared with traditional web applications is
> that at least some form validation can be done without submitting the
> form to the server.

When building a servlet that accepts these requests and parses the request XML document, you can use either the Reader or InputStream from the request, accessed with
getReader( ) and getInputStream( ), respectively. Although it doesn't actually do any
searching, Example 13-13 contains a servlet that accepts the XML document produced by Example 13-12 and echoes the search terms back to the browser. We use
JDOM's XPath support to extract the search terms from the request document.

Example 13-13. Servlet to accept XML posts

```
package javaxml3.ch13;

import java.io.IOException;

import javax.servlet.ServletException;
import javax.servlet.http.HttpServlet;
import javax.servlet.http.HttpServletRequest;
import javax.servlet.http.HttpServletResponse;

import org.jdom.Document;
```

Example 13-13. Servlet to accept XML posts (continued)

```
import org.jdom.JDOMException;
import org.jdom.input.SAXBuilder;
import org.jdom.xpath.XPath;

public class PostServlet extends HttpServlet {

    private SAXBuilder builder = new SAXBuilder();

    private XPath nameXPath;

    private XPath yearXPath;

    protected void doPost(HttpServletRequest request,
            HttpServletResponse response) throws ServletException, IOException {
        if (!"text/xml".equals(request.getContentType())) {
            response.getWriter().println("Please post as text/xml.");
        } else {
            try {
                Document doc = builder.build(request.getReader());
                StringBuffer buff = new StringBuffer();
                buff.append("You searched for name '" + nameXPath.valueOf(doc)
                    + "'");
                String year = yearXPath.valueOf(doc);
                if (!"notselected".equals(year)) {
                    buff.append(" and year '" + year + "'");
                }
                buff.append(".");
                response.getWriter().print(buff.toString());
            } catch (JDOMException e) {
                response.getWriter().print(
                        "Error getting search terms: " + e.getMessage());
            }
        }
    }

    public void init() throws ServletException {
        try {
            nameXPath = XPath.newInstance("/search/name/text()");
            yearXPath = XPath.newInstance("/search/year/text()");
        } catch (JDOMException e) {
            throw new ServletException("Unable to create XPaths", e);
        }
        super.init();
    }
}
```

Putting the HTML and servlet together gives us the output pictured in Figure 13-10.

This section has contained a quick overview of the use of XML in Ajax applications. There's a lot more involved in creating a complete Ajax application. Ajax is a rapidly growing area and there are a wide variety of online sources for more information, from blogs like Ajaxian.com to developer sites created by Mozilla and Microsoft.

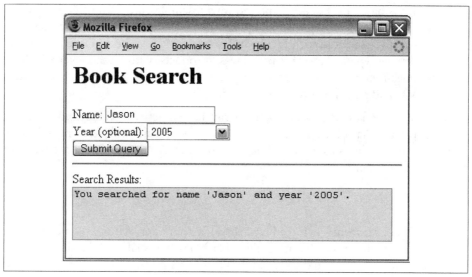

Figure 13-10. Result of XML post

Dozens of Ajax-related books are available for sale including, we should note, *Head Rush Ajax* by Brett McLaughlin (O'Reilly).

Flash

Since its introduction in 1996 under the name FutureSplash, Adobe Flash (formerly Macromedia Flash) has become the de facto standard for web animation and interactivity. With each subsequent release of the Flash platform, it has become more full-featured to the point where it can now be considered a platform for any kind of interactive application. The Flash platform is currently composed of three different components:

- A file format named SWF (files in this format are commonly called Flash movies)
- Applications for displaying SWF files, packaged as a standalone executable (Flash Player) and a browser plug-in
- Authoring tools

The specification for the SWF file format is available on Adobe's web site. However, the license terms prohibit the use of the specification to create alternatives to the Flash Player. It can be used to write applications that create SWF files. As a result, authoring tools for SWF files range from Adobe's tools (Flash Professional, Flash Standard, and Flex) to open source command-line compilers like MTASC.

ActionScript

Almost every version of Flash has included some level of scripting support. Flash 5, released in 2000, introduced a new scripting language named ActionScript.

ActionScript is based on ECMAScript and thus resembles JavaScript. Flash 7 (a.k.a. Flash MX 2004) introduced ActionScript 2.0 in 2003 supporting language features more commonly associated with Java than JavaScript such as class inheritance, interfaces, and strong typing. ActionScript 3.0 was introduced with Flash Player 9 in 2006 and continues this trend with better exception support, true runtime typing, a new API for XML, and regular expression support.

In addition to the language itself, ActionScript has an active developer community. You can produce Javadoc-style documentation with as2api and perform unit tests with AS2Unit. For links to these and other open source tools, check out the web site *http://www.osflash.org*.

Flex

In March 2004, Macromedia introduced the Flex server application as an alternative development platform for Flash. Unlike Flash Professional and Flash Standard, which use a binary file format called FLA and then compile the FLA file into a SWF file, Flex uses an XML file format called MXML, which is compiled into a SWF file. MXML files represent both the display and functionality of an application. Example 13-14 contains an example MXML file. You can see the result of compiling this MXML in Figure 13-11. Even if you've never used ActionScript, Flash, or Flex, it is pretty obvious what this application does.

Example 13-14. Simple MXML form application

```
<?xml version="1.0" encoding="utf-8"?>
<mx:Application xmlns:mx="http://www.adobe.com/2006/mxml" layout="absolute"
    width="331" height="258">

    <mx:Script>
        <![CDATA[
            import mx.collections.ArrayCollection;

            [Bindable]
            private var listData:ArrayCollection = new ArrayCollection();

            private function addText() : void {
                listData.addItem(text.text);
                text.text = "";
            }

            private function clearList() : void {
                listData.removeAll();
            }
        ]]>
    </mx:Script>

    <mx:List x="10" y="10" width="311" height="129" id="list"
        dataProvider="{listData}" />
    <mx:TextInput x="10" y="162" width="311" id="text"/>
    <mx:Button x="45" y="216" label="Add Text" click="addText()"/>
```

Example 13-14. Simple MXML form application (continued)

```
    <mx:Button x="194" y="216" label="Clear List" click="clearList( )"/>
</mx:Application>
```

Figure 13-11. Simple MXML application in a browser

Flex was originally packaged only as a J2EE web application. MXML files were compiled into SWF within a servlet process. In addition, the compiled applications could use a data gateway that was part of the web application to access server-side resources like databases, Enterprise JavaBeans (EJB), and, of course, XML data. The first version of Flex was targeted at large companies, with a large license fee per CPU. Along with the server license came a development tool called Flex Builder. However, since MXML is just XML, and XML is just text, any text editor can be used to write MXML.

With the release of Flex 2 in 2006, Adobe radically changed the structure and licensing model for Flex. The Flex compiler and documentation (what Adobe refers to as the Flex SDK or Flex Framework) can be freely downloaded after registering from *http://www.adobe.com/products/flex*. This free compiler can be used as a standalone application to create SWF files from MXML files. The resulting SWFs can be hosted on any web site (or not hosted at all); no server license is required. Flex Builder 2 can be purchased by itself and is built on top of the Eclipse platform. There is still a per-CPU licensed server component for Flex 2 used to facilitate communication between Flex applications and backend systems.

XML in ActionScript 3.0

The remainder of this chapter will explore several different ways of working with XML documents using Flex 2 and ActionScript 3.0. ActionScript 3.0 is supported by Flash Player 9 and the forthcoming Flash 9 development environment in addition to

Flex 2 (At the time of writing, an alpha version of Flash Professional 9 was available for download from *http://labs.adobe.com*. According to that web site, the sole purpose of this alpha release is to enable the creation of Flash applications using ActionScript 3.0..). Although ActionScript 2.0 is now quite prevalent, by the time this book is printed, that may no longer be the case. Because Flex 2's file format is XML-based, it seems a better fit, both with the subject of this book and its intended audience. Plus, using Flex 2 means that the examples can be compiled using a free download, which isn't the case if we were to use the normal Flash authoring tool.[*]

To demonstrate these features, we will build a simple application that views the book data used throughout this chapter. In addition to viewing a list of books, users of this application will be able to add new books. Finally, to show off the ability to push XML to Flash, we'll display the current date and time according to the server. Figures 13-12 and 13-13 contain screenshots of the application in use. Example 13-15 contains MXML to create the various form components. As with some of the Swing code from prior chapters, it's not necessary to understand these components completely. In most cases, the meanings are self-evident.

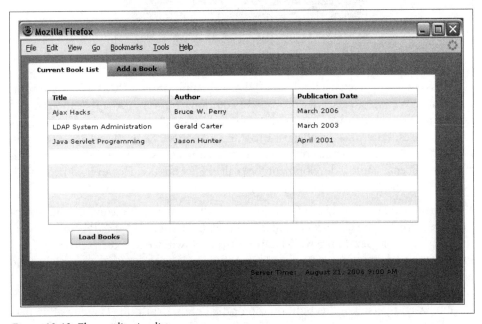

Figure 13-12. Flex application list page

---

[*] Although there are free trial versions available of Flash Professional and Flash Standard, that's not the same thing as just free.

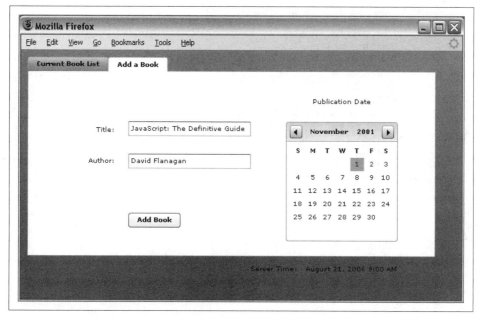

Figure 13-13. Flex application form page

Example 13-15. Form components in MXML

```
<?xml version="1.0" encoding="utf-8"?>
<mx:Application xmlns:mx="http://www.adobe.com/2006/mxml" layout="absolute">
    <mx:Script>
      <![CDATA[
        // our ActionScript will go here
        ]]>
    </mx:Script>
    <mx:Canvas x="10" y="10" width="635" height="350">
        <mx:TabNavigator id="tabs" width="100%" height="300">
            <mx:Canvas label="Current Book List" width="100%" height="100%">
                <mx:Button x="65" y="221" id="load" label="Load Books"/>
                <mx:DataGrid x="29" y="10" width="577" height="203" id="booklist">
                    <mx:columns>
                        <mx:DataGridColumn headerText="Title"/>
                        <mx:DataGridColumn headerText="Author"/>
                        <mx:DataGridColumn headerText="Publication Date"/>
                    </mx:columns>
                </mx:DataGrid>
            </mx:Canvas>
            <mx:Canvas label="Add a Book" width="100%" height="100%"
              id="addFormPage">
                <mx:Label x="10" y="69" text="Title:" width="128"
                  textAlign="right"/>
                <mx:TextInput x="156" y="65" width="190" id="title"/>
                <mx:Label x="10" y="116" text="Author:" width="128"
                  textAlign="right"/>
                <mx:TextInput x="156" y="114" width="190" id="author"/>
```

Example 13-15. Form components in MXML (continued)

```
                    <mx:Label x="439.5" y="26" text="Publication Date"/>
                    <mx:DateChooser x="400" y="65" id="pubdate"/>
                    <mx:Button x="156" y="203" label="Add Book" enabled="false"
                        id="add"/>
                </mx:Canvas>
            </mx:TabNavigator>
            <mx:Canvas y="300" width="100%" height="50">
                <mx:Label x="345" y="10" text="Server Time:"/>
                <mx:Text x="430" y="10" text="Waiting..." width="191"
                  textAlign="left"/>
            </mx:Canvas>
        </mx:Canvas>

</mx:Application>
```

E4X

ECMAScript for XML (E4X) is an extension to the ECMAScript standard upon
which ActionScript and JavaScript are based. E4X provides native support for XML
documents within ECMAScript. Creating a new document with E4X can be done
with code such as:

```
var doc=<content>
    <element attribute="1">
        <child>Here's some child text</child>
    </element>
    <element attribute="2">
        <child>Here's some more child text</child>
    </element>

</content>
```

In ActionScript, it's preferable to include the type definition, so the first line above
should really be:

```
var doc:XML=<content>
```

Accessing child elements uses a dot notation, such as:

```
doc.element[0].child;
```

Attributes are accessed using the @ symbol:

```
doc.element[0].@attribute;
```

This access can be used to read values from a document object or update the document:

```
doc.element[1].child = "Changing the child text. ";
```

Finally, in addition to the index-based access shown above, XPath expressions can be
used:

```
doc.element[@attribute="2"].child = "Changing the child text when attribute = 2";
```

Parsing is done with the XML constructor:

```
var docString:String = "<content><element><child>text</child></element></content>";
var doc:XML = new XML(docString);
```

E4X in Firefox

In addition to ActionScript, E4X has been implemented in the JavaScript engine used in the Mozilla Firefox browser. Firefox versions since 1.5 have contained E4X functionality. However, to use E4X in JavaScript, you must use a special type attribute to the script tag:

```
<script type="text/javascript; e4x=1">
```

As of the time of writing, Microsoft had not announced plans to include E4X support in any future version of Internet Explorer.

More information on E4X in general can be found on ECMA's web site: *http://www. ecma-international.org/publications/standards/Ecma-357.htm*.

XML data providers

ActionScript and Flex make it easy to bind the content of controls to portions of an XML document. In Example 13-15 above, we have a DataGrid control with three columns, which correspond to the child elements in our XML content. As a result of this correspondence, we can automatically populate the DataGrid control with XML content. In this case, we create a bindable list object and set the DataGrid control's dataProvider property with the list object's name:

```
// these two lines go inside <mx:script> tags
[Bindable]
private var gridData:ArrayCollection = new ArrayCollection();

<!-- this is the updated <mx:DataGrid> control -->
<mx:DataGrid x="29" y="10" width="577" height="203" id="booklist"
  dataProvider="{gridData}">
  <mx:columns>
    <mx:DataGridColumn headerText="Title" dataField="title"/>
    <mx:DataGridColumn headerText="Author" dataField="author"/>
    <mx:DataGridColumn headerText="Publication Date" dataField="pubdate"/>
  </mx:columns>
</mx:DataGrid>
```

Note that we also told each column what XML element to get its content from.

Sending and loading XML

ActionScript contains a generic URLLoader class that can be used to load data from an URL. There's a related class named URLRequest, which encapsulates all the parameters of an HTTP request. As with the XMLHttpRequest object discussed earlier in this chapter, it's possible to use URLRequest and URLLoader to retrieve XML data as well as to post XML data in the body of a request. In the sample application, we'll use these classes twice.

First, when a user clicks on the "Load Books" button, we need to request a URL and add each book defined in the resulting XML into the list we created above. Because we will be reusing the URL, we define it as a variable:

```
private var serviceURL:String = "http://localhost:8080/ch13-flex/books";
```

Then we create a loadBooks( ) function to be called when the user clicks the "Load Books" button:

```
function loadBooks( ) : void {
  // remove anything from our grid data
  gridData.removeAll( );

  // load the data
  var loader:URLLoader = new URLLoader( );
  loader.addEventListener("complete", getCompleteListener);
  loader.load(new URLRequest(serviceURL));
}

<!-- modified <mx:Button> control -->
<mx:Button x="65" y="221" id="load" label="Load Books" click="loadBooks( )"/>
```

You can see that, like XMLHttpRequest in asynchronous mode, URLLoader needs an event listener to be notified when the request is complete. But whereas XMLHttpRequest has a single function set as its onreadystatechange property, URLLoader can have different functions assigned to each of the six events it defines. These events are listed in Table 13-2. Each event has a name and an event class associated with it. An instance of this class is passed to the defined function. In the case of the complete event, the event class is the generic flash.events.Event class. So, our getCompleteListener( ) function looks like this:

```
function getCompleteListener(event:Event) : void {
  // cast the event target to a URLLoader object
  var loader:URLLoader = URLLoader(event.target);
  parseBookDoc(new XML(loader.data));
}
```

I've separated the parsing of the document from the listener function so that it can be reused later. In parseBookDoc( ), we simply loop through the book elements in the XML document and add each one to the gridData object.

```
function parseBookDoc(docXML:XML) : void {
  gridData.removeAll( );
  for (var i:String in docXML.book) {
    gridData.addItem(docXML.book[i]);
  }
}
```

Table 13-2. URLLoader events

Event name	Event class
complete	flash.events.Event
httpStatus	flash.events.HTTPStatusEvent
ioError	flash.events.IOErrorEvent
open	flash.events.Event
progress	flash.events.ProgressEvent
securityError	flash.events.SecurityErrorEvent

The second place we use URLLoader is to post new book information as XML to the server. We first assemble the XML document using E4X. As above, we create a function to be called upon a push of the "Add Book" button:

```
function addBook( ) : void {
  var newBookXML:XML = <book />
  newBookXML.title = title.text;
  newBookXML.author = author.text;

  var pickedDate:Date = pubdate.selectedDate;
  if (pickedDate == null)
    pickedDate = new Date( );
  newBookXML.pubdate = pubdateFormatter.format(pickedDate);

  var request:URLRequest = new URLRequest(serviceURL);
  request.method="POST";
  request.contentType="text/xml";
  request.data = newBookXML.toXMLString( );
  var loader:URLLoader = new URLLoader( );
  loader.addEventListener("complete", postCompleteListener);
  loader.load(request);
}

function postCompleteListener(event:Event) : void {
  var loader:URLLoader = URLLoader(event.target);
  parseBookDoc(new XML(loader.data));
}

<!-- updated <mx:Button> control -->
<mx:Button x="156" y="203" label="Add Book" enabled="false" id="add"
  click="addBook( )"/>
```

Using Flash XML sockets

Our final bit of XML is opening a socket to the server and listening for XML documents. In this case, these documents will contain the current date and time, like:

```
<current>
    <date>August 25, 2006</date>
    <time>6:00:03 PM EDT</time>
</current>
```

Our application needs to open the socket on startup and update the display every time it receives a new document from the server. We could use URLLoader to accomplish something similar, by regularly polling the server for an XML document. However, by using a persistent socket connection, the server is able to control when and how frequently documents are sent. To facilitate the case of sending and receiving XML documents over a persistent socket connection, ActionScript includes a class named XMLSocket.

Before we can use XMLSocket, we have to write a socket server. The class in Example 13-16 is not the best implementation of a server, but it will do for our purposes. If you were going to deploy this type of server for real use, you would want a multithreaded server. For more information on writing socket servers, see *Java Network Programming* by Elliotte Rusty Harold (O'Reilly).

Example 13-16. Simple socket server

```
package javaxml3;

import java.io.BufferedWriter;
import java.io.IOException;
import java.io.OutputStreamWriter;
import java.net.BindException;
import java.net.ServerSocket;
import java.net.Socket;
import java.text.DateFormat;
import java.util.Date;

import org.jdom.Document;
import org.jdom.Element;
import org.jdom.output.XMLOutputter;

public class DateTimeSocketServer extends Thread {

    private Document currentDocument;

    private Element dateElement;

    private DateFormat dateFormat = DateFormat.getDateInstance(DateFormat.LONG);

    private XMLOutputter outputter;

    private int port;

    private Element timeElement;

    private DateFormat timeFormat = DateFormat.getTimeInstance(DateFormat.LONG);

    public DateTimeSocketServer(int port) {
        this.port = port;
        outputter = new XMLOutputter( );
        currentDocument = new Document( );
```

Example 13-16. Simple socket server (continued)

```
        Element root = new Element("current");
        currentDocument.setRootElement(root);
        dateElement = new Element("date");
        root.addContent(dateElement);
        timeElement = new Element("time");
        root.addContent(timeElement);
    }

    public void run() {
        try {
            ServerSocket server = new ServerSocket(port);
            System.out.println("Listening for connections on port "
                    + server.getLocalPort());

            while (true) {
                try {
                    Socket socket = server.accept();

                    BufferedWriter out = new BufferedWriter(
                            new OutputStreamWriter(socket.getOutputStream()));
                    while (!socket.isClosed()) {
                        String current = updateCurrentXML();
                        System.out.println("sending XML");
                        out.write(current);
                        // must end on a zero byte for Flash to see this
                        // as a complete document
                        out.write(0);
                        out.flush();

                        try {
                            Thread.sleep(1000);
                        } catch (InterruptedException e) {
                        }
                    }
                } catch (IOException e) {
                    System.err.println("Exception while accepting: "
                            + e.getMessage());
                }
            }

        } catch (BindException e) {
            System.err.println("Could not start server. Port Occupied");
        } catch (IOException e) {
            System.err.println(e.getMessage());
        }

    }

    private String updateCurrentXML() {
        Date date = new Date();
        dateElement.setText(dateFormat.format(date));
        timeElement.setText(timeFormat.format(date));
```

Example 13-16. Simple socket server (continued)

```
        return outputter.outputString(currentDocument);
    }

    public static void main(String[] args) {
        int port;
        try {
            port = Integer.parseInt(args[0]);
        } catch (Exception ex) {
            port = 8900;
        }

        Thread t = new DateTimeSocketServer(port);
        t.start( );
    }

}
```

The key thing here is to output a zero byte following our XML document. If we do not do this, Flash will never know the document is complete.

To connect to the server when the application is loaded, we create an init( ) method and reference it in the mx:Application tag:

```
<mx:Application xmlns:mx="http://www.adobe.com/2006/mxml" layout="absolute"
    initialize="init( )">

private var xmlsocket:XMLSocket = new XMLSocket( );

function init( ) : void {
  xmlsocket.addEventListener("connect", onXMLConnect);
  xmlsocket.addEventListener("data", onXMLData);
  xmlsocket.connect("localhost", 8900);
}
```

As with URLLoader, we need to create event listeners. XMLSocket and URLLoader share many of the same events. The events available for XMLSocket are listed in Table 13-3.

Table 13-3. XMLSocket events

Event name	Event class
close	flash.events.Event
connect	flash.events.Event
data	flash.events.DataEvent
ioError	flash.events.IOErrorEvent
securityError	flash.events.SecurityErrorEvent

The full MXML source code for this application is contained in Example 13-17.

Example 13-17. Complete MXML source

```
<?xml version="1.0" encoding="utf-8"?>
<mx:Application xmlns:mx="http://www.adobe.com/2006/mxml" layout="absolute"
  initialize="init()">
  <mx:Script><![CDATA[
            import mx.formatters.DateFormatter;
            import mx.collections.ArrayCollection;

            private var serviceURL:String =
              "http://localhost:8080/ch13-flex/books";

            [Bindable]
            private var gridData:ArrayCollection = new ArrayCollection();

            private var pubdateFormatter:DateFormatter = new DateFormatter();

            private var xmlsocket:XMLSocket = new XMLSocket();

            function init() : void {
                pubdateFormatter.formatString = "MMMM YYYY";
                xmlsocket.addEventListener("connect", onXMLConnect);
                xmlsocket.addEventListener("data", onXMLData);
                xmlsocket.connect("localhost", 8900);
            }

            function onXMLConnect(event:Event) : void {
                serverTime.text = "connected to server";
            }

            function onXMLData(event:DataEvent) : void {
                var data:XML = XML(event.data);
                serverTime.text = data.date + " " + data.time;
            }

            function loadBooks() : void {
                // remove anything from our grid data
                gridData.removeAll();

                // load the data
                var loader:URLLoader = new URLLoader();
                loader.addEventListener("complete", getCompleteListener);
                loader.load(new URLRequest(serviceURL));
            }

            // this function is called when the data URL has been loaded
            function getCompleteListener(event:Event) : void {
                // cast the event target to a URLLoader object
                var loader:URLLoader = URLLoader(event.target);
                parseBookDoc(new XML(loader.data));
            }

            function parseBookDoc(docXML:XML) : void {
                gridData.removeAll();
```

Example 13-17. Complete MXML source (continued)

```
                for (var i:String in docXML.book) {
                    gridData.addItem(docXML.book[i]);
                }
            }

            function validateAddForm( ) : void {
                add.enabled = ((title.text.length > 0) &&
                  (author.text.length > 0));
            }

            function addBook( ) : void {
                disableForm( );

                var newBookXML:XML = <book />
                newBookXML.title = title.text;
                newBookXML.author = author.text;

                var pickedDate:Date = pubdate.selectedDate;
                if (pickedDate == null)
                    pickedDate = new Date( );
                newBookXML.pubdate = pubdateFormatter.format(pickedDate);

                var request:URLRequest = new URLRequest(serviceURL);
                request.method="POST";
                request.contentType="text/xml";
                request.data = newBookXML.toXMLString( );
                var loader:URLLoader = new URLLoader( );
                loader.addEventListener("complete", postCompleteListener);
                loader.load(request);
            }

            function postCompleteListener(event:Event) : void {
                var loader:URLLoader = URLLoader(event.target);
                parseBookDoc(new XML(loader.data));
                reenableForm( );
            }

            function disableForm( ) : void {
                title.enabled = false;
                author.enabled = false;
                pubdate.enabled = false;
                add.enabled = false;
                load.enabled = false;
            }

            function reenableForm( ) : void {
                load.enabled = true;
                title.enabled = true;
                author.enabled = true;
                pubdate.enabled = true;
                title.text = "";
                author.text = "";
```

Example 13-17. Complete MXML source (continued)

```
        }
      ]]></mx:Script>
  <mx:Canvas x="10" y="10" width="635" height="350">
    <mx:TabNavigator id="tabs" width="100%" height="300">
      <mx:Canvas label="Current Book List" width="100%" height="100%">
        <mx:Button x="65" y="221" id="load" label="Load Books"
          click="loadBooks( )"/>
        <mx:DataGrid x="29" y="10" width="577" height="203" id="booklist"
          dataProvider="{gridData}">
          <mx:columns>
            <mx:DataGridColumn headerText="Title" dataField="title"/>
            <mx:DataGridColumn headerText="Author" dataField="author"/>
            <mx:DataGridColumn headerText="Publication Date" dataField="pubdate"/>
          </mx:columns>
        </mx:DataGrid>
      </mx:Canvas>
      <mx:Canvas label="Add a Book" width="100%" height="100%" id="addFormPage">
        <mx:Label x="10" y="69" text="Title:" width="128" textAlign="right"/>
        <mx:TextInput x="156" y="65" width="190" id="title"
          change="validateAddForm( )"/>
        <mx:Label x="10" y="116" text="Author:" width="128" textAlign="right"/>
        <mx:TextInput x="156" y="114" width="190" id="author"
          change="validateAddForm( )"/>
        <mx:Button x="156" y="203" label="Add Book" enabled="false" id="add"
          click="addBook( )"/>
        <mx:Label x="439.5" y="26" text="Publication Date"/>
        <mx:DateChooser x="400" y="65" id="pubdate"/>
      </mx:Canvas>
    </mx:TabNavigator>
    <mx:Canvas y="300" width="100%" height="50">
      <mx:Label x="345" y="10" text="Server Time:"/>
      <mx:Text x="430" y="10" text="August 21, 2006 9:00 AM" width="191"
        textAlign="left" id="serverTime"/>
    </mx:Canvas>
  </mx:Canvas>
</mx:Application>
```

Cross-Domain Access

By default, the Flash Player has a fairly strict rule defining what network access is allowed: a Flash movie can only make network requests to the host with the *exact* same domain name from which it was loaded. If a Flash movie is loaded from *http:// www.example.com/flash/movie.swf*, for example, it could request *http://www. example.com/feed*, but not *http://www.othersite.com/feed* or even *http://data.example. com/feed*. To allow access to these other hosts, a cross-domain policy file must be created. This policy file is called *crossdomain.xml* and is located on the host to which Flash needs to be granted access. If you had a data feed on *http://www.othersite. com* and wanted to allow access to Flash movies loaded from *www.example.com*, this policy file would need to be downloadable from *http://www.othersite.com/ crossdomain.xml*:

```
<?xml version="1.0"?>
<!DOCTYPE cross-domain-policy SYSTEM
  "http://www.macromedia.com/xml/dtds/cross-domain-policy.dtd">
<cross-domain-policy>
  <allow-access-from domain="www.example.com" />
</cross-domain-policy>
```

Multiple allow-access-from-domain elements are permitted. In addition, you can use a wildcard to allow access to Flash movies loaded from any subdomain of *example.com*:

```
<?xml version="1.0"?>
<!DOCTYPE cross-domain-policy SYSTEM
  "http://www.macromedia.com/xml/dtds/cross-domain-policy.dtd">
<cross-domain-policy>
  <allow-access-from domain="*.example.com" />
</cross-domain-policy>
```

Using the wildcard, you can allow access to Flash movies loaded from any domain:

```
<?xml version="1.0"?>
<!DOCTYPE cross-domain-policy SYSTEM
  "http://www.macromedia.com/xml/dtds/cross-domain-policy.dtd">
<cross-domain-policy>
  <allow-access-from domain="*" />
</cross-domain-policy>
```

For more information on cross-domain policy files, see *http://www.adobe.com/ cfusion/knowledgebase/index.cfm?id=tn_14213*.

There is much more to learn about the technologies discussed in this chapter. Hopefully it has provided you a taste of where you can use XML in the presentation tier of your web applications, as well as some pointers to where you can find more information on each of the topics.

## CHAPTER 14

Looking Forward

It's almost time to wrap up the journey through Java and XML. I hope you've had fun. Before I leave you to mull over all the possibilities, I want to finish up with a few pointers to interesting XML-related technologies that we weren't able to discuss in this book.

XML Appliances

The various XML processing libraries discussed in this book have been implemented entirely in software, sometimes as part of the Java Runtime Environment (JRE) and sometimes as separate libraries. In addition to these options, there are also solutions for processing XML using specialized hardware. In some cases, this hardware is packaged as an add-in card that is installed in a server. In other cases, the hardware is a separate box, which is accessed over a network. Regardless of how it's packaged, your application uses a specialized library to offload processing onto the specialized XML hardware. With most hardware, these libraries include implementation of the JAXP interfaces discussed in Chapter 7, in which case your code may not need to be changed to take advantage of the hardware. XML appliances are made by companies such as DataPower and Sarvega, subsidiaries of IBM and Intel, respectively, as well as smaller companies like Layer 7 Technologies and Reactivity.

XML Databases

As you work with XML documents, you may find yourself needing to manage collections of documents. XML databases (sometimes called XML-native databases) are built for just this task. You can query a collection using XPath or XQuery (see below). Another specification, XUpdate, defines how collections get updated, although most XML databases support a variety of mechanisms for adding and updating documents. There are a variety of available XML databases, both open source and commercial.

In addition, many relational database servers support an XML datatype. With columns of this type, XML queries can be combined with traditional, relational queries. The disadvantage of XML support in relational databases is that, in general, the support has been bolted on and not fully integrated into the software.

XQuery

XQuery is a query language for extracting data from XML documents. It is similar in purpose to SQL (Structured Query Language). Although XQuery is related to XSLT—both use XPath extensively and can be used to accomplish some of the same things—XQuery queries are not in XML as XSLT stylesheets are. At the time of writing, the specification for XQuery is not yet finalized, although it is getting very close. This specification is available at *http://www.w3.org/TR/xquery*. You can also learn more about XQuery from the web site *http://www.xquery.com*. A standard Java API for XQuery is being developed under JSR 225 using the name XQuery for Java (XQJ).

Fast Infoset

Fast Infoset is an alternative encoding of the XML object model. Normally an XML document is written in plain text, just as we've seen throughout this book. With Fast Infoset, however, a binary, nonhuman readable, file format is used. In exchange for the loss of human readability, Fast Infoset-encoded documents are significantly smaller and require less processing effort to parse. The Fast Infoset specification is defined by two different standards bodies: the International Telecommunications Union (ITU) and the International Organization for Standards (ISO). There is an open source Java implementation of Fast Infoset at *https://fi.dev.java.net*. This implementation is included in the Java Web Services Developer Pack discussed in Chapter 11.

And Many More...

I could go on, but who knows what will happen between now and the time you're reading this? Without a doubt, something new and exciting will be developed. The best I can do is point you to a few web sites:

XML.com
> O'Reilly's XML news and information site. In addition to articles written for the site, XML.com contains links to XML-related entries throughout the blogosphere.

JRoller.com
> JRoller.com is one of the larger Java blog sites. JRoller.com hosts thousands of Java-oriented blogs.

TheServerSide.com

TheServerSide.com is a premiere enterprise Java news site.

Oracle's XML Technology Center

Located at *http://www.oracle.com/technology/tech/xml/index.html*, Oracle's XML site has a variety of technical articles and tutorials.

IBM developerWorks

developerWorks is IBM's developer community site. The XML section, located at *http://www-128.ibm.com/developerworks/xml*, contains tutorials, documentation, podcasts, and various pieces of software for download. IBM frequently uses developerWorks to preview technologies coming out of their vast research facilities.

If you keep up to date using these sites and the thousands of other related sites on the Web, you'll be aware of the next big thing before it's here. And if you have the inclination (and the time), all of these sites have healthy user communities and more are always welcome.

SAX Features and Properties

This appendix describes the SAX 2.0 standard features and properties. Although a vendor's parsing software can add additional features and properties for vendor-specific functionality, this list represents the core set of functionality that any SAX 2.0-compliant parser implementation should support.

 To be precise, these are drawn from the SAX 2.0.2 release 3. However, any SAX 2.x parser should provide these features and properties—or, at worst, recognize them and throw a SAXNotSupportedException.

Core Features

The core set of features supported by SAX 2.0 XMLReader implementations is listed here. These features can be set through setFeature( ), and the value of a feature can be obtained through getFeature( ). Any feature can be read-only or read/write; features also may be modifiable only when parsing is occurring, or only when parsing is not occurring. For more information on SAX features and properties, refer to Chapter 4.

External General Entity Processing

This feature tells a parser whether or not to process external general entities, such as:

```
<!ENTITY copyright    SYSTEM "legal/copyright.xml">
```

URI: http://xml.org/sax/features/external-general-entities
Access: read/write
Default: unspecified; always true if the parser is validating (see the "Validation" section)

External Parameter Entity Processing

This feature tells a parser whether or not to process external parameter entities, used to define DTDs by a system and/or public ID (rather than directly in an XML document by location):

```
<!DOCTYPE book [
  <!ENTITY % book SYSTEM "http://www.newInstance.com/dtd/book.dtd">
  %book;
]>
```

URI: http://xml.org/sax/features/external-parameter-entities
Access: read/write
Default: unspecified; always true if the parser is validating (see the "Validation" section)

Standalone

This feature reports whether a document is standalone, declared via the standalone attribute in the XML declaration:

```
<?xml version="1.0" standalone="yes"?>
```

URI: http://xml.org/sax/features/is-standalone
Access: read-only during parsing; not available otherwise
Default: not applicable

 This feature is a bit of an aberration; it's available only during parsing, and must be called *after* the startDocument( ) callback has been fired. Additionally, you can't set this feature on a parser; it has no meaning outside of the parsing context.

Parameter Entity Reporting

This features lets a parser know that parameter entity reporting (when they start, and when they stop) should be handled by a LexicalHandler (for more on LexicalHandlers, see Chapter 4, and the "Lexical Handler" property section).

URI: http://xml.org/sax/features/lexical-handler/parameter-entities
Access: read/write
Default: unspecified

Namespace Processing

This feature instructs a parser to perform namespace processing, which causes namespace prefixes, namespace URIs, and element local names to be available through the SAX namespace callbacks (startPrefixMapping( ) and endPrefixMapping( ), as well as certain parameters supplied to startElement( ) and endElement( )). When this feature is true, the processing will occur. When false, namespace processing will not occur (this implies that "Namespace Prefix Reporting" is on).

> URI: http://xml.org/sax/features/namespaces
> Access: read/write
> Default: true

Namespace Prefix Reporting

This feature instructs a parser to report the attributes used in namespace declarations, such as the xmlns:[namespace URI] attributes. When this feature is not on (false), namespace-related attributes are not reported, as the parser consumes them in order to discover a namespace prefix to URI mappings, and they are generally not of value to the wrapping application in that context. In addition, when namespace processing is turned on, generally namespace prefix mapping is turned off.

> URI: http://xml.org/sax/features/namespace-prefixes
> Access: read-only when parsing, read/write when not parsing
> Default: false

Absolute URI Declaration Resolution

If this feature is true, absolute paths are returned from the following methods (all on the DTDHandler interface, detailed in Chapter 4):

- notationDecl( )
- unparsedEntityDecl( )
- externalEntityDecl( )

 This feature has no effect on resolveEntity( ) in EntityResolver, which isn't used to report declarations (entities are not the same as declarations). Additionally, startDTD( ) in LexicalHandler always returns a nonabsolute URI, and is unaffected.

> URI: http://xml.org/sax/features/resolve-dtd-uris
> Access: read/write
> Default: true

String Interning

This feature dictates that all element raw and local names, namespace prefixes, and namespace URIs are interned using java.lang.String.intern( ). When not on (false), all XML components are left as is.

URI: http://xml.org/sax/features/string-interning
Access: read-only when parsing, read/write when not parsing
Default: unspecified; newer, high-performance parsers usually have this set to false by default, so they can perform their own optimizations for dealing with character data

Unicode Normalization Checking

Related largely to XML 1.1, this feature indicates whether a parser should report Unicode normalization errors (defined in section 2.13 and Appendix B of the XML 1.1 specification). If set to true, these errors are made visible via the error( ) callback on ErrorHandler.

URI: http://xml.org/sax/features/validation
Access: read-write
Default: false

Attributes2 Usage

SAX 2 defines an "enhanced" version of several core SAX interfaces in org.xml.sax. ext; the Attributes2 interface is one of those (it exposes extra constraint-related information, particularly about attributes). You can check to see if your parser is returning an implementation of this interface—and not of the normal Attributes interface—with this feature.

URI: http://xml.org/sax/features/use-attributes2
Access: read-only
Default: not applicable

Locator2 Usage

Like the Attributes2 interface (see the previoius section, "Attributes2 Usage"), Locator2 is an enhanced version of Locator. Located in the org.xml.sax.ext package, this interface provides information about entity character encoding (and in some cases, the XML version of parameter entities). You can check to see if your parser is returning an implementation of this interface—and not of the normal Locator interface—with this feature.

URI: http://xml.org/sax/features/use-locator2
Access: read-only
Default: not applicable

EntityResolver2 Usage

EntityResolver2 is another of the enhanced interfaces defined in org.xml.sax.ext. You can determine if your parser is returning an implementation of this interface—and not of EntityResolver—with this feature. This feature can also be set, specifying that the extra methods defined by EntityResolver2 should be used (assuming your parser supports them).

> URI: http://xml.org/sax/features/use-entity-resolver2
> Access: read/write
> Default: true

Validation

This feature requests that validation occur and that any errors as a result of broken constraints be reported through the SAX ErrorHandler interface (if an implementation is registered). When set to false, no validation occurs, which is generally the default setting. You'll need to check your parser vendor's documentation to determine if this feature applies to both DTD and XML Schema validation.

> URI: http://xml.org/sax/features/validation
> Access: read-only when parsing; read/write when not parsing
> Default: unspecified

Report Namespace on xmlns Attributes

If this feature is true, xmlns attributes are reported as being in http://www.w3.org/2000/xmlns/namespace. The namespaces in the XML recommendation specified that these attributes are *not* in a namespace, but an earlier version of that specification defined them as in the above namespace.

 This is largely for backward compatibility; don't use this feature unless you really need it.

> URI: http://xml.org/sax/features/xmlns-uris
> Access: read/write
> Default: false

XML 1.1 Support

This feature will return true if the parser supports XML 1.1 (and XML 1.0, obviously); otherwise, if only XML 1.0 is supported, it returns false.

> URI: http://xml.org/sax/features/xml-1.1

Access: read-only
Default: not applicable

Core Properties

Properties provide a way to deal with objects used in the parsing process, particularly when dealing with handlers such as LexicalHandler and DeclHandler that are not in the core set of SAX 2.0 handlers (EntityResolver, DTDHandler, ContentHandler, and ErrorHandler). Any property can be read-only or read/write; features also may be modifiable only when parsing is occurring, or only when parsing is not occurring.

Declaration Handler

This property allows the setting and retrieval of a DeclHandler implementation to be used for handling of constraints within a DTD.

URI: http://xml.org/sax/properties/declaration-handler
Datatype: org.xml.sax.ext.DeclHandler
Access: read/write

Document Version

This property returns the version string of the XML document, indicated by the version attribute in the XML declaration:

```
<?xml version="1.0"?>
```

 Like "Standalone," this property acts a bit abnormally; it's only available during parsing, and must be called *after* the startDocument( ) callback has been fired.

URI: http://xml.org/sax/properties/document-xml-version
Datatype: String
Access: read-only during parsing; not available otherwise

DOM Node

When parsing is occurring, this property retrieves the current DOM node (if a DOM iterator is being used). When parsing is not occurring, it retrieves the root DOM node.

 Most of the parsers I used in testing for this book did not support this property except in very special cases; you shouldn't rely on it providing useful information in the general case.

URI: http://xml.org/sax/properties/dom-node
Datatype: org.w3c.dom.Node
Access: read-only when parsing; read/write when not parsing

Lexical Handler

This property allows the setting and retrieval of a LexicalHandler implementation to be used for handling of comments and DTD references within an XML document.

URI: http://xml.org/sax/properties/lexical-handler
Datatype: org.xml.sax.ext.LexicalHandler
Access: read/write

Literal (XML) String

This retrieves the literal characters in the XML document that triggered the event in the process when this property is used.

Like the DOM node feature, I found little use and little support for this property. Don't depend on it, particularly across parsers.

URI: http://xml.org/sax/properties/xml-string
Datatype: java.lang.String
Access: read-only when parsing; not applicable outside of parsing

Index

Symbols

" (quotation marks, double)
" entity reference, 8
XML attributes, 6
$ (dollar sign), indicating variables, 183
& (ampersand) in XML entity references, 8
' (apostrophe), ' entity reference, 8
' (quotation marks, single)
' entity reference, 8
XML attributes, 6
* (asterisk), recurrence modifier, 22
+ (plus sign), recurrence modifier, 22
, (comma) operator, specifying order, 22
. (period), in Java property names, 249, 253
; (semicolon), in XML entity references, 8
< and > (angle brackets)
<!-- and --> comment delimiters, 82
<! opening of a DTD tag, 22
entity references in XML, 8
<![CDATA[and]]> for CDATA nodes, 106
? (question mark), recurrence operator, 22
| (pipe symbol)
combining constants defined by
ContentFilter, 275
OR operator, 22

A

A9 Open Search module, 370
AbstractView interface, 139
accept( ) method
EventFilter and StreamFilter, 224
Node interface, 290
acceptNode( ) (NodeFilter), 132
Action interface, 306

ActionScript, 415
XML in ActionScript 3.0, 417–429
E4X, 420
Flash XML sockets, 423–426
sending and loading XML, 421
XML data providers, 421
ActiveX control, XMLHttpRequest as, 402
addContent( ) method, 245, 252, 253, 263
addElement( ) (Branch), 293
addNamespace( ) (XPath, 273
Adobe Flash (see Flash)
AElfred2 (SAX parser), 84
afterMarshal( ) (Listener), 346
afterUnmarshal( ) (Listener), 346
aggregators, 384
building, 365–369
Ajax, 401–415
online sources for information, 414
posting XML to the server, 411–415
creating XML document in
JavaScript, 411
servlet to accept XML posts, 413
submitting XML document, 412–413
using DOM with, 406–409
using XSLT with, 408
XMLHttpRequest object, 402–407
allocate( ) method, 238
AndFilter class, 276
annotations, 315, 330–334
class-level, 330–332
XmlAccessorType, 331
XmlRootElement, 331
XmlType, 332
enabling binding of arbitrary Java
classes, 316

We'd like to hear your suggestions for improving our indexes. Send email to *index@oreilly.com*.

nodes (*continued*)
  types supporting validation, 148
  working with, 101
  XML, eliminating references from
    code, 310
NODESET (XPath return type), 178
NodeTypePattern class, 306
nodeValidity( ) method, 153
noNamespaceSchemaLocation attribute, 33
nonfatal errors in XML parsing, 237
  SAX handling of, 67
normalization (Unicode), 438
normalizing character data in XML
    document, 257
notation declarations, handling with
    DTDHandler, 78
NOTATION_DECLARATION event
    corresponding StAX interface, 212
    XMLStreamReader methods, 202
notationDecl( ) (DTDDHandler), 437
NotationDeclaration interface, 212
null return values (JDOM), 284
NullPointerExceptions, 284
NUMBER (XPath return type), 178

O

Object class
  Object properties of
    XMLInputFactory, 237
  SAX features and properties and StAX
    properties set to, 236
object model neutral, 176
ObjectFactory class, 328
  generated in JAXB 2.0, 329
objects
  plain-old Java objects (see POJOs)
  tree of Java objects, binding to XML
    document, 310
Odeo.com, 372
oneOrMore element, 35
opening XML tag, consolidating with closing
    tag in one element, 6
optional element, 35
order
  elements defined in XML Schema, 29
  of nested XML tags, 5
OrFilter class, 276
org.dom4j.tree package, 289
org.xml.sax.driver system property, 45

output escaping, HTML content in XML
    elements, 17
output( ) method, 258
OutputFormat class
  customized formatting, 296
  default formatting, 295

P

package-level annotations, 333
  XmlSchema, 333
parameter entity reporting, 436
parameterized types (generics), 315
parent elements, 59
Parent interface, 274
parse( ) method, 381
  DomParser class, 98
  XMLReader interface, 45
parser factory
  configuring, 158
  creating, 158
parsers
  changing implementation in JAXP, 165
  checking for DOM module
    support, 125–128
  DOM Level 3 support, 93
  dom4j, provided by another package, 292
  I/O streams as input, 48
  JTidy, 128
  obtaining a parser, 160
  Xerces, 43
parseText( ) (DocumentHelper), 292
parsing, 41
  dom4j, 292
  JAXP, 154, 156–165
    reading XML with SAX, 156–165
  pull parsing with StAX, 196–242
    cursor and event iterator APIs, 196
    download site for StAX, 197
    factory classes, 199
    obtaining StAX, 198
    parsing, 199–227
    StAX event types, 197
  pull parsing with XmlPull, 239–242
  SAX, 45–49
    event flow, 84
    instantiating a reader, 45–47
    parsing the document, 47–49
  warnings and nonfatal errors,
    capturing, 237

W

W3C (World Wide Web Consortium)
  DOM specification, 91
  XML 1.0 Recommendation, 1
  XML 1.1 specification, 9
  XML activity page, 19
  XML Schema
    complete support in JAXB 2.0, 316
    support by JAXB 1.0, 315
  XML Schema (XSD), 21
  XSL specification, 12
warnings in XML parsing, 237
  SAX, 66
web applications, XML as
    presentation, 384–430
  Ajax, 401–415
    posting XML to the server, 411–415
    using DOM with, 406–409
    using XSLT with, 408
    XMLHttpRequest, 402–407
  Flash, 415–430
    ActionScript, 415
    Flex, 416
    XML in ActionScript 3.0, 417–429
  MVC pattern, 384–391
    XML in, 385–391
  transforming to HTML with
    JSP, 391–393
  transforming to HTML with
    XSLT, 392–401
    client-side transformations, 393–395
    server-side transformations, 394–401
web page for this book, x
Web Services Developer Pack (see Java
    WSDP)
web technologies, 384
well-formed HTML, 130
well-formed XML, 5
  JSPs and, 390
whitespace
  dealing with in JDOM, 257
  SAX parser handling of, 60
width attribute (XML Schema), 29
Wiki, ROME, 370
Wikipedia page for RSS, 350
wire feeds, 359
WireFeed class, 359, 360
WireFeedInput class, 365
WireFeedOutput class, 360
Wireless Markup Language (WML), 10
World Wide Web Consortium (see W3C)

writeAttribute( ) (XMLStreamWriter), 229,
    231
writeEmptyElement( )
    (XMLStreamWriter), 230
writeEndDocument( )
    (XMLStreamWriter), 229, 231
Writer class, 89
Writer object, ROME feed output, 360
writers, SAX, 88
writeStartElement( )
    (XMLStreamWriter), 231

X

Xalan-J, 19
Xalan-Java processor, 176
Xerces (SAX parser), 43
  classpath, 43
  DOM Level 3 functionality, 103
  features and properties, online listing, 71
  implementation of XMLReader, 45
  versions used directly and with JAXP, 94
XHTML, 6, 19, 130
  DOM Level 2 HTML module, 93
  formatting in dom4j output, 297
XInclude processing, configuring for parser
    factory, 159
xjc application
  compiling a schema, 324
  JAXB 1.0 output, 326
  JAXB 2.0 output, 329
  output for JAXB 1.0 and 2.0, 326
  target namespace for schema, 325
  -use-runtime option, 329
XJCTask class, 324
XLink, 19
XML
  core Java APIs (see DOM; SAX)
  other related technologies, 19
  transformations, 10–19
    XPath, 13
    XSL, 11
    XSLT, 12
XML 1.0, 1–9
  attributes, 6
  elements, 4–6
  entity references, 8
  namespaces, 7
  root element, 3
  unparsed data (CDATA section), 9
XML 1.1, 9
  SAX support, 439
XML module (DOM), 126

About the Authors

Brett D. McLaughlin has worked in computers since the Logo days. (Remember the little triangle?) In recent years, he's become one of the most well-known authors and programmers in the Java and XML communities. He's worked for Nextel Communications, implementing complex enterprise systems; at Lutris Technologies, actually writing application servers; and most recently at O'Reilly Media, Inc., where he continues to write and edit books that matter. His list to date includes *Head Rush Ajax,* and *Java 5.0 Tiger: A Developer's Notebook.*

Justin Edelson has been a software developer for more than 10 years, specializing in web development for media and entertainment companies. He has contributed extensively to high-profile web sites and applications for brands such as MTV, VH1, Comedy Central, Showtime, The Movie Channel, Spike TV, Nickelodeon, and MSN. Recently, he was instrumental to MTV Networks' wide-ranging suite of mobile products, which includes messaging, ringtones, wallpapers, games, and mobile video channels, in partnership with all major U.S. carriers.

Colophon

The animals on the cover of *Java & XML,* Third Edition, are lions (*Panthera leo*). These great cats differ from other solitary felines in that they form family groups, called prides. Prides consist of as many as 30 to 40 lions, most of whom are females and their offspring. The life span of a lion is approximately 10 to 14 years (quite a bit more if in captivity). Full grown males can grow up to 10 feet in length; the only cat larger is the tiger. The lion's eye is particularly sensitive to movement, and it can detect the movement of its prey from a great distance. Special receptor cells in the cat's eye give it exceptional night vision.

Lions live in eastern and southern Africa, although some subspecies of the African lion are endangered. The Asiatic lion (*P.l. persica*) once lived throughout India, the Middle East, and Southern Asia. Today, with conservation efforts, its population still numbers only approximately 359 animals, which can be found in the Gir Forest National Park in Gujarat in western India. The Barbary and Cape lions are extinct.

Lions are carnivores and prey on large herd animals. They are at the apex of the food chain, the top predator of their environment. The females are the hunters, while the males' role is to protect the pride from other aggressive males. Lions are not as fast as other big cats, such as the cheetah. As a result, they concentrate on heavier, less agile animals, and ambush their prey by driving them toward concealed members of the hunting group. They use coordinated, cooperative techniques that enable the group to hunt with more success than an individual could. African lions eat wildebeest, zebra, antelope, gazelle, impala, and giraffe.

The cover image is from *Original Antique Engraving.* The cover font is Adobe ITC Garamond. The text font is Linotype Birka; the heading font is Adobe Myriad Condensed; and the code font is LucasFont's TheSans Mono Condensed.

Better than e-books

Buy *Java and XML*, 2nd Edition, and access
the digital edition FREE on Safari for 45 days.

Go to www.oreilly.com/go/safarienabled
and type in coupon code IMYSLZG

Search
thousands of
top tech books

Download
whole chapters

Cut and Paste
code examples

Find
answers fast

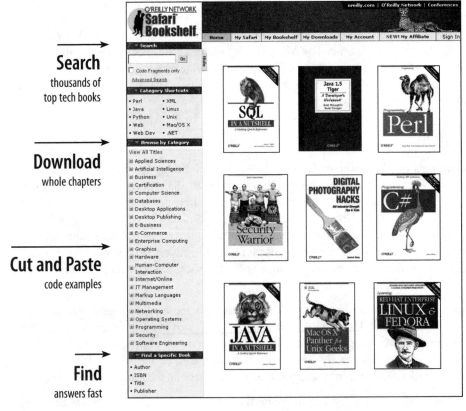

Search Safari! The premier electronic reference
library for programmers and IT professionals.